NOW THROUGH A GLASS DARKLY

NOW THROUGH A GLASS DARKLY

Specular Images of Being and Knowing
from Virgil to Chaucer

EDWARD PETER NOLAN

Ann Arbor

THE UNIVERSITY OF MICHIGAN PRESS

1993   1992   1991   1990   4   3   2   1

Library of Congress Cataloging-in-Publication Data

Nolan, Edward Peter, 1937–
     Now through a glass darkly : specular images of being and knowing
from Virgil to Chaucer / Edward Peter Nolan.
          p.   cm.
     Includes bibliographical references and index.
     ISBN 0-472-10170-6 (cloth : alk.)
          1. Literature, Medieval—History and criticism. 2. Latin
literature—History and criticism. 3. Literature, Medieval—Roman
influences. 4. Self-knowledge in literature. 5. Mirrors in
literature.   I. Title.
PN681.5.N65   1990
809'.93356—dc20   90-45224

Lines from "Poetry" are reprinted with permission of
Macmillan Publishing Company from *Collected Poems*
of Marianne Moore. Copyright 1935 by Marianne Moore,
renewed 1963 by Marianne Moore and T. S. Eliot.

for Liesel
—and for the two Charlottes—
donne ch'avete intelleto d'amore

He swept the mirror a half circle in the air to flash the tidings abroad in the sunlight now radiant on the sea. . . .
—Look at yourself, he said, you dreadful bard. . . .

. . . Laughing again, he brought the mirror away from Stephen's peering eyes. . . .
—The rage of Caliban at not seeing his face in a mirror, he said. If Wilde were only alive to see you.
Drawing back and pointing, Stephen said with bitterness:

—It is a symbol of Irish art. The cracked lookingglass of a servant.
—James Joyce, Ulysses, 1914–21

Languages of heteroglossia, like mirrors that face each other, each reflecting in its own way a piece, a tiny corner of the world, force us to guess at and grasp for a world behind their mutually reflecting aspects that is broader, more multi-leveled, containing more and varied horizons than would be available to a single language or a single mirror.
—Mikhail M. Bakhtin, "Discourse in the Novel," 1935

One image crossed the many-headed, sat
Under the tropic shade, grew round and slow
No Hamlet thin from eating flies, a fat
Dreamer of the Middle Ages. Empty eyeballs knew
That knowledge increases unreality, that
Mirror on mirror mirrored is all the show.
—W.B. Yeats, "The Statues," 1936

Acknowledgments

This is my chance to thank people for putting up with me over the many years I was putting up this book. First, my gratitude to Colorado colleagues. John L. Murphy, D. C. Baker, Richard J. Schoeck, and Julia Bolton Holloway read the entire work with extraordinary patience and wit; others helped with specific problems: Kaye Howe (almost daily in those years we taught together), Ulrich K. Goldsmith, Joy Kerler King, Constance Wright, William Calder III (now in Illinois), John D. Hoag, Hazel E. Barnes, Bruce Kawin, Michael Preston, C. David Benson (now in Connecticut), Sophia Morgan (now in Arizona), and James Kincaid (now in California).

A gifted cohort of graduate students, most now gone their ways, were unstinting in their supply of enthusiastic support and nagging questions: Reed Merrill, Lilika Marmaras, Helen Black, Joanne Karpinsky, Anne Scott, David Mogen, Jim Wilson, Tom Vallejos, Lorene Carpenter, Karin Boklund, Howie Movshovitz, Peter Burgess, Jean Sutherland, Linda Williams, Susan Linville, Nancy Nolte, Mark Bailey, Robin Kornman, and Roberto Cagliero.

And there are extramural colleagues, acquaintances, and friends who helped in special ways: Howell D. Chickering, Jr., at Amherst, who gave a sharp and careful reading at a very early stage; Gerhard Hahn, at the University of Regensburg, who invited me to share this book in its earlier stages with his Oberseminar in Mediävistik; and Paul Ruggiers, at Oklahoma, whose recent reading was most penetrating. And for years of intellectual, aesthetic, and familial comfort and support my warmest thanks go to Traute Maass of Hamburg and her daughter (and my dear niece), Esther.

I must also thank, knowing I can never really repay, the teachers who made a difference: Robert G. Owen, Rudolf Arnheim, Cleanth Brooks, W. K. Wimsatt, Maynard Mack, George Kubler, Vincent Scully, Peter Demetz, Marie Borroff, John Hollander, Alfred David, Newton Stallknecht, Frank Ryder, Norbert Fuerst, Richard O'Gorman, James Poag, Robert Fitzgerald, George Steiner and Frank Kermode. But the greatest debt here is to Allen

Mandelbaum, whose brilliant work, smart talk, and piquant nudges over the years helped so many (including me) to persevere.

There is a special debt owed to Holly Stevens and Alfred A. Knopf for permission to exploit the poetic genius of Wallace Stevens throughout the book as a kind of captive Virgil. For teachers, certain translations of the classics become canonical and I am grateful to the University of Chicago Press for permission to use Richmond Lattimore's translation of Homer's *Iliad*, to Vintage Books for permission to use Robert Fitzgerald's translation of Homer's *Odyssey*, and to Bantam Books for permission to use Allen Mandelbaum's translations of Virgil's *Aeneid* and Dante's *Divine Comedy*. I thank Houghton Mifflin for permission to use the *Riverside Chaucer* and Penguin for permission to use the Pine-Coffin translation of St. Augustine's *Confessions*. Special acknowledgment is also made to the Macmillan Publishing Company for permission to quote several lines from Marianne Moore's "Poetry."

A few arguments and discussions in this book have developed out of previously published essays. My thanks go to the Colorado Associated University Press for allowing me to use in chapters 4 and 9 several passages from an essay of mine on medieval *ordo* that originally appeared in *Hypatia*, a festschrift put together in honor of my colleague and friend, Hazel Barnes. For permission to use revised parts of an earlier article on Chrétien de Troyes in chapter 6, I am grateful to the editors of *Symposium* and the Helen Dwight Reid Education Foundation; and I am indebted to Mario di Cesare and CMERS at SUNY Binghamton for permission to expand a paper on embedded Latin in Dante and Langland for use in chapter 9 which first appeared in the *Acta Conventus Neo-Latini Bononiensis*. Full documentation of credit for all these acknowledgments appears in the notes.

I also owe thanks to Leslie Blake DiNella of the Birmingham Museum of Art and a great debt of gratitude to my editor, LeAnn Fields, to Linda Berauer, and to the outside readers and the copy editors at the University of Michigan Press.

Finally, I offer loving gratitude midst the regrets of omission to Char and Lottie. And for Sisi, sharer of the journey, borrowed words: "Trinkt, Ihr Augen, was die Wimper hält, von dem goldenen Überfluss dieser Welt!" To these ladies who possess such intelligence of love I dedicate this book. It was theirs to start with; it is theirs to end with.

Contents

CONTENTS

Introduction:
The Cracked Looking Glass

videmus nunc per speculum in aenigmate: tunc autem facie ad faciem.
Nunc cognosco ex parte: tunc autem cognoscam sicut et cognitus sum.
—Paul, 1 Corinthians 13.12

The King James translation of St. Paul's paradigm, "Now we see
through a glass darkly," has haunted the imagination of the English-
speaking world since the age of Shakespeare. The reverence we feel
toward it, however, can blind us to the fact that the closer we look for
precision of meaning, the less we find it. For greater clarity, one might
rather turn to the Revised Standard Version and its "Now we see in a
mirror dimly," or to the New English Bible with its "Now we see
puzzling reflections in a mirror." Yet many still prefer the King James
Version; for its beauty, some argue, and, as others argue, because it
protects, even as it illuminates, a central mystery. They may well be
right, if in fact the desire is to gain greater proximity to the force of
Paul's original language.

The central impenetrability of the verse in the King James Version
(how can we see through something darkly?) captures rather well the
deep and irresolvable ambiguity that resides in Jerome's "*per speculum
in aenigmate*," which in turn accurately reflects the crux at the center
of Paul's "*di' esóptrou en ainígmati*." Although an analysis of Paul's
Greek will lead us essentially to the same impasse, we do well here to
deal with the ambiguities embodied in the Vulgate. It was, after all,
not the Greek formulation but the Latin translation that became the
canonical icon in medieval western Europe of Paul's vision of the ontological and epistemological double bind we suffer now, this side of the

eschaton. The question remains: What does—or better—how can *"per speculum in aenigmate"* mean?

In one sense, the problem reduces to this question: What is the lexical force of the prepositions *per* and *in*? Are we now able to see *in* a mirror? or *through* a mirror? or *by means* of a mirror? And do we look *at* an enigma? or *from within* an enigma? There are no signals privileging any one sense; thus all "readings" must be simultaneously held. This is an eighth type of ambiguity, one that prohibits its own dissolving.

The epistle is written to Corinth, as famous then as Venice is now for the making of mirrors. And it is written by a man whose capacity for seeing was infinitely privileged on the road to Damascus. Yet as he writes the Corinthians the most important thing he knows about the hermeneutic situation in which we find ourselves, and tries to shed light on the matter with the help of verbal mirrors, we are left darkling. We discover that the utterance written to clarify an enigma is itself an enigma.[1]

Here we are, at the liminal frontier between being and knowing, at the node where ontology and epistemology share the same face. Nowhere do we require nonequivocal language more intensely than at the point where we bump up against the mystery of things, at the border between reader and text, subject and object, knower and known, creature and Creator. And it is precisely at this juncture, where we come to the absolute end of ourselves and touch the beginning of the radically Other, that language signals its fundamental limitation, its inevitable and final inability to bring us the object of our desire.

We face, whether implicit in Greco-Roman tradition or explicit in Judeo-Christian belief, divine interdiction: We cannot see God and live.[2] Only on the other side of death shall we see face to face, shall we know the Other as we ourselves are known. Here and now we must make do with the Creator's reflection in the mirrors of middle earth. Paul's lexical ambiguity reinforces the tenor of his argument; we must accommodate ourselves to this unrelenting verbal/existential crux, for speech and being unite in a belief system in which the Word has been made Flesh. Our project then is to reenact, continuously and incompletely, the central challenge offered us by the ambiguity inherent in our "happy fault." Language is, for fallen us, an unceasingly self-elaborating speculum in which we are both privileged and doomed to see only enigmas of Love.

At this point we do well to recall that Paul's mirror dictum only gradually developed into Christian orthodoxy, and that it can usefully be seen as a special case of a general anxiety combining a sense of alienation with a desire for mediation between divinity and humanity. This collective anxiety is not one with its Pauline naming, but reaches back, along one line of our heritage, to Genesis and along another, through mythic and discursive traditions, to Plato, Attic theater, Hesiod, and Homer.

To add a sense of narrative flesh to the schematics implied in Paul's mirror dictum we will often consider individual members of a quaternity of narrative figures who pervade the Western imagination before, during, and after the Christian dispensation: Narcissus, Pygmalion, Daedalus, and Orpheus. In each mythic configuration, the encounter of each figure with the desired Other involves the problem of partial knowledge and significant failure. Each "problem" reflects ways in which the image of the Other acts as barrier as well as bridge to any adequate sense of union with the Other. These four figures form important suballiances.

Narcissus and Pygmalion rhyme in the more explicitly erotic aspects of the human agenda: each encounters not the desired Other, but mirroring inadequations *of* the Other.

The fatality of the Narcissus narrative resides in the fact that at the heart of the recognition before the reflected image in the pool, we discover there *is* no bridging the desired Other and our image *of* it; in fact we see, with the armchair perspective of Lacan, that our faith has been radically misplaced, that the Other is a fiction only, a figment of our desiring imagination.[3]

The apparently happy ending of the mirroring narrative of Pygmalion may also turn out to be a fatal misprision; but at least within the confines of the myth the metamorphic powers of Venus, the figura of universal libido, turn the ivory sex doll into flesh and blood, and the bridge between the desired One and its image is completed.[4] The price of vivifying the doll is canceling the identity of the image as imago and replacing it by an act of transubstantiation that may or may not require the loss of the self in union with the newly (re)constituted Other.

A major difference between Narcissus and Pygmalion is Pygmalion's greater degree of self-awareness regarding the situation. This arises from the fact that Pygmalion is an active artist, whereas Narcissus is the paradigmatically male version of the Foolish Virgin, a cartoon of the passively adoring but noncritical Constant Reader.

With Narcissus remaining alone as a contrastive background figure of the cloud of unknowing, Pygmalion joins Daedalus and Orpheus as self-conscious makers. These figures comprise a powerful constellation in the Western imagination for that special case of representation in which the artist figures as Everyman.

The major projects of Daedalus as artist are three: (1) the labyrinth designed to contain the pollution of man and beast known as the Minotaur; (2) the wing constructs and the instructions for their care and use; and (3) the reconstitution of that artistic activity in the structures of remembrance as figured in Virgilian reliefs on the temple doors of Apollo. The partiality of knowledge and success is caught in corresponding moments: the labyrinth is undone for love, the boy falls to his death, and "twice the hand of the father failed" in the attempt to convert that fall into the stabilities of significant form.

If Daedalus is the artist of flying, Orpheus pursues the fatal art of flying in its radical aspect: resurrection. Orpheus's arts are not the arts of things (architecture, manufacture, bas-relief) but the arts of words and music: he sings a new and compelling reality for the king and queen of the dead in order to gain his wife reentry to the land of the living. The partiality of his knowing and doing is figured in the loss of Eurydice, his dismemberment, and the petrifaction, at the end of the narrative, of his singing, severed head on the shore of Lesbos.

These master figures involving only partial success in the fundamental acts of seeing, knowing, and doing haunt the imagination of the West. In conjunction with the onto/epistemological conundrum captured in Paul's mirror dictum contrasting the *nunc* of partial knowledge with the *tunc* anticipations of life on the other side of death, they provide an imagistic grid in which and through which our survey of reflexive strategies in the present study can gain greater coherence.

This book grows out of an effort, sustained over many years, to come to some kind of peace with the way in which Paul's sentence, by capturing so many different meanings in a single saying, became a kind of pivotal figure, with both culminating and seminal powers, for depicting our occidental understanding of the human project of "being there."[5] As one assesses the development of literary mirroring from Virgil's foundational text of the Roman empire to the full flowering of the brilliant, if disastrous, attempt at instituting a Christian imperium so dazzlingly depicted in the divine and human comedies of Dante and Chaucer, one gains, with Paul's paradigm echoing in the mind, a richer understanding of the speculative mode of seeing, thinking, and writing that dominated Europe for over two thousand years.

The project, then, is to scan the functions of intra- as well as intertextual literary mirroring, ranging from Virgil's indexing of Homer to Chaucer's indexing of Dante, with stops at way stations in between to explore key images of mirroring power in Ovid, Augustine, various medieval commentators, Chrétien de Troyes, Heinrich von Morungen, Alan of Lille, St. Bonaventure, Dante, and Langland.

In Virgil and Ovid we shall examine the functions of the Ivory Gate of False Dream and the severed head of Orpheus, both watershed images associated with the parabolic curve of falling and rising embodied in the descent into and return from Hell. These are paradigmatic narratives that echo back to the Nekyia of Homer's *Odyssey,* the Ur-catabasis of Western literary tradition, and forward to the central event in the credo of the new dispensation, the death and resurrection of Christ.

With the advent of incarnational thinking, Paul revealed each human as having a new mirroring power. The foundational formulae of St. John—*"Deus erat Verbum"* [God was Word] and *"Verbum caro factum est"* [Word was made Flesh]—pointed back toward, and fulfilled, in the minds of the early fathers, a redemptive promise inherent in the foundational language of Genesis: *"Faciamus hominem ad imaginem et similitudinem nostram"* [let us make man in our image and likeness]. As the implications of an *imago dei* relationship between creature and Creator developed in the Christian imagination, the redemptive possibilities inherent in reciprocity flowered: is not man himself a Pauline speculum by means of which we can see back into the enigma of God? Then every human, as an image of God, is both *like* God and, not *being* God, *un*like God. The fecundity of our bearing simultaneously both similitude and dissimilitude to God and to each other was not lost on St. Augustine, who then laid out, in his own foundational writings, the doctrine that makes of all of us imperfect mirrors of Christ's hypostasy, cracked looking glasses by means of which we can serve as redemptive mirrors for one another. In Christ is mirrored our perfectability; in each other, what we really are. St. Augustine calls that territory of discrepancy between the two mirrors the *regio dissimilitudinis,* or "region of unlikeness," and by assessing that dissimilitude with care and accuracy, we can muster salvatory agendas of reform.

The main body of the book, then, explores the range of implication

5

inherent in this idea; and we begin with Augustine's own concern with the ways in which the mirroring capability of the world, as figured in texts, people, and history, can help us increase our faculties for knowing and loving. The culmination of Augustine's relentless quest is to authenticate the self in the undeniably Other. The specific image of mirroring we shall focus on is his discovery of the ordinating power of the human mind in the universal schemes of time.

The fourth chapter bridges over eight hundred years. By a schematic investigation of the ways developed by medieval commentators of reading Virgil and Ovid between the twelfth and fourteenth centuries, one senses, in spite of what might seem an inordinate exegetical thirst, the development of a quiet but powerful conspiracy to shore up the domain of the literal meaning of the image. A glance at the twelfth-century Victorine program of biblical analysis reinforces this idea, and we see an ever-growing insistence on the autonomy of the literal dimension of the image in the ascent narratives of Alan of Lille's *Anticlaudianus* and in St. Bonaventure's *Itinerarium mentis in Deum* as well as in key mirror imagery in all three canticles of Dante's *Commedia*.

The next two chapters form a mirroring pair, exploring aspects of twelfth-century lyric and romance. In a notoriously ambiguous image, Heinrich von Morungen reflects the obsession of the medieval lyric with the psychopathology of erotic infatuation in the lover's horror on seeing a damaged "mirror-mouth" of his Lady in a dream. He begins to intuit that what he loves is not his Lady, but rather his image of her, a self-entrapping, self-deluding image of his own desiring. He senses, in this dream, brought by Love herself, and surrounded with images of children entranced by mirrors, that the beloved's eyes act more like the reflecting pool of Narcissus than the gateway to her heart and soul. The unsatisfied search for a univocal reading of Heinrich's damaged mouth both aids in and is aided by consideration of the contextual imagery of narcissistic perception that frames this extraordinary minnesinger: the anticipatory lyrics of Bernard de Ventadorn and the fulfilling catoptric allegories of Guillaume de Lorris.

In the romances of Chrétien de Troyes, we examine implications of a paradigmatically different image of perceiving the Lady: "her eyes were as bright as two stars . . . in truth she was made to be looked at; for in her one could have seen himself as in a mirror." To understand the broader functions of this "romance paradigm," we shall trace the increased use, within the frame of the romance, of intrusively fragmentary images which seem to mirror the quotidian world existing outside that frame.

Chrétien develops the interposition of such intrusive, broken images of the quotidian into the otherwise hermetically protected world of the romance in anticipation of the Brechtian alienation effect. He uses them to create a programmatic technique of category trespassing; as he does so, he multiplies readerly points of view on the implied range of narrative action and suggests a critical, humanistic, even subversive ethical function for the genre of romance. If the lyric expresses an *attritio cordis* in the face of threatening solipsism, the romance moves from celebration to liberating critique: Chrétien fashions a new image of marriage into a mirror of desired reconciliation between the demands of private passion and public virtue. We are asked to envision the expulsion from the Garden of Eden as a foregrounding of the romance hero's escape from the *hortus conclusus* of the love lyric—to see, in fact, the exit from the garden as a self-liberating act of humanity rather than a punitive act of God.

The next two chapters explore directly the figural as well as verisimilar capabilities of medieval literary characters to mirror one another in Pauline and Augustinian ways; Dante and Chaucer wed the techniques of representation and mimesis, of lyric and romance, as they recuperate, for the Middle Ages, a generically encyclopedic, epic style. In a reading of *Inferno* 5, we see Francesca reveal herself, by weaving a network of oblique literary quotation, as an infernally cracked looking glass capable of mirroring both the purgatorial Siren and the paradisal Beatrice. In like manner, we see Chaucer mirroring Dante, not structurally, or imagistically, or even thematically, but ethically, as his figures of the Pardoner, the Wife of Bath, and St. Cecilia mirror the aspects of human possibility figured forth by Francesca in Hell, Statius in Purgatory, and Beatrice in Paradise.

The book moves toward closure by addressing the mirroring powers of language itself, examining the figural functions of Latin in the vernacular texts of the *Vita Nuova,* the *Divina Commedia,* Langland's *Piers Plowman,* and a macaronic lyric of thirteenth-century England, "Of oon that is so fayre and bryht." The project concludes with a meditation on the problematics of closure generated by the texts considered throughout the book. At the liminal boundary between the text and the world to which it submits, we can more fully assess the reciprocal mirroring power of the world and the book, as figured forth in the *liber mundi* trope, a central and sustaining image of the Christian medieval imagination.

This study makes a considered but by no means systematic attempt to bridge those medieval and modern concerns that seem bridgeable. At key moments such apparent conjunctions across epochs are directly addressed in the text. A more subliminal set of suggestions and provocations are offered by the programmatic use of quotations from the work of Wallace Stevens as epigraphs to each numbered chapter. It is perhaps instructively ironic that in the poetry of this rather militantly secular humanist, who viewed any reliance on christological or paradisal consolations as an abrogation and betrayal of human freedom, there are so many shared concerns with the development, over a thousand years, of a coherent, theomimetic Christian poetics. In addition, each chapter, and the study itself, concludes with a brief recapitulation from a "postmodernist" point of view. Consistent efforts are made to avoid unduly compromising those true and crucial differences between then and now. Real alterities shed real illumination, perhaps most brilliantly, when most unrelenting.

Yet when all is said and done, this book is not a strictly disinterested series of objective essays in medieval studies. There is a deep and unalterable bias, as implied by the range of concern reflected in the table of contents. This book does not align with those who find revelation in the deep ruptures, dislocations, and sudden silences that undeniably and traumatically punctuated Western cultural history, but rather with those, however unfashionable they may be at the moment, who are convinced of the existence of an empowering continuity underlying Western tradition—at least until the end of the fourteenth century.

Having said this, it seems appropriate to share some methodological and conceptual concerns. This study assumes that one appropriate response to the cultural development of speculative thinking and writing is to engage in speculative reading. The term *speculative* has in its root *speculum,* or looking glass, and to read speculatively is to read literature as if it were mirroring something important in ways that are important. The primary risks in speculative reading are to catapult oneself into the heady yet extremely thin air of allegory or sink, in a wincing phrase of George Saintsbury, into "that reverse or seamy side of allegory, rationalistic interpretation."[6] Although it can be argued that such excesses are more a fault of taste than method, avoidance

8

appears called for, even though it must be admitted that such avoidance has not always been successful.

This study also avoids current polemics concerning the act of reading, the nature of the text, deconstruction—in fact, nearly all that has fired debate in literary theory over the last fifteen years or so. Given that this study generally views medieval culture as logocentric, such programmatic avoidance of theoretical polemics will prove problematic for some readers and requires some explanation. It is a matter of time and space; efficiency suggests that I state my general position regarding current theory now and then proceed with that position as read.

Let me at once declare unmitigated pragmatic, but not necessarily ideological, affection for the enormous amount of ground won by recent theory. Indispensable to medievalists is the gradual uncovering of the mirroring capabilities of alterity itself for the modern reader of medieval literature. Major links in this collective project include the adumbrations of Peter Haidu and Eugene Vance in the early 1970s, the fuller demonstrations of H. R. Jauss, published as *Alterität und Modernität* in 1977, and the conversation held by Vance, Jauss, Paul Zumthor, and others in the special issue of *New Literary History* devoted to that seminal work performed by Jauss and other members of the Konstanz school in "Rezeptionsaesthetik," what Stanley Fish has dubbed "reader response" theory. In addition, extraordinary and not unrelated insights have recently been won by Judson Boyce Allen's ground-breaking analysis of medieval commentaries.[7]

Theoretically, this book is a conservative study: it is structuralist and formalist in nature, pervaded by what materialists call an "essentialist" or humanist view, and altogether unabashed at the ways in which literary works often appear to be part of a coherent tradition. Hence this study is perhaps most vulnerable to attack by the anti-mimetic Marxist critique of mirror reading, most richly and recently laid out by Dieter Schlenstedt.[8] Yet even here, both sides would probably stipulate that the major force of that critique is aimed at post-medieval literature rather than the literature of the Middle Ages per se. As for Derrida, *vive la différance!* Like it or not, his influence is unavoidable. Our resurgent interest in the ludic, our unease in the face of univocal readings, our suspicions in the face of grand closures, and our tendency to defer conclusion until a full inventory has at least been adumbrated all testify to his pervasive presence. Finally, there is the Appendix, a critical review of some specific contemporary positions on mirroring, including brief analyses of key ideas put forward by Jacques Lacan, Umberto Eco, and Richard Rorty.

Of all the things to be learned from the critical uproar in literary theory over the past two decades, perhaps the most important is to recognize just how profoundly self-conscious literature always is. More than that: it seems to be precisely in the presence of the most effective stratagems of reflexivity that we see literature most clearly and diligently engaged in its fundamental business of being about something other than itself.

A second important idea derives ultimately from the first: any critical project that tries to recapture a sense of the past unadulterated by a sense of the present is doomed. Modern "impositions" on the past cannot, by the very nature of the enterprise, be avoided; they can be seen and understood, even highly valued, for what they are. Modern readings will, by necessity, if not by desire or design, remain modern readings: what else could they be? But they can and must be significantly enriched by our self-conscious appropriation of what is "other" in the past. For in just such an appropriation lies, in Jauss's words, "the particular repercussion of aesthetic enticement: to take in bit by bit an unfamiliar attitude and thus to broaden one's own horizon of experience."

Jauss suggests that the medieval reader found enjoyable what for us may only be felt as "endless didactic digressions" precisely because:

they told him what he already knew, and because it satisfied him deeply to find each thing in its correct place in the world-model. The aesthetic pleasure of such recognition certainly presupposes the experiential horizon of the medieval life-world, which is only . . . available for us if it is reconstructed. . . . It cannot again become imaginable for the modern reader without historical mediation.

Modern readers must make their peace with more modest goals; it may in fact be both a great deal and all we can ask to discover an acceptable "fusion of the past horizon of aesthetic experience with the present one."

Thus we may well be forced to reduce the scale of any project that purports to reconstruct or reconstitute the past as a grand design; at least we must reduce some of the pretensions of such projects. But that does not relieve anyone from the clear imperative of gaining, from all sources, as much information about the past as can be mustered—if only to enable us to exercise what Jauss calls our aesthetic "bill of rights: a pleasurable understanding and an understanding pleasure."[9]

In terms of this study, that meant acquiring a clearer sense of the often overlapping boundaries in medieval culture between text and context, between a given text and what Jauss has termed its "horizon of expectation." In search of a clearer focus on the relationships that obtained in the Middle Ages between a given text and all that was not that text but was somehow called up as witness to that text by that text, concentration on paired images, characters and situations, on structural doubling, and on other various and related methods of inter- and intratextual mirroring produced unexpectedly bright and wide-ranging illumination. But to focus on such medieval mirroring and doubling as a literary method poses some unavoidable procedural, and perhaps some irresolvable conceptual difficulties.

The biggest problem arises from the way in which the radical (e.g., mirror, speculum, miroir, spiegel, speglio, etc.) constantly escapes denotative as well as connotative control. It simply refuses to preside with any stability over a limited set of referents. In the minds of medieval Europeans, *speculatio* had as much to do with ways of writing, thinking, and knowing as it did with ways of seeing. In a search for what the act of mirroring meant to the medieval mind, one might think one need only collate an inventory of literary passages in which mirrors appear as instruments and, by means of feature analysis, derive a clear and limited set of functions. What such an exercise does, however, is only begin to demonstrate the extraordinary range of *mirror*'s denotation.

The term denotes not only an instrument, but almost always, and almost immediately, a correlative function of extraordinary metaphorical potential as well. Mirroring reveals itself at once both as activity and as sign, with significations ranging from experiencing self-consciousness to the processes involved in thinking itself; from the typological functioning of intertextuality to the processes of typology itself; from the means by which we acquire knowledge to the ontological relationships obtaining in cosmic time between the human and the divine.

Perhaps the strongest demonstration of this denotative range is to be found by analyzing the uses of the word *speculum* and its vernacular variants in medieval manuscript titles. This was first schematically performed in 1954 by Sister Ritamary Bradley, and recently much more ambitiously by first the German and then the English redactions of the monumental mirror studies of Herbert Grabes.[10] The briefest glance at these studies will reveal the bewildering extent of semantic range that mirroring enjoyed throughout the Middle Ages and the early Renaissance.

In any attempt to unravel the rich and varied semantic skein that common usage of terms for "mirroring" or "reflecting" developed over centuries, one needs to attempt a rehabilitation of the "literal," to get a firm idea of the "thing itself" we refer to as "mirror." It immediately becomes quite clear that our general handbag knowledge of mirrors will not do. For one thing, the technology of mirror making from the Egyptians, Greeks, and Etruscans onward is an evolving history.[11] For another, both the lay and specialist views of optics and catoptrics shifted wildly over time. One must gather a reasonably differentiated set of ideas together about what people thought light was, how it was one saw, what they thought happened to the eye when it saw things, what they thought the eye did when it saw, and what they thought happened when something got mirrored.[12] Over the centuries, the debates concerning the nature of light, sight, eye, soul, mind—in fact the entire dialectic between physics and metaphysics, between being and knowing—shifted around, looped in on themselves, stacked up, sorted out, died down, and always, incessantly, got born again.

To provide a schematic sense of this rich historical interplay, the Appendix reviews some major contributions by David Lindberg and Jurgis Baltrusaitis and gives shorter notes on Gustav Hartlaub, Herbert Grabes, Marcia Colish, Rosalie Colie, Norbert Hugedé, Robert Javelet, Hans Leisegang, and Julia Kristeva. Questions are raised regarding the relationships that obtained between the physics and metaphysics of medieval optics, and there are some preliminary probes into the ways in which medieval theories of optics and catoptrics impinged on theology and medieval notions of being and knowing.

Facts, as usual, refuse to speak for themselves, and the record, as always, must be extrapolated from extant texts and other chancy shards that lie about: that eyeless, brutally casual detritus of the past. Thus one requires, in a study of this sort, a conceptual framework that allows for a certain range of methodological flexibility.[13] The table of contents reveals that this is not a systematic study of the history of an idea or of a literary image, but rather a series of interrelated chapters in that mode of literary criticism that links literature and philosophy. Perhaps the biggest risk, in terms of exhausting the reader's patience and tolerance, is to be as widely ranging in my senses of mirroring and the processes of literary reflection as were the Europeans of the Middle Ages themselves. And yet only by stretching the denotative as well as connotative frames of reference to the fullest range of medieval applicability can one fully appreciate the richness and depth, as well as the brilliance and range, of the ontological and epistemological intuitions generated by the medieval mind as it both engaged in and thought about the acts of speculation and reflection.

So we begin, as promised, with Virgil and Ovid, not reading them as classical philologists or historians would, but as would medievalists, typologically, as they forecast a figural relationship to the medieval texts that will become our primary concern.

CHAPTER I

The Ivory Gate: Virgil, Daedalus, and the Limits of Art

> Oh! Blessed rage for order, pale Ramon,
> The maker's rage to order words of the sea,
> Words of the fragrant portals, dimly-starred,
> And of ourselves and of our origins,
> In ghostlier demarcations, keener sounds.
> —Wallace Stevens, *The Idea of Order at Key West*

A special case of literary mirroring occurs, probably at least once in any extended work, when an image or scene functions as an interior mirror of the work as a whole.[1] That interior image speaks to the work in which we find it by bearing either a reinforcing or an inverse relation to the whole it is mirroring, usually a bit of both. An obvious example in the *Iliad* is the way Achilles' style of presiding over the funeral games in book 23 mirrors inversely Agamemnon's style of managing the war. The Song of the Sirens performs a similar function in the *Odyssey,* mirroring directly the driving forces of the *Iliad* and inversely the procedures of the *Odyssey.* But surely, in the case of the *Odyssey,* the two greatest mirror images of the epic as a whole, images in which the quest of the hero is both radicalized and epitomized, are to be found in Menelaos's confrontation with Proteus in *Odyssey* 4 and in Odysseus's Nekyia, or descent into hell, in *Odyssey* 11.

Homer's link to the Middle Ages is, of course, extremely tenuous, passing as it does through Rome. In order to treat the tradition of interior mirroring as available to the Middle Ages, one needs to turn to the strategies of Virgil and Ovid. In these first two chapters, we shall focus on the Ivory Gate of False Dream in *Aeneid* 6 and on the moment in which Apollo transforms the severed, singing head of Orpheus to stone in book 11 of the *Metamorphoses*. Each of these master images reaches backward in filiation as well as seminally forward in the development, in European literature, of the visit to the underworld as an empowering episode that credentials the hero as a bearer of truth. They function both as *intra-* and *inter*textual mirrors. *Intra*textually, each image concludes a parabola of revelation.

In this chapter I shall argue, from an examination of an inventory of imagistic contexts surrounding the Ivory Gate, that Aeneas's three-part catabasis (the descent with the Cumaean Sibyl and the Golden Bough, the showings of Anchises, and the release up to the light of the living through the Ivory Gate of False Dream) mirrors the ways in which the revelatory truth of Virgil's image of Rome reaches the light of the living court of Augustus through the necessarily artificial strategies of the poet's craft. In the next, I suggest that the severed head of Orpheus, singing on the shores of Lesbos, functions as an interior mirror of the head of Ovid himself, severed from us by exile and death. In addition, these master images mirror *inter*textually: they call up other texts in witness. Orpheus persuades Hades to allow him to return to Earth, where he sings songs of art and inverted love. After dismemberment by outraged bacchantes, he returns to his Eurydice in Hell. This rise and fall of Orpheus is inversely mirrored in Aeneas's descent into Hell, the revelations of Anchises, and the return of the hero to the living in Virgil's epic. In his own poem, Virgil rewrites Penelope's description of the Gates of Dream in such a way as to bring Odysseus's famous Nekyia to mind even as we participate in Aeneas's catabasis. Thus both Virgil's and Ovid's narratives of descent and resurrection, although in relation of chiastic inversion to one another, echo backward against the Ur-model of Homer's descent into Hell. In addition, we, from our own vantage point, see how all these narratives figure forth a continuing tradition of falling and rising, reaching from the harrowing of Hell and ascent into Heaven lying at the heart of the Christological narrative all the way to Dante's infernal descent under the guidance of Virgil and his ascent, with Beatrice, to the stars.

Such central moments of reflexivity, mirroring *intra*textually the containing text as well as *inter*textually the surrounding contexts of that text, always remind us that we are in the self-conscious literary *world* of texts. Thus they provide us with a heightened sense of being in the presence of poetic artifice rather than nature, of being in the world of *signum* rather than the world of *res*. This is a world in which the significant gesture always points beyond itself, backward and forward in time, even as it points toward itself, urging, in the reader, the recognitions of self-discovery. And this is perhaps why the most Virgilian of the Roman gods was Janus. Long meditation upon a head that looks both backward and forward can have the effect, in the mind's eye, of a metaphysical coalescence. The perspectives meld, and the image that at first insists on opposition begins to suggest some underlying identity.

Although one might well seek other paths, one way to get to Paradise is to back away from Hell. At least through *Aeneid* 8, Aeneas moves toward Rome by backing away from Troy. We discover early on that this is a method, that the constant backward glance is not mere morbid nostalgia but the work of the hero as sibyl. Virgil's literary image of history is neither linear nor progressively cyclical but, in ways that resonate with certain aspects of contemporary Judaic mysticism and later Christian thinking, typological, even eschatological.[2] The sibylline leaves of Troy's terrible past have written on them the itinerary of ultimate release: a transformation of personal suffering into a significant form that in turn provides for the community, in the hero as figure, a sure knowledge of its valor and destiny, and for the hero, as burdened individual, a reasonable hope of death and oblivion.

A related aspect of Virgil's program is systematic undermining, at key points in his poem, of any claims his epic might make for unmediated or privileged access to truth. Only twice does Aeneas get what would appear to be direct access to the future: as forescreened by Anchises in Hades (*Aeneid* 6) and in the presentation of Vulcan's shield (*Aeneid* 8). In the case of Vulcan's shield, Virgil concludes a lengthy pas de deux with *Iliad* 18 by informing us that Aeneas, glad as he was for the shield, did not know what the images meant. At the end of *Aeneid* 6, Anchises, after having revealed the center of the cosmos and the glorious future of Rome, brings his son to the double exits of hell and sends him, not through the honest gate of horn, but through the Ivory Gate of False Dream.

This raises one of the most celebrated cruxes in Virgil: how can one read these images of deprecation as not seriously compromising the Augustan ideal the poem is so clearly in the service of celebrating? The quest for such a reading is the linchpin of this chapter. The troublesome image of the Gate of Ivory requires the development and examination of a context in which a series of images can be seen as having a similar symbolic function in the poem: the Caves of Aeolus, Furor in the temple of Janus, the pictures on the gates of Juno's temple in the new Carthage, the reliefs of Daedalus on the gates of Apollo's temple at Cumae, the Golden Bough, the lament for Marcellus, the Shield of Vulcan, the quotation from Penelope, and finally the Gate of Ivory itself. They are all partial figures for art in general and for the *Aeneid* in particular, and, like the *Aeneid* which they figure forth and are fulfilled by, they must, in a special way, be literally false in order to become portals for a higher truth. If compelling arguments can be marshalled for such a reading of this chain of images, then we can extrapolate a new dimension, not only of Virgil's own implied poetics, but of our general understanding of the great affinity Virgil bore to the explicit and implied poetics of Chrétien de Troyes, Heinrich von Morungen, Dante, Langland, and Chaucer. The Middle Ages assumed they had Virgil on their side: exploring this aspect of Virgil's legacy helps us see better how true this assumption was.[3]

Let us begin where many conversations about Virgil begin: with his use of Homer.[4] Knauer, who exhausts both direct and oblique citations of Homer in the *Aeneid,* concludes his magisterial study by suggesting, with judicious hesitation, that Virgil's use of both history and Homer was essentially typological. I suggest we accept this as a working hypothesis and go on to see what implication such a hypothesis has for a reading of Virgil. The reader must have Homer in his head, as any contemporary of Virgil would have had. The reader then must meditate on both the resonance and the dissonance that every significant use of Homer brings with it. It is not enough to see Elpenor in Palinurus and have done. It is the almost Derridean *différance* between Elpenor and Palinurus that brings us where Virgil would lead us. One may not merely note that Dido's cutting silence imitates that of Ajax: we must pursue the differences that the similarities bring to the forefront of our readerly/writerly imaginations with such compelling force.

Just as in later Christian exegesis *Eva* figures forth and is ultimately fulfilled, reversed, and corrected by Mary's *Ave,* so images recalled in Homer must be seen as both figuring forth and being fulfilled and, if not actually reversed, called into question by the corresponding images in Virgil.[5] The act of reading both the text of Virgil and the memory of Homer weaves a web in the mind: a text between texts. It is in this arachnid mental architecture, which overspans the physical texts as written and becomes the text as read, that we discover Virgil's "true" message about Rome, a message which escapes its "brilliant, shining, polished, false gate" unscathed. The locus of the text-as-read is then precisely where Socrates says it should be, not in the scrolls of Lysias hidden under the cloak of Phaedrus, but in the living mind.

Let us begin the odyssey to the Ivory Gate at the point of discovering the hero. Odysseus broods on love's bitter mysteries at land's end, that liminal space between the apparent stabilities of the ground and the transforming powers of the sea. His life is running out. He looks with longing across the sea to his horizon. In the face of Calypso's offer of immortality, he has chosen death. He will return to Penelope. What Penelope has that Calypso does not have is that she will die. Even when most pressed, as later in the raft in *Odyssey* 5 when he blesses the death of the Danaans and Achilles, he does not bless death as a release from life, but blesses a heroic death as a better death than the lonely humiliation of drowning. By choosing death as a part of life he chooses for the significant life, a life ethically superior to that of the gods. Only when death is absolute can human things really matter.

Aeneas is also in that liminal space that joins the sea and land, but he is at sea. Storm threatens shipwreck. His Ithaca is in ashes, his Penelope dead. As he looks at the breakers that threaten his ship, his horizon stares him in the face. His words also bless death, three and four times over, "O terque quaterque beati," but it is the death of those who have gone before, the death of cessation and release, a death at the end of life that denies any ultimate value to human experience by the relief imagined in superseding it. The similarities of the abstract mise-en-scène in which we discover our respective heroes point to enormous difference, a difference that only begins to become intelligible with the bare schematic similarities as guide: beginning in Homer reaches forward: it is the next step toward an ever-opening future; beginning in Virgil reaches backward: it embodies and figures the end.

As we read on in book 1 of Aeneas's encounter with pictures of the Trojan War on the newly built gates of the temple of Juno, we also recollect Odysseus in Phaiakia. In both epics we are in the presence of classic moments of reflexivity. Odysseus, who has not yet identified himself to the household of Alkinoös, has been moved to tears by the song of Demodokos who has sung of the deception of the Trojan horse and the central role of Menelaos and Odysseus in the rape of Troy—a song he specifically asked for. The tears of Odysseus are tears of recognition; he surely does not weep for Troy, but for the waste of time between himself then and himself now captured in song; between a recollected external Odysseus captured in song and the present internal self still thrashing in the webs of Poseidon here and now in Phaiakia. Alkinoös, ignorant, is eager to assuage with knowledge:

> Tell me why you should grieve so terribly
> over the Argives and the fall of Troy.
> That was all gods' work, weaving ruin there
> so it should make a song for men to come.[6]

This curious bit of hyperbole, if that is what it is, which states that Zeus weaves fate and history in the service of poets is itself reflected in *Iliad* 6 where Helen, in her attempt to provide some consolation to Hector, says:

> But come now, come in and rest on this chair, my brother
> since it is on your heart beyond all that the hard work has fallen
> for the sake of dishonoured me and the blind act of Alexandros,
> us two, on whom Zeus set a vile destiny, so that hereafter
> we shall be made into things of song for the men of the future.[7]

The Virgilian countermoment to these self-recognitions of Helen and Odysseus occurs when Aeneas sees himself and his confreres figured in the pictures decorating Juno's temple in Dido's new Carthage. What in Homer is song, time in action, is in Virgil *pictura,* space held still by the introspective gaze.

In Homer, the commentator is ignorant of the true situation: Alkinoös's advice is interesting but has no special privilege. In the *Aeneid,* Virgil himself intervenes and calls into question the status of his newly introduced hero in a breathtaking strategy worthy of the later Henry James:

> For while he waited for the queen, he studied
> everything in that huge sanctuary,
> marveling at a city rich enough
> for such a temple, at the handiwork
> of rival artists, at their skillful tasks.
> He sees the wars of Troy set out in order:

the battles now famous through all the world,
the son of Atreus and of Priam, and
Achilles, savage enemy to both.
He halted. As he wept, he cried: "Achates,
where on this earth is there a land, a place
that does not know our sorrows? Look! There is Priam!
Here too, the honorable finds its due
and there are tears for passing things; here, too,
things mortal touch the mind. Forget your fears;
this fame will bring you some deliverance."
He speaks. With many tears and sighs he feeds
his soul on what is nothing but a picture.

(Aeneid 1.454–65)[8]

He feeds his soul on an empty picture: "animum pictura pascit inani." This startling intrusion by the narrator not only calls the existential position of the hero into question; it calls into question the enterprise of art itself. Art here is one with the portal of entry, just as the *Aeneid* was designed to be the intellectual portal of entry into the *civitas* of Augustan Rome. So, after shipwreck, our hero enters the new city whose temple is filled with images of the siege and destruction of the old city. But to the Roman eye, this new city is a fictive mirror, a type of the old city. It is Carthage, destroyed by Rome in 146 B.C. More important, it is also Alexandria, defeated and torched at Actium in 31 B.C., a city ruled over by Cleopatra, who took as lover Marc Antony, a more than imaginable anti-Octavian. Part of the typological force of Aeneas's meditation on the artistic representation of the Trojan War is that we see him on the threshold of Carthage, himself a figure of dual recent historical aspect. Aeneas bears within him the potential of both Antonius and Octavian. Aeneas-as-Antonius, who allies with the claims of private passion and loses all for love, must be denied. He must be denied by his inverse sibling, Aeneas-as-Octavian, who by that very denial declares himself the true Anchises of Augustus.

Just as significant in the typological reading is the role of art itself and, by implication, of the artist who provides the *pictura inani* on which the hero feeds his soul. If the ultimate end of the typological arch of the hero's signification lies this side of the actual frontier of the fiction, i.e., the real Augustus, then the ultimate end of the typological arch of the *pictura inani,* on which Augustus also feeds his soul, is

21

the *Aeneid*, just as the artist at the end of this typological rainbow is Virgil. The underlying equation begins to take shape. The idea of Rome is the epic fiction of Augustus: the *Aeneid* is the epic fiction of Virgil. It is this parallel function of art and governance that assures the constant resonance of the poem with the state: for the poem is not only a figure of the state; the state is also a poem. The philosophical King idealized by Plato has become the philosophical artist: a co-invention of Virgil and Caesar Augustus. For Augustus to have acceded to Virgil's dying wish to burn the *Aeneid* would have been to engage in filo-genocide: he would have burned the map of Rome. For all its darkness and self-subversion, the *Aeneid* was the only intellectually valid map in hand.

Aeneas's next confrontation with art is in book 6 on the shores of Cumae, and it is a mirror of the first. Again memorial art appears as a pictorial program on the portals of a temple, this time Apollo's. But this time the artist has a history and a name. On his return from Crete, Daedalus built this temple:

> Upon the gates he carved Androgeos' death
> and then the men of Athens, made to pay
> each year with seven bodies of their sons;
> before them stands the urn, the lots are drawn.
> And facing this, he set another scene:
> the land of Crete, rising out of the sea;
> the inhuman longing of Pasiphae,
> the lust that made her mate the bull by craft;
> her mongrel son, the two-formed Minotaur,
> a monument to her polluted passion.
> And here the inextricable labyrinth,
> the house of toil was carved; but Daedalus
> took pity on the princess Ariadne's
> deep love, and he himself helped disentangle
> the wiles and mazes of the palace; with
> a thread he guided Theseus' blinded footsteps.
> And Icarus, you also would have played
> great part in such a work, had his grief allowed;
> twice he had tried to carve your trials in gold,
> and twice a father's hand had failed.
>
> (*Aeneid* 6.20–33)

22

These panels of Daedalus function not only as portals to the temple of Apollo, but also, in an extended sense, as portals of entry to *Aeneid* 6 as a whole. Thus they frame, with the Gates of Horn and Ivory at the end, the entire catabasis.

The passage is redolent with the death of sons.[9] We begin in Athens with Androgeos, the son of Minos of Crete, who, in the version surely on Virgil's mind, was sacrificed by Aegeus, king of Athens, to the Marathonian bull. On the opposite gate Daedalus has sculpted the grotesque engendering of the "new" son of Minos, the Minotaur. He is called *Veneris monumenta*, a monument not only to Love, but to Venus herself: the passion that brought his mother Pasiphae to bestial adultery was visited on her by Venus because Pasiphae, in turn, betrayed Venus's own adultery with Mars. Daedalus builds the *inextricabilis error* in verbal parody of, and hence in poignant allusion to, Catullus 64. The labyrinth is built to enclose, contain, and control the unnatural and unholy mixed form, this *contaminatio* of man and beast. Yet however grotesque, the Minotaur is also a son; he is sacrificed to and by Theseus. Daedalus, the artist, is the agent of mediation in both cases. Back on the Athenian panel, we see the father standing before the urn of chance to select the seven sons who will be sacrificed to the Minotaur. Then the *labor* of the labyrinth by Daedalus and his own undoing of it for the sake of Ariadne's love for Theseus, but it is an undoing that, as it leads to success, leads inexorably to Theseus's betrayal of Ariadne. The myth, as Catullus so brilliantly demonstrates, is as labyrinthine as the palace itself. Then in rare but effective use of apostrophe Virgil declares a bond between himself and Daedalus by addressing Icarus as *tu:*

> . . . tu quoque magnam
> partem opere in tanto, sineret dolor, Icare, haberes;
> bis conatus erat casus effingere in auro,
> bis patriae cecidere manus.
> (*Aeneid* 6.30–33)

Daedalus plays art for very high stakes: he builds structures to contain monsters that threaten the survival of civility itself. Yet he fails. Twice he attempts to capture the failure of his art; twice the grief at the loss of his son keeps him from completing his labor. Typologically this scene figures forth: in fiction, Aeneas's loss of Pallas and in history, Rome's loss of Marcellus.

That historical loss is of course directly dramatized as Anchises, after the show of heroes in Hell, answers Aeneas's question regarding the identity of the boy whose head is shadowed in darkness with these famous lines, which, we hear, drew tears in the court of Augustus:

> . . . no youth born
> of the seed of Ilium will so
> excite his Latin ancestors to hope;
> the land of Romulus will never boast
> with so much pride of any of her sons.
> I weep for righteousness, for ancient trust,
> for his unconquerable hand: no one
> could hope to war with him and go untouched,
> whether he faced the enemy on foot
> or dug his foaming horse's flank with spurs.
> O boy whom we lament, if only you
> could break the bonds of fate and be Marcellus.
> With full hands, give me lilies; let me scatter
> these purple flowers, with these gifts, at least,
> be generous with my descendant's spirit,
> complete this service, although it be useless.
>
> (*Aeneid* 6.875–86)

This passage raises several issues that require brief examination before we can proceed to the Ivory Gate. First, the close of Anchises's speech in which he asks for lilies reads "fungar inani munere" [complete this empty service]. This fulfills and points back to the pictures at an exhibition in book 1 where Aeneas "animum pictura pascit inani" [fed his soul on empty pictures]. The link implied here joins the priestly and poetic arts: marmorealization is part of memorialization. To pay tribute to an action, especially a future action, is in a way to complete its death, and it is the more honest part of ritual consolations such as poems and funerals that we realize both how real the consolation can seem and how empty such consolations in fact must be.

The other issues have to do with how the hero's necessitous unknowing meshes with both the ethical contexts and the clarifying powers of poetic art.

It is the rare reader who has not, if only in private moments of frustration, found Aeneas slow-witted. To some extent this is ungenerous. The reader has been given a steady diet of advanced and reliable information that is never available to Aeneas. The question then becomes whether or not such ignorance on the part of the hero is functional. The question of heroic possibility in the state of minimum awareness was often a central problem in Greek tragedy, and both Sophocles and Euripides should be present in our thinking as we look at those instances where Virgil seems to undermine his hero's awareness, if not actually his intelligence.

Three instances are of particular interest. One we have already glanced at: the authorial intrusion in *Aeneid* 1 concerning empty pictures that follows the moving lines on things mortal touching the mind. In *Aeneid* 8, Virgil engages in one of many full-scale exercises in Homeric resonance. As we read in the text of Virgil's Shield of Vulcan, which Venus brings to Aeneas, we call up to memory Homer's Shield of Hephaestos, which Thetis brings to Achilles. Achilles's shield is bifocular, a circle with dual centers: a city at peace and a city at war. Aeneas's shield has only one center: Actium and the triumph of Augustus. Both teem with imagery. Homer makes a point of the miracle of Hephaestos's work: all the figures really move. Virgil animates his imagery, but all movement is credited to the successful illusory powers of the engraver. But perhaps the greatest difference lies in the reaction of the respective heroes to the divine gift of arms. In *Iliad* 19 none of the myrmidons dares even look at the shield except for Achilles:

> . . . only Achilles
> looked, and as he looked the anger came harder upon him
> and his eyes glittered terribly under his lids, like sunflare.
> He was glad, holding in his hands the shining gifts of Haephaestos.
> (*Iliad*, 19.15–18)

Although it is difficult to prove whether or not the question of ignorance or knowledge is actually an issue for Homer, one can argue that the sudden flash of sunflare from under the eyelids of Achilles is a token of intuitive, semidivine anagnorisis. The question I ask is close to that which Yeats asks about Leda:

> Did she put on his knowledge with his power
> Before the indifferent beak could let her drop?[10]

Indeed, whatever one makes of anagnorisis at this moment of Homer's narrative, it is clear that it was very much on Virgil's mind. The reaction of Aeneas, in comparison to Achilles, is remarkably quiet:

> Aeneas marvels at his mother's gift,
> the scenes on Vulcan's shield, and he is glad
> for all these images though he does not
> know what they mean.
>
> (*Aeneid* 8.729–30)

In book 6, of course, Aeneas's ignorance is a narrative necessity if the pedagogical function of descent-as-revelation is to have any point. But there too Aeneas never really seems to learn anything—there is never any real response. If he did manage to learn anything, it would seem hopelessly compromised by Virgil's arrangement of having him exit Hades into the prosaic light of day through the Ivory Gate of False Dream. This brings us back to the crux with which we began.

If one turns to Greek tragedy rather than epic, and thinks of Oedipus, Philoctetes and Achilles, Theseus and Hippolytus, or Cadmus and Agave, one can see how deep ignorance of the designs of the gods need not subvert our sense of the hero's intelligence, but in fact rather amplifies the power and validity of his will. It brings the hero into scale: none of us knows the will or design of the gods. Yet action is imperative. If we knew in advance how it would all work out we might be as trivial, as powerless, or as paralyzed as Cassandra or Teiresias. Roman heroism depends for its own credibility on a high quotient of ignorance on the part of the actor. What would be heroic about doing what one knew in advance would work? Virgil's insistence on Aeneas's ignorance in the face of revelation does several things. It puts him into human scale. It accords with the tragic principle of exclusion: ignorance clarifies the ethical situation in which one tests the validity of native will and intelligence. And it provides a privileged and distanced view for the reader, who in turn is in danger of the same ethical complacence in which the gods themselves indulge. To remain at Virgil's ordained distance and retain one's humanity is one of the great challenges Virgil offers the reader.

The last issue in this discussion centering on the panels of Daedalus has to do with the nature and function of the image of the labyrinth. Again, a return to Homer. There is a sense, very difficult to document, that as one looks from Homer to Virgil one's inner eye passes from the heady freedoms and risks of time to the more modest sureties and consolations of space, and not without significant cost.[11] One recalls that Odysseus discovers himself in song, a medium of time, whereas Aeneas discovers himself in *pictura,* a medium of space. Virgil's spaces, in contrast to Homer's, seem often dense, static, multidimensional, architectural, almost penal. Homeric space is more often a simple platform on which to capture the choreographies of time. Recall the Phaiakian dancers:

> And next Alkinoös called upon his sons
> Halios and Leadamas, to show
> the dance no one could do as well as they
> handling a purple ball carved by Polybos.
> One made it shoot up under the shadowing clouds
> as he leaned backward; bounding high in the air
> the other cut its flight far off the ground
> and neither missed a step as the ball soared.
> The next turn was to keep it low, and shuttling
> hard between them, while the ring of boys
> gave them a steady stamping beat.

Odysseus now addressed Alkinoös:

> O Majesty, model of all your folk,
> your promise was to show me peerless dancers;
> here is the promise kept. I am all wonder.[12]

The floor in Homer is merely a place on which to dance. In Virgil such space is transformed into a figure of containment and control. Recall Virgil's Cave of Aeolus:

> . . . in his enormous cave King Aeolus
> restrains the wrestling winds, loud hurricanes;
> he tames and sways them with his chains and prison.
> They rage in indignation at their cages;
> the mountain answers with a mighty roar.
> Lord Aeolus sits in his high citadel;
> he holds his scepter, and he soothes their souls
> and calms their madness. Were it not for this

then surely they would carry off the sea
and lands and steepest heaven, sweeping them
across the emptiness. But fearing that,
the all-able father hid the winds within
dark caverns, heaping over them high mountains;
and he assigned to them a king who should,
by Jove's sure edict, understand just when
to jail and when, commanded, to set free.

(*Aeneid* 1.52–63)

In both passages there is stirring movement, passion, and control. In Homer, the control is one with the boys' stirring movement and passion. We have controlled tension within a unified source of energy: the dancer. In Virgil, the need for control can only be answered by the imposition of a governor who, on mandate from the god, imposes in turn the arts of governance. One more image completes this brief excursus on Virgilian space. It closes Jupiter's long prophetic speech in book 1 which promises the ultimate coming of Julius Caesar and the beginning of lasting peace. But the image of peace is somehow penulti-mate and is seriously compromised by a final image of associated brutal-ity:

... with battle forgotten
savage generations shall
grow generous. And aged Faith and Vesta
together with the brothers Romulus
and Remus shall make laws. The gruesome
gates of war, with tightly welded iron plates
shall be shut fast. Within, unholy Rage
shall sit on his ferocious weapons, bound
behind his back by a hundred knots of brass;
he shall groan horribly with bloody lips.

(*Aeneid* 1.291–96)

The grotesquerie attending the image of Furor is not there merely to provide a neoteric frisson, but indicates that the enemy is real and never dies. *Furor* is a radical image of *Amor,* of desire, and is for Virgil a metonym of the energies of the human mind that are beyond the control of reason. The imperatives of Virgil's art are ethically, politi-cally, and aesthetically severe. Reason alone cannot effectively govern instinct. It requires the structures of the art of state, which are the same as the state of art. Art, for Virgil, is in the service of a higher and sterner master than any isolated "truth" viewed merely as a philosophic position. Art is in the service of necessitous belief, "but with the nicer knowledge of belief, that what it believes in is not true."[13]

In one way, Virgil provides a justification of art as handmaiden that is very compatible with the cultural imperatives of the Christian Middle Ages. In another, he foreshadows the secular humanism of the mid-twentieth century by insisting that ultimate authenticity comes from action based on belief, yet also insisting that the claims of belief upon the intellect are not absolute. The dignity that reason thus maintains under such imperatives of authentic action comes in a kind of *resignatio* that is by no means incompatible with heroic action in which the quotient of ignorance on the part of the hero is high.

Such a system of contrapuntal tension is not that stable. The structures that reason devises for control of instinctual passion often fail in the face of love ("twice he tried to form your story in gold, twice the hands of the father failed"). The structures themselves also elicit ambivalent responses; thus the same image can have both negative and positive value. Bernard Knox has shown this brilliantly in his article on the images of fire and serpent in *Aeneid* 2.[14] Surely the image of the labyrinth has such multiple value. It conceals, sequesters, and controls an unspeakable force at its center, and yet its very structure provides form to the surrounding world and gives to the intellect a map of significant penetration to its center. It is the same structure that, with the thread provided by its creator, allows the hero to engage in the necessary pageant of mortal combat with the beast, which has as its implied double his own image. The labyrinth defines both the problem and the solution and as such is always about something other than itself, even when it seems to be most about itself. It is in this higher sense that the labyrinth, a radical figure for art, is then never true; but the beast it contains is always real. And this *labor* of the labyrinth ("hic labor ille domus inextricabilis error," [*Aeneid* 6.27]) figures forth and is fulfilled by the *labor* required to re-ascend out of hell:

> . . . facilis descensus Averno:
> noctes atque dies patet atri ianua Ditis;
> sed revocare gradum superasque evadere ad auras,
> hoc opus, *hic labor est.*

[Easy the way that leads into Avernus: day
and night the door of darkest Dis is open.
But to recall your steps, to rise again
into the upper air: *that is the labor;*
that is the task.]

(*Aeneid* 6.126–29, my emphasis)

The last station to the Ivory Gate is the Golden Bough. The classic essay on the Golden Bough was written in the fifties by Robert A. Brooks.[15] The key image is "crepitabat brattea vento" [the leaves rattled in the wind]. Brooks argues convincingly that the bough partakes both of the order of nature and the order of artifice. My more radical gloss would insist that in so doing it also partakes of the order of life and the order of death. The underlying equation, which declares an identity of artifice and death, also insists that nature and life themselves have no intelligible significance for us except in figures that unite them with the realms of artifice and death. As Aeneas raises the Golden Bough, this double-thing, and thereby gains access to the epistemology of the dead, so we raise this double-thing, the *Aeneid,* and thereby gain access to the secrets of our own descent into Hell. Brooks closes his brilliant essay with the following remarks:

The causes of things are never to be known with the same ecstatic certainty as Lucretius'. Neither causes nor things are the same in Virgil's world. They are revealed, not deduced and conceal themselves again in the act of revelation. . . . At the center of Virgil's poem, the golden bough, in all its density of suggestion, is the primary symbol of this splendid despair.[16]

I would agree that despair in Virgil is both real and splendid. But the bough, I would suggest, declares its meaning primarily by function, not by reference. And as it gains the hero entry to revelation, it signifies not despair, but the power of art itself as a mixed thing, partaking of opposite orders: nature and artifice, life and death. Like the labyrinth, which opens book 6, the medial image of the Golden Bough is a figure of the *Aeneid* itself: it is a troubled mirror, a *mise en abîme* within the work it is designed to reflect.

By this route of functionally linked images we arrive, with Virgil, at the Ivory Gate. Here is the passage:

> There are two gates of Sleep: the one is said
> to be of horn, through it an easy exit
> is given to true shades; the other is
> made of polished ivory, perfect, glittering,
> but through that way the Spirits send false
> dreams into the world above. And here Anchises,
> when he is done with words, accompanies
> the Sibyl and his son together; and
> he sends them through the gate of ivory.
>
> (*Aeneid* 6.893–98)

To repeat the thorny question, why send Aeneas through the Gate of False Dream? A small library could be built out of the critical discussions that have been held on this issue.[17]

I would like to begin the answer as we began the chapter, with a look at the Homeric resonance. Before we can answer the main question, we must ask why we suddenly find ourselves, at the end of this most Roman book of revelation, listening to Penelope lecture Odysseus in disguise on the nature of truth, dream, and the dead:

> Two gates for ghostly dreams there are: one gateway
> of honest horn, and one of ivory.
> Issuing by the ivory gate are dreams
> of glimmering illusion, fantasies,
> but those that come through solid polished horn
> may be borne out, if mortals only knew them.[18]

The effect of burdening Penelope with the narrative of the *Aeneid*, perhaps at its most vulnerable point, is double. First we are reminded generically of the road not taken. We are reminded, by mere consideration of the *Odyssey* at this crucial point, that Homer chose quite a different mode of exit for his hero. Odysseus notices that the spell of blood is breaking down and that the true *nullus ordo* that is Hell's "natural" state is beginning to manifest itself:

> But first came shades in thousands rustling
> in a pandemonium of whispers, blown together,
> and the horror took me that Persephone
> had brought from darker hell some saurian death's head.
> I whirled then, made for the ship.[19]

31

In the face of such ghastly breakdown, Odysseus flees in terror. By reminding us of Homer, Virgil signals to us that he has taken some pains to provide a different exit, that he knew what he was doing. The second effect of hearing Penelope speak is that we are suddenly made especially aware, by literary quotation, that we are not in the world of history but in the world of literature, of artifice: we are in two texts at once. This is an elegant, very Virgilian strategy of *Verfremdung*, or distancing, which reminds us that we are in the presence of *words* of the world, and not the world they would be words *of*. We are reminded of the necessary artificiality of the literary image at precisely the point where the distinction between true and false is surfaced in the narrative. This *deixis*, or pointing, at the nature of the game we are playing is anticipatory of Vaihinger and Wittgenstein. In addition, we have the aesthetic domain reinforced by the Virgilianized diction of Penelope, which attributes to the Ivory Gate of False Dream elements appropriate to a style—a style very much like Virgil's own: "altera *candenti perfecta nitens* elephanto" [the other of *glowing, perfect, shining* ivory].

While Homer's Penelope expends her valorizing adjectival energies on the honest Gate of Horn, Virgil attaches his aesthetic and illuminating values to the *falsa* of the Gate of Ivory. This is consistent with the simultaneous presence of positive and negative values in the image of the "empty pictures" in Carthage, the reliefs of Daedalus on the Cumean shore and the Golden Bough in the dark wood. The Ivory Gate of False Dream, like these other master images, is a figure of art in general and of the *Aeneid* in particular.

The defense of the aesthetically beautiful, ethically and politically utilitarian, but literally false vehicle is fundamentally an *argumentum ad necessitatem,* perhaps the strongest argument of them all.[20] It is the argument of the inner-sanctum stoic: There never was a "real" Aeneas who either entered or exited a "real" Hell, just as there will never be a "real" Rome or, for that matter, a "real" Republic. There will be, because there must be, the necessary fiction of Rome, which, by means of the false Ivory Gate of significant form, can and will reveal the structure of a just man's mind.[21] The hero of that fiction, whether Augustus or Aeneas, will function as a necessary angel of earth. He is necessary, he would say, because

> . . . in my sight, you see the earth again
> Cleared of its stiff and stubborn, man locked set,

And, in my hearing, you hear its tragic drone
Rise liquidly in liquid lingerings
Like watery words awash; like meanings said
By repetitions of half meanings. Am I not,
Myself, only half of a figure of a sort,
A figure half seen, or seen for a moment, a man
Of the mind, an apparition apparelled in
Apparels of such lightest look that a turn
Of my shoulder and quickly, too quickly, I am gone?[22]

CHAPTER 2

The Severed Head: Ovid, Orpheus, and the Powers of Art

This endlessly elaborating poem
Displays the theory of poetry,
As the life of poetry. A more severe,

More harassing master would extemporize
Subtler, more urgent proof that the theory
Of poetry is the theory of life,

As it is, in the intricate evasions of as,
In things seen and unseen, created from nothingness,
The heavens, the hells, the worlds, the longed-for lands.
    —Wallace Stevens, "An Ordinary Evening in New Haven"

Just as Virgil uses Homer as an attendant mirror in which to reflect his Roman poetics, so Virgil's *Aeneid* provides Ovid with a structure against which to play out his own poem so that we can see more closely what is new and different in the *Metamorphoses*. Just as the ivory gates can be read as an interior mirror of Virgil's program in the *Aeneid*, so the Orpheus panels in books 10 and 11 mirror the procedures of the *Metamorphoses*. And if the perfect, polished Ivory Gate of False Dream is an interior mirror of the gestalt of the entire *Aeneid*, so the lyre and severed head of Orpheus produce an unheard music that, in our imagination, provides an echo chamber for the *carmen perpetuum* of the *Metamorphoses*. As we meditate on an orphic music surviving the death of its maker, we hear Ovid's own valedictory voice at the end of his epic of transformation promising us that, as long as Rome shall live and man shall read, he will be living too: his life-promising last word in the *Metamorphoses* will reverberate in our memories with the imagined voice of Orpheus singing beyond the dead: *vivam!*

After a few remarks concerning the images of time and human history in Ovid, we will turn to the central and ultimately related subject of Ovid's explicit and implied ideas regarding the theory and practice of art and the metamorphic powers of the poet/artist in the face of nature.[1]

If Virgil's images of history function, in Roman Jakobson's sense of the terms, more metaphorically than metonymically, we often sense in them the almost palpable absence of an implied counter image. Ovid's images declare themselves the other way around.[2] If Virgil's images reveal a program resigned to the substitutability of one thing for another while under intense teleological pressure, Ovid's images celebrate the world's bizarre, grotesque, funny, and unexpectedly lovely and redemptive contiguity. Time is not as obviously necessitous in Ovid as in Virgil; time in Ovid is metamorphic, and metamorphic time is not so much a matter of progress toward closure as an ordering axis in the creation of an endlessly convoluting literary space in the reader's imagination.[3]

There is no single theory of history in Ovid; there are three: all mutually exclusive in any logical sense, all brazenly jumbled together with a surprisingly consistent result. The first theory is lifted from Hesiod: history as phasal descent, reality as entropic: the Four Ages of Man as they range downward from Gold to Silver to Bronze to Iron. And though Ovid sends Jove to redo the world early on and in that sense may seem to cancel out this Hesiodic pattern, once so strongly depicted, it cannot be erased by either divine or poetic fiat. In fact, the Hesiodic pattern remains pervasive in the general scheme of the fictions that make up the first four-fifths of the poem. That general scheme goes from early disorder (*amores deorum*) to a later sorrow (humans suffering in the absence, rather than in the mediating presence, of the gods).

At the same time, during the latter third of the poem there is the strong implication that history is also revealing itself as progressive: things are getting better and better: we leave the world of mythic gods and enter political history, and as we move from Achilles, Odysseus, and Aeneas, we move to Julius Caesar, Octavian, and the idealized *pax* of the Augustan principate. Ovid even insists, not altogether playfully, that Julius Caesar must be deified in order to justify the son.

Finally, in the last book, buried in a lecture on the virtues of the vegetarian, we find a third understanding of time, the Heraclitean theory of Pythagoras *redivivus,* in which history anticipates Newton's conservation of energy. In the extraordinary speech of Pythagoras, we are told that reality is driven by a natural and unified force, not unlike Dylan Thomas's "force that through the green fuse drives the flower." It is constant in its sum while its forms change eternally—neither for better nor for worse.

The copresence of these three theories of time, logically at war with one another and exerting radically different pressures on human exis-tence, is, at least in Ovid's hands, no more hypocritical or intellectually sloppy than the twentieth century's simultaneous use of both wave and particle theories to represent and account for the various phenomena of light. Ovid is, in a way, a prototype of Niels Bohr, generating, with his idea of a perpetual song running from Creation to our own day, his own reconciling principle of complementarity. The rashest aspect of Ovid's strategy in this connection is the way in which his promise at the beginning turns out to be the negative of what he actually delivers. He opens the *Metamorphoses* as if he truly believed in the explanatory power of etiology:

> In nova fert animus mutatas dicere formas
> corpora; di, coeptis (nam vos mutastis et illas)
> adspirate meis primaque ab origine mundi
> ad mea perpetuum deducite tempora carmen!

> [My mind moves me to speak of the new: forms changed
> to different bodies. Gods—you changed those forms—
> breathe into my work: help weave a never-ending song
> that links the origin of things to my own time.]
>
> (*Metamorphoses* 1.1–4, my translation)[4]

One way or another, he does manage to spin each story into the web or *textus* of the whole, and when the links are obviously forced, he offers explicit apology. In fact, that candid, shared, yet nonetheless intrusive sense of forced connection is a characteristically Ovidian alienation effect, and leads us to see that the actual flux of life in time has no inherent meaning at all, that it is the work of the poet as *vates* that gives order to the world. The *Metamorphoses* does not so much discover order in the world as create and subvert it as a "reality principle" of metamorphic art.

It is more than a little ironic that the *Metamorphoses* celebrates, at its center, art's ultimate disadvantage in the face of nature. In the "real time" of nature, flux continues and never ceases—hence there is no "real" end, no "real" meaning of anything beyond itself. Narrating art, in spite of all its splendid mimetic powers, has this fatal and magnificent flaw: the words and images come only one at a time and finally they stop. Yet as they cease at the last page and the surrounding silence begins, there remains a "fitful tracing" of the pattern generated by the moving words on the reader's mind: a residual shape in memory that does *not* change, that *does* end, and therefore *can* mean beyond itself. The disadvantaged strategies of narrative are also redemptive: they can convert real time to the memorial spaces of remembered time.

It is this final power that allows the artist, but *not* nature, to perform the vatic function of providing us with significant form in the face of disfiguring time. It is this metamorphic power of art that provides for the human condition both a tribute to its own collective valor and a private release from individual suffering. In anticipation of Augustine, narrative can literally save our lives by converting life's energies into the more lasting and stable shapes of artistic form. All the transformations in the *Metamorphoses* are variations on this central project. And so we shall see that although the strategies Ovid used are vastly different from those of Virgil, the ultimate functions and consolations of art remain, for both poets, much the same.

Ovid's image of the death and "resurrection" of Achilles not only indexes but also embodies this "saving" power of art:

> . . . the same god who armed him burned him [armarat deus idem idemque cremarat]. Now there's not enough left of him to fill a jar. But his fame's alive and his glory fills the world [non bene conpleat urnam / at vivit, totum quae gloria conpleat orbem]. (*Meta.* 12.614–17, my translation)

Over and over again, it is the literary *figura* of *Natura* that Ovid, for sound reasons, empowers with art's stratagems; but we shall see, through the lenses of many related images, that the net effect is to convince us, by having us see how artistic nature is, to see how natural art is.

The first great story of human failing in the *Metamorphoses* is also a story of artistic filiation: the story of Phaeton and Apollo. It is not by accident that this story rhymes with Virgil's Icarus and Daedalus. As in Virgil, pride of place is afforded to art by means of artwork carved on gateways: here the folding double doors of the palace of the sun. What Phaeton enters, in his search for his father, is the gate of the living world:

Design had conquered matter [*materiam superabat opus*]. The artist Vulcan *carved* the earth-encircling waters, the wheel of earth, the overarching skies. The sea holds cerulean gods, Triton's horn, ambiguous Proteus who changes always, and Aegaeon gripping the backs of whales, the sea-nymph Doris and her daughters, some could be seen swimming, others sitting on the rocks, green hair drying, still others riding fishes. They did not share one face, nor were they very different, as is the case with sisters. The land has *graven* men and cities, beasts and forests, rivers, nymphs and woodland gods. Above them the *image* of the shining sky *is set,* and zodiac signs: six on the right door, six on the left [haec super inposita est caeli fulgentis *imago* / *signaque* sex foribus dextris totidemque sinistris]. (*Meta.* 2.5–18, my translation and emphasis)

The gate is reminiscent of Virgil's temple doors (*Aeneid* 1 and 6), not in tonality, of course, but in emphasis on artifice and design. Ovid's imagery is lush, redolent of water, the mindless transformations of Proteus, and Doris with her seaside girls. We do not have, however, the images of nature but imagery of nature transformed by art. The girls by the sea, by the beautiful sea, come not from the beach but from frescoes painted on the walls of Roman villas. The diction of the artisan in the first and last lines of the passage reinforces our sense of art as a metamorphic ordinator of reality, with the *materiam* subject to the demands of the *opus* at the beginning, and with our fixed *pictura* at the end: the *signa* of the stars set in the *imago* of the sky. Through these images drawn from nature, but given new and stable form by the metamorphic powers of art, we enter, with Phaeton, the palace of the sun to read:

> Words of the fragrant portals, dimly-starred,
> And of ourselves and of our origins,
> In ghostlier demarcations, keener sounds.[5]

Later on, in book 3, there is a striking assertion of nature as mimetic artist in the depiction of Gargaphia, the pool where Actaeon sees more of Diana than he wishes:

There was a vale there, thick with pine and sharp-needled cypress, called Gargaphia, the sacred haunt of Diana. In its inmost nook, there was a shaded grotto, *no artist worked it: Nature, by her own genius, had imitated art [arte laboratum nulla: simulaverat artem ingenio natura suo]*; she had shaped a native arch of soft tufa and living rock. (*Meta.* 3.155–60, my translation and emphasis)

As we see here by the light but shifting attributions of agency from art to nature to art, one of the central functions of Ovid's literary images of art and nature in liminal cahoots with one another is to transform, in our minds, the stuff of the world of changing appearances into the stability of significant form and then to create compelling illusions that these stable forms have themselves become a natural part of the living, changing world.

In a systematic pursuit of a taxonomy of the varied metamorphic strategies pursued by Ovid across the vast canvas of his *Metamorphoses,* I found that the majority of his literary transformations clustered around three general kinds of change. I would like to explore briefly these three related modes of the metamorphic art, as they form a base of poetic procedure in the poem: reflection, crystallization, and elevation. Unlike the previous chapter on Virgilian reflexive poetics, there will be no arachnid spinning of argument; on the contrary, the discussion here will resemble more a guided tour of pictures at an exhibition.

Nonetheless, as we examine specific applications of these modes, one after another, we shall see that they share interpenetrating boundaries, that they do function together in complex and synthesizing ways. To show as well as argue the ways in which I perceive Ovid orchestrating these metamorphic modes as aspects of a unified poetic vision, I shall conclude the chapter by focusing on the extended panel of orphic narratives (book 10 and beginning of book 11), seeing it as an inverse mirror of the program of the *Metamorphoses* as a whole.

Reflection

Reflection involves recognition and transformation on the part of the observer who sees in the mirror of art some bit of the self crucial to the success or failure of his desire. A number of such moments in Ovid are fleeting and delicious. As poor Io slips into bovinity, the art of her own transformation begins to terrify her and she wanders until she has an opportunity for anagnorisis. And the outcome is an inverse anticipation of the denouement of Narcissus:

> Her woeful story fain she wou'd have told,
> With hands upheld, but had no hands to hold.
> Her head to her ungentle keeper bow'd,
> She strove to speak, she spoke not, but she low'd:
> Affrighted with the noise, she look'd around,
> And seem'd t'inquire the author of the sound.
> Once on the banks where often she had play'd
> (Her father's banks), she came, and there survey'd
> Her alter'd visage, and her branching head;
> And starting, from her self she wou'd have fled.
>
> (*Meta.* 1.635–41, Dryden)

Another high moment is the ameliorating effect upon world trade of Polyphemus's desperation in love: here the mirror of art works good in the world as long as its truth is imperceptible to the beholder: Galatea reports that the Cyclops

> . . . felt the force of love, and fierce desire,
> And burnt for me, with unrelenting fire.
> Forgot his caverns, and his wooly care,
> Assum'd the softness of a lover's air;
> And comb'd, with teeth of rakes, his rugged hair.
> Now with a crooked scythe his beard he sleeks;
> And mows the stubborn stubble of his cheeks:
> Now in the crystal stream he looks, to try
> His miagres, and rowls his glaring eye.
> His cruelty, and thirst of blood are lost;
> And ships securely sail along the coast.
>
> (*Meta.* 13.764–69, Dryden)

As the power of love saves the ships at sea, Polyphemus goes on to sing his hilarious panegyric to Galatea—elegant buffoonery that was aped, over fifteen hundred years later, by Caliban's sumptuous mooning over Miranda.

41

Perhaps the most telling panel in the early books concerning the reflexive and reflective powers of art is the narrative of Echo and Narcissus. The phonic mirrors of the dialogue between Narcissus and Echo lead nowhere.[6]

It happened that the boy, having strayed afar from friends, said, "Anybody here?" and Echo echoed "Here!" ["ecquis adest?," et "adest!" responderat Echo]. Amazed, he looked around in all directions. He called "Come here!" with rising voice. And she called his calling back to him. He looked back to see nobody coming. He asked, "Why flee from me" and heard again the self-same words. He stopped, deceived by an imagined other voice, and said, "Here let us come together." And never happier, Echo answered "Let us come. Together." ["Huc coeamus!" ait, nullique libentius umquam / Responsura sono "coeamus!" rettulit Echo] (*Meta.* 3.386–87, my translation)[7]

The boy who (de)reflects all who desire him will live just so long as he refuses the Delphic imperative, just so long, Teiresias says to his mother, "as he does not know himself" [si se non noverit]. This pretty nobody who has refused everybody then comes upon his image in the pool of his unknowing. It is an antiplace, a place where nobody lives, a pastoral without pastors.

There was a fountain, clear, with silver waters, to which no shepherds came, nor she-goats feeding on the mountain, nor any other cattle, nor did bird nor beast disturb it, nor falling branch. . . . (*Meta.* 3.407–10, my translation)

This is the negative landscape that inspired Dante's wood of the suicides with its full inventory of all that is not there. The confrontation of the boy and his image in the nameless reflecting pool at the center of this nowhere place proceeds in a Latin filled with the echoing ricochets of alliterations, internal rhymes, and chiastic repetitions.

> Dumque *sitim sedare* **cupit,** *sitis* altera **crevit,**
> **dumque** bibit, visae conreptus imagine formae
> *s*pem *s*ine **corpore** amat, **corpus** putat *esse,* quod umbra *est.*

> [While he tries to soothe his thirst, he thirsts again;

and while he drinks, his sight is raped by imaged form;
he loves a hope without a body, thinks it's body, but it's not.]
(*Meta.* 3.415–17, my translation and emphasis)

And:

Se cupit in*pru*dens et, qui *probat,* ipse *probat*ur,
dumque *petit, petitur pariter*que *accendit et ardet.*

[Unknowing, he desires himself; praising, he has praised
himself; while he seeks, he's sought; as he kindles, he's consumed.]
(*Meta.* 3.425–26, my translation and emphasis)

The visible linguistic forms and the audible sounds of the narrative discourse create a visual and phonic labyrinth; and our encounter with this textual labyrinth recapitulates the catoptric encounter of the boy before the pool. When he learns the identity of his water-image, he weeps and literally flows into the earth: he dies of knowing who he isn't.

The glowing beauties of his breast he spies,
And with a new redoubled passion dies.
As wax dissolves, as ice begins to run,
And trickle into drops before the sun;
So melts the youth, and languishes away.
. . . .
Then on th' wholsome earth he gasping lyes,
'Till death shuts up those self-admiring eyes.
(*Meta.* 3.486–90, 502–3, Addison)

It is important to remember the precision of the Latin at the beginning of his encounter with his mirror-image:

Adstupet ipse sibi vultuque *inmotus eodem*
haeret, ut e Pario formatum marmore signum.

[He looks in wonder, charmed by himself, *no more moving
than a sign formed of Parian marble.*]
(*Meta.* 3.418–19, my translation and emphasis)

As one thinks of the boy looking at his image in the pool as a figure of pure mimesis, one notices that the diction surrounding the boy's encounter with his image is delicately drawn from the realm of poetry and sculpture. Such artistic diction calls to mind an image of the poet himself seeking truth in the imaged world of his own making. The vatic poet, like the boy, and like ourselves, is always in danger of waking up to find himself trapped in a vision of his own design.

Crystallization

The second major mirroring function of art is that of crystallization; art marmorealizes as it memorializes; one thing it does to the world, in the flux of time, is freeze it, stop it, fix it. Ovid is fond of adjusting his own pyrotechnics of transformation in this direction—in ways that can be refulgent and splendid, or dark and ironic. One memorable moment of such fixing is a lovely image in which Callisto is immortalized. Her son, who does not know she has been transformed into a bear, is hunting; he is close on her trail and about to spear her, whose eyes seem somehow to contain recognition when:

> She knew her son, and kept him in her sight,
> And fondly gaz'd: the boy was in a fright,
> And aim'd a pointed arrow at her breast,
> And would have slain his mother in the beast;
> But Jove forbad, and snatch'd 'em through the air
> In whirlwinds up to Heav'n, and fix'd 'em there!
> Where the new constellations nightly rise,
> And add a lustre to the northern skies.
> (*Meta.* 2.501–7, Addison)

In the act of transformation, the crime or *nefas* (in this case, inadvertent matricide) is expunged by the translation from life on earth to sidereal splendor; the human suffering of the mother is voided along with the new-won guilt of the son, but the value inherent in their suffering is saved in this divine artistic economy by being rendered into significant, but no longer personal, form. A similar gesture of magnanimity is employed by Bacchus as he rescues Ariadne, nearly insane with grief at her betrayal by Theseus on Naxos:

44

> He left his fair consort in the isle behind,
> Whom Bacchus saw, and straining in his arms
> Her rifled bloom, and violated charms,
> Resolves, for this, the dear engaging dame
> Sho'd shine for ever in the rolls of Fame;
> And bids her crown among the stars be plac'd,
> With an eternal constellation grac'd.
> The golden circlet mounts; and, as it flies,
> Its diamonds twinkle in the distant skies;
> There, in their pristine form, the gemmy rays
> Between Alcides, and the dragon blaze.
>
> (*Meta.* 8.176–82, Addison)

In imitation of (and commentary on) paradigmatic portrayals of the abandoned female (Medea in the *Argonautica,* Dido in *Aeneid* 4, as well as Ariadne in Catullus 64), Ovid depicts the limits of human passion. The crime is once again expunged, and the agony is for her assuaged, for us memorialized, in the spectacular diction by which Ovid effects her apotheosis.

The same mechanism of crystallizing the moment can work in dark and ironic ways. Such is the instance in which Perseus uses the head of Medusa in an infernal act of sculpting:

> . . . and Perseus thus replies:
> Coward, what is in me to grant, I will,
> Nor blood, unworthy of my valour, spill:
> Fear not to perish by my vengeful sword,
> From that secure; 'tis all the Fates afford.
> Where I now see thee, thou shalt still be seen,
> A lasting monument to please our queen;
> There still shall thy betroth'd behold her spouse,
> And find his image in her father's house.
> This said; where Phineus turn'd to shun the shield
> Full in his face the staring head he held;
> As here and there he strove to turn aside,
> The wonder wrought, the man was petrify'd
> All marble was his frame, his humid eyes
> Drop'd tears, which hung upon the stone like ice.
> In suppliant posture, with uplifted hands,
> And fearful look the guilty statue stands.
>
> (*Meta.* 5.224–35, Mainwaring)

45

Elevation

The remaining aspect of art to be discussed is metamorphic art as elevation, the way in which the artist's powers may raise the soul in sublimity. Ovid himself seems to distrust this power of art—although he clearly admires it in Virgil and, on occasion, seeks it himself. The most interesting references are by indirect figuration, and we see Ovid treating this power with ironic resonance in two central episodes: the narratives of Daedalus and Orpheus. These two figures are the master artists present in the *Metamorphoses* and together with the philosopher Pythagoras, are extremely informative when it comes to extrapolating Ovid's poetics.

If the master image of art's elevating power for Orpheus is resurrection, for Daedalus it is flight. In both cases the result is failure; in both, the failure is instructive. The perverse haunts the art of each. Ovid's Daedalus could barely find the way out of his own labyrinth, "so false was his web" [*tanta est fallacia tecti*]. And when, hating his exile, he thinks of escape from Minos, his thinking involves an abstract kind of inversion: "and he turns his mind to unknown arts and changes nature's laws" [*et ignotas animum dimmittit in artes naturamque novat*]. When he teaches Icarus, he gives him "flying lessons" [*praecepta volandi*] as if they were rules of composition and, by example, "teaches and encourages him in those fatal arts" [*hortaturque sequi damnosasque erudit artes*] (8.168, 188–89, 208, 215). We turn now to the multivalent arts of Orpheus.

Metamorphic Narrative

The three aspects of metamorphic art so far discussed serially (reflection, crystallization and elevation) have been separated only for heuristic purposes; they are in reality facets of a unified artistic program, and, like colors on a palette, simultaneously serve, in various mixes, the demands of the poet. To sense this fully, I would like to turn finally to book 10 and the first lines of book 11, which constitute the panel of fictions framed by the first and second descents of Orpheus into Hell.

Orpheus is the human version of Apollo: he is the master of light, of love, of the lyre, and of death. In his first descent into Hell to rescue

Eurydice, he captures the memories and imaginations of the lords of death by the mimetic powers of his art. By stunning achievements of verisimilitude, he creates the illusion of life in the realm of the dead, becoming the daemon-mediator of life and death through his fictions.[8] As he turns, and loses Eurydice forever, we see that the limits of his power reside only, but irrevocably, in his humanity.

In his resurrection, Orpheus loses Eurydice the second time, and he vows to sing songs only of inverted love, denaturing nature in mimetic retaliation for her double death. As Orpheus completes his canon, consisting essentially of the narratives of Cyparissus, Hyacinth, Pygmalion, Myrrha, and Adonis, we see that the orphic oeuvre reveals itself as an inverted mirror of the program of the *Metamorphoses* as a whole.

First there is the chiastic parallelism of the beasts and their subtle contamination with love at the beginning and at the end of the series: the boy perversely puts a spear into the heart of the trusting stag in the narrative of Cyparissus, and, in the narrative of Venus and Adonis, the boar kills Adonis by plunging his tusk deep into the young man's groin. Shakespeare's erotic descant on the boar's attack on his own Adonis is firmly anchored in Ovid's plainly delivered narrative.

These symmetrical tales of love interrupted by death and the beast frame the narratives of Hyacinth and Myrrha, which in turn, and in a pattern similar to the Chinese box puzzle, frame the central narrative of Pygmalion. The tales of Hyacinth and Myrrha have their own inverse symmetry as well. Each tale is about a victim of hapless compulsion; each moves through the vortex of intense human agony and emerges in a new sense of beauty and promise.

Hyacinth feels compelled to catch the discus thrown in sport by Apollo and receives a death blow instead. Apollo's lament over Hyacinth resolves itself into the promise of a greater hero to come (Ajax), who will wear the flower of Hyacinth.

Myrrha's terrible compulsion to sleep with her father is followed by an even more terrible guilt as she carries her father's child into exile. Her anguish, her own sense of guilt burdened by the knowledge of her father's contempt and disgust upon learning of the trick whereby she entered his bed, is amplified by the grotesque physical depiction of the way in which her huge belly strains to give birth to the fruit of her forbidden coupling. As she has compared herself to Pasiphae earlier on, we await the outcome of this pregnancy with no little interest.

47

Then, as she passes through the vortex of human suffering, the agency of *melior natura* provides the releasing shape of the fragrant myrrh tree into which she enters, her belly straining against the growing bark with which she is slowly being encased. Lucina, the goddess of midwifery and an internal figure here for Ovid himself, releases the child from the tree. The product of Myrrha's violation of the fundamental laws of love is no Minotaur, but Adonis, the most beautiful boy in the world.

This is paradigmatic. Hideous suffering is transformed, at the point of no further bearing, into a lovely form of nature, unsullied by the errors of human volition; and, to quote Yeats's refrain from "Easter 1916": "a terrible beauty is born." The transformation of such erotic violation into the child born of the myrrh tree echoes back to another metamorphosis in which the mourning sisters of Phaeton transform into trees in their grief at the death of their brother. Their mother attempts to stop their transformation by plucking away the growing bark and leaves, so that the line of generation will not come to an end (*Meta.* 2.361–66). Their tears, which continue to drop from the trees upon completion of the transformation, are crystallized by the sun and polished by the waters of metamorphic nature and become amber, adornments for later Roman rituals of marriage, fecundity, and continuance.

Situated at the center of these enclosing narratives is the story of Pygmalion. Galinsky suggests that the Pygmalion narrative is the only one in which Orpheus appears to wander from his original intent: i.e., to sing of boys loved by the gods and of girls punished for forbidden lust.[9] I would argue that by appearing to break the "rule" at the center of his narrative program Ovid's Orpheus signals a reflexive function for his "portrait of the artist." Pygmalion is a sculptor who falls in love with his own creation: he wants his statue to live, and Venus accedes to this impossible desire.[10] Through a series of mirroring symmetries, Orpheus gradually reveals that the fulfillment of Pygmalion's desire is a comedic reversal of the dark narrative of his own loss of Eurydice. If Orpheus's song bridges life and death, his Pygmalion, through the mediation of Venus, bridges art and life. But these are ambiguous, even dubious bridges.

As I suggested the breaking of the rule is only apparent. The rule is to sing of forbidden love; and Orpheus sings of no love more forbidden than that of Pygmalion. The infatuation with an ivory doll, deep at the center of Orpheus's narratives of perverse love, mirrors inversely Orpheus's own libidinous powers over death. Pygmalion, who shudders at the bad reputation of real women, makes an ivory doll to play with, while Orpheus, bereft of the real but dead Eurydice, sings songs of inverted, ersatz love. Venus grants life to Pygmalion's artificial playmate and the two of them marry and have real children. But Pygmalion's happy ending as narrated by Orpheus is framed by the darker endings and narrative of Ovid, in which Pluto and Proserpine give Eurydice another chance at life, but Orpheus loses her and is dismembered by the maenads of Bacchus. These two triangulations of death, art, and life as mediated by love, one containing the other, create a structure analagous to the heraldic *mise en abîme:* the high comedy of Pygmalion is an interior mirror image of Orpheus's enclosing tragic program. Together the tragicomic resonances between the fastidious Pygmalion and the desolate Orpheus reflect and illuminate Ovid's own philosophical program for the *Metamorphoses* as a whole.

Our sense of a mirroring relationship of the center to the whole is further intensified as we visualize the curve generated by Ovid's narrative structure. Here is a schematic map of the rising and falling pattern of the orphic narratives as framed by Ovid's chiastic narratives of the double descent of Orpheus:

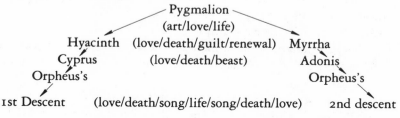

Ovid's Orpheus, like Virgil's Aeneas, ascends from Hell (*hic labor est*), but only to fall again. In the Chinese box of enclosed narrative, Pygmalion, as he makes his art live by loving it, functions as an internal mirror of Orpheus, who sends his wife back to death by loving her: both act as inverse interior mirrors of Ovid's metamorphic program. This is the intratextual relation that obtains within the *Metamorphoses.* Intertextually, Ovid's rising and falling of Orpheus mirrors inversely the falling and rising of the catabasis of *Aeneid* 6. It may not be too outlandish to suggest that this was part of Ovid's design: to show us, by means of this inverse speculum, his tactful critique of the Virgilian program.

In his first descent Orpheus sings with such power that Hell is stilled:

> Thus, while the bard melodiously complains,
> And to his lyre accords his vocal strains,
> The very bloodless shades attention keep,
> And silent, seem compassionate to weep;
> Eve'n Tantalus his flood unthirsty views,
> Nor flies the stream, nor he the stream pursues;
> Ixion's wond'ring wheel its whirl suspends,
> And the voracious vulture, charm'd attends;
> No more the Belides their toil bemoan,
> And Sisiphus reclin'd, sits list'ning on his stone.
> Then first ('tis said) by sacred verse subdu'd,
> The Furies felt their cheeks with tears bedew'd:
> Nor could the rigid king, or queen of Hell,
> Th' impulse of pity in their hearts repell.
>
> (*Meta.* 10.40–47, Congreve)

The comic tone is highly serious, and the extraordinary balance of detail and implied emotion is characteristic of the way in which Ovid allows us to imagine well, but somehow not actually feel, the suffering of his personae. Orpheus's art triumphs and its elevating power resurrects Eurydice almost to the brink of day. It is the failure of his personal will, not his art, that undoes the spell and releases Eurydice to her final death.

Later, in the scene leading to Orpheus's own death, we are treated to a full-blown Ovidian spectacular. Wild maenads are resentful of his turn from women to boys and his songs of homoerotic love and the forbidden loves of women. In erotic reversal, they pierce him to death with the horns of bulls they have slain and deconstruct him with their bare hands. As for his lyre and severed head:

> His mangled limbs lay scatter'd all around,
> His head, and harp a better fortune found;
> in Hebrus' streams they gently roul'd along,
> And sooth'd the waters with a mournful song.
> Soft deadly notes the lifeless tongue inspire,

A doleful tune sounds from the floating lyre;
The hollow banks in solemn consort mourn,
And the sad strain in echoing groans return. . . .
And driv'n where waves round rocky Lesbos roar,
They strand, and lodge upon Methymna's shore.
But here, when landed on the foreign soil,
A venom'd snake, the product of the isle
Attempts the head, and sacred locks embru'd
With clotted gore, and still fresh-dropping blood.
Phoebus, at last, his kind protection gives,
And from the fact the greedy monster drives:
Whose marbled jaws his impious crime atone,
Still grinning ghastly, tho' transform'd to stone.

(Meta. 11.50–60, Croxall)

All the powers of art discussed above—transformation, elevation, reflection, and crystallization—are simultaneously at work in this tour de force of orphic death and transfiguration. The maenads are the worshippers of Bacchus, the god of transformations; they use their thyrsis wands as spears, plows as weapons, bullhorns as swords. They reverse the process of erotic penetration of the female by the male, bringing death rather than life. Above the clamor and the shrieking and the tearing of flesh, Orpheus sings and sings, the music of his art elevating the brutality into mystery, bridging the ultimate transformation of life into death. The music continues from the lyre and the severed head in the flow of the river, finding reflection in the flow of the tears of the naiads, the mourning song of Orpheus phonically mirrored by the song of Orpheus's mourners on the banks as the head and the lyre float by. As the head seems to have at last found refuge on the shores of Lesbos, the island later made famous by the songs of Sappho, nature appears to threaten the final power of art in the form of the venomous worm. As the jaws of the serpent grin to devour the singing, severed head of the artist, Apollo, the divine avatar of both Orpheus and Ovid, crystallizes the moment into the stone of eternity.

The metamorphic shift from personal suffering into stable and significant form is complete, and the individual is released from the pressures of becoming. As the death song and the frozen image of the snake and head flare in our minds, we are provided with the final comic moment, the simultaneous image of Orpheus and Eurydice in Hell, happy and irresponsible as any nameless lovers in the park:

51

His ghost flies downward to the Stygian shore,
And knows the places it had seen before:
Among the shadows of the pious train
He finds Eurydice, and loves again;
With pleasure views the beauteous phantom's charms,
And clasps her in his unsubstantial arms.
There side by side they unmolested walk,
Or pass their blissful hours in pleasing talk;
Aft or before the bard securely goes,
And, without danger, can review his spouse.

(*Meta.* 11.61–66, Croxall)

As Ovid brings the *Metamorphoses* to its close, we sense his transfer of orphic power first to Vertumnus and finally back to himself as vatic poet.

Vertumnus sighs for the love of Pomona, a veiled figure for the city of Rome. Disguised as an old woman, he cajoles Pomona with all his transforming, narrative arts, to return the love of her unrequited lover, who is, of course, none other than Vertumnus himself, the god of the changing year. Ovid's language at the point of transformation is subtly adorned with the diction of art's stratagems. Just at the point where art seems to fail—and the god abandons his disguise to turn to naked force—the nymph chooses to love the "real" god who shines forth through the fictive weavings of his ever-changing form:

When the god in the *form* [*formae*] of age had told his story in vain, he returned to more youthful *equipment* [*instrumenta*], put off old women's clothes, and stood revealed, as when opposing clouds are conquered by the *image* [*imago*] of the sun which shines with nothing to mar its *radiance* [*reluxit*]. He was ready to love her by force, but no force was necessary, the *figure* [*figura*] of the god had captured the nymph and she feels an answering passion. (*Meta.* 14.765– 71, my translation and emphasis)

Finally, by means of the combined transforming, reflexive, crystallizing, and elevating powers of art, the image of the death head of Orpheus coalesces in the mind's eye with the vibrant figure of Vertumnus, whose love of Rome and life in change transforms the necessary failures of art into powers of adequation. Together both images figure forth and are fulfilled by the persona of Ovid himself, both retroactively at the beginning, in which he promises to effect, by his *carmen perpetuum,* the transformation of chaos into the created world, and at the end of this extraordinary philosophic epic comedy of Rome, in which his song commits and submits both itself and its singer to *natura,* the eternal force of life:

The work is done. Neither Jove's wrath, nor fire, nor sword, nor the gnawing tooth of time can undo it. Let that day come, when it will, which only has power over my body, and cut off my uncertain span of years. In my better part, I shall be carried beyond the stars, and my name shall never die. Wherever in the world Rome extends her powers, people will read, and through eternal fame, if vatic intuitions [vatum praesagia] carry any truth, I shall live [vivam].

(*Meta.* 15.871–79, my translation)[11]

* * *

Perhaps a summary of findings will prove useful as we move forward to St. Augustine and the Middle Ages.

Virgil proceeds by principles and strategies of exclusion. He carves away all that does not define the hard, clear lines of the minimal situation we face of "being there, together, in the dark." He uses Homer and other texts as mirrors to clarify his portrait of what it is to be Roman. One may feel, on occasion, the temptation to apply the word "tragic" to Virgil, but resists it because such a tag would prove both baroque and reductive. The glow of Virgilian heroism illuminates the statesman and the artist at once and is thus as circumscribed as it is circumspect. A major and nagging crux in the *Aeneid* asks why Virgil, after showing his hero (and us) the glorious future of Rome, has his hero leave Hades through the Ivory Gate of False Dream. Examination of a series of interlocking images in the epic shows the Ivory Gate to be an internal, reconciling mirror of the *Aeneid* as a whole. But this function of the gate can only be seen in the external mirror of the Homeric presence.

As Homer for Virgil, so Virgil for Ovid. Examination of the Orpheus panel shows it as both a reforming mirror of the catabasis of *Aeneid* 6 and an internal, inverted image of the furthering mechanisms driving the *Metamorphoses* as a whole. Ovid provides a "gaiety transfiguring all that dread." He counters Virgil's *gravitas* by parodying him, not corrosively but in the interest of producing balance. For all the huge, if rubber, brickbats Ovid throws at the *Aeneid,* his splendid play is absolutely dependent upon the dark and brooding Virgilian presence that impels it. Ovid operates on the principle of inclusion and generates multiplication, concatenation, mad juxtaposition, outrageous linking: the mind suffers a kind of vertigo when it attempts, at all systematically, to follow the literal threading of the narratives that make up Ovid's *carmen perpetuum.* Yet his philosophic center is very close to Virgil's: the speech of Pythagoras in praise of vegetarianism is in fact an encomium to cosmic flux in constant limits and thus fulfills as well as reflects the speech of Anchises that illuminates the dome of Virgil's heaven. The balm Ovid brings to the deep wounds figured forth by Virgil are the ministrations of transformation itself.

Like any epoch, the Middle Ages required mirrors, formal *conjointures* of competing yet coalescing views to awake its collective mind into self-recognition. Dark Virgil and irrepressibly gay Ovid provided the pole stars of an imaginable continuum of intellectual and ethical possibility. What those living in the Middle Ages also saw, from the particular vantage point articulated by St. John and systematically deployed over the thousand years between Augustine and Dante, was the centrality of love in both Virgil's and Ovid's worlds. The pressure of Christian thinking forced, early on, the establishment of a triune lexis for love that was not, of course, systematically played out in Virgil or Ovid. In Augustine, *amor* moves toward self-fulfillment in the direction of either *cupiditas* or *caritas.* Yet in both Virgil and Ovid such a dialectic is more than merely latent. In both, all that goes wrong and all that goes right is love's doing. Not only is *amor,* for each poet, the wellspring of all significant external action; it also evolves into a figure of that power of the mind that both creates and destroys its worlds.

Dante imagined sin in terms of love: love deficient, excessive, or misdirected. Such thinking came in part from profound and systematic meditation on the double world figured forth by Virgil and Ovid. Only in the profound resignations of Virgil and the penetrating delights of Ovid does the Roman world provide a sufficient model of a whole for that later Middle Age that appropriated to itself the mission of celebrating the world as the word made flesh by love.

CHAPTER 3

The Book in the Garden:
St. Augustine and the
Authentication of Self in the Other

The poem refreshes life so that we share,
For a moment, the first idea . . . It satisfies
Belief in an immaculate beginning

And sends us, winged by an unconscious will,
To an immaculate end. We move between these points;
From that ever-early candor to its late plural

And the candor of them is the strong exhilaration
Of what we feel from what we think, of thought
Beating in the heart, as if blood newly came,

An elixir, an excitation, a pure power.
The poem, through candor, brings back a power again
That gives a candid kind to everything
    —Wallace Stevens, "Notes toward a Supreme Fiction"

omnis mundi creatura
quasi liber et pictura
nobis est et speculum
nostrae vitae, nostrae mortis
nostri status, nostrae sortis
fidele signaculum

[All creation is to us as a book, a picture,
a mirror: a faithful signal of our life, our death,
our state, our fate.]
    —Alan of Lille, *De Incarnatione Christi* (my translation)

Perhaps what pleases most about Augustine is the neverending dialectic between the unflagging energy of his desire and his unflinching insistence upon intellectual control. Gifted with lyric power, he soars, in the grip of revelation, as high as any. Yet for him the time before and after mystic vision is never sad or waste. His devotion to the external, hard physicalities of the world complements an insatiable longing for internal elevation and transfiguration. He never betrays the brilliant autonomy of experience by belittling it cheaply in favor of the sublime. The delight in the gleanings of observation and analysis is matched only by the ecstasies of holy intuition. This equilibrium mediates a fecund reciprocity in his work between analysis and synthesis, interiority and exteriority, faith and reason, self and other. His work exudes a realism that accepts the knowledge that we can never complete the project, and radiates a faith that forbids abandoning it. The characteristic way in which he reconciles the ongoing, often competing demands of faith and reason is well illustrated in the progress of his career-long fascination with the link that he saw between the *imago dei* formulation of the relationship between God and humanity as instituted in Genesis: "*et creavit Deus hominem ad imaginem suam*," and the epistemological implications inherent in the Corinthian mirror-dictum of St. Paul: "*videmus nunc per speculum in aenigmate.*"

Augustine pursued his projects with a difficulty symptomatic of his times. He focused on life-and-death issues without benefit of a universally accepted physics upon which to ground his more metaphysical understandings about the created world.

This need to speculate on first and last things without a physics of the middle led to a discourse in which distinctions between the physical and the metaphysical appear to our eyes as quite tricky, much less obvious, less pronounced, than in the speculative discourse of post-Keplerian Europe. I have tried to recapitulate a sense of this heady instability in the Appendix, particularly in my remarks concerning the ground-breaking contributions of David Lindberg. For the moment, let us consider the following case in point.

When Augustine, in the full maturity of his career, discusses mind and its faculties of self-knowing in book 9 of *De Trinitate*, we see him face straightforwardly the fact that he must speak of vision without having a satisfactory theory or physics of vision at hand:

56

For whence does a mind know another mind, if it does not know itself. For the mind does not know other minds and not know itself, as the eye of the body sees other eyes and does not see itself; for we see bodies through the eyes of the body, because, unless we are looking into a mirror, we cannot refract and reflect the rays into themselves which shine forth through those eyes, and touch whatever we discern—*a subject, indeed, which is to be treated of most subtly and obscurely, until it be clearly demonstrated whether it be rays or anything else*—we cannot discern with the eyes that power itself; but we inquire into it with the mind, and if possible, understand, even this, with the mind. (My emphasis)[1]

This is a telling and difficult passage. It is important to sense fully the shaky ground upon which his understanding of the phenomena of reflection and perception stands.[2] But one must not allow oneself to be distracted by that from what his real concern here is. The shakiness of his physics must remain merely an ironically apt backdrop for an even more central liminality: the mental landscape into which Augustine has led us is one in which things are at once both like and unlike each other. To paraphrase a famous passage in *Confessions* 7, we discover ourselves, in this paragraph, in a region of unlikeness, *in regione dissimilitudinis*. Similarity leads us to hypothesize an underlying intelligibility; the attendant dissimilarity brings wrenching anxiety, and leads us to think we may be considering two aspects of the same activity, or two different activities with a shared aspect, or both of these things at once.

For Augustine, all analogies are cracked looking glasses. Indeed, it is the perception of the crack, the way in which the one member of an analogy is *false* to the other, in which the image is *false* to the original, that allows us to make any epistemological headway at all.[3] It is the very discrepancy between the model and the thing it is a model of that triggers the speculative mind into useful and creative action. In this case, as he allows that minds, like eyes, can learn much about themselves by perceiving other minds, he also insists that minds, *un*like eyes, which can *only* see other eyes, but not themselves, *can* know themselves directly as well as being reflected in other minds. And then of course there occurs, in the middle of this slowly developing negative simile, the telling digression that we started with, by which he informs us he is only tentatively holding to the Neoplatonic extramission theory of perception and is clearly willing to accept a better theory should it come along. One must admire the candor with which, in the pursuit of a particularly knotty issue of metaphysical analogies, he shares the tentative status of his underpinning physics.[4]

A little later on in *De Trinitate,* in his spectacular essay on mind in book 10, he repeats this "antisimilitude":

For eyes can never see themselves except in looking glasses; but it cannot be supposed in any way that anything of that kind can also be applied to the contemplation of incorporeal things, so that the mind should know itself, as it were, in a looking glass.[5]

As he continues exfoliating, he plays at length with the ways in which reflection on both the similarity and the difference inherent in the analogue of "mind as eye but also not as eye" brings the intellect into a state of awareness of its true ignorance about the matter. As the mind is purely human, it is like the eye and requires external mirrors for its recognitions of self. As the mind is divine, i.e. retains vestiges of its creating deity, it is both one (*mens*) and three (*intelligentia, memoria,* and *voluntas*) and thus *can* know and love itself because it is the *imago,* the type, the imperfect figure of the Trinity. The relation between mind and eye in Augustine's discourse is a figure of speech, perhaps even a figure of thought. But the relation between *mens* and its Creator, of the *imago* to its original is *not* metaphorical for Augustine, it is *real.* God, not man, is the author of creation and when He "speaks," His "words" become worlds, human history. Here we see the intricate dance in medieval discourse between earthly and heavenly kinds of signification and can begin to see how Dante, nearly a thousand years later, can claim to use the allegory of the theologians as the figural mode of the *Commedia.*

The last book of *De Trinitate* functions, in a sense, as an extended, fully orchestrated gloss on Paul's mirror saying:

What has been said relates to the words of the apostle, that "*nunc videmus per speculum*" but whereas he has added, "*in aenigmate,*" the meaning of this addition is unknown to any who are unacquainted with the books that contain the doctrine of those modes of speech, which the Greeks call *tropos.* For as we more commonly speak of *schemata* than *figuras,* so we more commonly speak of *tropos* rather than *modos.*[6]

Augustine moves relatively quickly from definitions and equivalencies of rhetorical terms to the more interesting issues they imply:

> While any likenesses may be understood as signified by the apostle when he speaks of a glass and in enigma, so that they are adapted to the understanding of God, in such a way as he can be understood; yet nothing is better adapted to this purpose than that which is not vainly called His image.[7]

Having now definitively linked the *speculum* of Paul to the *imago* of Genesis, Augustine then engages in a symphony of ternaries of the human mind and soul, which darkly mirror but which, for that very reason, can never be identical to God. It is just this simultaneity of like and unlike which provides the epistemological matrix of figural power inherent in the great autobiographical narrative of Augustine and which now becomes our central concern.

The *Confessions* of Augustine is a liminal work, at once valedictory to the classical world of Greece and Rome and harbinger of the Middle Ages. Its central forwarding strategy is unique in its time: the narrative voice of the author recollects the self in the image of a personal history.

In some ways, putting the self at the center was necessitous. If the Christian wishes to explore the drama of salvation, redemption is first of all piercingly personal and must be depicted so. Out of the exact examination of the personal experience comes the revelation of the power each has of mirroring the other.

As to effect, putting the self at the center of an epic narrative engenders two points of view: the self as writer and the self as character. We can imagine the journey from the point of view of the cartographer and from the point of view of the pilot on the bench holding the tiller.[8] The distance inherent in the cartographer's view can bring a sense of control, the proximity to the event shared with the helmsman, a sense of immediacy. The potential advantages of this duality of view in autobiographical narrative already lurk in the Ur-model of the journey, Homer's *Odyssey*. For over a third of the epic, Homer relinquishes the narrative to his hero, and we share the intensity of the experience as lived even as we share it as remembered by the narrator, alive and safe at the dinner table in Phaiakia. Curiously, it was not until the *Confessions* of Augustine that western Europe was offered a full-scale narrative of the self in the act of recollecting the self.

There is a slight irony inherent in the fact that the first self-sustained narrative of the self as hero enters into history just as the classical heroics of pride in the self's achievements give way to the claims of higher orders of humility. And it is of course not pride but humility that urges Augustine to offer up the privacy of his past, which was exquisitely his own, as public spectacle. Part of the drama of Christian redemption implies that as we are all imperfect types of Christ, we can function as types of imperfection for our fellows, as mirrors in which all can see their own imperfection. Augustine incorporates this in his mode of address:

To whom am I telling all this [*cui narro haec*]? Not to thee my God. But in thy presence I tell it to my kind, that small part of human kind [*generi meo, generi humano*] that might pick up my book. And why? That I and all who read may know the depths from which we are to cry to thee [*de quam profundo clamandum sit ad te*].[9]

The brilliant exprofessor of rhetoric at Rome and Milan, the celebrated ex-Manichee, the recently mitred bishop can, like anyone, be Everyman, especially as he weds, in his prelatical life, the active mode of the pastoral priest with the contemplative mode of the doctor of divinity. In his sacrifice of his own private, vividly personal past on the altar of figuration, he is engaged in a fundamentally Christian mimesis: the *imitatio Christi.*

As his narrative converts private experience into public figure, he reaches, in the process, deeply into both realms: the unique, hence unshareable moment of experience and the typical, hence shareable image of the figure. He so narrates that we see constantly from both his own points of view, the more spatial vision of the "Lebenskünstler" of structuralizing memory and that more temporal sense of the helmsman in the vivid process of becoming. The experience completes itself as it gets narrated and enters into a new order of being. As the process of telling exhausts itself, it leaves the structure in the memory as a completed, hence significant, thus redeemed form. As the life is narrated, it is saved.

We also watch the growth of Augustine's talent for mediating oppositions, the deepening affiliations with the Plato who shimmers behind his "books of the Platonists" as well as with the Aristotle who shines behind his Cicero.[10] We sense his growing allegiance to John as well as Paul, to love as well as intellect, to mercy as well as justice. And as we see that power of mediating opposition develop throughout the *Confessions,* we begin to see that power itself as an imperfect figure of the radical mediating power inherent in Christ: His hypostasy, the copresence in His dual nature of His humanity and His divinity.

We need to see not only how this double sense of event as both lived experience and reconstituted recollection works as a procedure but also how it develops into a kind of icon, a figure with its *own* signifying values. We see the powers and limitations of each track best from the vantage point of the other. The relationship between the tracks is a mirroring one: seeing in alternation each point of view from the other is what speculative reading is all about. As we see the method better by practicing it, we also begin to see its value and power as figure. And a great deal can be learned about this dualistic mode, both as method and as figure, as we examine the speculative functions of "language," appropriated "text," and narrated "situation" in the *Confessions.*

Speculative Language

One of the most important characteristics of the *Confessions* is the constituent presence of two languages, both of them written in Latin: the private language of experience and the public language of revelation. Although the first reading of the *Confessions* may strike the reader as excessively Bible-thumping, further readings show that the constant quotation from Scripture forms part of a massive, formal scheme of counterpointing. It is precisely by the antiphonal orchestration of two languages that the text praises, in an act of mimesis, the dual nature of its ultimate model, Christ, the Word made Flesh. The utterances of experience, the narrative of Augustine's life, come in complete and finished sentences and never need to be said again. Against these unique sentences indexing a singular life come the interventions of fragmented quotations from the revelation of the *Vita Christi,* which are partial because they never, in our world of time and space, end. They are never completed because they never cease being uttered: they echo the cosmic, eternal reality of the divine plan. It is precisely this power of language that Augustine addresses directly in book 15 of *De Trinitate,* using the mirror dictum of Paul to gloss the great *Deus erat verbum* formula of St. John:

Whoever is able to understand a word, not only before it is uttered in sound, but also before the images of its sounds are considered in thought . . . is able *now to see through this glass* and *in this enigma* [iam videre *per* hoc *speculum* atque *in* hoc *aenigmate*] some likeness of the Word of whom it is said, "In the beginning was the Word, and the Word was with God, and the Word was God" [*et verbum erat apud deum, et deus erat verbum*].[11]

The copresence of these two languages, the private language of recalled experience and the public language of revelation together acts as a speculum of Christ's hypostasy to redeem the private life and to reveal its place and cogency in the divine scheme of things. This is not so much an argument in the *Confessions* as a demonstration. The work begins:

Great art thou, Lord and most worthy to be praised: great is thy power and thy wisdom has no limit [Magnus es, domine, et laudabilis ualde, Ps. 144(145).3; magna virtus tua et sapientiae tuae non est numerus, Ps. 146.5] and man wishes to praise you. Being a part of your creation, man carries his mortality around with him as testimony of his sin, which is a testimony that *thou resisteth the proud* [superbis resistis, 1 Pet. 5.5; James 4.6]. And still man wishes to praise you, being a part of your creation. You excite him so that he delights in praising you; because you made us in your likeness, our heart is unquiet until it rests in you. Give me, Lord, the intelligence to know which is prior: to praise you or to invoke your aid? And how can one invoke you without knowing you? . . . *How shall they call on him in whom they have not believed? and how shall they believe without a preacher?* [quomodo autem invocabunt in quem non crediderunt? aut quomodo credent sine praedicante? Rom. 10.14]. *And they will praise the Lord who seek Him* [et laudabunt dominum qui requirunt eum, Ps. 21.27]. For surely those who seek him will find him, and those who find him will praise him.[12]

These opening words of the *Confessions* reveal themselves as a rich amalgam of quotation from Psalms, 1 Peter, James, Romans, and Matthew on the one hand, and on the other hand, a near jumble of private words in which it is difficult to distinguish anguish, confusion, and doubt from prayer, thanksgiving, and praise. By the end of the *Confessions,* Augustine will have worked the alternation of both narrative and meditative modes into a clarifying program for the redemption of the language of private experience [*"de profundis clamavi ad te"*] by means of a gradual but radical metamorphosis into the significant form of sacramental prayer [*"laudamus te"*].

Augustine narrates his infancy in terms of a growing ability to generate signs, thus reflecting the depth of his intuition that semiotic power arises naturally out of the need to mediate self and other even in the Ur-situations involving primal sustenance:

In those days all I knew was how to suck, and how to lie still when my body sensed comfort or cry when it felt pain. Later on I began to smile. . . . Little by little I began to realize where I was and to want to make my wishes known to others, who might satisfy them. But this I could not do, because my wishes were inside me, while other people were outside, and they had no faculty which could penetrate my mind [*animam meam*]. So I would toss my arms and legs about and make noises [*itaque jactabam et membra et voces*], hoping that such few signs as I could make would show my meaning [*signa similia*].[13]

He is subtle as he manipulates our senses of proximity to, and distance from, the narrated action. In the passage just quoted we are very close; just a little later he removes us from the squalling infant to let us join him in a mature meditation on his infancy. The sense of distance increases as we are told that he remembers nothing himself, but must rely on the recollections of others. That meditation is couched in an imagined conversation with God that occurs in the "now" of narrating while the "now" of narrated action is temporarily suspended.

O God . . . tell me whether my infancy followed upon some other stage of life that died before it. . . . Was it the stage of my life that I spent in my mother's womb . . . O God my Delight? Was I anywhere? Was I anybody? You have allowed men to discover these things about themselves by watching other babies, and also to learn much from what women have to tell. . . . I tried to find signs to convey my feelings to others.[14]

Having engaged in a characteristic dislocation of narrative by moving to a free meditation arising out of that narrative, Augustine goes on to undermine any remaining complacency felt by the reader:

Surely we can only derive [our life] from our Maker, from you, Lord, to whom living and being are not different things, since infinite life and infinite being are one and the same. For you are infinite and never change. In you "today" never comes to an end: and yet our "today" does come to an end in you, because time, as well as everything else, exists in you. If it did not, it would have no means of passing. . . . Need it concern me if some people cannot understand this? Let them ask what it means, and be glad to ask: but they may content themselves with the question alone. For it is better for them to find you and leave the question unanswered than to find the answer without finding you [*gaudeat etiam sic et amet non inveniendo invenire potius quam inveniendo non invenire te*].[15]

Ten books later he will return to this conundrum of time and eternity and provide us not so much the answer, but a narrative of the process of discovery of the self in the other. We shall return to this. Before we do, we need to consider the function of the destabilizing effect of meditative intervention on the basic forwarding strategies of the narrative. First, he shows the absolute importance of language and its primacy as the child moves toward an ability to function as a human being. Second, and almost casually, he makes us realize at the same time how vulnerable the project of language learning is by showing us how unstable the meaning of words is in the scheme of things. Language ordinates the mundane problems of getting the next meal as well as the highest mysteries of the universe. This sets up the echo chamber needed later in the *Confessions* when we hear the opening salvo of John: "*in principio erat verbum.*"

Augustine combines, in very revealing ways, the two basic attitudes concerning language that descended from the ambivalence of Plato and the confidence of Aristotle. As a Christian, Augustine is attracted to Plato insofar as Plato locates ultimate reality elsewhere, not in time or space, but in some eternal order of ideas and forms. At the same time, he is not subject to the melancholy of any Platonic nostalgias because he has been refreshed by the etiologies of Genesis in which the world created is not only real, but good.

For Augustine, there are two "real" worlds. Ours is not less real simply because through our sin it has ceased to be Paradise and has become a theater in which to play out our drama of salvation. Augustine's knowledge of the eternal mystery of the Christian Godhead allows him to be deeply Platonic in certain ways, but his sure sense of the reality of the here and now—no need, for the moment, to consider its transience—allows equally deep affiliations with Aristotle. One must remember that both Plato and Aristotle are theoreticians of mimesis and differ not on whether words imitate action, but on the relative quotient of value it is appropriate to allocate to either the words or the actions in the midst of that mimetic process. And they also disagree on the parameters of accuracy and reliability of mimetic action. Aristotle is surprisingly airy in his confidence about this matter and Plato deeply ambivalent. Few have failed to note the fundamental ironies inherent in the fact that Plato, himself a master of the poetic figure, banished the poet from his ideal republic.

Both philosophers considered language as mirrors, but of different sorts. When Aristotle offers reasoned arguments, for example, in book I of the *Physics,* he is as likely to plead grammatical as well as logical necessity; the implication is that the order of syntax mirrors the order of the world.[16]

Plato thought of language rather as mediating souls by mirroring minds, and right discourse was a matter of making sure that language accurately imitated the thoughts of the speaker's mind in that vital territory occupied by the dialectic process of intellectual intercourse. Both the *Symposium* and the *Phaedrus* are classic texts that demonstrate perhaps even more powerfully than they argue that right discourse is a mirror of the mediating daemon of right love. But it is particularly in the *Phaedrus* that we have inverse demonstrations and can see quite graphically how ignoble discourse becomes a living mirror of fatal loving. The importance of this negative image is enhanced by Socrates' heuristic participation in it. After convincing Phaedrus that his speech is superior to that of Lysias, Socrates pretends to leave, uttering first a prayer in propitiation to Eros. But the daemon of love prevents him from leaving; he returns and addresses both the speech of Lysias and his own:

Socrates: And now I have come to realize the sin.
Phaedrus: What do you mean?
Socrates: Phaedrus, it was a dreadful, dreadful speech, both the one you brought and the one you forced me to deliver.
Phaedrus: How, please?
Socrates: It was fatuous, and also concealed something impious. What could be more dreadful than that?
Phaedrus: Nothing, if you're right about it.[17]

And, of course, he is right about it. Both Aristotle and Plato know that language is more than merely capable of deceit. But for Plato that unreliability goes deeply to the heart of things and has serious, possibly fatal implications for the soul as it seeks to partake of the eternal banquet of the gods. For Plato, the system is fundamentally corrupt, because of the slippage between the world of here and now and the ultimately real. For Aristotle, there is only the here and now and thus his enthymemes, his propositions about actions, are either correct or the errors are detectable and corrigible.

For Plato that is not always so, and the stakes are considerably higher: we recall, for example, that Alcibiades, at the end of his speech in praise of Socrates, says he knew that Socrates' warnings to him were true, but knowing that made no difference to him—knowing the truth did not make him free. Plato demonstrates over and over, in the most famous of his dialogic narratives, that language is not all we wish, yet it is what we have and must be used with cunning, care, irony, and good will.

There is a special moment in the *Iliad* that readers have found as disturbing as they have found it charming: as we leave the catalogue of ships in *Iliad* 2, we turn to the place where the Trojans are marshalled for battle:

Near the city but apart from it there is a steep hill in the plain by itself, so you pass one side or the other. This men call the Hill of the Thicket, but the immortal gods have named it the burial ground of dancing Myrina.[18]

The way one thing, by having different names in two radically different lexica, participates in two radically different orders of reality is itself an image of the partiality of language. It does not embody the world, but can only mediate its edges. That demonstrable imperfection manages to mirror the unimaginable hiatus between our reality and the reality of the gods.

This Homeric sense of things is accepted and lightly touched upon at several points in the *Phaedrus;* but nowhere is it more indicative of the problem concerning word and world as Augustine later faced it as in that moment when Socrates suggests the pragmatic need, and not any romantic desire, for adequate poetic figures: he stages an advance defense for his gorgeous images of the banquet of the gods, the dome of heaven, and the soul as charioteer of the black and white winged horses:

As for the soul's immortality, enough has been said. But about its form, the following must be stated: To tell what it really is would be a theme for a divine and a very long discourse; what it resembles, however, may be expressed more briefly and in human language. [19]

This moment in turn is echoed in an early and crucial moment of Augustine's *De Doctrina Christiana,* the first three books of which were completed by 397, about the time of the writing of the *Confessions.* In one of his characteristic maneuvers, Augustine moves from meditative discourse to the language of prayer and seeks to address the mystery of the Trinity:

Thus there are the Father, the Son and the Holy Ghost, and each is God and at the same time all are one God; and each of them is a full substance, and at the same time all are one substance. The Father is neither the Son nor the Holy Ghost; the Son is neither the Father nor the Son. But the Father is the Father uniquely, the Son is the Son uniquely, and the Holy Spirit is the Holy Spirit uniquely. All three have the same eternity, the same immutability, the same majesty, and the same power. In the Father is unity, in the Son is equality, and in the Holy Spirit a concord of unity and equality; and these three qualities are all one because of the Father, all equal because of the Son, and all united, because of the Holy Spirit. [20]

Augustine then begins a new chapter, and suddenly one realizes that he has not changed his topic so much as begun to address it from a radically different angle. He has left, momentarily, the mystery of the Trinity only to enter upon the inadequacies of language as it strives to mediate that mystery, and we have arrived at one of the most significant moments of reflexivity in the treatise:

Have we spoken or announced anything worthy of God? Rather I feel that I have done nothing but wish to speak. If I have spoken, I have not said what I wished to say. Whence do I know this, except because God is ineffable. If what I said were ineffable, it would not be said. And for this reason God should not be said to be ineffable, for when this is said something is said. And a contradiction in terms is created, since if that is ineffable which cannot be spoken, then that is not ineffable which can be called ineffable. [21]

The way out of this trap is articulated by Augustine with a dazzling combination of wit and humility:

This contradiction is to be passed over in silence rather than be resolved verbally. For God, although nothing worthy may be spoken of Him, has accepted the tribute of the human voice.[22]

Thus for Augustine as well as Plato, human language mirrors rather than embodies truth; for both it is the speculum by which we reach toward the enigma, a speculum whose necessity must be affirmed, even in the face of its inadequacy.

Speculative Texts

As important as language qua language is for Augustine, it becomes even more important when canonized in texts of authority. After all, the central event of the narrative of the *Confessions* is the encounter in the garden with the text of God. We will concentrate on the speculative function in the *Confessions* of the following texts: Virgil's *Aeneid*, the books of the Platonists, Genesis, Psalms, and the New Testament texts of John and Paul.

We have already touched on the central figural function of the antiphonal use of broken quotation from the Psalms as part of the creation of a running background figure of the Incarnation, a mirror in which we see Christ's hypostasy imperfectly reflected. The second category of text is more directly involved with the life of the child as recollected and narrated by Augustine. Having learned verbal language, which Augustine gratefully accepts as a major advance over the more primitive semiosis of laughing and crying, his first real confrontation with text is not with anything from Scripture, but with Virgil's *Aeneid*. Augustine is very effective in allowing us to see this confrontation from the dual perspective of the quickening mind of the boy with the quickening body, and of the recollecting theologian who has managed to save classical learning for Christianity.

Early in his *Confessions*, Augustine recalls his schooling. He was never able to feel confident in Greek, but loved Latin. Yet his beginning courses in grammar, rhetoric, and mathematics he found as burdensome as Greek. But they were useful. And in other subjects he was compelled to read Virgil:

I read of the wanderings [*errores*] of Aeneas oblivious of my own wanderings [*errorum meorum*] and wept at Dido dead who killed herself for love, while in the midst of those things I myself was dying to thee, O God my life, with dry eyes.[23]

Even as the narrator rejects the inexperienced hate of remembered youth for mathematics and the misplaced ardor for the plight of Dido—and, perhaps closer to home, the plight of Iulus's mother, Creusa—he does so strangely echoing by actual partial quotation the metrical cadences of the very poet being rejected:

Iam vero unum et unum duo, duo et duo quattuor odiosa cantio mihi erat et dulcissimum spectaculum uanitatis equus ligneus plenus armatis et Troaie incendium atque ipsius umbra Creusae.

[One and one are two, two and two are four was truly an odious song for me, but how sweet the vain spectacle of the wooden horse full of soldiers, and Troy in flames, and the veriest shade of Creusa.][24]

It may at first appear that Virgil is merely condemned by the mature man recollecting the excitement and attraction that the Roman epic of exile had for the boy he once was, yet further consideration reveals a profoundly important use of Virgil. The epic of Aeneas, after all, is an inverse mirror of the correct journey. Troy is in ashes and he must move forward, in exile, under divine impulsion, to found the promised city of Rome.

For the young Christian-to-be (and future writer of *De Civitate Dei*) the overarching structure of the *Aeneid* is "right," encapsulating as it does the miseries of exile, the fata morgana of temporary attraction and the necessity of the denial and death of Dido, the exertions of the pilgrimage, the founding of the City, the sacrifice of Pallas and Turnus, attending well to the will of divinity as voiced by the father, etc., etc. What is "wrong" is the specific ethical content of the pilgrimage, not its mirroring structure. The narrative of textual confrontation, the positivities of the boy's response and the negativities of the remembering narrator as well as the symmetry of what was "wrong" in alternation with what was "right," helps the Virgilian text perform as a corrective mirror: we see an inverted image in Virgil that, when turned around, reveals the true image of the *itinerarium* necessary for Christian salvation. That agenda we find explicitly outlined by Augustine even as he criticizes its absence in Platonism:

The books of the Platonists tell nothing of this. Their pages do not contain the expression of this kind of godliness—the tears of confession, thy sacrifice, a troubled spirit, a broken and a contrite heart, the salvation of thy people, the espoused City, the earnest of the Holy Spirit, the cup of our redemption.[25]

And it is to these "books of the Platonists" we now turn. As Augustine begins to prepare us for the great conversion scene in the garden of book 8, he recalls for us a major encounter with what he calls "Platonicorum libros ex graeca lingua in latinum versos" [books of Platonists translated into Latin from the Greek]. He then engages in an extremely curious mode of quotation. He does not quote his Platonist texts, but asks us to imagine the words that would result from a kind of ideal abstraction of all the reasonings and proofs he found there. In such an ideal abstract, he says, we would read:

In principio erat verbum et verbum erat apud deum et deus erat verbum: hoc erat in principio apud deum; omnis per ipsum facta sunt, et sine ipso factum est nihil, quod factum est; in eo uita est, et uita erat lux hominum; et lux in tenebris lucet, et tenebrae eam non conprehenderunt.[26]

How are we to understand that a condensation of Platonist texts eventuates in the Gospel according to St. John? And yet, not quite John but a prefiguration of John, although the actual words of this imaginary abstract of Plotinus are John's. The Platonist texts had only "some" of John, but not the central fact that distinguishes them from the complete John and makes all the difference:

Similarly I read there that the word, God, was born "not of flesh nor of blood, nor of the will of man, nor of the will of the flesh but of God." But that "the Word was made flesh, and dwelt among us"—I found this nowhere there.[27]

The text of John functions in both epitomizing and typological ways: it is the text that the Platonic texts imperfectly figure forth and it is the text that fulfills and corrects the Platonic texts. By using John in this pyrotechnical way, Augustine avoids the need for quoting or dealing with imperfect texts while at the same time indicating, by a special kind of absence, their existence and mediating importance.

When we move to the beginning of book 8 and the culmination of the conversion, we find Augustine inspired to seek out Simplicianus—because, although he had accepted the spiritual substance of divinity, the flesh was weak: "The Way of the Savior was pleasing, but I was reluctant to pass through the strait gate." Simplicianus was the spiritual father of Ambrose (who played the same role for Augustine and baptized him later in the cathedral of Milan). But Simplicianus was also the leader of a circle of Christ' ` Platonists. Augustine says:

I mentioned to him that I had read certain books of the Platonists which Victorinus, a former professor of rhetoric at Rome, who I had heard died a Christian, had translated into the Latin tongue. He congratulated me that I had not fallen upon the writings of other philosophers, which were full of fallacies and deceit, "after the rudiments of the world," whereas in these [the Platonists] all their texts insinuate God and his word.[28]

We shall shortly see how the public confession of Victorinus becomes a speculative figure in which we see mirrored Augustine's own. Both suffered fastidiousness to excess. Victorinus translated the *Enneads* of Plotinus, and it is this work that most scholars believe is alluded to by Augustine's oblique reference to the *libros Platonicorum*.

But the point regarding the unusual metamorphosis of the "books of the Platonists" into the Gospel of John is this: John signals an extraordinarily powerful figural function of text and language, even more so because of the particular passage in John that Augustine used—"*In principio erat verbum*"—John's replication of the opening cadence of Genesis (and the resulting sense of a momentary annihilation of all intervening text and history), which identifies Light (Spirit), Word (Christ), and God (Father) as a protofigure of the Trinity at the point of the world's beginning. This power of John's, of engaging in the articulation of radical identities, goes beyond mere metaphor and creates a context for two thousand years of meditation on a new dispensation for language and its jurisdictions and powers. To say that God is Word, God is Love, and that the Word is made Flesh was to say words that called all previous words into question and opened up a new lexicon for mediation between man and God. These articulations of John are prime examples of a special case of figural "writing" that Augustine terms *aenigma*.

Some of his understanding of that term probably comes from the *De Oratore* of Cicero. His master text for the term, of course, is Paul's Corinthian mirror dictum: *"videmus nunc per speculum in aenigmate: tunc autem facie ad faciem"* [Now we see by means of a mirror into an obscure image: then face to face].[29]

As I have suggested, the burden of Paul's mirror dictum is not so much argued as demonstrated in the *Confessions*. His first use of it occurs as he seeks to explain to God his difficulty in believing in the possibility of a God with spiritual substance. He alludes to Paul as he quotes and seeks an understanding of the key articulation of the *imago dei* linkage in Genesis: "So God created man in His own image, in the image of God created He him, male and female created He them" [*Et creavit Deus hominem ad imaginem suam; ad imaginem Dei creavit illum, masculum et feminam creavit eos*] (Gen. 1:27):

Everywhere the truth of the statement that "you made man after your own image" [*ad imaginem tuam hominem ad te factum*] had passed by your spiritual children. . . . as if they believed and imagined that you were bound by a human form, although what the nature of a spiritual substance could be, I could get no idea, *not even by the technique of allegorical reading [atque aenigmate suspicabar].*[30]

The text from Genesis guarantees even as it figures forth the imagistic relationship between the created world and the Creator. It is important that the text of Genesis allows us to see the inherent mutuality of the imago relationship even in the text of Paul. The ternary involving God, the external world, and our interior minds reveals the completions of the triangle as each mirrors the other's presence. God in us impels us out to God and world: as we look within we see enigmas of the world and God, just as we see enigmas of God and ourselves in the world. Only Dante, in the final image of the *Commedia,* in which our collective *imago* is limned in the tricolored circles, dares to imagine seeing ourselves in the image of God. But Augustine is here preparing the way. It is the process of reading the images of the book of the world as enigma that allows him to achieve peace in the face of Scripture. Part of his excessive fastidiousness comes from the literalness of his imagination. As a well-trained Latinist, he finds the central images of Scripture killing in their crassness. Under tutelage of Ambrose he is made aware of a new mode of reading those images: *"per speculum in aenigmate"*:

I began to believe that the Catholic faith, which I had thought impossible to defend against the objections of the Manichees, might fairly be maintained, especially since I had heard one passage after another in the Old Testament figuratively explained. These passages had been death to me when I took them literally, but once I had heard them explained in their spiritual meaning I began to blame myself for my despair.[31]

At the beginning of *Confessions* 8, the portal to the book of conversion, Augustine quotes the Pauline text again, in the same context. He has now, he says, been able to overcome the failure of his intellect, imagination, and faith by means of his new Pauline mode of vision:

About thine eternal life I was certain, for I had seen *in aenigmate* in so far as I had seen *per speculum,* and all doubts were gone regarding incorruptible substance, from which all substance derives.[32]

Not only do the "dark glasses" of Paul mediate man and God, but the text itself functions as a mirror mediating the created world of substance with its incorruptible Creator in the mind of the eager convert.

All preparations for the conversion in the garden are now complete, and we see language and text together conspiring to create a dramatic figure in which we can see the dark image of our own possible conversion in that of Augustine. In this Edenic reminiscence, we also find anticipation of the garden in Eliot's *Burnt Norton,* where the leaves are "full of children, hidden excitedly, containing laughter":

Suddenly I hear a voice, of a boy or a girl—I don't know—coming from a nearby house, a sing-song, chanting over and over again, "Pick it up, read it; pick it up, read it" [*tolle, lege, tolle, lege*]. I quieted down, and began to think whether it was usual for children at play to sing such a song, but I couldn't remember ever hearing anything like it before. . . . I stopped the tears and got up, interpreting this as nothing but a divine command to open the Bible and read the first passage I should find there. . . . So I quickly

73

returned to where Alypius was sitting, for that's where I had put down the apostle's book. . . . I picked it up, opened it, and in silence read the chapter that first came to my eyes: "not in rioting and drunkenness, not in chambering and wantonness, not in strife and envying but put on the Lord Jesus Christ, and make no provision for the flesh to fulfill the lusts thereof." There was no wish nor need to read more.[33]

Speculative Situations

Just as one finds at the center of the confession of sin a reenactment of conversion, at the center of conversion there resides the confession of faith. This sacramental mirroring is itself mirrored in Augustine's *Confessions*. At the ethical center of the narrative of books 1–10, there is conversion in the garden, which involves a confession of faith that both fulfills and corrects the failure of faith in Eden. The meaning of Augustine's conversion is both foreshadowed and affirmed by surrounding narrated situations that function as speculative figures in which we can see, darkly, the true nature and significance of the conversion itself.

It is useful to note that at the crucial moments in the narrative part of the *Confessions* (books 1–10), Augustine is never alone; he has always someone with him. As he struggles to the light, he finds the rhythm of his partial successes and devastating failures intelligible primarily through the relationships he has, or fails to have, with others. It is the record of these relationships with others that become figural mirrors for the radical drama of self and other that is at the center of his conversion to the Christian God.

There is the boy whose early death leaves Augustine desolate and whose loss sets him on a radical course of discovery of the true relationship he wants to bear with the other he loves. In a moving moment of grief he imagines that his sudden and fervent reluctance to die stems not from self-centered fear, but from a fear that if he dies, the last living vestige of the boy will die with him.

There is in addition the narrative of Victorinus, a professor of rhetoric and literature, for whom conversion was most difficult because it was so publicly verbal. Surely that is a prefiguration of Augustine's own conversion and surely that is why he is told the story by Simplicianus in the context of the *translatio studii* of Plato (Victorinus had

74

translated the *Enneads* of Plotinus a year or so before his conversion). The narrative of the conversion of Victorinus, who himself "converted" the inaccessible Greek of the Platonists into the common Latin of the community, is fittingly, even figuratively, told by the spiritual father of Ambrose (who performed in turn that function for Augustine). He is thus the ideal figure to use in constructing a prefiguration scene in which Augustine, also a former professor of rhetoric and literature, witnesses, in a glass darkly, the conversion of a man of old words to the new Word.

Finally, there is the relationship with his mother, Monica, which, although an easy target for cynics, triumphs nonetheless in the extraordinary postconversion scene at the window at Ostia. The figural density of the scene is executed with an amazingly light touch when one considers how obviously "symbolic" the elements of the scene actually are when abstracted: Ostia is the port to the City (Rome, the antitype to the New Jerusalem). Monica is mortally ill, waiting for the boat home. Her newly converted son, aged thirty-three, joins her at a window, and as they look at the sky together they experience a moment of joint ecstatic elevation. The language and imagery, which Augustine admits is not one with what they said and saw, but only in imitation of his felt sense of the scene as recollected, shimmers with resonance backward to both Plato and Paul, and forward to the Dante of paradisal memories:

Suppose, we said . . . they [all dreams and visions, tongues and transient signs] fell silent and he alone should speak to us, not through them but in his own voice, so that we should hear him speaking, not by any tongue of the flesh or by an angel's voice, not in the sound of thunder nor in some veiled parable but in his own voice {nec *per aenigma* similitudines, sed ipsum}, the voice of the one whom we love in all these created things; suppose, we said, that we heard his voice alone with none of these things between ourselves and him?[34]

This extraordinary sentence, an interlace of "suppose, we said's," never quite grammatically ends, but keeps generating chains of subjunctive "contrary to fact" suppositions until it imperceptibly shifts into scriptural quotation as the deep realization comes that the desire that lies at the center of the discourse is the unquenchable desire for unmediated union with the unspeakable. This dance of words itself functions as a speculative mirror of the limitations as well as the powers of earthly mediation, of language in love as it traces its impossible desire to speak with the silence of the ineffable.

The autobiographical narrative proper concludes with the tenth book of the *Confessions.* Augustine proceeds with three additional books that have not been altogether comfortably related by the major commentators to the ten narrative books. They are three essays devoted to reading figuratively, seeing in the world of the here and now, dark images of the other; and they move in an ascending scale. Taken as a whole, they are a kind of demonstration of the success of the *Confessions'* major breakthrough: the conversion of private experience into a usable *figura* for others.

Once converted and confessed, he has his own affairs in order and is able to move from self-absorption to meditation on the truly Other. What he discovers, in three differing ways, is that full meditation on the Other reveals redeeming bridges back to the self. In book 11 he examines the nature of time against the backdrop of eternity. In book 12, he examines creation itself as it implies the Creator. In book 13 he examines the text of creation and finds the opening lines of Genesis to be an enigma, a speculative figure of the Trinity.

These essays have two modes of being or, at least, two modes of understanding: they are at once intriguing meditations with their own inherent interest and value; at the same time, in the economy of the doctrine of Christian use, they function as three variations on the same theme, a figure of the Trinity they praise in and by the very act of mimesis. These last books are lessons, emblems on the way to read the book of the world once one has gone through the vortex of conversion, of making one's private life a public good. We shall examine briefly the speculative figure of the discovery of the self in the Other as Augustine completes his meditation on the nature of time in book 11.

He asks what sense time makes as we perceive it in its three aspects of past, present, and future, and he fails, again and again, to come up with any image that adequately mediates understanding. Finally, after prayer, he reports a breakthrough. He sees that the three aspects of time are the result of the ordinating power of our own mental process of engaging the world. This discovery links the self to the Other of Creator and creation intelligibly, yet in no way celebrates the success of the intellect at the cost of belittling the essential mystery at the center. On the contrary, analysis submits to prayer.

Discovery in Augustine is a dialectical process, hence difficult to capture in a single, telling quotation. Here are several passages with minimal commentary that should reflect Augustine's image of discovery of the Other as a process of self-discovery:

What is it that shines into me and pierces my heart without wounding? I am both in terror and afire. In terror, insofar as I am different from it, afire insofar as I am similar to it.

[Quid est illud, quod interlucet mihi et percutit cor meum sine laesione? et inhorresco et inardesco: inhorresco, in quantum dissimilis ei sum, inardesco, in quantum similis ei sum.][35]

He begins not with an idea but an experience: the burning but nonconsuming light of God. This veiled reminiscence of the burning bush links his unique experience to its paradigm on Mt. Sinai, yet it does so gently enough that one retains the sense of the experience as personally felt as well as universally figural. In this lies the force of the truly typological, speculative figure: one's sense of individuation, of the figure occurring uniquely in history, is enhanced rather than diminished, precisely because one also, and simultaneously, senses its signifying power.

In addition, the imagery, that of piercing the heart, draws on the realm of secular, erotic experience so as to use it as a mirror in which we can begin to imagine the unknowns of mystical experience. The reaction is a simultaneously apprehended feeling of terror and desire: one recognizes the light as somehow one's own even as one sees it as impossibly alien; one is like it and not like it at all. Recognition in the face of deity, however accommodating to our limitations, is and must always be partial. The light shines in and pierces the heart, bringing illumination from above as it pierces to the dark core of the center. This is a propitious beginning.

You are the Maker of all time . . . but if there was no time before heaven and earth was created, how can anyone ask what you were doing "then"? If there was no time, there was no "then."[36]

This is not merely the rhetorical, obligatory demur of a creature doomed to suffer the contingencies of time and space excusing his crassness in the face of divinity; rather Augustine is building into our sense of the issue the negative aspect of the inventory. The clear if tacit implication of saying that time is *not* part of God's nature is to say that it belongs to the created world, as do we. As he breaks the issue down into its constituent parts, we run immediately into a *reductio ad absurdum.*

Of these three divisions of time . . . how can two, the past and the future *be,* when the past no longer is and the future is not yet? As for the present, if it were always present and never moved on to become the past, it would not be time but eternity. If, therefore, the present is time only by reason of the fact that it moves on to become the past, how can we say that even the present *is,* when the reason why it *is,* is that it is *not to be?* In other words, we cannot rightly say that time *is,* except by reason of its impending state of *not being.*[37]

This is not just flimflam. There is some of that, of course, but the verbal razzle-dazzle is deeply functional: it shows us just how quickly we can come to the edge of the abyss, the limit of language's powers as a mediator of reality. Like the lessons of the *Phaedrus,* the written word may act as a kind of mirror for the truth, but it can only mediate that truth, never embody it.

By chapter 20 of book 11, he seems to be making some progress out of these crystalline but hopelessly regressive arguments:

It might be correct to say that there are three times, a present of past things, a present of present things, and a present of future things. Some such different times do exist in the mind, but nowhere else that I can see. The present of past things is the memory, the present of present things is direct perception; and the present of future things is expectation.[38]

And then:

It seems to me, then, that time is merely an extension, though of what it is an extension I do not know. I begin to wonder whether it is an extension of the mind itself.[39]

Now the interior dialectic closes in, mixing interrogative, indicative, and imperative modes of discourse:

It is in my own mind, then, that I measure time. I must not allow my mind to insist that time is something objective. I must not let it thwart me because of all the different notions and impressions that are lodged in it. I say that I measure time in my mind.[40]

But how can the future be diminished or absorbed when it does not exist? And how can the past increase when it no longer exists? It can only be that the mind, which regulates this process, performs three functions, those of expectation, attention, and memory.[41]

That this intellectual clarity is still part of an all-encompassing mystery is reflected by the characteristically Augustinian move, at the close of the "argument," to prayer and supplication:

You my Father are eternal. But I am divided between time gone by and time to come, and its course is a mystery to me. My thoughts, the intimate life of my soul, are torn this way and that in the havoc of change. And so it will be until I am purified and melted by the fire of your love and fused into one with you.[42]

What he sees in his meditation on time, that aspect of reality that seems to be so integral to the *otherness* of the created world in which we find ourselves, is that we are centrally and undeniably *there*. He sees in time the imago of our own mind, our interior ordinating mental power. There is nothing more absolutely and undeniably other for most of us than the infinite backward and forward abysms of time—and Augustine clarifies our being by correct *consideratione:* if we look at time well we shall see our mind mirrored in it. We are present in the Object even as we meditate upon it as Subject. We find ourselves authenticated by virtue of our inextricable presence in the undeniably Other.

The entire process of intellectual meditation on the nature of time reveals itself as an act of the mind in the process of discovering its own nature. Later, in the explosions of ternaries with which he brings his treatise on the Trinity to a close, we find in Mind a unity of three faculties, Will, Memory and Intellect—a speculative figure of the Trinity itself. These mirrors are reversible and mutual. The central interdiction of Exodus stands: "Thou shall not see God and live." Yet the Incarnation, in its speculum of the hypostasy of Christ, redeems the world and allows Paul his triumph of partial knowledge: we can now, by way of mirrors, see into the enigma of God.

* * * *

The encounter with the mirror in any epoch can be read as a special-case encounter with the Other in which we play out the drama, often as a kind of grief therapy, of seeing our hopes of authenticating ourselves in the undeniably Other both raised and shattered. For us to follow the Delphic imperative, for the eye to truly know itself, it must see itself. And Augustine articulates as well as anyone the tedious, universal truth of that particular epistemology: "For eyes can never see themselves except in looking glasses" [*Numquam enim se oculi praeter specula videbunt*] (*De Trinitate,* 10.3). And although mirrors are never adequate to the project of knowing ourselves, the project appears incapable of initiation without them.

It was perhaps only in the special status granted to the things of this world by the medieval Christian dispensation that it was possible to so reify relation that, for a time, one could imagine the desolate hiatus between a word and its referent as redeemed. For a while it became imaginable that putting the words together was more than a mere metaphor for putting the world together and that to tell past experience in narrative actually transformed that experience into a stable and usable figure of meaning. In fact, meaning in the Middle Ages often seems to have ventured from the very process of narrating. To tell the world a story was to convert the incessant flow of exterior time into a structured, stable, mental space. To tell the world was to save it, to perform in true typological action the mimetics of both genesis and Redemption: to engage in that highest and surely most dangerous act of divine praise: the *imitatio dei*.

The danger was real. The Middle Ages had its quotient of dark intimations of the looming threat of solipsism: witness the catoptric anticipations of Gottfried von Strassburg's *Tristan* and the "Donna mi prega" of Dante's first friend, Guido Cavalcante. And what happens when the looking glass is not only cracked, but shattered altogether?

For that we shall examine the twelfth-century passage to Dante and Chaucer by means of sojourns in the lyric of Heinrich von Morungen and the romance of Chrétien de Troyes. But before we turn to the arts of writing lyric and romance in the high Middle Ages, we need to get a sense of parallel developments, between the twelfth and fourteenth centuries, in the medieval arts of reading.

CHAPTER 4

Self as Other: Medieval Commentary and the Domain of the Letter

> There would still remain the never-resting mind,
> So that one would want to escape, come back
> To what had been so long composed.
> The imperfect is our paradise.
> Note that, in this bitterness, delight,
> Since the imperfect is so hot in us,
> Lies in flawed words and stubborn sounds.
> —Wallace Stevens, "The Poems of Our Climate"

> Dal centro al cerchio, e sì dal cerchio al centro
> movesi l'acqua in un ritondo vaso,
> secondo ch'è percosso fuori o dentro
> [From rim to center, center out to rim,
> so does the water move in a round vessel,
> as it is struck without, or struck within]
> —Dante, *Paradiso* 14.1–3 (Mandelbaum)

At this juncture, we move from fourth-century St. Augustine to late twelfth- and early thirteenth-century Heinrich von Morungen. This is a leap of over eight hundred years and cries for a sense, however schematic, of historical transition. Thus this chapter seeks to bridge St. Augustine's culminating yet seminal image of his recollected divided self-image encountering the enabling mirror of Pauline text in the garden of the *Confessions* and Heinrich's equally fecund, if dislocating, encounters with the weeping eye and damaged mouth of his Lady. To construct such a heuristic schematic, we shall deal very selectively with what in fact is a vast topic: the ways medieval acts of reading and writing became informing mirrors of one another.

We shall move first backward and then forward in time, beginning with medieval commentary on Ovid and Virgil by Pierre Bersuire, John of Garland, Arnulf of Orleans, and Bernardus Silvestris; finding a turning point in Hugh, Richard, and Andrew of St. Victor; and returning by the way stations of Pauline mirror imagery in Alan of Lille's twelfth-century *Anticlaudianus'* the thirteenth-century *Itinerarium mentis in Deum* of St. Bonaventure, and three major encounters with the mirror in Dante's fourteenth-century *Divina Commedia*. We shall see how the attention paid by these writers to the acts of reading secular as well as sacred texts embodied a profound intuition of the coordinating powers of Paul's catoptric imagery in 1 Corinthians 13.12.

The focus will be on the ways in which medieval acts of reading and writing protected, recuperated, and rehabilitated the autonomous value (and mystery) of the signifying image even as these writers expended great energy in exploring both the techniques and the ethical implications of the exegetical act of seeking the meaning of those images. And although there is a radical difference in the medieval attitude toward secular texts and the extraordinarily privileged status of biblical texts, nonetheless the act of reading images points not only outward and, in the mental sense of the word, forward from the image to our own personal understanding of it as readers; the act of reading also points backward and inward to its original as a cynosure of the world.

This duality of signifying direction, outward and inward, both reflects and celebrates, in a reverse kind of *imitatio* of praise, that relation of sign to signified captured in the foundational image of reflexive *representatio* that medieval men and women believed informed the relationship they bore to their Maker. The *imago dei* of Genesis 1.27 haunts the medieval pilgrimage to self-knowing: "*et creavit hominem ad imaginem suam; ad imaginem Dei creavit illum, masculum et feminam creavit eos*" [and He created man in His image, in the image of God created He him, male and female created He them].

This foundational link between Creator and creature survives the Fall in the image of nature retaining her identity as a mirror of God, but a mirror now cracked. That crack in the mirror both reveals the imperfection in the image of the human seeker looking into the mirror and suggests tantalizing hints of the perfection of its Maker. This

84

mirror of middle earth can reflect the depravity that led to the Fall and help the mirrored seeker devise a program for reform and salvation.[1]

The central Christian image of this lapsarian sense of things, at least for the purposes of this study, is the paradigmatic mirror dictum of St. Paul in 1 Corinthians 13:

Videmus nunc per speculum in aenigmate: tunc facies ad faciem. Nunc cognosco ex parte: tunc autem cognoscam sicut et cognitus sum. Nunc autem manent fides, spes, caritas: tria haic; major autem horum est caritas.

[Now we see *per speculum:* "through" and/or "by means of" a mirror; *in aenigmate:* "into" and/or "from within" a riddle or mystery,
Then face to face;
Now I know *ex parte:* "in part" and/or "from outside"
Then I shall be known even as I am known.
Now there remain faith, hope and love: these three;
But (then) the greatest of these is (will be) love.][2]

The first part of this chapter will concentrate on both implicit and explicit concerns medieval commentators had in relating the literal meaning of a given image to its range of wider signification. The concluding section will test any ground won by the first part by means of a brief excursus into the mirror images in Allan of Lille, St. Bonaventura, and Dante. The test will be to examine the degree to which the Pauline mirror dictum offered these writers a coherent matrix of eschatological implication regarding that dislocating gap that yawns between the literal and spiritual senses of images linking the orders of time and eternity.

Virgil and Ovid among the Exegetes

H. R. Jauss suggests that a major source of pleasure in reading medieval texts stems from encounters with true alterity; our sense of a "surprising otherness" triggers an awareness of a significant gap in sensibility between then and now. Such encounters make us reassess our idea of the "horizon of expectation" of the imagined contemporary medieval reader; it is this effort at historical reconstitution that enriches our own "horizon of experience" and increases our pleasure now, in more adequate readings of the texts of then.[3]

John Block Friedman narrates just such an encounter; it led him to his indispensable study of Orpheus in the Middle Ages. He recalls reading the famous fourteenth-century allegorizations of Ovid by Pierre Bersuire (d. 1362):

Bersuire wrote that Eurydice, that is, human nature, had been tempted by a forbidden fruit while gathering flowers, that she had been bitten by Satan disguised as a serpent, and that Satan had carried her off to the underworld. Then Orpheus-Christus—for so he is called by the commentator—went down and took back his wife from the rule of hell, greeting her with these words from the Song of Songs: "Rise up, my love, my fair one, and come away."[4]

Most would go along with Friedman's initial reaction: the blatant eclecticism reflects a "need to find Christian doctrine in the fables of the pagan gods." But it is his double take that led him and leads us to fresh insight: "the fusion of pagan and Christian imagery in the story seemed too apt, too resonant . . . to have come unaided from Bersuire's pen."[5] The need of any reader to link a given image to some counter in a hermeneutic program of his own or his culture's devising is a fact of literary life and as such always of some interest. But just as intriguing as the voracious impulse of medieval culture to interpret images is for us, so is the capacity of literary images themselves to excite and accommodate such a vast array of different readings.

In fact, Friedman is a bit unjust to Bersuire. From the beginning, Bersuire is openly reductive, and he remains single-mindedly faithful to his expressed project. He intends to interpret pagan fables in such a way as to clarify the way they present the issues and options humanity faces as it seeks to understand and reform personal action in accord with the moral life. In fact, in his accessus, or introduction, he expressly says that "only rarely will he touch on the literal sense" of Ovid's narratives: "*hinc est quod in presenti opusculo non intendo nisi rarissime literalem sensum fabularum tangere, sed solum circa moralem expositionem at allegoricam laborare sequendo librum Ovidii qui Metamorfoseos dicitur.*"[6]

What proves stable in the project of medieval Ovidian commentary is to seek readings of narrative detail that reflect general situations in human behavior involving ethical choice. What proves surprisingly flexible, given the inflexible imperative to allegorize in the first place, is the range of possibility allowed to the particular allegorical identification. That appears to be left rather open to choice; even a

86

single commentator can present a range of candidates for election to the status of "the signified." In fact, one of the more intriguing aspects of Bersuire's own reading is precisely the fact that the menu of signification he offers is often so varied.

Here is Bersuire on the allegorical ramifications of Teiresias's warning against self-knowing, Echo's self-offering to Narcissus, and Narcissus's rejection of Echo:

The truth of Tiresias' words is demonstrated daily in many things. . . . there are many who flourish spiritually. They watch out for their own lofty beauty . . . that is they care for their own physical beauty as much as. . . . for the condition of their souls or their learning. . . . This may be said about many in . . . holy orders. Whoever has the same beauty and virtue as they do, they find guilty of vanity. These people they condemn and despise . . . but for their own empty glory and pride they perish as vain hypocrites and become as flowers which pass away and their souls fall with certainty into hell. . . . *Or you may also think that* such material shadows signify the world's delights (*vel dic quod ista umbra temporalia mundi bona designat*). Indeed whoever is accustomed to laugh at men in the wordly fountain of prosperity and whoever offers kisses and embraces and is scarcely about to gain any in return, this person . . . will certainly perish and, as it is said, be tranformed into a flower. (My emphasis)

When Bersuire deals with Echo herself he combines the moral certitude of a fundamentalist when writing about the meaning of this figure and the disinterest appropriate to a scholar when indicating the *range* of that meaning:

Echo was a certain talkative nymph. . . . Historically this is a charge against whores and pimps and lusty old women who encourage adultery. While they do their filthy work they capture with their words Juno—that is those who are jealous and the parents of young people. . . . *Or you may even say that* Echo signifies those who flatter [*vel dic aliter quod Echo signat adulatores*].[7]

As he promised, Bersuire pays little or no attention to the literal aspect of the image that triggers his exegetical habit of mind. Even when he says he asserts the "historical" meaning of Echo, he in fact continues his radical allegoresis. He is simply uninterested in the letter or in the problems involved in reading the sign as signifier. But neither is he interested in singling out the "correct" or canonical allegorical counter.

On the contrary, he seems rather more concerned with casting his sharp eye over the ethical seascape of human action and gathering together as complete an inventory as possible of conceivably relevant signifieds: counting, ordering, and displaying for sale the fish he has caught in his allegorizing net.

Kenneth Knoespel's recent work on medieval understandings of Narcissus is as indispensable as Friedman's book on Orpheus and should be considered a necessary complement to the relevant sections of Julia Kristeva's *Tales of Love* (discussed briefly in the Appendix) and Charles Segal's recent book on the Orpheus myth.[8] In terms of the current inquiry, Knoespel guides us well through two of our way stations on the journey backward to a new understanding of the sense of the letter developed by the early twelfth-century school of St. Victor: John of Garland, writing in the last half of the thirteenth century, and Arnulf of Orleans, writing in the last quarter of the twelfth century.

The title of John of Garland's commentary on the *Metamorphoses*—*Integumenta Ovidii*—is itself indicative of an important medieval "alterity" in conceiving the act of reading texts. Knoespel quotes and translates John of Garland's own gloss on *integumentum* from his *Poetria Parisiana,* in which he links the term, by the participle *palliata,* to a much more popular metaphor for the imagined relation that the truth of a narrative bears to the narrative itself: that of an implied body covered by a cloak:

If a whole narrative is obscure, it may be made plain by means of a suitable story or fable, through the device known as Integument which is truth cloaked in the outward form of a story [*si narratio fuerit obscura, per fabulam appositam vel per appologum clerificetur, per Integumentum quod est veritas in specie fabule palliata*].[9]

For most modern readers, the act of "allegorizing" an image is viewed as a move that begins by considering the particular image as part of an integrated, autonomous text and then moves out, beyond the text, to the world of reality that is the context of that text, in order to identify and celebrate a relation between the image of the text and some "real" thing in the world beyond that text. In this view of things, one considers the text autonomous, yet enclosed within the real encircling world. Thus the text is seen, for a moment, as the world's cynosure, and the act of reading as essentially a centrifugal act, moving from the text outward to the surrounding world in search of signified equivalents somehow implied by the signifying image from which we start.

But there is very strong evidence that the medieval imagination also viewed the act of reading inversely, as essentially moving in a centripetal direction. This is indicated by the popular metaphor of the text as nutshell and the seeking of meaning as cracking the shell in the interest of getting at the meat of the nut, or the image of the fruit within the chaff, or the idea of the narrative surface of a fable as an "integument," or covering. All these images indicate that the direction of finding the signified meaning is not upward and outward, but rather downward and inward.[10] This difference in conceiving the gestalt of the act of determining the meaning of an image helps us to see a bit better how it was possible for the medieval imagination to conceive of the sense of the letter as *including,* or encircling (rather than pointing outward toward) the sentential, moral, tropological, or even the anagogical senses of the image.

Perhaps the most important of John of Garland's integuments brought forward by Knoespel is not that regarding Narcissus, but that which he weaves around Prometheus, that liminal figure whose narrative links the micro- and macrocosm:

Prometheus was the first to make a little doll of clay. The fable originates man [*fabula fert hominem*]. It holds things hidden. The fable's language seems fictive to you [*est sermo fictus tibi fabula*] because it conceals or delights, or does both. History narrates the deeds of the great and is written as a reminder for men to come. For you these verses are an allegory of human behavior cloaked in the language of history; an integument cloaked in the voice of fable, hiding things for you which are true teachings [*fabula voce tenus tibi palliat integumentum, / clausa doctrine res tibi vera latet*]. A key opens the fable. Prometheus, your teaching taught us how to shape material into form; you affirmed that the light of reason comes from heaven, and that it is reason that seeks the celestial zone [*celestesque plagas a ratione peti*].[11]

One of the most intriguing aspects of this integument is the explicit manner in which the act of reading and understanding *integumentum sui generis* is itself a central function of the discourse designed to help us understand this particular integument. It is still difficult to tell if integument for John is the same as the actual verbal narrative of the telling itself, or if it is the structure of the parable left etched on the memory after the tale is told. What is clear is that we feel no desire to abandon the fable upon arriving at its signification; somehow the fable and its signification have become part of a contiguous and ongoing process of reading, thinking and writing, and belong to an interior whole within the reader's mind. The fable is not conceived as a stepping stone which one leaves behind as one moves toward truth; it is that the fable embodies, rather than points toward, its own significance.

Arnulf of Orleans (fl. 1156) most clearly links the exterior and interior worlds as he reads Ovid both as physics lesson and as psychological narrative.

The point of talking about transformation is so we may not think that metamorphosis only occurs in corporeal things [*ut non intelligamus de mutacione que fit extrinsecus tantum in rebus corporeis*] but also internally in the mind [*sed etiam de mutacione que fit intrinsecus ut in anima*]. Ovid wants to show us the internal motion of the mind by means of his fabulous narratives [*fabulosam narrationem*].[12]

Knoespel is compelling as he argues that Arnulf's plea to read Ovid as a narrative of the interior mind was the most telling counterargument to Conrad of Hirsau, who argued that reading Ovid's *Metamorphoses* was "dangerous" because it "represented human deformation into stones, plants, beasts, and birds, and challenged scripture which said that man's form in God's image was perfect and not susceptible to change."[13] Arnulf argues that Ovid is using a *fabulosa narratio,* a tradition reaching back to Macrobius for justifying fabulous narrative in terms of philosophical (but not necessarily theological) potential. For Arnulf, then, the act of reading the "exterior" narrative was to see in it an *imago* or mirror of the interior of the reader's own mind: this marks the fable even more emphatically as an external enclosure of its internal range of signification. Arnulf's eagerness to argue for internalization of exterior narratives as an appropriate act of exegesis is not as new as it might sound. After all, psychomachic allegory, an extremely important and popular genre of writing ranging from Prudentius through Alan of Lille to Guillaume de Lorris, depended upon a reader's willingness to appropriate a narrative that purports to occur in the exterior world of nature and "reconstitute" it "back" into the mind as an interior image of the soul moving forward in its pilgrimage to God.

The more one reads medieval Ovidian commentary, the easier it is to see how the commonplace arose that says that the medieval reader trivialized classical literature by reductive acts of allegorizing that often strike the modern mind as nearly obsessive in avoiding any real encounter with the enabling image itself. And though there is more than a little truth to this commonplace, we have also begun to trace the presence of an important and powerful counterimpulse to vary, to defer, even to resist the itch of mechanical allegoresis. This resistance can be seen and felt in some of the equivocations, deferrals, and oscillations commentators indulge in when approaching the target head-on; and what might be seen as merely exegetical dithering can then be understood as performing an important function: it protects and enriches the power and range of what we have learned from the Middle Ages to call the spirit of the letter: the "literal" senses of the image.

We find this more tentative—perhaps, for the modern eye and ear, more welcome—approach to the text in the Virgilian commentary attributed to Bernardus Sylvestris.[14] Here Bernardus is glossing the famous reliefs of *Aeneid* 6, which Daedalus carved into the doors of the temple of Apollo on the shores of Cumae:

Dedalus ut fama est: according to historians, Daedalus was a certain wise man who prospered in mechanics after he gained experience in the other sciences. We read that he made a cow for Queen Pasiphae, who, enclosed in it, was violated by a bull. I think that this means nothing more than that he made a chamber in the shape of a cow, in which a young man named Taurus violated her. Then Minos, seeing him, very prudently threw him into chains that is, he bound him into service. Finding himself in chains (that is, in service), Daedalus travelled the aerial paths with feathers (*pennis*) and came to Apollo's temple—that is, by reason and intellect he contemplated the sublime and inwardly moved himself to philosophical study, and he there dedicated the oarage of his wings *alarum remigium sacravit,* the exercise of reason and intellect. . . . *Immania templa:* the arts—instruction, theory, or anything philosophical. *In foribus:* in the approach to the arts, namely, in the authors. *Letum Androgei:* these fables outside the temple represent all the fables of the poets and hence are not to be understood allegorically. . . . *Omnia perlegerent:* Aeneas and those who came to the temple with him, that is, those who propose to come to philosophy, read all the playful fables of the authors.[15]

In addition to the more conventional medieval delight in firmly nailing down an array of univocal identities in terms of signifiers and signifieds (e.g., *in vincula* [in chains] = *muneribus* [in service]), Bernardus also indulges in the more subtle and equivocal pleasures of deferring such identification, in skirting the perimeters (and parameters) of his literal imagery, and sharing his exegetical hesitancy with his reader. We probably shouldn't seek an allegorical reading of the bull's violation of Pasiphae. In fact we might already *have* an allegorical reading of an alleged literal occurrence in Virgil's text, and the appropriate act of reading is then not to find an allegorical signification but to undo one, to realize we need to reverse the process and understand the bull as an allegorization of a reginal seduction of a fully human young man whose name happened to be Taurus. This can strike one as an illusory explanation, raising more questions than it answers about either Bernardus's sense of the mores of Crete, or his own erotic imagination, or both. But there seems little possibility, or point, in pursuing the issue any further.

Finally, it turns out not to be terribly important that we be particularly precise in how we trope *immania templa*: it will do if we consider the phrase as meaning "instruction, theory, or anything philosophical" [*artes, theoricas vel quaslibet philosophicas*]. As for *in foribus*, that means "the approach to the arts, you know, into the authors" [*id est in introitu ad artes, scilicet in actoribus*]. By such little acts of mild equivocation and deferral, Bernardus actually does much to protect the territory of the literal, to shore up the boundary between the image under observation and the structures to which a medieval reader might seek to refer it. As he comes to the end of this famous Virgilian passage devoted to the reliefs of Daedalus on the Cumaean temple of Apollo, an implication begins to grow that we are to join not only Bernardus but also somehow Aeneas and his followers as they gaze on those Carthaginian pictures at an exhibition, and we, like them, are not supposed to read a mystical or allegorical signification in Daedalus's images because they are outside the temple. We too have come to Philosophy and not to Theology, as we can assume by the conspicuous presence of the one term and absence of the other. By this delicate dance of proto-Derridean *différance*, we are gradually, if only implicitly, reminded that Virgil's own text, the very text upon which we are engaged in commentary, is also one of the "playful fables of the authors" [*ludicras actorum fabulas*]; that it is also outside the temple, implying that we feed on an empty picture, as Virgil says that Aeneas does [*animum pictura pascit inani*]. The final, quiet implication then, is that if Virgil can be usefully read philosophically, he is, for Bernardus, nonetheless theologically beyond the pale and thus capable of tropological but not truly allegorical or anagogical exegesis.

As Bernardus resists the allegorical leap and defers identification of the image within his text to an image or idea outside the text, he helps us see more richly the range of implication present within the image; he expands the domain of attention we are invited to devote to the letter of the image, to its full, autonomous power as a signifier, to its Pauline quiddity as *speculum,* as a mirror, and to our equally Pauline difficulty in reading it in the dark, as being quintessentially *in aenigmate,* caught in the quotidian enigma within which we work, trapped as we are in the space/time contingencies of *nunc,* of the Now.

The Victorine Recuperation and Rehabilitation of the Letter

Perhaps one reason for Bersuire's massive disinterest in the *sensus literalis* may be that by the time of his *Ovidius Moralizatus,* nearly a century had passed since the twelfth-century explosion of exegetical interest in the sense of the letter had illuminated the Paris of the school of St. Victor. In fact, as we move backward in this rapid review of medieval commentary on Ovid and Virgil we sense an ever richer concern with the autonomous power of the enabling image. We find that much of this concern can be attributed to the Victorine program of rethinking the meaning of the Bible as reflected in some of the more provocative articulations of Hugh, Richard, and Andrew of St. Victor. The ground-breaking work of Beryl Smalley has shown us that if all of the answers regarding the importance of the letter were not definitively answered by the Victorines, most of the questions were magnificently raised. [16]

In the passages quoted above, Pierre Bersuire, John of Garland, Arnulf of Orleans, and Bernardus Silvestris use with ease phrases such as *"literalis sensus"* or *"multi sunt qui spiritualiter viguerunt."* And when discussing medieval theories of reading we tend to borrow the same medieval terminology regarding signification. Surely it is meet and right to do this, as long as we agree, however roughly, on the matrix or grid of implication when we do it. When Hugh of St. Victor (ca.

1096–1141) refers to the correct mode of reading texts he suggests a threefold impulse, shifting his terminology, it would seem, when discussing sacred and secular texts. When referring to the Bible, he speaks of the historical, allegorical, and moral senses; when discussing secular texts he refers to the letter, the sense, and the sentential. The basic difference, although Hugh is not explicit about this, is that in the Bible the "literal" level is usually, but not always, historical (the Bible does make use of *fictio* when it speaks figuratively to start with). The literal level of secular literature is usually fictive (though it is surely evident that secular literature can and does recount historical events).[17] Other traditions, earlier and later, make do with twofold systems of signification; still others expand the levels to four.

Dante (in his Letter to Can Grande della Scala) combines the twofold and fourfold systems. His overriding schemata are binary: literal and allegorical (the letter and some referenced "other" level). He then enriches this fundamental opposition by dividing the referenced "other" [*alienum*] into three: moral, tropological and anagogical.[18] In this discussion I propose we leave it at that level of complexity with the following codicil drawn from Hugh's advice to his students concerning three-fold understanding of texts:

First of all, it ought to be known that Sacred Scripture has three ways of conveying meaning—namely, history, allegory, and tropology. To be sure, all things in the divine utterance must not be wrenched to an interpretation such that each of them is held to contain history, allegory, and tropology all at once. Even if a triple meaning can appropriately be assigned in many passages, nevertheless it is either difficult or impossible to see it everywhere. . . . It is necessary, therefore, so to handle the Sacred Scripture that we do not try to find history everywhere, nor allegory everywhere, nor tropology everywhere but rather that we assign individual things fittingly in their own places, as reason demands.[19]

Although Hugh had a wide reputation for being a gentle and flexible teacher, he was more than merely capable of putting an edge on his voice. That edge cuts rather sharply when he speaks of the eagerness of certain student exegetes to abandon the text in front of them and leap to the stars of mystical interpretation. Here is Smalley's exquisitely just translation from *De Scripturis:*

The mystical sense is only gathered from what the letter says in the first place. I wonder how people have the face to boast themselves teachers of allegory, when they do not know the primary meaning of the letter. "We read the Scriptures," they say, "but we don't read the letter. The letter does not interest us. We teach allegory." How do you read Scripture then, if you don't read the letter? Subtract the letter and what is left?[20]

In Hugh's mind the problematic inherent in the relationship between the letter and the spirit is analogous to that in Paul between the *nunc* of "*per speculum in aenigmate*" and the *tunc* of "*facies ad faciem.*" In fact, he alludes to Paul's First Epistle to the Corinthians precisely in this context and quotes from a chapter that immediately follows the famous mirror dictum:

If, as they say, we ought to leap straight from the letter to its spiritual meaning, then the metaphors and similes, which educate us spiritually, would have been included in the Scriptures by the Holy Spirit in vain. As the Apostle says, "That was first which is fleshly, afterwards that which is spiritual" [1 Cor. 15.46]. Do not despise what is lowly in God's word, for by lowliness you will be enlightened to divinity. The outward form of God's word seems to you, perhaps, like dirt, so you trample it underfoot, like dirt, and despise what the letter tells you was done physically and visibly. But hear! That dirt, which you trample, opened the eyes of the blind. Read Scripture then, and first learn carefully what was done in the flesh.[21]

The project, for Hugh of St. Victor, was to redress an imbalance caused by excessive Gregorian enthusiasm for exegetical interpretation. Things in the eleventh century had apparently reached a kind of exegetical extreme similar to the one reached by the early decades of our own that led Archibald MacLeish to propound that "A poem must not mean, but be," and Susan Sontag to decide to enter the lists against modern exegetes in *Against Interpretation*. At the same time, it would be a mistake to overreact to Hugh's rhetorical fervor; as Smalley insists:

Hugh's philosophy teaches him to value the letter. It does not teach him to regard the letter as a good in itself. His great service to exegesis was to lay more stress on the literal interpretation *relatively* to the spiritual, and to develop the sources for it.[22]

True balance in any collective program of reform is difficult, if not impossible, to maintain, and Hugh's desire for biblical exegesis to reflect what he felt was a tensive dialectic between the literal and spiritual meanings of the biblical text was more powerful as an idea or an attitude than as a systematic method. He was followed by Richard, both a consummate if mystical reader and a very successful administrator of the priory, and by Andrew, who was, at least early on, very unsuccessful as an administrator, yet enormously powerful as a theoretician of the literal sense of the biblical text. Each, in very different ways, revealed himself as a true inheritor of Hugh's legacy as protector of the letter.

The greatest moments of challenge, in a program that seeks some equipoise between the claims of the literal and spiritual senses of the text, come when the running narrative appears either extremely figural or extremely mundane. St. Augustine, in *De Doctrina,* is conservative, allowing for figural reading only when the literal sense does not *make* any sense in terms of the world of ordinary experience and authority. Richard and Andrew of St. Victor are most interesting when coming at the problem from the other way around: when seeking the "literal sense" of extremely figurative imagery. Perhaps the most difficult challenge, in terms of isolating a "literal" reading, is offered by visionary prophecy. In Richard's prologue to his commentary on the vision of Ezekiel, we note a guarded self-consciousness as he argues against authority:

Lo! Blessed Gregory expounds the wonderful vision of celestial creatures, seen by the prophet Ezekiel, according to the mystical sense. But what it means literally he does not say. Of the second vision he says that it cannot mean anything according to the letter. This is true, but only according to the way he takes it here. If we decide to consider the same passage in a different way, perhaps we may be able to extract some suitable literal meaning. [23]

Here Richard is a faithful student of his teacher Hugh. Both have learned what is perhaps the most important lesson of Augustine's semiotics: Although all things are not signs, all signs are things. There is no utterance without a literal dimension, and Richard will have it even if he has to fly in the face of eminent exegetical authority. Of course there is more to it than that. The Victorine reverence for the letter of the divinely instituted text reflects a reverence for Creation itself as the Word/World of God because when God speaks worlds appear. Our idea of the Creator derived from our point of view of the creature reads our image back into its Maker. As we ponder the gap between that which we have and are and that which we desire to have and become, we enter the realm of Paul's meditations on *nunc* and *tunc* in 1 Corinthians. It is the very resistance of the image to the onslaught of our interpretive desire that triggers our reason and intelligence so that we may, once again, more correctly assess our real situation. This is what Richard seems to be praising when he praises the dimension of the Bible's figurative style *as* letter:

For they describe unseen things by the forms of visible things and impress them upon our memories by the beauty of desirable forms. Thus they promise a land flowing with milk and honey; sometimes they name flowers or odours and describe the harmony of celestial joys either by human song or by the harmony of birds. . . . Yet we know that none of these things are in that place from which no good thing is absent. . . . And we can immediately imagine these things as we like. The imagination can never be more useful to the reason than when she ministers to it in this way. [24]

Beryl Smalley gave us the first full portrait of the life and work of Andrew of St. Victor in 1941. Even more than Richard, Andrew senses the sheer power of the letter for both the intellect and imagination. Part of its mystery is its very inexhaustibility, and this too, in the ardor of his rhetoric, can be sensed as a reflection of the God behind the Word: the more we find there, the more there is to find. As he speaks of Jerome's willingness to go beyond Origen in his search for the literal meaning of the prophets, Andrew is speaking, sub rosa, of his own willingness to go beyond his own prior authorities as well. What Andrew admires in Jerome is clearly a mirror of what we admire in Andrew:

Yes! He knew, the learned man, he knew, full well he knew, how hidden is truth, how deep she dwells, how far she screens herself from mortal sight, how few she receives, how laboriously they seek her, how few (they are almost none) may reach her, how partially and piecemeal they drag her forth. She hides, yet so as never wholly to be hidden. Careful seekers find her, that, carefully sought, she may again be found. None may draw her forth in her completeness [*nemini tota contingit*], but by degrees. The fathers and fore-fathers have found her; something is left for the sons and descendents to find.

97

So always: she is sought; something is still to seek; found, and there is something still to find [*Sic semper queritur, ut semper supersit quod queratur. Sic semper invenitur, ut semper supersit quod inveniatur*].[25]

Andrew's *veritas* anticipates the image that haunted Baudelaire, of the stately swan trapped in the gutters of Paris. That image triggered inexhaustable images of exile, ranging from Virgil's Andromache, bereft of Hector ("Andromaque, je pense à vous!"), through a catalogue of resonant images, to the final admission of the fact that the image defies, ultimately, any attempt of man's intellect or imagination to control it by completing its inventory of signification: "et à biens d'autres encore."[26]

If Hugh's irritability with too-early foreclosure in the act of reading the letter anticipates the antimimetic itch of current literary theory, then both Richard's sense of how the edge of the image mirrors the edge of our own readerly situation and Andrew's delight in the inexhaustible plenitude of the letter anticipate symbolists such as Paul Valéry, Mallarmé, and Wallace Stevens. There is a mixture of fear and ecstasy in the face of it. We remember that Virgil says: "*hic labor est*" [this is the project] both about the arachnid labyrinth of Daedalus that encloses the Minotaur and about the liberating effort required to ascend out of Hell.

The Pauline Mirror in Alan of Lille, St. Bonaventure, and Dante

The concluding step in this chapter is to test briefly the degree to which medieval writers, acting now more as creators than as commentators, reveal this impulse to expand and protect the domain of the letter by means of their use of mirror imagery at the liminal borders between the orders of time and the orders of eternity. Judson Boyce Allen, in his ground-breaking book on medieval commentary, helps expand our sense of the letter in Dante. First he quotes the famous Latin passage from Dante's letter to Can Grande della Scala, in which the poet lays out his plan of the *Paradiso;* here is my translation:

Therefore the subject of the entire work, insofar as we take it literally, is simply the state of souls after death. For the entire process of the work turns on this or around this. If we take the work allegorically, the subject is man

98

rewarded or punished in justice because of the merit or demerit exhibited in the exercise of his free will.[27]

Then Allen goes on to say:

Dante's subject is man. . . . It is surprising that so little notice has been given to the fact that anagogy, for Dante, is the letter. That level, by the norms of exegesis, to which we should attain only at the mystical end, is for Dante the starting place. That this literal place, the *"status animarum post mortem,"* has itself a clear hierarchical arrangement, does not alter the fact that it is all anagogy, and it is all literal. The *Commedia* is—shocking truth—only literally about hell, purgatory, and heaven. It is only literally a journey, only literally ordered in terms of an ascent, and that into a heaven which literally presents itself, not as it is, but in a metaphoric or similitudinous manner suited to the capability of its observer. . . . The allegorical subject of the poem is man in this life, man deserving of reward and punishment as a political animal.[28]

Earlier on, Allen presents the work of another twelfth-century thinker, Giles of Rome (Aegidius Romanus, d. 1316) who, in his *De regimine principum* [*On the Training of Princes*], speaks of the moral process of instruction in terms of the kinds of images best used for that instruction:

Therefore it is known, *in all moral matters* [*in toto morali negotio*], that according to the Philosopher *the mode of proceeding is figural and proximate* [*modus procedendi est figuralis et grossus*]: for it is appropriate to deal in types and figures because moral action is not completely captured by mere narrative [my translation and emphasis].[29]

So Giles of Rome argues that the density of figures calls the mind to meditation around the approximations that they imply, that there is an aspect of the image that holds the attention to itself *qua imago* in addition to the outward-pointing referentiality of didactic language. If we return to Paul's mirror dictum for a moment, the fact is that there the *tunc* is present only as the word that references outward to a world after death, a world that may indeed come, but that is not in fact yet here. This, after all, is what Paul is talking about. We are *here,* not there; *now,* not then. Insofar as Paul's dictum is concerned, all the words, those clustering around the *tunc* as well as around the *nunc,* are words of the here and now: they work together to comprise the domain of the letter, which is both *figuralis* and *grossus:* "figural" and "proximate."

Alan of Lille's *Anticlaudianus*

Bernardus Silvestris may not be the author of the *Commentary on Virgil's Aeneid,* but he is indisputably the author of the *Cosmographia,* which is the base and inspiration of Alan of Lille's (ca. 1116–1202) *Anticlaudianus.* The hero of Alan's poem is not the hotly sought New and Perfect Man, but rather the Lady who seeks him. Nature, with the contrivance of Reason, persuades the heroine, who is known by three names—Prudentia, Phronesis, and Sophia—to seek the help of God in instilling a soul into a new redemptive Man. Gillian Evans overstates the danger that, in imagining a Perfect Man, Alan was skirting heresy, that he was ignoring the fact that the quest for the perfect man had already been won in history and that the prize is Christ, the Word made Flesh.[30] What Evans fails to account for sufficiently is the allegorical aspect of Alan's narrative. For Alan, who expressly enjoins the reader to read his text literally, morally, and allegorically, the object of Nature's quest is, in its ultimate allegorical sense, always already Christ. And humanity, figured forth by Alan in the image of the three-named heroine, seeks through the mediating mirrors of Faith and Reason her Original. The fact that she has three names reveals her to be a reflection of the triune nature of her originating Divinity. Prudentia, Phronesis, and Sophia are all aspects of an integrated *mens* or Mind, and perform in the narrative as an ongoing figure for the Lady as an Augustinian *imago dei.* We see here a prudentially narcissan (rather than narcissistic) use of the self's reflexive capacities to ascend to God.

What we discover in the mirrors of the *Anticlaudianus* are liminal fields in which temporal mutations miraculously adhere to eternal stability. Two crucial mirrors will do for the purposes of discussion: the Mirror of Reason and the Mirror of Faith.

In book 1, Nature deplores the depravity of man and the imperfection of the world as the result of the Fall and asks help to build a New Man. Reason comes forth to speak: in her left hand she holds a book:

Her right hand is resplendent, aflame with the brightness of a threefold mirror. . . . With unruffled countenance and profound mind, she perceives how the composite is simple: the heavenly, mortal; the different, identical; the heavy, light; the moving, stationary; the dark, bright . . . the eternal, temporal; the revolving, fixed. . . . Here it was possible to see how the image of the idea is reflected in the universe and the idea's pure splendour is sensed in its copy.[31]

The rhythm here is not an alternating one, not an oscillation from here to there, from time to eternity and back, but rather the rhythm of recognition, of the response of the eye to what it sees. We imagine Reason meditating on an imagined image in which both orders are somehow copresent. Reason is not moving back and forth from the letter to the spirit; she is not, in any progressive sense, moving at all; she is contemplating the full domain of the letter in which the eternal is temporal and the revolving is fixed.

When Prudence, with the help of the seven liberal arts and the seven virtues, manages to ascend to the Empyrean to ask God for the ensouling of the New Man, the brilliance she encounters blinds her, and Faith, in order to restore her faculties, presents her with a mirror:

In this mirror is reflected everything which the fiery region encompasses . . . but the appearance of these things differs from the real objects. Here one sees reality, here a shadow; here the thing, here appearance; here light, there an image of light [*hic res, hic umbra videtur, hic res, hic species, hic lux, ubi lucis imago*]. . . . The mirror acts as an intermediary to prevent a flood of fiery light from beaming on her eyes and robbing them of sight.[32]

This mirror, the Mirror of Faith, is used to protect Prudence-Phrone-sis-Sophia, i.e., to defend her triune mind from the unmediated light of God: Prudence cannot see God and live. There must be mediation, an accommodation to the fact that she *exists* in the realm of the letter, whereas God *is* in the realm of the spirit. She is trapped in the contingencies of time and space, of her five wits, limited to sensual data that have been specially encoded, originating as it does from a world of grace beyond space, or time, or sense. In this Mirror of Faith she can see, as Reason saw in hers, the miracle of the coexistence of radically differing orders. Her gaze is drawn to the mirror image of the miracle of the Virgin: both maid and mother. By what ordinance of heaven, she asks, can the father be born of the daughter or

God by earthly power, the permanent by the transitory, the cedar by the bloom, the sun by a star, the fire by a spark and how can the rock exude liquid honey. She is astonished that God clothes himself in our shape and that the lord of flaming Olympus dwells in our huts, that the flower of the rose lies hidden beneath the sea-weed, that clay covers the gem, that the violet is hidden in the hemlock, that life dies and the sun darkens.[33]

The letter, which this all is, figures forth a truth beyond itself and yet protects its own autonomy, its own mystery, as it does so. As we see the mirror performing the double function of protection and mediation, we enrich our sense of the image of the enigma and the mirror as captured in Paul:

Near to God, then, she can scarce endure His immortal radiance, can scarce abide the light that floods the court of His majesty. However, the surface of the mirror which she places before her eyes protects her from its flash, dulling the light by means of reflection [sed eam defendit ab isto / fulgere planities speculi, quam visibus offert / illa suis, lucem speculo mediante retardans].[34]

We recall Alan's contemporary, Andrew of St. Victor: in this integument of placing the mirror before the eyes the truth is never quite hidden; sought, it is never quite found. The Mirror of Faith allows us to see "into" God [in aenigmate] indirectly [per speculum] and live. Alan neither quotes nor comments on the Pauline mirror dictum; he embodies it as a fundamental poetic strategy whose power we only discover in the active process of exegetical reading.

Bonaventure's *Itinerarium mentis in Deum*

As Alan builds on the *Cosmographia* of Bernardus Silvestris, St. Bonaventure (1217–74) builds his *Itinerarium mentis in Deum* on Alan's *Anticlaudianus*. The *Itinerarium* begins and ends with prayer and mystic vision. We come out of the darkness of unknowing, ascend the six steps of ever-increasing light and understanding, and leap into the Noys. This imagined entry into the ineffable is couched by Bonaventure in Dionysian language of ecstasy, signalling that language itself is reaching the limits of its powers: he tells us that we will ascend to the superessential gleam of the divine darkness by an incommensurable and absolute transport of pure mind [*etenim te ipso et omnibus immensurabili et absoluto purae mentis excessu, ad superessentialem divinarum tenebrarum radium, omnia deserens et ab omnibus absolutus, ascendes*].[35]

All in the middle is reasoned and clear; ordinary language mediates the clarity of ordinary day. But in terms of beginnings and ends we move from mystery to mystery, from the visitation of the stigmata upon the body of St. Frances to a prevision of passing the barrier of the *eschaton,* in which imagined ending both promises and veils the brilliance of the Second Coming. The visions of *aitios* and *eschaton* may well help us make sense of the middle, but it does not work the other way. The middle remains the middle. Here, in this haunting work that is part treatise, part prayer, and part poem, Bonaventure shows that what we usually mean by form can render what we usually mean by the content clearer by mirroring it.[36]

The seraph repeated its visitation to Bonaventure, he says, when he went up to Mount Alverno to meditate on the vision that illuminated Francis, precisely thirty-three years (the number of years in Christ's life) after the saint's death. Bonaventure's reaction to the apocalyptic image of the living God in the form of a six-winged angel was to note that its fearful, telling symmetries mirrored the steps of the soul's ascent to God:

The six wings of the seraph can be rightly understood as signifying the six uplifting illuminations by which the soul is disposed, as by certain grades or steps, to pass over to peace through the ecstatic transports of Christian wisdom. The road to this peace is through nothing else than a most ardent love of the Crucified, the love which so transformed Paul into Christ when he was rapt to the third heaven that he declared: "With Christ I am nailed to the Cross. It is now no longer I that live, but Christ lives in me."[37]

The allusion to Paul fits both aspects of the *forma duplex:* the *forma tractatus* and *forma tractandi.* In a chain of figural anticipation and fulfillment of love, Bonaventure fulfills Francis, who fulfills Paul, who fulfills Christ. But Paul also looms in theory as well as history when Bonaventure explains the underlying method of his project and how the form of it does in fact mirror its meaning (all of it to be seen in the letter). The primary form is the Seven, the four and three Man-God number that is a *representatio* of the hypostasy of Christ. The Seven is also the One of unity and the One of the Sabbath, which follows the Six of Creation: a trinity doubled.

As for the Three: the mind draws its knowing from three epistemological realms: the world that is outside of us [*extra nos*], the world within the mind [*intra nos*], and the world of revelation from above [*supra nos*]. A modern terminology for the disciplines of inquiry appropriate to these universes of experience might be science, psychology, and theology. So much for the ontological-epistemological trinity. This trinity gets doubled by viewing each realm as a mirror that needs two kinds of seeing: we need to look *in* it and *through* it; we need to see the letter as well as the spiritual sense that it implies. And Bonaventure couches these two kinds of seeing in the mirror by a direct play of allusion to the language of Paul's Corinthian mirror dictum, *"per speculum in aenigmate"*:

Each of the foregoing ways of seeing may be subdivided according to whether we consider God as the Alpha and the Omega, or whether we consider Him in any one of the aforesaid ways as *through* and as *in* a mirror [*seu in quantum contingit videre Deum in unoquoque praedictorum modorum ut per speculum et ut in speculo*].[38]

Bonaventure's coordination of the three realms of ontology along the Pauline axis of the prepositions *in* and *through* appropriates the problematics of Paul's Corinthian mirror dictum directly into the structural scaffold of his image of ascent into the Noys, the One, the *Monos pros Monon*. The metaphor Bonaventure uses for the epistemological tools required to see into these mirrors are themselves mirrors as well, and they must be continually polished. The way and the goal reflect one another; this relation creates a coherent and intelligible structure of the pilgrimage: Christ is both the End and the Means: the Goal and the Way. Thus Paul's fecund articulation, which captures in the irresolvable ambiguities of its language the very image of the enigma *into* which and *by* which we look, resolves for Bonaventure, at least in words, the conundrum of being and knowing, and can therefore function as an enabling grammatical superstructure by which the seraphic Doctor erects his ladder to the Mind of God.

Dante's *Divina Commedia*

Dante creates an unforgettable chiastic vignette for Sts. Bonaventure and Thomas Aquinas in Paradise. In the Cantos of the Sun, Bonaventure pays tribute to his rival order, the Dominicans, while St. Thomas, the great Dominican theologian, pays tribute to the foundation of the order of St. Francis. Both saints then join their separate circles and the circles turn, in contrary motion, one inside the other, as a tribute to the rose windows of Paris and Chartres where mystical and scholastic theology had their greatest triumphs. These cantos constitute one of the most spectacular examples of Pauline mirroring in the *Paradiso*.

Yet Dante makes no direct allusion to Paul's Corinthian mirror dictum anywhere in his oeuvre. Of course he alludes frequently to Paul, but always with regard to other questions, other issues. For a poet as centrally concerned with meaning, both in theory (*Convivio*, etc.) and in practice (all of his poetry contains the seeds of its own commentary), why this silence about Paul's most provocative utterance about the nature of and quest for meaning?

Frequency of direct presence has often little to do with the power of more indirect forms of presence, or even unexpected absence. Preparatory to dealing with the "absence" of Paul's mirror dictum, let us briefly discuss the function of oblique and minimal presence of Narcissus and Orpheus in the *Commedia*.

Narcissus is mentioned directly only once in the *Commedia*: Master Adam, the counterfeiter, suggests that Sinon of Troy is eager, in the thirst of his dropsy, to "lick the mirror of Narcissus" (*Inferno* 30.129). Although the boy is named only once, his presence haunts the entire poem. R. A. Shoaf, for example, is able to construct, in a demonstration running over four chapters, a rich and illuminating reading of the entire *Commedia* while limiting himself essentially to those images that reverberate with the Narcissus narrative; and even so he does not exhaust the inventory.[39]

For instance, the narrative of the lost boy is indirectly alluded to again in *Paradiso* 3, where Dante the Pilgrim seems to reverse the error of the boy at the pool when he mistakes the "real" visage of Piccarda and the moon's inhabitants for "shadows," only to turn around to seek the originals and find nothing. But in a way, of course, he also makes the *same* error as the lost boy. As we learn from Beatrice in *Paradiso* 4, these souls do *not* in fact inhabit the moon; when he sees them there he is not seeing *them,* but only *segna,* signs of their being. These souls, Beatrice says in the very next canto, are "really" where all souls are, together as one in direct contemplation of their Maker. They are shown "as being here" in a gesture of divine accommodation: the grace (and poetic wit) of God as stooping to the limitations of Dante's humanity, trapped as it is in the warp and woof of space and time. It would probably be misleading to call the image of Dante's misprision of the souls in the moon is narcissistic, but it is, in one of Kristeva's more useful distinctions, profoundly narcissan.[40] By means of these images, God is providing Dante (allegorically) even as Dante is providing us (quite literally) with Pauline mirrors in which he-as-we can gain some partial knowledge, the only knowledge really possible this side of death.

Finally, the ultimate image of the *Paradiso* functions as a glorious inversion and redemption of the Narcissus image even as Narcissus himself is, by poetic necessity, conspicuously absent. Dante can "see our image" in the "pool" limned by the Circles of God and becomes, as our representative Everyman, the Anti-Narcissus: not the boy who sees his empty visual echo in the pool where nobody ever is, but a *figura* for all of us; who can see, on our behalf, a dark mirror fore-figuring the final fulfillment of our foundational status as the *imago dei* of Genesis in the final resurrection of the body, a peace passing all understanding.

So there is very important narcissan imagery in the *Commedia* even if the boy himself makes only one minimal direct appearance in the Hell of the counterfeiters. The equally minimal presence of Orpheus generates an equally powerful poetic effect. Orpheus is tidily placed in a list of many others wandering the Elysian fields of Limbo in *Inferno* 4.130: " . . . e vidi Orfeo . . . ," and that's that. The only important actual presence of Orpheus in the rest of the Dantean canon is in the *Convivio:* but that presence is all important and sustains a suspicion that the minimal indicator of Orpheus's Elysian location is much more telling for the enormous hole in the reader's imagination that it leaves behind than for the small, insignificant space it fills in canto 4.

In the *Convivio,* Orpheus is used as the prime exemplum in Dante's display of the machinery of allegorical signification:

Writings can be understood and ought to be expounded chiefly in four senses. The first is called literal, and this is that sense which does not go beyond the strict limits of the letter; the second is called allegorical, and this is disguised under the cloak of such stories, and is a truth hidden under a beautiful fiction. Thus Ovid says that Orpheus with his lyre made beasts tame, and trees and stones move towards himself, that is to say that the wise man by the instrument of his voice makes cruel hearts grow mild and humble, and those who have not the life of Science and of Art move to his will, while they who have no rational life are as it were like stones.[41]

What orphic aspects are present? Orpheus as artist in the face of death; the artist as shapeshifter, as he works his will on others, as he moves the beasts and the stones. What is absent? The lost Eurydice, the failed promise not to turn and look, the desolation as Orpheus sings alone, his dismemberment by the maenads, the lyre and severed head floating down the Hebros, the mourning, echoing landscape, the worm and head frozen by Apollo on the beach of Lesbos. This crucial subset of the orphic inventory is absent in the *Convivio*. But all these missing pieces, along with the pieces that are present in the *Convivio,* come together in our heads and create an extremely rich horizon of expectation as we begin to read of Dante's descent in the *Commedia*. This vast orphic horizon is then met by the tidy isolation of Orpheus as merely another face in the Elysian crowd of *Inferno* 4. And so we are made ready for his necessary reduction and displacement: we realize that Orpheus must be shunted aside so that his role in our collective memory can be appropriated by Dante himself, the Hero-Pilgrim-Poet of the poem.[42]

And even among the carefully selected aspects of the orphic inventory that are present in the *Convivio,* there remains a minor, nagging question. Although Dante *speaks* of the Orpheus of Ovid, his diction obliquely *quotes* the *Commentary* of Bernardus Silvestris on Virgil. Bernardus is much more likely thinking of the Orpheus of Virgil's fourth *Georgic* than the Orpheus of Ovid's *Metamorphoses,* and my hunch is that Dante is too. The role of Orpheus in the fourth *Georgic* is not autonomous, but openly exemplary. Virgil's Orpheus acts as a mirror agenda of self-understanding and reform for Aristaeus; he is an essentially negative model about whom Aristaeus must gain greater, more sympathetic understanding, and to whom he must even pay homage, but from whom he must also learn to do better. The fourth *Georgic* contains not only the narrative of Orpheus but also Virgil's famous valedictory to the lyric and his intention to take on the burden of epic. These lines of farewell follow immediately upon the impressionistic, elegiac rendering of the narrative of Orpheus's failure to resurrect Eurydice and Aristaeus's countering success in resurrecting his bees from the desiccated corpse of the bull.

In the *Aeneid*, Orpheus's presence is as minimal in the catabasis of book 6 as it is later in the limbo of Dante's *Commedia*, and for similar poetic reasons. As Aeneas pleads with the Sibyl to grant him descent, he summons up a short list of exemplary figures—which include Pollux, Theseus, Hercules, and Orpheus—saying " . . . If Orpheus could recall the spirit of his wife, relying / upon his Thracian lyre's enchanting strings . . ." (6.119–20). This casual and minor reference to Orpheus in the *Aeneid*, suppressing all but the poetic triumph before Pluto and Persephone, reminds us of the singer's haunting centrality in the recent fourth *Georgics*, that lyric valedictory to a bygone world, or at least a bygone project. Thus the sudden marginalizing of Orpheus to near-absence in the *Aeneid*, the imperial foundational epic of the future, reveals itself just as deeply functional for Virgil as it was later to prove for Dante: it figures forth, is corrected, and fulfilled by the central presence of Aeneas/Aristaeus, the Anti-Orpheus, who brings up from Hell, not a dead Creusa/Eurydice, but the busy-bee labor of founding Rome.

In terms of the implied political allegory of the *Aeneid*, the absent Orpheus evokes that aspect of Aeneas who is infatuated with Dido and must be denied: Mark Antony. Thus Antony/Orpheus figures forth and is corrected, displaced, and fulfilled by *his* necessary alter ego, Aristaeus/Aeneas/Augustus. And we have seen how this Virgilian pattern of metaphoric absence and substitution is later replicated by Dante, where the echoing absence of the marginalized Thracian also figures forth, and is displaced and fulfilled: this time by Dante himself, now both Poet/Subject (author) and Pilgrim/Object (hero) of his epic of redemption.

As with Narcissus and Orpheus, so with Paul's Corinthian mirror dictum. Although there is no direct reference to the phrase "now we see through a glass darkly" in the *Commedia*, the presence of the apostle himself is frequently called to mind. As we examine a master image of actual mirroring in each canticle, we sense the ways in which Dante appropriates, in a rich if silent set of implications, Paul's mirror dictum in profound and intuitive ways.

There may even be a faint echo of Paul's actual language in the first two lines of the *Commedia:*

Nel mezzo del cammin di nostra vita
mi ritrovai *per una selva oscura.* . . .

[*In the middle of the road* of our life
I found myself *by a darkened forest.* . . .]
(*Inferno* 1.1–2, my translation and emphasis)

Judson Boyce Allen recalls R. A. Shoaf saying Dante began his epic
with verbal punning and that the "mi retrovai" [finding myself] of the
second line echoes etymologically the poetic making of the "trouvères"
so that "the word 'per' makes the dark wood an agent of means as well
as a location."[43] If something of that sort is going on—and it seems,
given the long tradition begun by Virgil's lyric/epic transference in the
fourth *Georgic,* that it very well might be going on—then it would also
be possible to read the first two lines backward with catoptric Pauline
ambiguity: "It was by means of that darkened forest [per selva oscura
(*per speculum*)]—that I found myself in the middle of the road of life
[nel mezzo del cammin (*in aenigmate*)]." As canto 1 introduces the
entire epic undertaking of the *Commedia,* and not merely the *Inferno,*
every nuance is important, even if every nuance is not equally compelling. However faint, the reversibility of the two halves of the Pauline
formula—along with the undeniable presence of the Italian equivalents
of the problematic Latin prepositions *per* and *in*—create, in the opening
lines of the *Commedia,* an echo chamber that expands our horizon of
expectation to accommodate the rhythms of lexical ambiguity generated for the Middle Ages by the mirror dictum of Paul.

Inferno 14.94–120: "e Roma guarda come süo speglio . . ."

Nearly halfway through the *Inferno,* Virgil pauses to paint an extended
narrative image: that of the statue of the Old Man of Crete. His body
reflects the entropy of Hesiodic ideas of human history: the head of
gold, the neck of silver, the torso of bronze, and the legs of iron. His
feet are of clay; one of them, the one "on which he chiefly stands," is
cracked. He looks on Rome as on a looking glass; and he weeps. The
eyes that weep these tears of implied recognition function as the source
of all the rivers of Hell.

It is a truly hellish image: inverted and circular. The implication is
that deteriorating human history recognizes its pattern in the particular
history of *Roma,* the *civitas* of the human center; and that the recogni-

tion of the aptness of that mirror relation triggers the tears that flow through, and thus give shape and order to but cannot cleanse the landscapes of perdition. It is a dark mirror, this City, and it functions as the pool of Narcissus: only here the boy is an old man, and there is only recognition, no desire—and no new dispensation that can offer any promise of restitution or redemption. There will be no face-to-face, no knowing as we are known. The intense claustrophobia engendered here is infernally appropriate: the agony of Hell can only express itself through inverse grotesques, such parodies of the real. Otherwise it would reflect an ontological status that must be denied to evil. This issue is raised in greater detail in my discussion of Francesca and the poetics of evil in chapter 7. Suffice it here that at the center of the *Inferno,* we have a master counter image of Narcissus in the Vecchio di Creta. The original Narcissus melts into the ground as he weeps with knowing. The Old Man of Crete is no metamorphic flower. The source of the rivers of Hell is a golden eye that cannot close: its gaze is locked forever on its image.

Purgatorio 31.106–26: "Come in lo specchio il sol . . ."

If the *Inferno*'s epistemological realm is Bonaventure's *extra nos,* that of *Purgatorio* is *intra nos,* the interior world of the mind. The task here is for intellect and memory to instruct the will to the point where it can have confidence in the exercise of freedom—so that it may reach, in difficult love, that crucial point, the highest act of free will: its awful, daring self-submission to the Other. After Virgil mitres and crowns Dante with his own freedom, Matilda leads him through the baptismal immersion in Lethe so that he is freed of the remembrance of his sins. He encounters the pageant of revelation, his attention centering on the Cart of the Church, bearing Beatrice and drawn by the Griffin, a beast whose upper body is shaped like an eagle, whose lower body is shaped like a lion. In order to "see" the Griffin for what it "is," the four cardinal (or classical) virtues lead him to Beatrice, promising their "guidance to her eyes," but warning that the three theological (or Christian) virtues will be needed in order to complete the "penetration of her joyous light."

> So singing they began; then, leading me
> together with them to the griffin's breast,
> where Beatrice, turned toward us, stood, they said:

"See that you are not sparing of your gaze:
before you we have set those emeralds
from which Love once had aimed his shafts at you. . . ."
　　Just like the sun within a mirror, so
the double-natured creature gleamed within,
now showing one, and now the other guise.
　　Consider, reader, if I did not wonder
when I saw something that displayed no movement
though its reflected image kept on changing.
　　　　　　　　　(*Purgatorio* 31.112–18, 121–26)[44]

The dual nature of the Griffin figures forth the dual nature of Christ's hypostasy. Seen directly, the beast appears to be stable in its image; seen in the eyes of Beatrice, it appears to Dante in a protocinematic series of oscillations in which the beast reveals itself alternately as entirely lion and entirely eagle in extremely rapid succession. In front of him is a set-piece allegory out of any bestiary. But as Beatrice looks on the beast, and Dante looks at its reflection in Beatrice's eyes, these eyes become a Pauline mirror of partial revelation, and he begins to get a more profound sense of the enigma of the hypostatic union. But it is still "figural" and "proximate": we rest, in a restless sort of way, with an image of a constantly shifting figure: we are at the extreme edge of the domain of the letter, but still within that domain—not in a state of, but on the brink of, revelation. It is important, even though we know that Beatrice will later insist, in the *Paradiso*, that "not in my eyes alone is Paradise," that we understand the difference between the two realms on just this point. Here, in Purgatory, at this stage of Dante's progress, her eyes mediate a new vision that must first be worked through before it can be safely overgone. Two earlier mirror images in canto 15, which begins the great series of purgatorial lectures on the nature of love and free will, help prepare us for the kind of love that Beatrice's eyes are both reflecting and mediating. The first is an elaborate astronomical image that allows us to extrapolate the time of day here in Eden by means of understanding, through the catoprics of the sun, the time of day in Rome. The image, though severe in its mathematical precision, is graced by the presence of children at play:

As many as the hours in which the sphere
that's always playing like a child appears

from daybreak to the end of the third hour,
    so many were the hours of light still left
before the course of day had reached sunset;
vespers was there; and where we are, midnight.

(Purgatorio 15.1–6)

This ludic dimension of reciprocal mirroring among the stars is itself mirrored in the catoptric possibilities we, as humans, have for one another. Some seventy lines later, Virgil is expounding the ways in which the economy of love runs counter to that of more mundane commodities. The more one loves, the more love there is:

Where ardor is, that Good gives of Itself;
and where more love is, there that Good confers
a greater measure of eternal worth.
    And when there are more souls above who love,
there's more to love well there, and they love more,
and, mirror-like, each soul reflects the other.

(Purgatorio 15.70–76)

Paradiso 30.61–132: "Son di lor vero umbriferi prefazi . . ."

According to the model provided by Bonaventure, the epistemological realm of *Paradiso* is the *supra nos* of revelation. Once Dante passes the still point of the turning world, he has "won beyond the sun." One of the things this means is that he has passed the realm of physics and entered into a metaphysical *lux nova* of "pure intellectual light." As Dante writes to Can Grande della Scala, in this realm a special kind of image must be developed to match the special state of the experience one is trying to image forth. And so Dante develops a poetics of ecstasy, in which a river of sparkling lights winds up and around and turns into a rose seating the company of heaven. The light blinds him, so he splashes the light of the river into the lids of his eyes so that he may see it. This act shows how light, in the Middle Ages, can act as an image of both the thing seen and the means of seeing it; the image of Dante bathing his eyes in the very light he wishes to see reconciles the seeing with the thing seen, knowing and loving with being. Mazzeo put it well:

". . . Light is both the principle of cognition and the principle of vision, the principle of being and the principle of 'being-known,' the principle of beauty and the principle of knowledge. . . . The same light which swathes him and which he sees is also the light by which he sees."[45]

> And I saw light that took a river's form—
> light flashing, reddish-gold, between two banks
> painted with wonderful spring flowerings . . .
>   " . . . that you may satisfy your mighty thirst
> you must drink of these waters." So did she
> who is the sun of my eyes speak to me.
>   She added this: "The river and the gems
> of topaz entering and leaving, and
> the grasses' laughter—these are shadowy
>   prefaces of their truth: not that these things
> are lacking in themselves; the defect lies
> in you, whose sight is not yet that sublime."
>   . . . . I hurried toward that stream
> to make still finer mirrors of my eyes.
>   (*Paradiso* 33.61–63, 73–81, 84–85)

As gorgeous as these final images are, Judson Boyce Allen is still correct: all is anagogy and all is literal. Mazzeo, no doubt carried away with Dante's poetic power, suggests we actually leave the domain of the implied at this point in the poem and cross over into the ultimately real. We begin indeed to witness a metamorphic collective shift of the form in which the souls reveal themselves to Dante as shifting, in collective good will, from the linear image of the river, a figure of becoming in time, to the circular form of the rose, a figure of being in eternity. But of course we do not have the actual passing itself, only the literary passage: a dark mirror of that passing. Not the *Deus*, but an *imago dei*. Not the *facies*, but a *speculum in aenigmate*, however drenched in light. The whole passage from *nunc* to *tunc* is captured in a series of images that move from a river to a rose to the Circles of God. But it is an image sequence whose mode of existence is absolutely limited to the *nunc*. At the end, like Oedipus and Lear, Dante is gone, we know not where, but we are left holding on to the words, longing for more, yet hoping against hope that Yeats was right when he said that the "words alone are certain good."

The bridge is now complete: it spans the text of Paul, found by Augustine in the garden of his nameless host, to the shadowy prefaces of the eyes of Beatrice, found by Dante in the Garden of Eden. We have gained our required access to Heinrich's terror upon seeing his Lady in a dream, always already waiting with her damaged mouth, and to Chrétien's gaiety as he depicts Enide as a prudential mirror of reform. We move now to twelfth-century lyric and romance.

The Damaged Mouth: Heinrich von Morungen, Narcissus, and the Catastrophe of Recognition

I am the woman stripped more nakedly
Than nakedness, standing before an inflexible
Order, saying I am the contemplated spouse.

Speak to me that, which spoken, will array me
In its own only precious ornament.
Set on me the spirit's diamond coronal.

Clothe me entire in the final filament,
So that I tremble with such love so known
And myself am precious for your perfecting.

Then Ozymandias said the spouse, the bride
Is never naked. A fictive covering
Weaves always glistening from the heart and mind.
　　　　—Wallace Stevens, *Notes toward a Supreme Fiction*

The central concerns in this chapter and the one following will focus on the speculative strategies of the two major secular genres of the twelfth century: the lyric and the romance. Although one must accept the full force of recent arguments by Colie, Jauss, Hult, and others that medieval genres are processes rather than structures, and thus have extremely tenuous, even interpenetrating boundaries, nonetheless, their centers remain remarkably stable and well differentiated.[1] As Rosalie Colie has so compellingly argued, insofar as genres reflect developing conventions for putting the words together, they reflect a culture's ways of putting the world together.[2]

In the Middle Ages, the genres of the lyric and romance developed in a dialectical relationship to one another. It proves heuristically useful to think of the romance as centrifugal, fundamentally concerned with a culture's modes of collective self-preservation. Romance, while often extremely concerned with the interior life of its *dramatis personae*, is itself more centered on plot and event, on contextual exteriority, on the world, in St. Bonaventure's terms, of *extra nos*. If romance is centrifugal in moment, lyric is centripetal. Although stipulating the contextual necessities of exteriority, the lyric deals centrally with attempts to capture the modes of interior reflection, mirroring the world of *intra nos*. The focal point for these chapters on the specular power of medieval genres will be that pivotal occasion in which the Lover beholds his Lady. This act of looking is speculative, and quickly became a medieval master figure capturing the subject in the face of the desired object.

One saw, in medieval mirrors, either an image that showed the world as it is or one that showed the world as it should be; mirrors reflected either reality or ideality. And one saw images of the Other (God or neighbor) or of the self. Thus one could extrapolate, by contemplating the discrepancy between what one saw and what one was, agendas for reform or despair. In the developing iconography of reflection, the literary figure that came to be associated with the agenda of life-giving reform was Prudentia; with death-dealing despair, Narcissus.

As one looks into the eye of the beloved, one physically as well as metaphysically looks into a mirror; one actually sees a miniature reflection of one's own image. From Plato's *Phaedrus,* through the summary commandments of the New Testament, to the latest tabloid scandal, the process of appropriately loving the Other has involved negotiating the reflecting difficulties of appropriately loving the self.[3] In the lyric, the confrontation with the mirroring power of the Lady is narcissistic, reaffirming the separation between the Lover and the object of his desire. In the romance, the same confrontation is narcissan, prudential, and potentially redemptive, leading to greater knowledge, both of the self and of the Other.[4]

We shall shortly consider two notoriously difficult lyrics of Heinrich von Morungen, beginning with the heavily anthologized "meadow" poem, *Des Minnesangs Frühling* (*MF*) 139.19, and concluding with *MF* 145.1, his famous "Narcissus" poem. We shall explore the darker side of twelfth-century concerns with the hiatus between appearance and reality by examining the representative as well as mimetic uses Heinrich makes of mirror images as he constructs his poems. In these constructions, and in the act of reading, which recapitulates the poetic act of these constructions, both he and we engage in acts of criticism: of contemporary experience and literary models of authority.

Heinrich is fascinated by the essentially unreliable nature of the modes of mediation that link the self to the Other. His fear of the mediating mirror as unreliable bridge is paralleled by his sense of the literary conventions of genre as being not only necessary, but eventually self-defeating and deluding. The agon between the poet and his art is figured forth both in the Lover's adoration of the Beloved and in Narcissus's adoration of his own image in the pool. These three images of relation coalesce and form an unholy trinity of desire. The poet's relationship to his art, the Lover's relationship to his Lady, and Narcissus's relationship to the pool combine into a mediating trope of our relation to our world. As the poet confronts, with *attritio cordis*, the *nullus ordo* at the center of an imagined self without God, he faces the ever-looming dark night of the soul, the *noche oscura*, which is the medieval anticipation of our twentieth-century nightmare of solipsism. An illuminating and not altogether peripheral irony arises as we discover the Virgilian ways in which Heinrich uses images of Ovid, just as we will discover, in the next chapter, the redemptive, Ovidian ways in which Chrétien de Troyes uses Virgil.

For a satisfactory analysis of the lyrics of Heinrich, we require a brief theoretical excursion to account for the representational power of the almost intrusive presence of formal manipulation in and of itself. The formal design of the medieval lyric, from Bernard de Ventadorn and Arnaut Daniel to Guido Cavalcante and Dante, is as important to its signifying power as its mimetic capability of mirroring interiority.

There appears, in the medieval imagination, to have been a contradiction of attitude toward the image. In opposition to the continuous tradition of creating, in various media, recognizable imagistic representations of the world came the often violent counterpressures of iconoclasm, which feared, even despised, the impulse of humanity to image itself forth in verisimilitude.

This double sense of things can be traced to medieval reading of biblical etiology and imperative. The opening salvos of Genesis would seem to legitimize the processes of imitation beyond question: "Let us make man in our image, after our own likeness; and let them have dominion" (1.26). The created creature then imitates his Maker in the generation of Seth: "And Adam . . . begat a son in his own likeness, after his image" (5.3). And yet the same God commands, albeit later on, "Thou shalt not make unto thee any graven image, or any likeness of any thing that is in the heaven above, or that is in the earth beneath, or that is in the water under the earth" (Exodus 20.4). That this Mosaic prohibition referred (in historical contexts provided by higher criticism) to the worship of molten or graven idols among the early Hebrews has little to do with its profound if diffuse impact on the medieval imagination, which was, at its height, more apocalyptic than historical and possessed of a collective passion for abstracting and universalizing the particular.

In a search for medieval modes of expression other than lexical referencing and the construction of literary images of verisimilitude, we find another major mode of signification: the principle of representation underlying the disposition or ordination of form itself. Again, biblical literature provides the enabling text: "Thou hast disposed the world in number, weight and measure" (Wisd. of Sol. 11.21). As the bits composing an artifice were put next to one another (whether musical tones, pieces of glass, stress-bearing arches, or words in a poem), a net of internal relation was declared. That relation, or *ratio*, among the parts was itself perceived as capable of a highly privileged kind of signification.[5] The numerical "ratios" among the world's parts reveal, according to St. Bonaventure, the vestiges of its creating deity.[6] In Gregorian chant, for example, it is the structure of intervals *between* the notes, and not the notes themselves, that imitates, as praise, the divine mind at work. Unheard ratios are generated in the mind by the notes actually heard in the ear, and thus the adequacy of this music as an act of praise resides precisely in the structure of holy silence "measured off" by the mundane notes as heard.

Let us take one of the last, great figures in the *Inferno* as a particularly illuminating example of *ordo*'s power. When Ugolino recounts the death of his sons by starvation in the notorious tower, he weaves a figure in the carpet of his recitation, which has been brought brilliantly to light by Allen Mandelbaum in the introduction to his *California Dante:*

But after we had reached the *fourth* day, Gaddo,
throwing himself, outstretched, down at my feet,
implored me: "Father, why do you not help me?"
And there he died; and just as you see me,
I saw the other *three* fall *one* by one
between the *fifth* day and the *sixth,* at which,
now blind, I started groping over each;
and after they were dead, I called them for
two days; then fasting had more force than grief.

[Poscia che fummo al *quarto* dì venuti,
Gaddo mi si gittò disteso a' piedi,
dicendo: "Padre mio, ché non m'aiuti?"
Quivi morì; e come tu mi vedi,
vid'io cascar li *tre* ad *uno* ad uno
tra 'l *quinto* dì e 'l *sesto:* ond'io mi diedi
Già cieco, a brancolar sovra ciascuno,
e *due* dì li chiamai, poi che fur morti.
Poscia, più che 'l dolor, poté 'l digiuno.]
(*Inferno* 33.67–75, my emphasis)

As Mandelbaum notes, "the sequence of ordinal and cardinal numbers obeys an all-enclosing law—no element escapes—it is as if even accidental elements combine to become a vice that locks Ugolino into the ineluctable."[7] Even more germane to the current consideration of *ordo* is that although the embedded numbers themselves are extremely significant to the medieval mind, the particular sequence—431562— is not. In fact, it is the very randomness of the sequence that calls to mind the "real" serial six of Creation, which is here parodied and which then, in our mind's eye, points back to Hell as an image of deconstructed reality. Once Creation is so invoked, the presence of the six also calls to mind the absence of the seven, a fine indicator that Hell's sorrow is without number, has no surcease or completion. This passage thus represents as well as imitates the vestigial traces of divine *ordo,* even in the *nullus ordo* of Hell.

What occurred, then, in medieval arts, especially the arts of the word, was a double game. Verisimilitude and formal ordination proceeded simultaneously yet independently as principles of composition and often acted in mutually tensive as well as reconciling and reinforcing ways. This double play, in which the same signifying urge could manifest itself both in mimetic systems of lexical signification and in representational systems of formal ordination, had enormous specular power, and provided a theater for the deployment of the dialectic generated by related oppositions within the culture: vernacular and latinity, cupidity and charity, self and other, constraint and freedom, interiority and exteriority, time and eternity, man and God.

Hugo Kuhn, until his death the dean of German medieval studies, argued in lectures that everything in Heinrich von Morungen is ultimately about art. Heinrich's darker message may well be that there never *is* anything but art; that only in and through the mirrors of art do we discover the central reality of the fatal hiatus that obtains between ourselves and the objects of our desire.

In *MF* 139.19, a famous but diversely read lyric, Heinrich von Morungen orchestrates a counterpoint between linkage and alienation that warrants consideration:

Ich hôrte ûf der heide	I heard in the meadow
lûte stimme und süezen sanc	bright voices and lovely sound
dâ von wart ich beide	that made me both
vröiden rîch und an trûren kranc	rich in joy and sick in grief
nâch der mîn gedánc	she for whom my thought
sê're ránc	had fought
ùnde swanc	and reeled
die vant ich ze tanze	I found her dancing
dâ si sanc	as she sang
âne leide ich dô spranc	without sorrow I danced too
Ich vant sî verborgen	I found her hidden
eine únd ir wéngel von	all alone her cheeks
tréhen naz	wet with tears
dâ si an dem morgen	where she foresaw me dead
mînes tôdes sich vermaz	that morning
der vil lieben ház	my beloved's hate
tùot mir báz	feels better
dànne daz	than that
dô ich vor ir kniewete	and then I knelt before her
dâ si saz	where she sat
und ir sorgen vergaz	and let her trouble go

Ich vant si an der zinne	I found her on the battlement
eine und ich was zuo zaln gesant	alone and I was sent for then
dâ mehte ichs ir minne	I could have claimed love's
wol mit vuoge hân gepfant	pledge by rights
dô wânde ich diu lánt	I thought I'd fired
hân verbránt	the land
sâ zehant	to ash
wan daz mich ir süezen minne bant	no her sweet love's bind
an den sinnen hât erblant	had blinded my mind[8]

The basic literary situation is this. In terms of the principle of verisimilitude, we witness three unique, autonomous strophes of re-called perception and discovery—a discovery that is always both can-didly physical and clearly more than physical. In the strophe, the speaker hears, in the lush landscape of the traditional *reverdie* of spring-time, words and music, and he responds, in an almost stipulated way, with a Thuringian trope out of Ovid: he is rich in joy and sick with sorrow. It is only at the end of the stanza that self-absorption turns into a moment of discovery of the truly Other: he finds her dancing; freed of suffering by that finding, he dances too.

The strophe is a complete poem in itself. It depicts a man caught in the received imagery of springtime, an essentially literary imagery that, even as it renders the world intelligible, leaves, in the pressures of its conventionality, little room for freedom.[9] Nonetheless he finds a real lady in his imaginary garden and is thereby freed to dance. The phrase *ane leit,* "without sorrow," which works, in its pointing, both back to the Lady and forward to the Lover, is the shared ground for the possibility of dancing in the face of the world.

As the moment of discovery in the first strophe is at the end ("I found her dancing"), in the second strophe it is at the beginning ("I found her hidden"). The enhanced proximity of the events of discovery emphasizes the dramatic opposition of the nature of those discoveries. If the first stanza celebrates the gift of freedom by way of the Beloved's example, the second eulogizes love's free surrender of itself in the sure foreknowledge of the Beloved's death.

Both strophes 1 and 2 close in tableaux of impressive physical ges-ture ("I danced...I kneeled"). The third also opens with physical placement; but in opposition to the kneeling figure of amatory submis-sion in strophe 2, we find ourselves with the lovers as apparent equals on a castellated height. Moreover, the external images of physical gesture that close strophes 1 and 2 are countered with the internal drama of perception and discovery that so memorably closes strophe 3: "I thought I had burnt the world, but no, it was that her love's binding power had blinded my mind."

If the mimetic principle governing verisimilitude is painting intense, autonomous moments and emphasizing, by means of image contrasts, the *difference* between them, the representative principle of ordination insists on an essential *identity* among the experiences of each strophe. Above all, there are the extremely obvious patterns of repetition governing the structure of the poem. Except for lines 1 and 3, all lines in each strophe have the same dominant rhyme. Line 5 always has triple internal rhyme, which is the same rhyme as the rhymes in lines 2, 4, 6, and 7. In addition, as one looks across strophe boundaries, although the final consonants of the rhyme scheme differ, all three strophes share the assonance of final /a/ at the dominant rhyme points (*a*nc, *a*z, *a*nt). Finally, the sound of the initial rhymes of lines 1 and 3 find an affirming echo in the incipit, or beginning, of the last line of each strphe (*ûf der heide* and *wart ich beide* are echoed in the opening phrase of 1.7, *âne leide,* and so on for the other strophes).

This repeated sounding of the tonic with the dominant at the end makes the final line of each strophe act as a kind of phonic mirror of the whole so that beginning is regularly recalled precisely in the cadences of ending. These shimmering patterns are more than brilliant virtuosity, they are functional—they insist upon the presence of ordered identities, of a plan.

Thus the mimetic principle of verisimilitude insists on the uniqueness of each moment, on the highly valued sense of differentiation in the experiences of our individual lives; the representational principle of ordination, here primarily exhibited by *repetitio,* simultaneously insists on the universality, the ultimate identity of these experiences. As we observe both orders at work, the clarity of the patterns of ordination render the imagistically depicted disorder of the impassioned speaker-lover into a narrower, more accurately human scale. We see an enclosing order that the Lover does not see and that results, for us, in a sympathetic yet therapeutically distancing irony. This is mature medieval dialectics in poetic action: the events of our lives seem central and unique as they form our personal history, yet they become intelligible and significant only as we learn to perceive them in an encompassing order. The formal ordering in Heinrich's poem can then be seen for what such ordering can always become in the Middle Ages: a trope for a providential order beyond our understanding.

In the great volume of medieval lyric manuscripts known as the Grosse Heidelberger Liederhandschrift, most of the poets whose texts are represented are also depicted in gorgeous full-page miniatures. It is not, I think, by accident that the miniature portrait of Heinrich von Morungen (folio 76v.) has the poet seated, full-face to us, while his Lady stands off to the right, slightly behind him, gazing in another direction, her hand raised in greeting to someone or something implied beyond the ornate border of the illumination. He cannot see her because there floats between them a partially unrolled scroll on which there is not a mark written, yet upon which his eyes are intensely fixed. It is an interesting assembly of medieval images and reinforces our modern sense that Heinrich is a poet of the isolated figure, of distance, of barriers, of absence, of the space between; that his words achieve always and only tenuous and indirect mediation between the Poet-lover and the Other, that object of deepest desire.

We have seen this in the "meadow" poem. His extraordinary "Narcissus" poem, MF 145.1, pushes things even further in this direction. The sequence of images in the poem shows that the very conventions of mediation we use to reach out to one another turn out to be inseparable from the very barriers between each other we are seeking to overcome. There may well be those who argue that attributing such a protosolipsistic view to a medieval poet is anachronistic. But I would argue that there is much in both the comic modes of Chrétien de Troyes and Wolfram von Eschenbach and in the darker modes of Gottfried von Strassburg that suggests that such a concern with slippage between reality and appearance, between our desire and its object, cuts deeply into the mental worldview of the twelfth century:

> Mir ist geschehen als einem kindelîne,
> daz sîn schoenez bilde in einem glase gesach
> unde greif dar nâch sîn selbes schîne
> sô lange vntz daz sîn hant den spiegel gar zerbrach.
> dô wart al sîn wunne ein leitlich ungemach.
> alsô dâhte ich iemer vrô ze sîne,
> dô ich gesach die lieben vrouwen mîne,
> von der mir bî liebe leides vil geschach.

[It's gone with me as with a little child
that saw its lovely image in a glass
and reached so often for that shining look of his
until he broke the mirror with his hand.
Then all his laughter turned to sorrow.
Just so I thought I'd always live in joy
gazing on my lovely, loving lady
from whom, through love, came bitter misery.]

Minne, diu der werelde ir vröude mêret,
seht, diu brâhte in troumes wîs die vrouwen mîn,
dâ mîn lîp an slâfen was gekêret
und ersach sich an der besten wunne sîn.
dô sach ich ir liehten tugende, ir werden schîn,
schoen unde ouch vür alle wîp gehêret,
niuwen daz ein lützel was versêret
ir vil vröuden rîchez <rôtez> mündelîn.

[Love, who brings joy's increase to the world
look, she brought my lady in a dream
as my body turned to sleep
to seek in her its greatest joy.
I saw her perfect virtue, her shining look—
lovely, noblest of all women—
except her mouth was slightly damaged,
usually so full and rich <and red> with joy]

Grô'z ángest hân ich des gewunnen,
daz verblîchen süle ir mündelîn sô rôt.
des hân ich nu niuwer klage begunnen,
sît mîn herze sich ze sülcher swaere bôt,
daz ich durch mîn ouge schouwe sülche nôt
sam ein kint, daz wîsheit unversunnen
sînen schaten ersach in einem brunnen
und den minnen múoz únz an sînen tôt.

[A huge fear took me then
because the mouth that was so red had paled
and so began now newer sorts of lamentation.
My heart led itself to such dispair
because I'd seen such pain with my own eyes
like a child unlit by wisdom

who saw his image in a pool
and had to love it till he died.]

Hôher wîp von tugenden und von sinne,
die enkan der himel niender ummevân,
sô die guoten, die ich vor ungewinne
vremden muoz und immer doch an ir bestân.
owê leider, jô wânde ichs ein ende hân
ir vil wunnenclîchen werden minne.
nû bin ich vil kûme an dem beginne,
des ist hin mîn wunne und ouch mîn gerender wân.

[A woman of greater sense and virtue
heaven does not know—so good she is,
She, whose distance is forever sealed by this loss,
although I'll stand by her forever.
O God, my God. I thought I'd reached the finish line.
I thought I had her perfect, joyful love.
I've only reached a miserable point of starting.
My joy and crazy, bubbling hope are gone.][10]

The basic curve of the interior poetic narrative runs thus: the first three strophes delineate a moment of recollected recognition that is imaged forth in a dream. Framing that dream are two images involving encounters with mirrors.

The first mirror encounter, at the beginning of the poem, depicts an image from the experience of childhood—epitomizing the moment when the child first sees that the image in a mirror is *only* an image (see my discussion of Lacan's mirror-stage in the Appendix). That recognition comes only by cracking the looking glass in the very desire to possess what he misreads as the thing itself, not its image. He reaches out in desire for the image, and the move outward eventuates in the destruction, not of the thing desired, but of the vehicle of its mediation. By breaking it, he sees the mirror for what it is; this empowers him to see the image that was *in* the mirror for what *it* is. He sees that his soul, as Virgil says of Aeneas gazing on his own image carved on the door of Juno's temple, "feeds on empty pictures" [*animum pascit pictura inani*] (*Aeneid* 1.464). The recognition that this is so brings tears. This recalls the same Virgilian scene yet again (even though Aeneas's recognition does not cut as deep as that of Heinrich, or our own, for that matter): "here too there are tears, and mortal things have touched the mind" [*sunt lacrimae rerum et mentem mortalia tangunt*] (*Aeneid* 1.462).

This image of childhood recognition is presented in the conventional form of a simile: "It's gone with me like a child." The image of the child and the broken mirror is a strong one, recalling an important event we all recognize in one way or another. Normally, the strategy of such similes is to provide a similar but not identical image drawn from the realm of the known to assist us in seeing something new. But this particular image from childhood, compelling as it is, does not "attach" to anything. There is only the general assertion of appropriateness in the biography of the speaker. There is an asserted loop, but one of the ends of the loop is missing: we have an opening image in simile that poses as an explanatory image, without a specific image of the counterpart that this image is supposed to explain. It is as if we had a precise and vivid vehicle, but only the promise of a tenor.

There follows the central image of confrontation: the Lady is brought by Love to the mind of the sleeping Lover in a dream. The image of the Lady in the dream is an almost perfect template of the Lady as remembered in the dreamer's mind: he knows who she is; she is his Beloved. The only difference is that in the dream, the Lady's countenance is marred by some small damage to the mouth; it is pale, instead of the customary and expected red.

This leads to the third image of the interior narrative arc, the allusion, again in simile, to yet another encounter with a mirror, this time from the collective memory of literature rather than of personal experience: called to mind is the plight of Narcissus before his image in the pool. Here again, the image of the vehicle in the simile is far more explicitly represented than the moment in the speaker's life it is intended to illustrate, though we do know more this time. This time the Narcissus situation is to be equated to his situation as he encountered his Lady in the dream. For whatever reasons of interior recognition or increased understanding about the nature of things, the speaker now knows that he has radically misconstrued his situation.

The poem closes with a fourth strophe in which (*a*) the qualities of the Lady are praised, implying that concerning *her* nothing has changed as a result of what the poet has seen and/or understood, and (*b*) all has changed utterly for *him* as a result of what he saw in his dream, though we are tantalized by his refusal to provide us with any clearer sense of what it was he saw. He had thought he was close to his courtly goal of union, one presumes, with his Beloved. But now, as a result of what he learned from the dream (whatever it is), he realizes he is only at the beginning of the quest and that the quest is of such a nature that he must despair of any hope of achieving it in any previously understood sense of what it might have meant.

In the center of the poem, as recollected event, stands the crucial yet bewildering dream. Although quite fashionable in medieval France and England, the dream is rare in medieval German lyric. This example constitutes one of only three dreams in the entire corpus represented by *Des Minnesangs Frühling* and the extant work of Walther von der Vogelweide. Thus Heinrich's use of the dream image is rare, but not unique. At the center of the dream is displayed the image of his Lady with a damaged mouth. This *is* unique. Nowhere in the canon of medieval lyric have I been able to find such a negative physical image of the desired Lady. And what this striking, disturbing image means in this poem is a crux that has generated a minor flurry of commentary.[11] Perhaps the most generally accepted readings are variations on the idea that the poet was brought an image of his beloved in which he foresees her inevitable death; that the recognition of that death shatters the stabilizing and controlling images that we all erect to maintain the illusion of our immortality, and that the speaker has made a fresh realization about the hard facts of reality as they reflect the certain biological future of his Lady.

Such a reading is surely not in basic disharmony with the interior disquiet revealed in the speaker. But what about the mirrors? A dark sense of impending danger is surely present, but is it in the Lady? Or is it in the dream? Or does it arise within the Lover as he sees the Lady in the dream? Let us turn briefly to Heinrich's Provençal model. My suggestion is that a careful look at a Provençal poem that Heinrich was probably pointing at is essential for an understanding of what he is doing here. Essential, but not sufficient. For sufficiency we will require the corresponding mirror of Ovid's Latin text. The Provençal model reads:

> Aissi m'ave cum al enfan petit
> que dins l'espelh esgarda son vizatge
> ei tast'ades e tan l'a assalhit,
> tro que l'espelhs so franh per son folatge;

adoncas pren a plorar son damnatge:
tot enaissi m'avia enriquit
us bels semblans, qu'er an de mi partit
li lauzengier per lor fals vilanatge.

[It's gone with me as with a little child
that watched his visage in a looking glass
and reached for it and played with it
until he broke it in his foolishness;
then he began to weep at what he'd done.
Just so I too had been delighted
by a lovely image, that's been taken from me
by the false villany of envious bastards.]

E per so ai conques gran consirier
e per so tem perdre sa drudaria
et aissom fai chantar per dezirier:
car la bela tan m'a vencut em lia
que per mos olhs tem que perda la vida
com Narcisi que dedins lo potz cler
vi sa ombra el amet tot entier
e per fol' amor mori d'aital guia.

[And that's why I'm extremely worried,
and that's why I'm afraid I'll lose her love,
and all that leads me to sing, out of desire,
for she has so defeated me there, where
my eyes see her, that I could lose my life
like Narcissus, who saw his shadow in the clear pool
and loved it so entirely he died
for foolish loving in this way.]

Be fora de son perdo cobeitos,
car l'an de mi fals lauzengiers partida.
dues lor do mal, car ses los enojos
agra gran gaug de leis e gran jauzida
quem fetz baizar vostras belas fiassos:
aissom ten en esperansa jojos
que nostr' amors sia per be fenida.

A la bela t'en iras, ma chansos,
e digas li que sai sui de joy blos,
si nom reve qualsque bona jauzida.

[I surely would do anything to get her pardon,
but those bitchy gossips have parted us.
God send them evil, for without those liars,
I would have had great joy from her, great pleasure.
Remember, Beauteous One, our sweet hours together
When you allowed me to come close and kiss.
And I will remain happy in high hopes
we'll have our happy ending after all.

Go to the Lovely One, my Song,
and say to her that all my joy is gone
if something good doesn't come my way.][12]

With one crucial exception, this poem has been accepted as a model for Heinrich von Morungen since the middle of the nineteenth century.[13] I have yet to see, however, a reasonably systematic comparison made in an effort to see what Heinrich was doing in his poem by tracking what he sustained and what he changed.

In the Provençal poem we also have the device of framing the Lady by a set of mirrors—the same mirrors: one from childhood observation, the other from literary history. Four major differences are at once apparent: the first three have to do, not so much with the frame, but with the Lady. In the Provençal poem she is recollected as she is, not as an image, and by a Lover who is awake, and not in dream. The third difference is that she is unmediated, simply there, whereas in Heinrich's poem she is "brought by Love." And although the Lady here is also separated from the Lover, it is by conventional backbiting at court, and not by some terrible ontological conundrum arising out of the dream in which she appears. Finally, in the comparison of the separation of the Lady to the breaking of the childhood mirror, the only aspect of this powerful image from childhood activated in the Provençal model is the attraction of the image.

The disappearance of this image when the mirror is broken and the implied interior recognition, so central to any ontological or epistemological concerns, are simply ignored. The same holds true for the second image, that of Narcissus: there is no interest in Narcissus's discovery of the true nature of the image in the pool or of his horror at that discovery. The Provençal poet merely castigates Narcissus for *fol amors*, loving foolishly. As for the deeper implication of catastrophic recognition that bothered Ovid, the Provençal poet simply shows no interest, or even awareness. He has taken an image that embodies what is for us perhaps the central epistemological crux of the human situation and done nothing but trivialize it in the interests of bitching at his rivals and, perhaps, impressing his Lady with a bit of literary name-dropping. We learn, however, that medieval neglect of the cognitive aspect of the narrative is in itself not particularly surprising. In fact, a pair of recent studies show that such neglect is more the rule than the exception. [14] It is more than merely conceivable that Heinrich is recalling the conventional use of the image to our minds in order to call it into question.

By quoting the Provençal poet with such accuracy and at such length at the beginning and at the conclusion of the third strophe, Heinrich von Morungen holds up his model to us as a steady mirror. But by substituting the dream of the damaged mouth for the Provençal emphasis on the political separation of the Lady, and by suggesting in the first and fourth strophes that some deep and terrifying catastrophe has occurred to the child upon breaking the mirror and to himself upon looking at the dream image, he recuperates for us the truly Ovidian Narcissus. Just as we can see in the Latin mirror of Ovid's text, as well as in the mirror of Heinrich's poem, just how callow the Provençal poem is, we see, by Ovid's absence in the Provençal poem and his implied presence in Heinrich's poem, just how penetrating Ovid is. And in the hiatus between Ovid and the Provençal model, which is Heinrich's poem as read, we see both how necessary and how self-defeating poetry is in the face of the need for reciprocal mediations between the self and the Other. We see afresh how close we always are to the abyss of solipsism. We see how dependent we are on received conventions of intelligibility—and how inevitably betrayed we are and must be by them.

Ovid goes to great, even baroque lengths in his descant on the philosophic implications of Narcissus's cloud of unknowing. I quote here a telling passage from the Golding translation (used by Shakespeare); it is still the finest in English:

> He knowes not what it was he sawe. And yet the foolishe elfe
> Doth burne in ardent love thereof. The verie selfe same thing
> That doth bewitch and blinde his eyes, encreaseth all his sting,
> Thou fondling, thou, why doest thou raught the fickle image so?
> The thing thou seekest is not there. And if aside thou go,

The thing thou lovest straight is gone. It is none other matter
That thou dost see, than of thy selfe the shadow in the water.
The thing is nothing of it self: with thee it doth abide,
With thee it would departe if thou withdrew thy selfe aside.
No care of meate could draw him thense, nor yet desire of rest.
But lying flat against the ground, and leaning on his breast,
With greedie eyes he gazeth still upon the falced face,
And through his sight is wrought his bane. [15]

Using the crucial discrepancy between the Ovidian and the Provençal images of the love-struck boy, we can perhaps become better readers of Heinrich von Morungen's troubling images, particularly that of the damaged mouth, the "verseret mündeline." As already suggested, what is present in Ovid and absent in the Provençal model is the catastrophic event of self-recognition as part of fatal knowing triggered in the boy as he perceives the image for what it really is:

Iste ego sum, sensi, nec me mea fallit imago.
[It's me! I feel it. It's nothing but my image!]

If we look at Heinrich's speaker looking, in memory, at dream's image, we see him see, as the child sees, and as Narcissus finally saw, that at the virtual center of things the image reflects not the truly Other, but merely, *per speculum,* a dark image of the Other, the Other *in aenigmate.*

As the Lover sees the image brought by Love, he matches it with his own image of the Lady stored in memory. The images mirror each other perfectly but for one detail, a detail that shows these looking glasses to be cracked, which in turn makes them truly revelatory: the mouth in Love's image is white; in his memory's image it is red. The Lover sees, by means of this discrepancy, where he really is: in Augustine's *regione dissimilitudinis,* the land of unlikeness.

The realization that comes with seeing the discrepancy between the two images is that both of the images are only images, and neither of the images is the "always already" desired Lady. The *pictura* on which he has fed his soul is *inanis,* empty. He has before him a version of the Lady, the Other as desired by the self, but not as she in her otherness really is, or could be. The Lady exists all right; there is no finer woman on earth, as the fourth strophe so eloquently affirms. It is just that she is forever separated from the Lover by the very mirror in and through which she is mediated. All he really knows or can ever have of her is an image of his own devising, drawn from his own desiring. As *Minne,* or Love, shows him this terrible truth in dream, his own memory and creative intelligence provide framing similes of mirrors for understanding that crucial message: the one from the domain of experience, a recollected image of the broken mirror of childhood; the other from the domain of authority, the Narcissus of literary history.

There is no possibility of a Provençal "happy ending" for the speaker in Heinrich von Morungen's poem—only the terrible recognition that the object of desire is simultaneously made present to our minds by our image of it and doomed to eternal separation from us by the irrevocable *différance* that obtains between the original and its image. This is the onto/epistemological conundrum that obsesses not just the lover, but also the poet, that mediator of love through the images of his art. There is only the numbing recognition of both the pressing need and the ultimate futility of such mediation by word and image, and a stoic resignation is born to go on with it in the face of that knowledge. As Virgil says of both the Daedalian labyrinth and the Orphic reascent from Hell: "*hic labor est*": this is the project.

* * * * *

In the broader curves of literary history, we must wait another century for the saving intimations of Dante. In the *Vita Nuova,* he struggles past the same recognition Heinrich experienced as he viewed his own ghastly dream: the lamentation of the frightful women mourning, in sure anticipation, the death of Beatrice. It is only in that internal drama of the mind's quest for an understanding of its own powers and limitations, the *Purgatorio,* that Dante the Poet provides to that recollected image of his own youth, Dante the Pilgrim, more saving dreams: of the eagle, the Siren, and the Lady in the meadow with flowers. It is by learning to read correctly the mirrors of such dreams that he develops power sufficient to see Beatrice correctly, to see reflected in her eyes the Griffin in its true duality, as a moving figure of the hypostasy of the redeeming Christ, and to hear in joy from his Lady that stunning, yet ultimately saving truth: "not in my eyes alone is Paradise."

CHAPTER 6

Toads in the Garden: Chrétien de Troyes, Anagnorisis, and Epithalamion

Each must the other take as sign, short sign
To stop the whirlwind, balk the elements.

The great captain loved the ever-hill Catawba
And therefore married Bawda, whom he found there,
And Bawda loved the captain as she loved the sun.

They married well because the marriage-place
Was what they loved. It was neither heaven nor hell.
They were love's characters come face to face.
—Wallace Stevens, *Notes toward a Supreme Fiction*

This chapter continues exploration of lyric and romance, two generic impulses by which and in which medieval culture mirrored itself. If lyric is more centered on registering the range of individual experience, romance speaks to the needs, fears, and joys of the collective. These genres are all the more interesting because they are interdependent: even sharing, on occasion, overlapping boundaries. Chrétien de Troyes, writing in the great literary courts of twelfth-century France, is exquisitely aware of the ambivalent delight his contemporaries took in the lyric; his romances reflect a never-ending, ever-elaborating dialogue between the lyric demands of the individual sensibility in quest of self-fulfillment, and the countermoves that society must make, in the interests of collective survival, against those imperious demands made upon it by the essentially self-absorbed, antisocial idealities of *fin amors*.

Chrétien de Troyes moves, in his four completed romances, from the emblematic marriage of Erec and Enide to the strained but reconstituted marriage of Yvain and Laudine.[1] In the course that he charts between the early *Erec et Enide* and the later *Yvain* he veers around, and thereby draws a certain attention to, the hopelessly compromised marriages of Alis and Arthur by passing through the *trobar clus* of the adulterous liaisons at the narrative center of the *Cligés* and the *Lancelot*.[2]

Chrétien's litany of tested, broken, and mended marriages reflects a basic move from a hermetic to an open poetic, from a fairly univocal mode of celebration to increasingly equivocal modes of social and literary criticism. In this chapter, I would like to approach that shift in poetics from three points of view, in the hope of illumination at a point of convergence in a brief coda dealing with the *Roman de la Rose*. The first tracks the placement of a series of disruptively "nonce" images scattered with stunning, reductive effect, and with increasing frequency, across the oeuvre. The second explores a set of troubling vignettes, occurring in each romance, of pseudo-death and pseudo-resurrection. These vignettes engender resonance with Christological narrative, a fact that has proved embarrassing for most critics; I suggest it is more useful to deal with this imagery as parodistic rather than imitative of Christology. The parody I speak of is not corrosive; rather it is an efficient vehicle developed by Chrétien for carrying self-deprecating Christian irony. The third view considers key moments in the four romances in which the Lover beholds his Beloved, allowing us to compare a paradigmatic event in the romance with its counterimage in the lyric. Finally, in a recapitulative codicil, we shall look briefly at Amant, the Lover, gazing in wonder at the crystals that he sees in the Fountain of Narcissus in Guillaume de Lorris's *Roman de la Rose,* and Pygmalion gazing in love at the ivory doll of his own making near the close of Jean de Meun's continuation of the *Rose*. We shall see in these images culminative figures of the speculative impulses shared by the romance of Chrétien de Troyes and the lyric of Heinrich von Morungen.

Toads in the Garden

A shift in Chrétien's poetics from a program essentially closed and celebratory to one that is more open and critical can be mapped by tracing the strategic placement of certain reductive strategies, minor stumbling blocks in the otherwise reasonably smooth and accessible curve of romance narrative. These reductive strategies, which shall be discussed in greater detail below, include such troubling images as the shearing off of a bit of a grateful lion's tail, a brutally severed leg falling into an Edenic garden, and a magic ring whose sole power is to denote and thereby dispel the presence of magic. Such images do not quite "compute" with the romance world in which we find them; rather they remind us of another world that exists beyond romance: our own world, the very world from which we seek temporary escape, the same world that impelled romance and to which, in the end, it must return and submit.

These reductive strategies surprise our generic "horizons of expectation." By doing so, they open up readerly perspective; they increase readerly capacity for perceiving things from multiple points of view. This opening of multiple points of view cracks the verisimilitude of the romance as a looking glass of courtly ideality and calls into question the very relation that obtains between the image and the original it is supposed to be an image of. This in turn reflects increasing tensions developing elsewhere in the twelfth century between a sense of truth as "unicity" and a darker, companion sense that truth is a plurality of realities.

We also begin to see a pattern to these disturbing and reductive stumbling blocks; this in turn leads us to think of them as part of a strategy of dislocation.[3] They kick us out of the euphoric forwarding consolations of the literal continuum as "virtual," but without providing a sufficient alternative structure for successful "interpretation." We are then left darkling in the hermeneutic gap, somewhere between vehicle and tenor, in a readerly space very much like Augustine's *regione dissimilitudinis*. The anatomy and program of the romance enterprise is freshly revealed by such defamiliarizing of the "olde daunce." And such demystification of the romancier's bag of literary tricks brings a restorative power that promises much by way of spiritual antidote to the psychic dislocations de/in/forming much medieval erotic lyric of the twelfth and thirteenth centuries. Chrétien disturbs the reader's ease, but he anticipates not the narcissistic lyric dead ends of Guillaume de Poitou, Heinrich von Morungen, and Guido Cavalcante, but rather the prudential, epic efforts of Wolfram von Eschenbach's *Parzival*, or Chaucer's Franklyn, Clerk, and Wife of Bath.

Marianne Moore, in the little she let stand of her famous poem entitled "Poetry," pleads for her version of the desired product:

> . . . when dragged into prominence by half poets, the
> result is
> not poetry
> nor til the poets among us can be
> "literalists of
> the imagination"—above
> insolence and triviality and can present
> for inspection, "imaginary gardens with real toads in them,"
> shall we have
> it.[4]

Chrétien is not above insolence and triviality. Yet he does become, in his later works, a "literalist of the imagination." All his works can be viewed as imaginary gardens. But as we read his completed works in succession, the *Erec et Enide*, the *Cligés*, and those nearly simultaneously composed twins, the *Lancelot* and the *Yvain*, we note a startling increase in the number of real toads we find there.

In the *Erec*, Chrétien develops his gardens more or less within the tradition, reinforcing and satisfying cultural expectations in a straightforward and systematic way. Starting with the obligatory dwarf who turns on the narrative machine and ending with the satisfying C-major chords of affirmation provided by the extended allegorical coronation of the hero, the principles of decorum governing medieval romance are never threatened. As a result, the world of the *Erec* appears coherent, romantic if you will, and almost totally impregnable. And the answers to the ethical problems involving a man's duty to his love and to his society seem pleasantly and predictably unambiguous.

As we pass through the *Cligés* and the *Lancelot* to the *Yvain*, we find that Chrétien undercuts the symmetrical designs of his gardens with increasing frequency and systematic rigor. As a result, the world of these later romances seems far less coherent. It is an increasingly unstable world whose fictive credibility is in constant danger of being shattered altogether by the real world outside whose fragmented nature is mirrored by the presence of these toadlike, dislocating images. As a result of this dislocation, viewpoints are multiplied, and the answers to the ethical problems arising from the hegemonistic claims of private passion in contention with the calls of public duty become very ambiguous indeed, perhaps more closely attuned to the way things are.

The *Erec* is constructed in the form of a triptych.[5] The opening section of the romance is a world of spring; Arthur seeks to provide a fitting end to the Easter celebration by hunting for the White Stag. Whoever kills the stag will be allowed to kiss the most beautiful lady in court. Gawain points out that diplomatic problems will arise when deciding just who that lady is, but Arthur shrugs this off, and early next morning nearly everyone joins the hunt. The queen, however, follows at a distance and Erec accompanies her. They encounter an ugly knight, a lovely lady, and an ill-mannered dwarf. Insult leads to injury, and Erec is off in chase to regain the honor of the queen. The chase turns into a full-fledged adventure. He meets a poor but honest vavasor who has a beautiful and intelligent daughter. It happens that on the next day there is to be a celebratory joust for a Sparrow Hawk, apparently an annual affair. It also happens that the favorable odds are on the very same knight whose dwarf insulted the queen. Erec gets a number of birds with one stone by defeating the knight: the honor of the queen, the Sparrow Hawk itself, and the vavasor's daughter Enide.

In the meantime, we learn that Arthur himself killed the White Stag, and the problem foreseen by Gawain has indeed arisen. The solution is provided by the arrival of Erec and Enide: Enide wins the royal kiss, of which much is made. The Bestowal of the Royal Kiss is so amplified, in fact, that it assumes ritual proportions. Enide is presented and accepted by the court as a type of courtly femininity, a type that she struggles against through the rest of the romance.

This pretty prologue is a romance in little. The double plot is cleverly sewn together: the exploit of the Sparrow Hawk provides structural balance to the adventure of the White Stag as well as a solution to the problem it raises. The prelude is, in fact, a paradigm of the Arthurian quest itself, providing us with all the norms of the genre, and throughout the *Erec* these norms are never betrayed.

The major narrative begins with the marriage of Erec and Enide. They are blissfully happy: this curiously provides the trigger for the narrative. The honeymoon lasts for months, apparently, most of it (except for meals and sundries) spent in bed. Erec has forgotten his duty to chivalry, a clear analogue in this romance for society. His companions blame Enide; she overhears some kitchen-talk, and thinking her husband asleep, rebukes herself aloud. But Erec is not asleep.

He overhears what she says to herself and, angry, forces the story out of her and makes a peremptory decision to return to the life of *avanture*, taking Enide with him. He thinks he can undo his own recreancy by teaching *her* a lesson. She must ride ahead and not speak unless spoken to. At first this smacks of the mindless testing of Griselda, but the contours of the narrative give the test and its meaning a radically different shape. On their way they run into danger after danger, and Enide proves her devotion (and her intelligence) by *dis*obeying his commands: she regularly breaks the rule of silence, and her male-forbidden, female discourse saves their lives. A joke looms; action and talk turn out to be mirrors of each other. And the whole series of adventures—certainly the reason lying behind them—seems to end when, after a particularly devastating trial in which her silence is mirrored in his apparent death, Erec makes peace with Enide and they ride off into the moonlight. Their joint adventures have formed an apt model of a husband and wife forging a meaningful life together; their ride into the evening would appear to be an obvious close. But it is not the close. The *sens* of the *matière* must be amplified. The marriage of private passion and public virtue discovered by Erec and Enide must be tested. Thus the third panel of the triptych: the *Joie de la Court*.

The final panel opens with Erec, Enide, and a train of friends making their way back to the court of Arthur. As evening falls, they come to Brandigan, an island fortress. Erec is informed that within this town there is a perilous and difficult adventure. His informant tells him that it is called the *Joie de la Court*, and that though the name is fair to say, its execution is hard. Erec determines to essay the adventure. That night the king also warns him away from the Joy. All the warning, along with the preparatory anxieties of the court, makes the next day's procession through town to the garden where the adventure is to be staged reminiscent of a *via dolorosa*.

The garden is supersaturated with significance. There are no walls except of air, but the air is as protective as iron of what is inside. There is abundant fruit in all seasons, but it can only be eaten in the garden. This fine and private place, however, is ringed with stakes capped with rotting skulls. Not Eden, then, but its antitype, a trap with strange fruits and severed heads. The affair is extremely public. The entire court enters the garden, and Enide, after some touching words of assurance from Erec, takes her place among the spectators, who appear to be in a state of centripetal gaze.[6] The adventure proceeds as if it were some outdoor mystery play. A fair maiden is draped upon a silver couch. One of the stakes is headless and supports instead a golden horn. As Erec looks at the maiden, a knight rides up and challenges him. The fight is long and arduous; Erec wins the final fall.

We feel, correctly, that we are in the midst of an arcanum and are grateful when Erec demands some explanations. The knight's name is Mabonagrain, and he supplies us the necessary background:

> That girl sitting there loved me from childhood, and I loved her. This pleased each of us, and our love grew until she asked me for a favor—but she didn't say what it was. Who can refuse anything to the beloved? . . . I promised her, without knowing what. The time came to be made a knight: King Evrain, I'm his nephew, dubbed me before many a noble man in this very garden. My mistress, sitting there, recalled to me my pledge, and said that unknowingly I had promised never to leave until a knight came and conquered me by force of arms. . . . By this means she hoped to hold me prisoner all my life.
>
> (*Erec et Enide*, 6002–8, 6018–22, 6046–47)

This recital of Mabonagrain's arrangement with his lady is not gratuitous, but in fact is a speculum in which we see the inverse image of Erec and Enide's tested marriage. Chrétien insists on our seeing them so, not only by the obviously contrasting congruencies in the structural configurations of their respective stories, but also by revealing to us that Mabonagrain was trained at the court of Erec's father and that the damsel in the garden is Enide's cousin.

The horn is sounded, and a song is sung. The defeat of Mabonagrain in the garden by Erec is the defeat of lyric by romance. The secret, hothouse code of adulterous love is defeated by the countercode by which romance provides a model for society's successful mediation between the demands of private passion and public responsibility. The sounding of the horn signals release from the garden; it is this that brings joy to the court. Mabonagrain and his damsel attempted to solve the dilemma of private passion in a public context by simply ignoring the public context. Chrétien indicates that this solution is self-defeating, both to society and the individuals involved, by painting for us, in such amplified detail, the kind of garden such people are forced to live in. This garden is no imitation, but a parody of Eden, and expulsion from it no punishment, but a new and needed freedom.[7]

139

Erec and Enide have discovered that the secret of reconciliation lies in the public rituals of marriage—but with a new understanding of the issues. Erec has learned the wisdom of granting Enide a role that reconciles opposing claims: that of wife and mistress, of *fame* and *amie*. This is allegorically figured by her horse and its trappings: the head is black on one side, white on the other, with a stripe of green down the middle; the saddle has figured on it images of both Dido and Lavinia. It is only this new knowledge of reconciliation of the claims of private passion and public virtue that is powerful enough to break the Gordian knot of Mabonagrain's garden, the self-entrapping syndrome of *fin amors*. Chrétien has displaced one myth with another, that of courtly love with that of a loving court. He reinforces our sense of this by a parallel and reaffirming displacement of the old model of marriage with a new one. In the final images of the poem, Arthur and Guinever graciously surrender their thrones for the rituals of coronation. In this courtly game of musical chairs, we see the saving marriage of Erec and Enide as an inverse mirror image, a briefly imagined displacement of that ruined marriage of Arthur and Guinever, which destroyed Camelot as inevitably as the broken marriage of Helen and Menelaos destroyed Troy.

This *sens* of the *conjointure* is amplified by the magnificent coronation of Erec, which concludes the romance.[8] The royal investiture of Erec is elevated to secular apotheosis by means of allegorical figures. He is robed in watered silk, the description of which can be found in no less an authority than Macrobius. Four fays had embroidered the robe: one with the figure of geometry, which measures space; the second with arithmetic, which measures time; the third with music, which reconciles the discords between space and time; and the fourth with astronomy, which gives the measures of cause. Arthur has a scepter brought, clearer than glass, all of one emerald, as large as a man's fist. There is no manner of fish, beast, man, or bird not worked and chiselled on this emerald ark with its proper figure. Enide is placed on Guinever's throne, Erec on that of Arthur. After gazing upon the scepter briefly, Arthur puts it into Erec's right hand, and Erec is king. The significance is clear. The green scepter in the right hand is a figure of the green world—of things as they are. The robe is a figure of the quadrivium, the controlling discipline of the knowledge of that world. As mentioned above, the seating arrangement temporarily displaces the centering power of Arthur and Guinever with the ordering principle of marriage figured forth by Erec and Enide, while the coronation, itself a figure of general *anagnorisis,* figures forth society's welcoming recognition of Universal Man. Thus we follow Chrétien's own directive for a successful reading of this romance, a directive he placed early on in the prologue:

So Chrétien says it is right that each of us should think and study and speak well and teach well and he draws from a tale of adventure a pretty lesson [tret d'un conte d'avanture / une molt bele conjointure] by which one can know and prove that it is in no way wise to abandon one's knowledge as long as God gives him grace.

(*Erec et Enide,* 9–18)

The *Erec* is a near-perfect work of its kind. It is lapidarian, radiantly clear, and early. We have a writer who has not only invented a genre, but also explored and exhausted its possibilities on its own terms. Everything indicates that Chrétien never wrote with this degree of literary innocence again.

The next completed work we possess is the *Cligés.* In this troubling romance, we find evidence of a transition, a shift to a new strategy of narrative that only later in the *Lancelot* and the *Yvain* is systematically employed.[9] This new strategy forces on the narrative functions other than delectation and social affirmation; narrative is freed to act not only as mirror of social engagement and celebration, but also as a tool of literary as well as social criticism.

The *Cligés* is deeply ambiguous, though it purports to be as straightforward as the *Erec.* It is one of Chrétien's two major excursions into the world of adulterous love. It is at once the most original and most parasitic of the poet's works: original in the sense that as far as actual fictive content is concerned, there are no literary models; parasitic in the sense that the entire production hinges upon a continuing and parodistic resonance with the Tristan narrative—perhaps the version of Thomas of Britain; certainly a version very much like it. The narrative of the *Tristan* acts throughout the romance as a mirror in which to reflect what "nouveles" Chrétien is up to.

The first allusion to the Tristan narrative occurs in the opening lines of the poem. Chrétien gives us an intriguing and at least partially fictive catalogue of his previous works:

He who composed the Erec and Enide, and put into romance form the
commands of Ovid and the Art of Love, and wrote the Shoulder Bite, and
about Mark and Iseut the Blonde, and about the metamorphosis of the
lapwing, the nightingale and the swallow, will tell another story now about
a youth in Greece who was a member of King Arthur's line.

(Cligés, 1–10)

This little home library describes a thematically darkening arc that
takes us from the safe port of the *Erec* to the more dubious ministrations
of Ovid, to the partial deconstruction of Pelops, to a Tristan narrative
with no Tristan in the title, and closes with one of the most brutal
narratives of rape, betrayal, infanticide, and cannibalism in our culture,
that of Ovid's Tereus, Procne, and Philomela. Displayed here is growing interest in shifting and darker narrative points of view. The question is not whether Chrétien wrote a now-missing Tristan, but
whether, if he had, it would have really centered on Mark. That would
have made it an early experiment along the lines of *Rosenkranz and
Guildenstern Are Dead*, for it is precisely Mark's point of view that is
systematically suppressed in the *Tristan* tradition. Yet once called into
question, it is a point of view that the imagination can no longer
suppress, and its presence, as mere and naked possibility in the mind's
eye, seriously jeopardizes any attempt to seduce the reader into a noncritical acceptance of the narrative from the vantage point of Tristan
and Isolt.

Other allusions to the Tristan complex, formal as well as thematic,
abound. The first third of the narrative, like that of the Tristan story,
deals with the love affair of the hero's parents. Alexander and Soredamors fall in love at sea, there are puns on *la mer,* love comes in
through the eyes, their love-dangers are seared and chilled with
Ovidian fire and ice, their monologues threaded with Andrean casuistry. Finally Guinever recognizes their plight as love and forces them
to declare it; they are married in perfect propriety and live happily
until death does, in fact, them part. So much for the similarities to the
narrative of Tristan's parents, Rivalin and Blancheflor. Unlike them,
Alexander and Soredamors put up with no wounds to the groin; nor is
their child conceived during the death throes of the father, nor is he
delivered into the world by means of the death throes of the mother.
In fact, there is nothing at all *triste* about Cligés until the reasonably
natural death of his parents.

He is then left heir and ward to his uncle Alis, the emperor of Greece. Alis has promised his elder brother Alexander to remain unmarried so that Cligés can ascend his father's throne. But as time goes by, Alis, like Mark, decides marriage might be a good thing and courts Fenice, the lovely daughter of the emperor of Germany. Like Tristan, his prototype, Cligés is not resentful; he is helpful. His prowess in arms saves the day and makes the marriage possible. He has by then, of course, himself fallen in love with Fenice and she with him. They do this all by themselves; no fatal love potions seem to be necessary. The problem, as formulated by Fenice, is how to avoid the triangular tangle. Fenice is determined that it will not be solved in the manner of its literary model:

I'd rather be dismembered than have people, because of us, recall the loves of Isolt and Tristan — about whom they tell such folly, it is a shame to retell it.

> [Mialz voldroie estre desmanbree
> Que de nos deus fust remanbree
> L'amors d'Ysolt et de Tristan
> Don mainte folie dit an,
> Et honte en est a reconter . . .]

(*Cligés*, 3109–13)

Ironically enough, she is later very nearly, and quite literally, *desmanbree* by three skeptical doctors who, after one look at her, suspect just such a relationship. What is essential to remember here is that for Fenice, adultery itself is not the problem. What she wishes to avoid is *partage*, sexual sharing, and she determines to avoid it in her own way, not that of Isolt.

What Fenice manages, with the help of Thessala, the obligatory nurse-confidente-Brangwin figure, is to produce not a substitute for the marriage bed on the wedding night but an *anti*love philter, one that the king drinks, and which gives him the illusion he is making love to his bride when in fact all he is clasping is unshaped air. In addition, one must remember that at this point in the narrative the mutual love between Fenice and Cligés, although it exists, remains undeclared by either party. Fenice is simply taking precautions against *partage*, hedging her bets. It is only after some time has passed, when

Cligés has returned from a visit to Arthur's court where he has made his name, that love declarations are made and plans are laid. The presence of a pedagogical trip to Camelot at this point in the narrative reminds us that this narrative, like its model concerning Tristan, Mark, and Isolt, functions as an imagined displacement for a love that hovers but dares not speak its name: that triangulation of desire that bound Lancelot, Arthur, and Guinever together and brought down Camelot.

In the face of such a love as theirs, Cligés sensibly advises flight. But Fenice has scruples, largely literary: she again refuses to suffer the reputation of Isolt. Her plan involves another philter that she herself will drink, allowing her to feign death. After burial, she will be exhumed and removed to a hidden tower with all modern conveniences. Carefully engineered, the deception does come off, but not without a painful last-minute hitch. Just as the pseudo dead Fenice is about to be buried, three doctors arrive in town, prove skeptical, and arrange a private audience with the corpse in which they indulge in torture tests for vital signs that one can only call medieval. At the last moment Fenice is rescued by the ladies of the court and, to her extreme relief, is carted off and buried.

After secret exhumation, life goes on in the tower, an extremely intricate and impressive tower built by that architect of exotic fictions, Prester John. Its whole *raison d'être* is to succeed in looking like what it isn't. Rooms that to the naked eye appear doorless prove, in fact, to have doors. There are anterooms to anterooms. After a year in the tower, Cligés and Fenice discover that one of the disguised doors leads out into a garden. It doesn't take long for the reader to realize that this tower is an internal speculum of the romance genre itself, a prototype of Henry James's house of fiction where the walls don't quite meet the floor. After they discover the garden, they choose it as the center of their love life, making it over and over again under a post-Edenic apple/pear tree whose branches have been grafted so that they point downward rather than upward, providing the pair with a dome-like screen. The narrator is entranced by the cleverness of it all, but the reader, by now a horticultural specialist when it comes to medieval romance narrative, is chary about upside-down trees in enclosed gardens.[10]

A knight of the court, out hunting, leaps over the garden wall in chase of a bird. He finds a bird of a sort. He discovers the lovers, *post flagrante,* naked and asleep under the grafted tree. There is recognition. Cligés awakes. The knight takes flight over the garden wall, but Cligés, naked as Adam, leaps up in his little Eden, sword in hand. He does not manage to prevent the knight's escape, but he does chop off, in this inverse miniparody of the Expulsion, a leg at the thigh, and this leg, one assumes, does not evaporate into thin air, but drops back, toadlike, into the garden.

Cligés and Fenice then make good their escape, and where else but to the court of Arthur. Arthur is prepared to lend the lovers military aid, but before they set sail, news arrives of the death of Uncle Alis. He died, we are told, of a broken heart. And the messenger informs us that Alis's heart broke not in grief at the loss of Fenice but in rage because he failed to get his hands on Cligés. Fenice and Cligés return in triumph to Greece, are crowned, and live out happily married lives. And in the same tone of pretended innocence in which we hear of their connubial bliss, the narrator concludes the romance:

Since then there hasn't been an emperor who did not fear his wife would deceive him when he heard how Fenice deceived Alis, first with the philtre and then with that other betrayal. Because of this every empress, no matter how upper-crust or noble she may be, is guarded in Constantinople as in a prison.

(*Cligés*, 6645–55)

Fenice is convinced she has found a morally acceptable mode of avoiding contamination with her literary model, but the narrator informs us that her later reputation was every bit as bad as Isolt's. Things are out of phase. What to make of Fenice's advance work, the parody of a martyr's death, the tower, the grafted tree and the severed leg in the garden—and the final casual pretence that the entire romance is merely an etiological fable supplying us with sufficient reason for the institution of harems?

The key, as suggested at the beginning, lies in point of view. The *Cligés* is not only a parody of the *Tristan*, it is also an anti-*Erec:* it is as if we viewed the *Erec* from inside out, as an entire romance fielded from Mabonagrain's point of view. Erec is the minister of Arthur's court and represents its needs as he intrudes into the garden of Mabonagrain, the *Joie de la Court.* Cligés is the minister of the lyric code of adulterous love, and the minister of the court in his romance is the intruder in the garden who loses his leg. The toads strewn about the landscape of the *Cligés*, and only partially listed in the paragraph above, act as mirrors of our own world, including the lubricating mechanisms of our narrative and decorative arts (the tower and the grafted tree) behind and in which we try to hide ourselves. The catalog of books at the beginning includes the closed text of Chrétien's own early *Erec* as well as the more open texts of Ovid, so that we may begin the romance with a plurality of viewing options. To see the same event from multiple points of view is to gain the critical purchase that comes with increased distance.[11] This opening catalogue of books points to the inner mechanisms of the *Cligés*, signifying at once the range as well as the limitations of the genre. When Chrétien returns to the theme of married love in the *Yvain*, this expansion of the literary playing field won in the *Cligés* is developed even further.

The *Lancelot* is a brilliant, hilarious adventure in the purely outrageous. From beginning to end Chrétien plays games of avoidance and cheats on the truth. The romance opens with a clear assignment of responsibility for both the *sens* and the *matière* of the romance to his patroness, Marie de Champagne. The romance ends with the discovery that Chrétien has abandoned it when Lancelot was in the tower; we are informed in the last few lines that a clerk by the name of Godefroi de Leigni has taken over the narrative and brought it to conclusion. Credulity is strained at the beginning by Arthur's idiocy in entrusting the queen to Sir Kay and at the end by Arthur's own credulity as he watches Meleagant ritually beheaded by the hero who has cuckolded him.

In between, the hero mounts a dwarf-drawn penal cart, lifts the stone cover, twice his weight, of his own sarcophagus, gets nearly sewn to the sheets of a magic bed by a flaming lance darting down from a high canopy, and crawls across a bridge consisting solely of the upturned edge of a giant sword. News ricochets back and forth, informing one set of characters that Lancelot is dead (he is not) and another that the queen is dead (she is not), and a letter arrives informing everyone that Lancelot is free and in Camelot (he is not). In this romance, one can scarcely see the garden for the toads. The only hope of a corrective is a magic ring worn by Lancelot. The virtue of this magic ring is to discover and dispel the presence of magic: when one gazes on it, all that is present as a result of magic disappears; only the "really real" remains behind. Lancelot looks upon his mirror-ring twice: the first time things are just as bad as we feared; all the threats are real. The second time, we discover an elaborate inventory of all that is not there. After Lancelot has crawled on hands and knees over the sword bridge, two threatening leopards that were there at the beginning of the passage have disappeared. Lancelot is worried about them, thinking they may still be there although made magically invisible. However, after gazing into his magic mirror-ring, he sees that they continue not to be there, proving that they weren't really there at the beginning either, but only seemed to be there. There is absolutely no interest in identifying the conjurer, or in why leopards appeared to be there in the first place: the leopards have disappeared; after checking, they remain gone, one is relieved, even grateful, and that is that.

Dislocation in the *Lancelot* has become an organizing principle, equivocation a rule of composition. There are no tests of validity; all is ambiguously self-deconstructing even as the words continue to appear on the page. Even the ending, in which a voice insists it is a voice other than the author's, cannot be tested: we have no real way of knowing whether the closing voice identifying itself as Godefroi de Leigni is really someone other than the poet or merely a useful fictive screen for Chrétien himself. Chrétien, in the *Lancelot*, seems to have obliterated any stable boundaries to our horizon of expectation; he has expanded that horizon to a game of "anything goes," and the pleasure of the text is to test the capability of romance for dreaming up ever-escalating examples of outrage. The hilarity is qualified only by a sense of vertigo as we see the romance approach the borders, occasionally shared with the lyric, of dream and hallucination.

In the *Yvain*, things are back under control; we have returned, in a sense, to the *Erec*. But it is an inverted mirror: an *Erec* the other way round. There is an anti-*Erec* strategy driving both the *Cligés* and the *Yvain*, but in the case of the *Yvain*, it is not only different; it is more effective. By subtle means of omission, commission, and change, Chrétien drains the magic and romanticism out of much of the traditional building material of his genre and thereby, indirectly, explores the ambiguous relationships that obtain between the real world and the world of fiction. By introducing these ambiguities, Chrétien by no means destroys the tradition in which he is working; he develops it by using it critically. He broadens the base of operations and admits the possibility of a broader moral vision, possible because the reader can now systematically view the action and implication of that action from an aesthetic and moral distance, from a more inclusive and comic perspective than is possible when viewing imaginary gardens unblessed by real toads.

The *Yvain* opens with a scene at Arthur's court in Carduel. A young knight named Calogrenant rehearses an adventure that happened to him seven years previously and which brought him shame. He had set out, found the path to the Right, and was received by a hospitable vavasor and a lovely daughter. After a chaste night's sleep, he rose early to seek adventure and encountered a frightful herd of oxen, which was kept in line by a frightful Vilain. Calogrenant asks the Vilain if he knows the whereabouts of any adventure and is told about a particular fountain that is guaranteed to do the trick. Calogrenant proceeds to the fountain and performs a ritual of pouring water over a stone; a storm rages and clears, birds sing, a knight rides out and challenges him, and Calogrenant is knocked off his horse to return the way he came.

Yvain, who is cousin-german to Calogrenant, has been listening and swears to recapture the young man's honor. Arthur, listening too, thinks it a good idea for everybody to see the Magic Fountain. Yvain skips out early, undercover, to get there first. He too finds the Right Way, the vavasor and daughter, the Vilain, and the fountain. He pours the obligatory water on the predetermined stone, the awaited storm takes place and abates, birds sing, and the expected knight rides out. This time it goes the other way. Yvain wounds the knight mortally, gives chase, and finds himself trapped between the two portcullises of the knight's castle. He is saved by Lunete, a maid and confidant to Laudine, the local queen. Lunete gives him a ring of invisible-making power, and Yvain is thus able to look on at the funeral rites of his late antagonist as well as view the public grief of the widow, Laudine. He falls in love with her at once, on sight. Lunete then acts as a go-between, and as a result of some quick thinking and quicker talking on her part, we find that Laudine has not only forgiven Yvain for killing her husband, but has fallen in love with him (sight unseen) and marries him, all within three days of her husband's death. Arthur and the court arrive to see the fountain, and now Yvain is the knight who rides out. Yvain unseats the unpleasant Sir Kay, and all return to Laudine's castle for marriage and celebration.

A week later, Gawain upbraids Yvain for chivalric degeneration in marriage (note that in the *Erec* this takes some number of months). Gawain urges Yvain to return to Arthur's court in order to repair his reputation; Laudine assents, but gives him a deadline of a year for return. The year goes by. A messenger from Laudine arrives and denounces Yvain as a traitor. He is so devastated that he goes mad and runs stark naked into the wildwood. He is cured by a magic salve supplied by a passing noble lady whose city he later defends. He rescues a lion from a serpent, and the beast then acts as his companion. At this point Yvain takes on the title "Knight of the Lion" and performs one rescue service after another. There are no fewer than four full-fledged adventures of rescue, each joined by a series of interlocking deadlines. The element of narrative tension is always the same: Will he be able to save Gawain's cousin from Harpin of the Mountain in time to rescue Lunete from the stake? Will he have enough time to defeat the devil's sons and free three hundred maidens before he must defend the daughter of "la Noire Espine" against her mendacious sister? He manages. And now that he has learned to keep a deadline, he and Laudine can be reconciled. Curiously, this is only possible by means of another bit of deception on the part of Lunete. Not realizing who he is, Laudine is anxious to employ the now famous Knight of the Lion to defend her castle. She tells Lunete that she will agree to his terms, namely, to do everything in her power to reconcile him to his estranged Lady. Of course the knight is none other than Yvain, and the Lady is none other than Laudine herself. So Laudine is tricked into a second marriage, or rather the same marriage for the second time, and the romance ends—without any massive allegorical affirmations of coronation.

Clearly this all runs programmatically contrary to the *Erec*. In the *Erec*, Chrétien amplifies time-honored devices; in the *Yvain*, he reduces such devices to empty paradigms of themselves. What creep into the literary vacuum in this situation are certain elements that traditionally belong outside the world of romance. When seen and judged from the point of view of the *Erec*, these elements look like gross breaches of decorum. If, however, one entertains the possibility of a new narrative strategy, tantamount to a radical shift in poetics, these outside elements assume a logical and literarily defensible place in the poem.

As in the *Erec*, the *Yvain* opens with a brief independent protonarrative. One must note that it is Calogrenant, not Chrétien, who narrates this *petite conjointure*. This is a distinction Auerbach neglected to make and which accounts for his radically divergent reading of the poem.[12]

At the time of his narration, Calogrenant would appear to be a fairly young man; at the time of his narrative, he was seven years younger. One can catch, with no trouble, the hyper-romantic idealism of the young man seeking adventure. The amusement comes when he stumbles over so many paradigms of courtly adventure without seeing them for what they are:

It's over seven years now since I, lonely as a peasant, went seeking adventures, armed to the teeth as a knight should be, and took my way to the right into a thick forest. The way was very hard, full of thorns and brambles; and the trouble, the hardships encountered on that path. . . .

(*Yvain*, 173–83)

Compare the tone of Calogrenant above with that of Chrétien after he takes over the narrative; note the tongue-in-cheek aridity of tone when Yvain finds the path:

My Lord Yvain, when armed, did not delay. Each day he quickly made his way over mountains and valleys, through forests long and wide; he passed through many a dangerous passage, many a peril, many a strait, until he came directly to the path that was so full of brambles and so dark, that he felt he was safe at last and could not lose his way.

(*Yvain*, 760–71)

More evidence of this occurs when Calogrenant narrates his encounter with the Vilain. According to him, the Vilain is an incredible creature, but in his description of the encounter he reports the Vilain's own responses accurately, and we see that Calogrenant is a victim of his own romantic perspective.

Sitting on a rock, I saw a Vilain, who resembled a Moor, indescribably huge and hideous (so ugly, no description could do him justice)—with a great club in his hand. I approached and saw that his head was bigger than that of a horse or other beast, his hair was in tufts, his forehead bare and more than two spans in breadth. His enormous ears were hairy, just like an elephant. His eyebrows were heavy, his face flat; eyes like a screech owl, nose like a cat. His jaws hung open like those of a wolf; teeth like a boar, sharp and yellow; black beard, twisted moustache; chin meeting his chest; his back long, but twisted and humped. He stood stock still, on a tree trunk; didn't move an inch. He was fully seventeen feet tall. He stared at me; didn't speak a word, any more than a beast would have. I took it that he didn't have the power of thought or speech. Anyway, I pulled myself together and asked him: "Hey! What kind of thing are you?" And he answered me: "I am a man." "But what kind of man?" "Just what you see, nothing else."[13]

The Vilain appears to Calogrenant as a fantastic giant, but to himself, and to us, the Vilain is "just a man," an inhabitant of the real world. The oxen that this Vilain guards are, in the eyes of Calogrenant, the fiercest ever seen on land or sea. Calogrenant marvels how any man could control such fabulous beasts, and he asks the Vilain how it is done. In his reply the Vilain betrays the realistic attitude of a shrewd if disillusioned cattleman:

None of them dares move when they see me coming. When I get my hands on one of them I give its horns such a twist that the others shake in their boots and gather round as if to ask for mercy.

(Yvain, 342–49)

The contrast of attitude is maintained in the dialogue that follows. The Vilain asks:

"What are you looking for?" "Adventures to prove my prowess and strength. Now I ask you, beg you to give me some advice concerning the whereabouts of some adventure or marvelous thing." "You've made a mistake. I don't know about any 'adventure' nor have I ever heard tell of such. But down the road a piece there is a fountain, and if you give it its due, you'll have a time of it getting back."

(Yvain, 361–73)

There are two attitudes toward the marvelous here. The "romantic" style belongs to Calogrenant, the "realistic" style to the Vilain. Chrétien, responsible for both styles, allows the reader a perspective broader than that of either.

One thing that has bothered many readers is the haste with which Laudine marries Yvain, only three days after he killed her husband. As a queen, Laudine may well stem from some sort of Celtic fountain fay; as a woman, however, she is very closely related to the Widow of

Ephesus. Frappier, it seems to me, bends a bit far over backwards in his defense of her majesty:

It was contemporary reality and contemporary custom which made it possible for Chrétien to render plausible and even commendable the marriage of Laudine to her husband's slayer three days after her husband's death. Too much has been said about the Widow of Ephesus.[14]

He then goes on to list the practical considerations that help Laudine to change her mind. Now these practical considerations may be compelling in their own way, but Chrétien himself suggests that they are in large part simply rationalizations that allow her to do what she instinctively *wants* to do in the first place:

Thus by these very arguments she discovers Justice, Common Sense and Reason; how she has no business hating him [Yvain]; and thus she put the matter in a light that conforms to her own desire.

(*Yvain*, 1775–78)

As a matter of fact, the verisimilitude of Laudine's rather abrupt about-face is brilliantly prepared for by Yvain himself while biding his time in Lunete's hideaway. Yvain's mood swings depend upon frequent infusions from the inherited repertoire of antifeminist tradition. He consoles himself with a bit of conventional knowledge concerning the fickleness of woman: it is part of her nature to change her mind. At first Yvain despairs, with Ovidian elegance, of ever winning the wife of the man he has just killed. Then, however, he is reminded of some additional antifeminist wisdom, and despair flies out the window:

It is madness to want what I cannot have. I've just killed her husband and nonetheless believe I can make it up to her! What an idea! At the moment she hates me more than anything else on earth. And she's right. "At the moment." Now there I have spoken like a sage. Because a woman has more than a thousand minds. Please God she'll change the mind she has "at the moment." No. She'll change it without any "Please Gods." It's madness to despair. Please God she'll change it soon.

(*Yvain*, 1432–45)

Here again is the contamination of the Romantic and the Real. Laudine is a "type" figure if there ever was one, but her actions are also motivated by conventional psychology. And it is precisely this contamination, Laudine at once as Fairy Queen, Chief Executive Officer, and man's Image of Woman, that adds to the humor of the situation.

Laudine could not have acted so quickly without the aid of Lunete; and without her the structure of the romance would fall to pieces. Lunete is a "realistic" character who finds herself in a universe of romantic "types"—a situation somewhat anticipatory to that of Alice, with the exception that Lunete is at home in her particular wonderland. She is quite as eager to save her neck as to save her Lady, and in the process of doing both, her manipulations ironically lubricate the somewhat rusty mechanism of the world of romance in which she lives. She survives by mediating the very romantic mechanisms that entrap her. Ojars Kratins intimates as much:

The final question mark in Chrétien's treatment of Courtly Love is the character and role of Lunete. When the go-between is a character with as ambiguous qualifications to represent an exemplary courtly figure as Lunete, and when this character very deliberately sets about creating an artificial atmosphere of tension before she discharges it by prodding the lover to declare himself, the treatment of the theme of Courtly Love in this section of the romance comes near to being a parody. [15]

But this is not just any section of the romance. This is precisely the crucial part of the narrative in which the norms of "courtly love" are set for the entire story. One has to consider the possibility that parody was part of Chrétien's intention. Whitehead, in his analysis of Chrétien's debt to the *Roman de Thèbes,* suggests:

Yvain is such a light-hearted and paradoxical production that it will not do to take anything the characters do *au grand tragique.* There is irony in the work, but it is directed not against the characters, but against the plot, romantically refurbished, that Chrétien borrowed from *Thèbes,* The crowning irony is of course the comic reversal, involving a complete shift of viewpoint when Lunete persuades Laudine to marry again. [16]

Much of this irony arises from the differences that exist, Chrétien implies, between the real world and the world that obtains within the genre of traditional romance. At several points in the poem, the contrast between the Real and the Romantic comes to the surface. A particularly interesting example of this occurs when Chrétien, tongue deep in cheek, lays a little trap for the allegory hunter. The marriage ceremony is complete, and we hear of backstairs intrigue:

But I would like to mention briefly an acquaintance made in private between the sun and the moon. Do you know of whom I speak? He who was lord of the knights, and who was famed above all ought surely to be called the sun. I refer, of course, to my lord Gawain; for chivalry is enhanced by him just as when the morning sun sheds its rays abroad and lights all places where it shines. And I call her the moon, who cannot be otherwise because of her great good sense and courtesy. However, I call her so not only because of her good repute, but because her name is, in fact, Lunete.

(*Yvain*, 2397–416)

The joke on Lunete's name is a fine one. For Gawain, the type-hero, the *sens* of the allegory, made painfully explicit, grinds pompously along in the conventional direction: chivalry is glorified by him just as the sun illuminates wherever it shines. In the contrasting case of Lunete, the "real" figure of *grant san,* the interpretive *subscriptio* proceeds in mirror fashion: "she is the moon because that is what her name means." This kind of contrast between the real and the typical is a conventional tool of literary satire. The dimensions of the joke increase when one notes that Chrétien is also poking fun at the convention of the allegorical set-piece itself.

A number of readers view the mad scene as Yvain's *noche oscura,* and his cure by the magic salve as the beginning of moral recovery.[17] Certainly something of the sort threatens, but the handling of the detail suggests that Chrétien is treating the theme as a commonplace. It has to do with the salve. The Dame gives precise instructions to the servant girl to use the salve sparingly; it is a gift from Morgan la Fay and the most priceless possession she owns. It must only be used on the forehead in order to cure the knight's madness. But the maid gleefully rubs it all over Yvain's unconscious and stark-naked body, and Chrétien dryly notes that if she had had five times the amount she would have used it all.

If we were to take Yvain's cure in a straightforward, serious manner, Chrétien would have omitted the detail about the maid's excess. But there it is: he didn't. In poking fun at the traditional trappings of herbal magic, Chrétien is also poking fun at the traditional stories, like the *Erec,* in which herbal magic is taken seriously. The funny business has drained out the potential literary magic or *sens* of the salve, quite within the confines of the romance itself—leaving only the letter of the action, an empty paradigm, which, without the proper spirit, kills any urge to allegorize.

The motif of the Grateful Lion is handled with equal skill, and in an analogous manner. The lion is a very common figure in medieval symbolism. As it is at the top of the hierarchy of beasts, so it has been used, via theories of hermetic correspondence, as a kind of hieroglyph for the top of the political hierarchy (king), the chivalric (honor), the divine (Christ), etc., etc. One cannot talk about a lion, especially a grateful lion, without bringing these symbolic potentials to the fore. And Chrétien makes excellent capital on this. Yvain discovers a lion in mortal combat with a serpent. The reader cannot resist drawing obvious parallels: Honor versus Shame, Good versus Evil, Christ (or at least Michael) versus Satan, etc., etc. Oddly enough, Yvain himself hesitates and stumbles in his first attempt to read this rather obvious allegory, although he finally does so correctly:

And he went toward the place where he had heard the cry. When he got there, he saw, in a clearing, a lion and a serpent who had the lion by the tail, scorching his hind-parts with a burning flame. My lord Yvain did not simply gape at this spectacle, but took serious counsel as to which he should aid.

(*Yvain,* 3342–51)

Yvain of course eventually attacks the serpent and frees the lion, but not without a slight hitch:

With his sword which cleanly cuts, he attacks the evil serpent, hacking him through to the earth and slicing him in two, then continuing the blows until he reduces him to bits. But he had to cut off a piece of the lion's tail to get at the serpent's head. But he cut off only so much as was absolutely necessary and unavoidable.

(*Yvain,* 3372–83)

One cannot cut off a piece of a symbol's tail without shearing off a bit of its purity, and the idea of Yvain's honor, piety, or compassion is slyly compromised by imaging it forth as a pet lion lolling after him with a slightly truncated tail.

Finally, and again quite within the dimensions of the romance itself, the physical gestures involved in activating the Magic Fountain descend from something vaguely mythic to an antimyth. I have yet to find a reader who has satisfied himself with a metaphorical or allegorical reading of the fountain that fits comfortably at all places in the text. Part of the reason for this lies in the *manner* in which its activation is presented throughout the poem. The first occurrence is a glowingly romantic presentation of a magical mythical phenomenon. The description is long and full of marvelous detail. But one must not forget that at this point Calogrenant, not Chrétien, is telling the story. After this initial episode, the fountain gradually dwindles into a kind of complicated door-knocker: the way into Laudine's place. As the motif is repeated, detail is shed, and, in conformance with the mode of reduction I was talking about earlier, humor builds. A knight rides up and dumps water on the block of emerald, the storm follows, and contact is made. First Yvain:

Then to the spring he made his way, and found all he desired to see. Without a pause, with no hesitation, he poured the basin full of water upon the stone, when straightaway it began to blow and rain, and such a storm was raised as had been expected. And when God had appeased the storm, the birds came to perch upon the pine and sang their joyous songs up above the perilous fountain. But before the jubilee had ceased, out came a knight, blazing with wrath like a burning log. . . .

(*Yvain*, 800–813)

Then Arthur:

And the king, in order to see the rain, poured a whole basin full of water on the stone beneath the pine, and at once it began to storm. It wasn't long before my lord Yvain, without delay, entered the forest fully armed . . .

(*Yvain*, 2220–26)

And finally, at the end of the romance, Yvain and the lion; the storm motif is later amplified, but note what has happened to the activating gesture:

They travelled until they caught sight of the fountain, and then they turned on the rain.

(*Yvain*, 6523–24)

156

One may argue that Chrétien could not give a lengthy description each time the fountain is approached. This may be true. But like it or not, this device of reduction, this repetition of formulae with descending intensity, is part of the stock in trade of the literary satirist. No matter what particular tenor the fountain may be carrying on an allegorical level, no critical interpretation can afford to overlook the increasingly cavalier attitude with which the narrator presents the motif.

The mirroring power of these dislocating toads in the imaginary garden of the *Yvain* has a telling effect on the modern critic. If nothing else it cuts short any attempt to construct massive, consequential, allegorical readings; even attempts to construct local figurations are fleeting and incomplete. We are facing an early form of generic self-parody; we have here the essence of an antiromance, in which the final consolations of closure are both precluded and "always already" there.

Death and Resurrection

In all four romances, there are central moments in which the hero and heroine participate in ordeals that are clear analogues of death and resurrection. Yet in each romance, the configuration of event and related signifying power seem to differ. My contention is that these ordeals do make a kind of collective sense if one reads them in the context of the shift in poetics tracked in the previous section of this chapter. Close to these liminal moments when heros reach simultaneously into the domains of life and death hover related liminalities bridging the domains of male and female, of speech and silence.

In the *Erec,* the hero's apparent death informs the scene in which Enide is forcibly married to the count of Limors (whose name reverberates as a quasi pun on death). Enide has been instructed by Erec, over and over, to maintain silence; over and over she has disobeyed this command and broken silence by speaking in order to warn him of one impending danger after another. After a particularly difficult encounter, Erec falls from his horse into a deathlike swoon from his wounds; the appearance of death convinces Enide that he is indeed dead, and her response is to link Erec's death with her own decision to leave the order of silence and enter into discourse: she blames herself for speaking and feels her only justified course is now to enter into the final silence of death:

I have murdered my lord, killed him with my speech. He would be alive had I not spoken the word which engaged him in adventure. Silence hurts no-one; speech often harms many. . . . Since Death does not take me, I must avenge my sinful deed. I shall die in spite of Death, who will not listen to my call for help. But I cannot die by desire alone . . . the sword my lord has on shall avenge his death.

(Erec et Enide, 4584–4628)

Her suicide is prevented by the arrival of Count Limors. He asks her if she is the wife or the mistress of the dead man: "Both one and the other," she replies. He decides on the spot to bury Erec with high honors and marry Enide at once. In his hall, with Erec on his bier, the count marries Enide and attempts to force her to eat a meal that is simultaneously funeral meat and wedding feast; she refuses. He slaps her and she shrieks, moving from the ordered mediations of civil discourse to the primal scream of unmediated self-projection. Her "new" voice wakes the dead: Erec recovers from his swoon and silences Limors forever with bloody death.

This is the final passage for both Erec and Enide; after surviving this, they are prepared to return to the court of Arthur with their new-won knowledge of a marriage in which the bride can function as both wife and lover, and in which the reconciliation of speech and silence, man and wife, can mirror the courtly desire of other unions in freedom: between art and nature, interiority and exteriority, past and future, humanity and divinity.

In the *Cligés,* it is Fenice who rises from her own ashes; it is the female who speaks and arranges for the necessity of her own silence. In her determination to avoid the reputation of Isolt, Fenice, with the help of her nurse, Thessala, devises a strategy using *two* potions: one for the king, by which he is charmed into the illusion that he is making love; the other for her, in order that she may appear dead. The plan is to go through the ritual of funeral and burial and, anticipatory of *Romeo and Juliet,* effect her own resurrection. Three doctors are brought in to test the validity of her death, and her body is submitted to a series of brutalities, one of which (pouring molten lead into her hands) is suggestive of the stigmata of Christ.[18] Even if the narrative outline of Fenice's suffering bears a strong structural resemblance to Christ's Passion, the presence of so many dislocating "toads," although sending

158

us out of the purely literal dimension of the narrative, forbids any satisfactory, consequential allegorizing of Fenice (her very name promises endlessly repeatable resurrection) as Christ. Chrétien is drawing on the universal figural power granted all humanity by the Incarnation of figuring forth, albeit imperfectly, the hypostasy of Christ: to function as cracked looking glasses of God. Yet here we are to see not the enigma we imperfectly reflect but our own imperfection, our cracked natures as mirrors. Fenice is not an *imitatio Christi;* she is a parody of Christ, just as she is a parody of Isolt. For Fenice, there is no self-knowing. For us there is. Fenice functions as a prudential mirror in which we can see our own pretensions, our own imperfections, rise up phoenixlike, over and over again.

In the case of *Lancelot,* images of his death and ressurection are fore-figured as he discovers, early on, his own tomb in the cemetery. But the later, central moment of erotic consummation between Lancelot and Guinever is the pivotal moment both in Chrétien's romance and in the myth of Camelot. It is both the ecstatic culmination of their courtly love and the trigger of the doomsday machine that will render Arthur vulnerable to the later treasons of Mordred, which will annihilate the court, leaving Lancelot and Guinever in their respective monastic isolations. These eschatological images are not present in the actual fictive confines of Chrétien's *Lancelot,* but subtle hints remind us that they belong in our horizon of expectation. This climactic moment of ecstatic betrayal is preceded, in Chrétien's romance, by a swirling, zigzag confusion of false reports of death, which in turn lead to near-suicides and providential recoveries on the part of both the hero and the heroine, as each hears false reports of the deaths of the other. The false reports of death are followed by a letter announcing Lancelot's freedom and return to Camelot; this also is false.

All this false news subverts the positive, univocal tone in which the climactic scene of reconciliation between Lancelot and Guinever and their erotic consummation is depicted. It also calls into fatal question the serenity and reliabililty of the narrator at the end of the romance. After so many false reports, what *is* truth? On what ground can we test *any* news? At the end of the romance, when we learn that Chrétien had abandoned the narrative with Lancelot locked up securely in his penal (penile) tower, we cannot fail to suspect Godefroi de Leigni's confidence at closure. Surely the jubilant celebration following Lancelot's beheading of Meleagant rings hollow as we recall, from our reading of William of Malmesbury, Geoffrey of Monmouth, and Wace, quite other, and universally catastrophic, endings to this story.

In the *Yvain,* the first death is that of Esclados li Ros, husband of Laudine and guardian of the liminal frontier of that ubiquitous, mythic region of unlikeness that both opposes and delimits the domain of Arthur in all of the romances. There is no resurrection of Esclados li Ros, but within three days Laudine has a new husband. The picture of Laudine mourning over his body, a dark mirror of the pietà, becomes for Yvain the speculum of the Desired Woman, whose arrow strikes him with the wound of love. In precisely three days after the burial of Esclados li Ros, Laudine, with the mediating trickery of Lunete, marries Yvain: the king is dead; long live the king.

After a week of honeymoon, Gawain upbraids Yvain for chivalric recreancy, and Yvain, like Erec, returns to the pursuit of *aventure;* unlike Erec, he leaves his bride at home. He promises to return in a year, and six weeks after he misses that deadline, a lady arrives with the news that Laudine is now "dead" to him. He then tears off his clothes and runs naked into the woods and, in anticipatory reverbera-tion with the Perceval narrative, runs into a local boy with five arrows, which he steals, and, madder than a hare, he hunts up food for a bewildered hermit in the forest. His recovery is providential; a passing noblewoman takes pity and sends a serving-woman to him with a curative salve concocted by Morgan la Fay. She rubs it all over his naked body, and he is returned to life. He meets a lion engaged in a life-and-death struggle with a serpent, and he saves the lion. In yet another reverberating image, this time recalling Ovid's Pyramus and Thisbe myth, the lion mistakes Yvain for dead and takes his sword, lodges it in a tree with the point extended outward, and is about to run himself on it when Yvain "awakes" and saves him yet again. After Yvain learns how to keep a deadline, he can be reunited with the "dead-to-him" Laudine, but only by a repetition of the mediating trickery of Lunete.

The parodistic function of Yvain's deaths and resurrections is similar to that of Fenice's. We are not to attempt any grand allegorizing of Yvain as Christ, but to see in his parodic imitations of the passion of Christ a prudential mirror of our own unknowing. Yvain is delighted to have his second chance; that is what redemption is all about. But Laudine's silence in the face of his joy is an eloquent dislocation for the reader; she remains true to her own honor and word even though tricked into marrying this lout a second time. We see quite clearly her anger and contempt. Yvain, all agrin, does not.

In the epic tradition as well as in the Christological narrative, the descent and resurrection from Hell (*hic labor est*) credentials the hero and provides him with the authority that comes from the privileged knowing we assign to those who have conversed with, and returned from, the dead. All of Chrétien's deaths and resurrections are parodies of this double tradition. Their net effect is to kick us into the hermeneutic gap—a comic region of unlikeness from whose vantage point we can see the absurdity of human pretension and yet delight in its mad charm. As the Wife of Bath would say, "it tickleth us about the heart's root." We move toward the conclusion of this chapter by examining briefly the ways the romances of Chrétien treat the moment in which the Lover sees his Beloved.

Beholding the Lady

When beauty is found in the eyes of the beheld, as Socrates insists in the *Phaedrus,* its perception is inseparable from the tiny images of the self-as-beholder that one sees there. Love of the Other involves in its subtle calculus a quotient of self-love, of *amour propre.* Even in the ideality of selfless love captured in the Christian imperative, the self remains at the center of the equation: recall the second summary commandment, "Love thy neighbor as thyself." What has become evident during this investigation of the lyric and romance is that in the interior mode of the lyric, the discovery of the self at the center of the Other tends toward the narcissistic. In its severest form, the image of the self is perceived as a barrier in front of the Other even as it acts as a mediating bridge *to* the Other: one arrives, at best, not at the quiddity of the Other but only an image, or idea, of the Other as created by the self's own desire. In the romance the same paradigmatic act of beholding the self in the Other tends toward the prudential: the discrepancy between what one desires to find in the image of the Beloved and what one in fact finds there can lead to a program of personal and collective reform. The new and providential self-knowledge may not accrue to the Lover; more often than not the image of the Lover beholding the Beloved acts as a speculum of possibility for the reader; and it is the reader *of* the fiction, rather than the Lover *in* the fiction, who is blessed with the shock of recognition.

Enide, the first Beloved as Mirror in Chrétien's canon, is also the ultimate ideal. She is presented as paradigm, in both natural and literary terms:

> Nature herself used all her skill in forming her. . . . The golden hair of Isolt the Fair had no radiance comparable to hers. . . . Her face was clearer than the lily . . . her eyes so brilliant that they shone like stars. . . . She was made to be looked at . . . for in her one could have seen oneself as in a mirror.
>
> (*Erec et Enide,* 421–41)

This rhapsodic description admits of no problematic, and that is precisely the point resulting from our investigation. The *Erec* has a place in Chrétien's canon much like the speech of Phaedrus in Plato's *Symposium:* Love is praised enthusiastically, and univocally. In this kind of praise there is no room for discriminations, for questions, for the critical, analytic process of the mind.

After the Erec, the pivotal event of the Lover beholding the Beloved is never again that invulnerable. In the prologue to the *Cligés* a moment of beholding occurs that has become, for twentieth-century scholars, one of the chief paradigms of medieval looking. This is the brilliant and extensively amplified "complaint" of Cligés's father, Alisandre, which contains a full analysis of what happened to him on beholding Soredamors. After a lengthy disquisition on love as sickness and madness, on the hopeless need for an adequate physician, on love as the wound of erotic arrows, and on love as teacher, the question is asked: But how did love wound my heart with his arrow and leave no external sign?

> Tell me that! . . . How did he make the arrow enter in? Through the eye. Through the eye? . . . If it passed through the eye, why does the heart complain, when the eye, which received the first effect, makes no complaint at all? . . . The eye is not concerned with the understanding, nor has it any part in it; but it is the mirror of the heart, and through this mirror passes, without doing any harm or injury, the flame which sets the heart afire.
>
> (*Cligés,* 695–706)

In terms of Alisandre's theory of light and reflection, he is a Neoplaton-ist, holding to a theory that combines intromission and extramission. For him the heart is like a candle in a lantern, sending out light. Light from outside must be greater than that light to enter in. The eyes act either like stained-glass windows or like periscopic mirrors, mediating interior and exterior sources, and in this role they reflect rays that enter from without down into the heart.

Know that eyes are like the glass and the lantern; for the light strikes the eyes in which the heart is accustomed to see itself reflected, and lo! it sees some light outside, and many other things, some green some purple, others red or blue; and some it dislikes and some it likes, scorning some and prizing others. . . . My mirror has greatly deceived me; for in it my heart saw a ray of light [a golden arrow] with which I am afflicted, and which has penetrated deep within me, causing me to lose my wits.

(Cligés, 724–41)

The golden arrow is what D. W. Robertson calls a "phantasmata" of the Lady—a mediating, enabling, yet dislocating image of the Lady— not the Lady herself.[19] Later on, when Alisandre's son Cligés first beholds his Beloved, the ever-rising Fenice, Chrétien presents the hero and heroine as themselves a source of radiating light:

The day outside was somewhat dark, but he and the maiden were both so fair that a ray shone forth from their beauty which illumined the palace, just as the morning sun shines clear and red.

(Cligés, 2714–20)

And Cligés himself is presented in specular terms of literary dissimili-tude, unlike both Narcissus and Tristan:

He was in his flower. . . . He was more comely and charming than Narcis-sus—who saw his reflection in the spring beneath the elm-tree, and when he saw it, he loved it so that he died, they say, because he could not get it. Narcissus was fair, but had little sense; but as gold surpasses copper, so was Cligés better endowed with wisdom. . . . He possessed the wood as well as the bark; he knew more of fencing and of the bow than did Tristan, King Mark's nephew, and more about birds and hounds than he.

(Cligés, 2724–51)

Even though compared to Narcissus and Tristan in terms of *un*likeness, the juxtapositions remain in the mind; there remains a *contaminatio* of the imagery. Robertson goes on to suggest that when Cligés sees Fenice, in the "flower of his age," however much Cligés is *not* like Narcissus, Chrétien is implying that a bit of the narcissistic aura clings: "what Cligés actually loves is an image created within himself, and the self-satisfaction it suggests, rather than Fenice."[20] This is a lyric posture quite close to that of Heinrich von Morungen.

Lancelot first sees the queen from a window; he gazes upon her until she disappears, after which he feels compelled to jump out the window to his death. As he is restrained by Gawain and others, words are said that haunt the memory for the rest of the romance:

As they leaned on the window sill, they saw a knight lying on a bier, accompanied by three mourning ladies. Behind the bier, a crowd approached, with a tall knight in front, leading a fair lady by the horse's rein. The knight at the window knew it was the Queen. He gazed at her with delight as long as she was visible. When he could no longer see her, he decided to throw himself out the window and break his body below. And would have done so had not my lord Gawain seen him, and stopped him, saying: "Be quiet now. Never think again of committing such a mad deed. It is wrong for you to despise your life." The damsel says [to Lancelot] "he's right." [And to Gawain] "Since he has been upon the cart, he has good reason to wish to die, for he would be better off dead. His life henceforth is sure to be one of shame, vexation, and unhappiness."

(*Lancelot*, 550–82)

The tableau in which Lancelot here first beholds his Lady is a *pictura inanis* prefiguring the breakdown of Camelot. In the processional of the bier with the body of the dead knight and the three bitterly mourning ladies, followed by a tall knight and the queen, we see a paradigmatic image of death and betrayal, a kind of fore-screening of the dead Arthur being borne by the ladies who will accompany him to Avalon, followed by fore-figurations of Lancelot/Mordred, Guinever, and the courtiers of ruined Camelot. The sight of his Lady in this sombre prevision of desolation jolts Lancelot into a new and insane mode of perception; he suffers an intensity of experience that, when over, calls for death; for nothing short of death can imaginably be borne upon denial of the sight of the Lady's image in this particular configuration. This sense of image-as-forecast is reinforced when we are given a preview of Lancelot's own death a bit later on in the romance, when we see him prove his power by lifting up the heavy stone lid of what we are laconically told is his own predestined sarcophagus.

In the *Yvain,* there is no revelation at all, only the arrow's wound. In fact, the tableau in which Yvain first sees his Lady is the funereal image of Laudine tearing her hair over the corpse of her husband, whom Yvain himself has just dispatched. As she tears her hair and face, the arrow of love enters Yvain's heart through the eyes and wounds him into love, but not into insight. His "complaint" is almost as long and as detailed as that of Alisandre's in the *Cligés,* but it never gets past the entry of love's image as wounding arrow. Suffering brings no wisdom. And that is precisely what we have seen in the *Yvain* as the capstone of Chrétien's canon of completed works, all of which center on the dialectic between adulterous and married modes of loving. At the end of his ordeal of marriage, Erec seems to have learned something; Yvain not. We can see this in the mirrors of the ladies: Enide is one with Erec; Laudine is deeply angry and contemptuous and only goes along with the second marriage because she has given her word, not because she loves Yvain. So we move from the ideal to the real. Erec and Enide are "pretty pictures never before assembled by law or marriage" [onques deus si beles ymages / n'asanbla lois ne mariage] (1495–96). We move from the ideality of the *Erec* to a much more realistic assessment of Yvain's intelligence and heart and his capacity to deal with the Other. His capacity is not very great, and that's the way things are. The comic forms of Chrétien move from one form of reformational didacticism to another: from the presentation of an imaginable revolution or renovation of human mores in the *Erec* to a more modest program in the *Yvain:* the revelation of human foible so that we may be stronger for the acceptance, in a comic understanding, of our own weakness, our stupidity, our cracked human nature.

The Lyric Romance of the *Rose*

In a celebrated moment in Guillaume de Lorris's *Roman de la Rose,* Amant, the Lover, comes upon a fountain encased in marble on the border of which Nature has discreetly incised: "this is the place where

Narcissus died" [illec dessus / se mourut li beaux Narcisus] (1460–61).
At first he hesitates looking into the fountain, for fear of succumbing
to the same fate as Narcissus. But then he decides that knowing the
story of Narcissus will itself protect him from that fate, and so he looks
into the fountain.

He sees two faceted crystals that reflect, without deception, the
entire garden. He looks and looks, and feels deceived after all. His
gaze at length perceives, in the crystals, a bush of roses, one of which
increasingly draws his attention and becomes the object of his desire
for the rest of the poem, into and through the continuation of Jean de
Meun. How can the crystals at once reflect the entire garden without
deception and yet deceive the Lover utterly? The crystals, of course, are
not in the pool at all. He is seeing a reflection of his own eyes. The
eyes themselves reflect without distortion. But they cannot reflect their
own nature or the nature of reflection itself. The world he sees is there,
all right, but he is deceived into thinking that he views it in an
unmediated fashion. What he sees are *images* of reality, not reality
itself; he sees, not face to face, but darkly, into the enigma of the real
by way of the mirrors of his eyes.

As Knoespel points out brilliantly, it becomes clear in the course
of Jean de Meun's continuation of the *Rose* that an alternative image for
Narcissus is required for satisfactory closure.[21] Jean de Meun chooses
the narrative of Pygmalion as both an apparent solution to and an ironic
inversion of the problematic posed by Narcissus. Through the grace of
Venus, the image of the artist's own making comes to life and can be
safely and fruitfully adored. But this miracle remains a merely literary
fulfillment of desire, fooling nobody. As D. W. Robertson argues, the
mediations of Venus in this transaction are dubious at best.[22] Thirteenth-century Europe was a world that believed not in the literal truth
of pagan gods but in another dispensation altogether.

The rich and empowering irony at the end of the *Rose* has much to
do with the equivocal nature of the transformation of the artificial idol
of the artist into the apparently living and willing but nameless girl.
The ironic reversals of the creation of Eve in the Eden of Genesis must
not escape us; it is quite likely that we are to understand the transformation of the image into its "original" as an illusory transformation
effected by the faculty of desire itself, as figured forth by Venus. That
this "alternative" to the Narcissus bind is not a real solution at all is
slyly indicated in the way in which Pygmalion compares himself as

"not really all that much like Narcissus" and by the fashion in which Jean de Meun's dialogue between the Lover and the Beloved echoes the echoing dialogue of Narcissus and Echo. We recall the moment when the Lover discovers that the image appears to be alive:

"What is this?" he said. "Am I being tempted? Am I awake? No, not awake, but dreaming. But no one ever saw so lifelike a dream. Dream! In faith, I do not dream, but wake. Then where does this wonder come from? Is it a phantom or enemy who has been put into my image?" [She answers] "I'm neither demon nor phantom, sweet friend, but your friend." ["Est ce fantosme ou anemis / Ques s'est en mon image mis?" . . . "Ce n'est anemis ne fantosme, / Douz amis, ainz sui vostre ami."]

(*Rose*, 2144ff.)[23]

The principle of echoed inversion implied in the placement of "fantosme" and "amis" (phantom and friend) is even further concentrated, although more heavily veiled, in the phonetic palindrome our ear discovers in elided "image" and "mis" that surfaces as one pronounces the final *e* in "image" in the question "Ques s'est en mon *image mis* (*imazhami*)?" The phonetic mirroring in an absence of ordering syntax leaves the important ideas echoed in the Old French words for "image," "has made," "friend," "enemy," "lover," and "mistress" inseparably clustered: all partial yet reinforcing images of one another in a phonic hall of infinitely reflecting mirrors.

The way the "solution" of Pygmalion and his Image/Lady echoes the "problem" of Narcissus and his Image/Echo tells us that this "miracle," this saving metamorphosis, cannot be taken as the "real" solution. It must be read instead as epideictic parody of the real solution. To move from the parody to an understanding of its original, we must read, within the parodic image, significant patterns of inversion.

On the one hand, the Pygmalion narrative is a deeply ironic inversion of the problem involved in beholding the Beloved as depicted by Heinrich von Morungen. Pygmalion's image of the Lady, through the equivocal mediations of Venus, comes to life; Heinrich, on the other hand, thought he loved a living Lady and dreams to discover, to his horror, that what he loves is only his image of her. The Pygmalion narrative also anticipates, inversely, Dante beholding the Siren in the *Purgatorio:* an image in which the dreaming artist/pilgrim invests the ugly "real" image with fictive beauty by exercising his artistic powers in the fulfillment of his own desire, at the cost, or at least at the risk, of self-deception.

And it is, of course, Dante who will provide images of increasing adequation of the "real" solution. First, at the beginning of the *Paradiso*, Dante the Pilgrim attends to the figure of Beatrice, who teaches Dante the most important lesson he has to learn about her. She will teach him to reject her as an idol, a substitute for God, and reread and accept her as a prudential and providential *imago dei;* teach him that her eyes are not the end of the quest, but glasses in which he can bear to observe darkly the splendor of the divine enigma. Finally, with Beatrice's mediative role complete, he will be prepared to see the final image of the poem: our collective *imago* in the Circles of God. This image of Dante seeing our image within the image of God will function for us as a mirror of the true fulfillment and corrective of the problematic generated by the image of Narcissus dying in front of his image in the pool.

Rosalie Colie eloquently argued for the extraordinary values inherent in what she styled *genera mixta,* mixed genres.[24] The genres, or kinds, reflect differing, and in their purer forms, exclusionary modes by which a culture perceives itself and reality. But unless they are called into question, they also mask the limitations and partiality of their own procedures. When they collide and mix, their anatomies and codes are revealed, and these *genera mixta* help us see, in perceiving alternative procedures operating simultaneously, a mirror of our own existential partialities and inadequacies for what they are. The ultimate utility of this hybridization is to empower literary art to help us lead more examined lives.

The *Roman de la Rose* is a prime example of *genera mixta,* an extraordinarily informative hybrid that bridges the lyric and romance horizons of expectation. It is precisely because of its haunting liminality in this regard that it can act so powerfully as a culminative confirmation of the fruits of our inquiry into the mirroring powers of medieval lyric and romance. It remains for Dante and Chaucer to reintroduce the divine and human comedy of encyclopedic epic, *genus mixtus non plus ultra,* which includes and transcends all other genres and provides a more adequate speculum of continuance and possibility for the Middle Ages—and for ourselves.

In summary, it is the contention here that Chrétien is presenting in all of his romances a confrontation between the duties of a man to his love and to his society. But by the time of the *Yvain*, he is also presenting, by the very *manner* of his presentation, a more fundamental, yet curiously and closely related, confrontation between illusion and reality, and he is doing so from a perspective that renders his vision cosmic as well as comic. It is a perspective that leads to recognition, that evokes a saving kind of laughter—much like that of the court on the return of Gawain in *Sir Gawain and the Green Knight;* much like that of Chaucer's Troilus looking down from the eighth sphere upon the scene of his own death. It also requires the creation of a certain distance between the "eigthe sphere" of our observational vantage point as readers, and "this litel spot of erthe" that grounds our text.

CHAPTER 7

The Descending Dove: Dante's Francesca as the Anti-Beatrice

But let the poet on his balcony
Speak and the sleepers in their sleep shall move,
Waken, and watch the moonlight on their floors.
This may be benediction, sepulcher,
And epitaph. It may, however, be
An incantation that the moon defines
By mere example opulently clear.
And the old casino likewise may define
An infinite incantation of our selves
In the grand decadence of the perished swans.
　　　—Wallace Stevens, "Academic Discourse at Havana"

The major concerns of this chapter and the next have to do with how medieval literature represented figures—what we might call literary characters—both as texts and as mirrors of *recte legendi,* or right reading. The reciprocal figural power that humans had for mirroring each other in the medieval imagination is perhaps most clearly etched by Virgil in his first lecture on love in *Purgatorio* 15:

And when there are more souls above who love,
there's more to love well there, and they love more,
and, mirror-like, each soul reflects the other.[1]

We shall track the ways in which literary characters in Dante and Chaucer signal themselves as "textual mirrors," both in their discourse and in the authoritative texts they quote and allude to for the purposes

171

of representing their thoughts and feeling. "Reading" these characters as "texts," we can better assess them both as literary constructs and as implied human beings suffering into truth. The specific challenge in this chapter will be to establish a right reading of the confrontation between Dante the Pilgrim and Francesca da Rimini in *Inferno* 5; we shall see how this haunting confrontation figures forth a double paradigm of infernal misreading.[2]

One best senses the ways in which the fictive world of the *Commedia* is fraught with text by attending to the pervasive network of textual allusion: direct quotation, translation, or obvious paraphrase (what one might call oblique quotation). Recall, for instance, the moment near the end of the *Purgatorio* when the entire company of the Pageant of Earthly Paradise bursts into Latin song:

> . . . From the godly chariot, eternal
> life's messengers and ministers arose:
> one hundred stood *ad vocem tanti senis.*
>   All of them cried: *"Benedictus qui venis,"*
> and, scattering flowers upward and around,
> *"Manibus,* oh, *date lilia plenis."*
>
> (*Purgatorio* 30.16–21)

To the sacred Latin text "Blessed is he who comes," from Matt. 21.4–9, slightly adjusted by Dante into "Blessed art thou who comest," is added a tag whose source remains, I believe, uncovered: *"ad vocem tanti senis"* [at the voice of so great an elder]. These sacred Latin fragments are then "topped off" by *"Manibus date lilia plenis"* [Bring me lilies with full hands], a famous line of Virgil from perhaps the most plangent scene in the *Aeneid* (in which Anchises laments the early death of Augustus's presumptive heir, Marcellus—see Chapter 1).

This extraordinary tribute paid by the collective personae of Revelation to a pagan poet by quoting his pagan text is, in Erich Auerbach's important distinction, both theologically and dramatically "right."[3] Considering first the dramatic aspect, we note that immediately following this quotation, Dante sees Beatrice for the first time in the epic. On turning to Virgil to share his delight on seeing her many years after her death, he also pays tribute to Virgil by translating Dido's equally famous *"agnosco veteris vestigia flammae"* into "conosco i segni de l'antica fiamma" [I recognize the token of an ancient flame]. The act of quoting

Aeneid 1 in the current context is filled with comic irony. It implies a subtext, as if Dante the Pilgrim were also saying the following *mots sous les mots:* "Remember this line of yours? But in my case it is the man, not the woman, who says it. And it is not another love (love for Aeneas, which recalled in Dido her earlier love for the dead Sycheus) but the *same* love: for I see now that my 'new' Beatrice, transfigured by death and resurrection in the Cart of the Church, recalls and fulfills the self-same, earlier Beatrice lost years ago in Florence . . ."—but Virgil is gone.

Both quotations from Virgil's epic, the one alluding to the death of Sycheus in *Aeneid* 1 and the other to the death of Marcellus in *Aeneid* 6, signal radical absence and are thus dramatically appropriate mirrors as we discover Virgil's sudden absence from Dante's side. But there is more. In Dante's Augustinian method of writing for "oure doctrine" and to extend the domain of love, the embedding of these pagan textual fragments is doctrinally "right" as well. They have been given a new context, and hence a new meaning. As Virgilian text, they once referred back and forth in historical time to the deaths of Sycheus and Marcellus. But as Dante appropriates them into the new testament of his own epic, their original figural potential is now fulfilled and corrected by the new contexts of a Christian text, the *Commedia* itself. Read typologically, Virgil's original lines commemorating the death of the old as a context for perceiving the need for the new now celebrate the advent of the new life (vita nuova) as a sufficient context for understanding the necessitous departure from the old.

Dante, as poet *of* the *Commedia,* also quotes himself on occasion as author of works written *before* the *Commedia:* in *Inferno* 4 he signals his own capacity as textural authority by having Virgil welcome him as one of "the six," including Homer, Horace, Virgil, Ovid, and Lucan. Self-quotation here is not, however, an instance of poetic grandstanding. Early on in the *Purgatorio,* the angelic ship lands a fresh crew of souls, among whom Dante recognizes the musician and friend Casella. After their greeting, and while the angelic strains of Psalm 114 are still ringing in our ears ("*In exitu Israel de Aegypto*" [when Israel came out of Egypt]), Dante asks Casella for a song. Casella begins to sing one of Dante's own canzone from the *Convivio:* "Amor che ne la mente mi ragiona" [Love that speaks to me in my mind]. From the limited point of view of the two friends meeting on the shores of ante-Purgatory, the positive nature of Casella's tribute of quotation to Dante the Pilgrim is unequivocal: not so from the controlling point of view of Dante the Poet; he has Cato bring them up short. This is not the song, nor the sort of song, they are in Purgatory to sing. The Italian line sung in self-quotation, originally a secular paeon to "love's reasons," now reverberates in quiet irony with the Latin echoes of Psalm 114, filled with the *ragione,* or "reasonable discourse" of the more embracing sacred love that awaits our release from the Egyptian bondage of this life.

Later on we learn that Dante's *Vita Nuova* is also required reading for the *Commedia.* In *Purgatorio* 24, Bonagiunta da Lucca asks Dante if he is the composer of the lines "Donne ch'avete intelletto d'amore" [Ladies who have intelligence of love] (*Vita Nuova* 19). Dante, in what is surely an important widening of the semantic fields of *amore, spira, noto,* and *significando,* answers:

> I' mi son un che, quando
> Amor mi spira, noto, e a quel modo
> ch'e' ditta dentro vo significando.
>
> [I am one who, when Love breathes
> in me, takes note: what he, within, dictates,
> I, in that way, without, would speak and shape.]
> (*Purgatorio* 24.52–54)

In Bonagiunta's lexicon, Amor is purely literary, secular, and pagan, but Dante's new lexis expands the denotative power of Amor to include the Holy Spirit. Bonagiunta accepts this new expansion of the imperatives of art and concedes that a radical shift in the source of inspiration is all that is needed to effect a radical correction in poetics and create a "sweet new style" [dolce stil nuovo].

For many the *Vita Nuova* is as much an analysis of self-absorbed adolescence as it is an analysis of insufficient codes of love, and I believe Beatrice is referring to the title of his book as well as twitting him about the state of his soul when she says to the Graces in Earthly Paradise:

> questi fu tal *ne la sua vita nova*
> virtüalmente, ch'ogne abito destro
> fatto averebbe in lui mirabil prova.

[This man was virtually so instituted *in his new life* that every right disposition should have proved wonderful in him.]
(*Purgatorio* 30.115–17, my translation and emphasis)

Such referencing to the texts of both self and other in the *Commedia* always keeps the literary dimension of the poem in the foreground. And it is precisely the literary function of this network of textual allusion that has yet to receive sufficient discussion in relation to the extraordinary confrontation Dante the Pilgrim has with Francesca da Rimini in canto 5.[4]

Although on the edge of Hell, Francesca is central to the entire enterprise of the *Commedia*. Novelistically compelling as she is, she is central because her function is figural. She stands, at the first major portal of discovery, as the infernal anti-Beatrice: local, with a notorious past, she figures forth and is ultimately fulfilled and corrected by Beatrice just as Eve figures forth and is ultimately fulfilled and corrected by Mary.

Robert Hollander, over fifteen years ago, saw clearly into the controversy surrounding Dante's kind of allegory and insisted we see the efficacy of Singleton's own insistence that Dante's procedure must not be seen literally as either the "allegory of the poets" or the "allegory of the theologians" but as *mimetic* of the allegory of the theologians. In the allegory of the theologians, all historical events of the Old Testament figure forth equally historical events of the New Testament. Hollander suggests that a literary imitation of this essentially theological mode of exegesis in the *Commedia* might well be called "verbal figuralism."[5] By analogy with biblical exegesis, every event in one part of the poem should figure forth and be fulfilled by another event in the poem. Few would question the existence of such figural density within the *Commedia:* just as few would grant that such verbal figuralism is driving the poem in any strictly systematic way. Others deserve my apologies for what I see as a necessary extrapolation of verbal figuralism for the "special case" that governs Hell.

Documentation of such special-case status for infernal figuration requires a brief review of the chief doctrinal constraints within which Dante worked, and an articulation of the resulting literary problem— and its solution. One of the most difficult things to get across to American students reading the *Inferno* is the important theological sense in which Hell can participate in the domain of Becoming, but not in the domain of Being. Orthodoxy insists that pure Being be attributable only to Divinity. To invest Evil or its locus with Being would be to diminish Divinity, to engage in Manichean heresy. The literary problem can be stated thus: if Evil is denied Being, how can Hell manifest itself? Dante's solution is to have Hell manifest itself in reversals, in parodistic mirror images of the Real. In the *Commedia,* the only images of quotidian reality as we know it are delineated in the *Purgatorio.* The imagined realities of *Paradiso* and *Inferno* are radically different from either our normal sense of reality or our usual modes of perceiving and representing that sense. In the *Commedia,* the mode of *Paradiso* is the imperfect imperfectly (Dante is, after all, a living poet) perfected; the mode of the *Inferno* is the imperfect perfectly parodied.

Paradiso presents itself to us as a progress of images by which Dante's imagined heaven stoops to conquer. In the lower paradisal circle of the moon, Piccarda is happy: God's will is her peace. To Dante's question regarding Piccarda's satisfaction with less than the highest status, Beatrice, with some paradisal warmth, answers for the worlds both containing and contained by the *Commedia:*

These spirits showed themselves here, not because they are assigned this sphere, but to signify their less celestial grade. Such speech best meets your mind, for only through sensation can you transmit what fits the intellect. So Scripture stoops to accommodate your faculties, and attributes hands and feet to God, intending something altogether different.

(*Paradiso* 4.37–45, my translation)

Thus the *Paradiso* comprises a succession of accommodating images that mediates true reality to the imperfect world of finite space and ticking time. As we assent to the power of the final images—the river of light, the mystic rose, and the triple Circles of God—we ascend a ladder of ever-increasing poetic adequacy. But we cannot see God and live; holy fiction has its limits: it can bring us only to the brink of salvation. This is a great deal, however, and may well be, if not all we desire, all we require.

The last canto of Hell opens with a parody of "Vexilla Regis Prodeunt," a famous hymn of Venantius Fortunatus.[6] By adding the word for Hell, "Vexilla regis prodeunt inferni" [The banners of the king of hell march forth], he appropriates the corporate language of paradise to infernal purpose. In one sense, Hell is a desperately willed

176

illusion, and here Hell's vernacular feeds, in a kind of parodic, linguistic cannibalism, on the Latin Real in order to make a mouth through which to speak.

If the *Paradiso* represents ultimate Being accommodating our essential poverty in fictive glass, in images always figural and only proximate to the Real, then the *Inferno* is a hall of darkly inverted mirrors in which we must learn the art of rereading for the Real. The *Commedia* requires a prior reading of itself; only then can we reenter the *Inferno* and reread it for what it really figures forth. If to read the infernal image correctly is to reread it, that is the same as saying that in some part of our heads we rewrite it. Parody is parasitic; it makes no sense without reference to some original; the original of the *Inferno* is the Real. To admire Dante's mastery of the grotesque for its own sake is a trivial admiration. Just as Evil is said to be in the higher and ultimate service of the Good, so close examination of the grotesquely false allows us to rewrite, reread, and leap, by *recte legendi,* to the True.

The ultimate infernal figure at the bottom of Hell is perhaps the most telling example. Recall the figure of Lucifer, stuck in his hole in the frozen floor of the world, his leathern wings flapping, causing a constant and deadening cold wind. His three heads forever gnaw the flesh of Brutus, Cassius, and Judas. Dante the Pilgrim shares his sense of cosmic vertigo as he proceeds to follow Virgil down the gigantic, hairy flanks of the Arch-Denier:

> When we had reached the point at which the thigh
> revolves, just at the swelling of the hip,
> my guide, with heavy strain and rugged work,
>   reversed his head to where his legs had been
> and grappled on the hair, as one who climbs—
> I thought that we were going back to hell.

> (*Inferno* 34.76–81)

In lines 110–11, Virgil amplifies this positioning of Lucifer: "when I turned, that's when you passed the point / to which, from every part, all weights are drawn." Lucifer, by right rereading, is revealed as a dark and enigmatic glass, a parodic mirror of Divinity itself: his three heads are an infernal figure of the Trinity, the chewing on the bodies of the sacred and imperial betrayers a parodistic reflection of the community of the Eucharist, the cold wind an inverted figure of the Holy

177

Spirit, and the geocentric anus an infernal mirror of the "still point of the turning world." It is in just such terms and complexities of inverse figuration that one understands Francesca to be an infernal mirror, or antitype, of Beatrice.

To close this excursus on special-case status of infernal figuration, let me suggest there are two tests of reading infernal figures: external inversion and internal reinforcement. One test of Hell is Paradise: evil manifests its intelligibility by means of inverse figuration. We have seen that Dante's genius at wedding doctrine and drama in this manner is severe and harrowing: as one descends further into Hell, one finds at the center a banality, a nullity that is, in Auerbach's terms, both dramatically terrifying and doctrinally satisfying. Inside Hell, however, evil manifests its intelligibility by means of reinforcing replication and resonance. Thus all figures in Hell function typologically at face value within the infernal systems: they participate in "verbal figuralism" by a congruence of reinforcing images. *Inferno* 5, for instance, divides exactly in half. The first half has no Francesca; the second half is all Francesca. In the internal test of reading Hell, both halves should mirror each other in reinforcing ways; we find they do.

At close of *Inferno* 5, Dante "responds" to the recital of Francesca by a deathlike swoon. Most would agree that Dante's swoon is a fourteenth-century equivalent of a psychosomatic reaction triggered by a profound and complex recognition of certain truths. Two facts make it difficult to ascertain just what those truths might be. First, on nearly every other occasion that embodies a central lesson for Dante, Virgil glosses; here he is silent. Second, Minos, on Dante's entry to the circle of the lustful (an entry that mirrors our own), has just warned us, "guarda com' entri e di cui tu ti fide" [take care how you enter, and in whom you trust]. With such warning on the part of Minos and silence on the part of Virgil, how are we to read the swoon?

The mere undoing of Paolo and Francesca, two of the beautiful people in Italian high society, might itself move Dante, as author of the *Vita Nuova*, to the *pietade* for which "io venni men così com' io morisse. / E caddi come corpo morto cade" [I fainted, as if I had met my death. And then I fell as a dead body falls] (*Inferno* 5.141–42). More central to the recognition leading to the shadow death of the swoon is the pornographic role that reading played in their undoing. The fatal slip came as Paolo and Francesca read the romance of Lancelot. The moment they read about is as central a moment for the ultimate breakdown of Camelot as the betrayal of Menelaos by Helen and Paris was for that of Troy. Even Chrétien de Troyes, usually refreshingly candid in the depiction of sexual bliss, pulls back in the case of Lancelot and Guinever:

A joy and a marvel such satisfaction of which has never been heard nor known; but it will never be revealed by me: *for it may not be spoken of in this story* [*qu'an conte non doit estre dite*]. (*Lancelot*, 4677–81, my translation and emphasis)[7]

Chrétien points, by such massive avoidance of it, to the main issue. This radical example of courtly, adulterous love, the name of which epic stories dare not speak, but which is sanctified by the love ethic of the medieval lyric, inexorably subverts political stability. This betrayal of the royal marriage bed is the "unspeakable" canker at the center of the Arthurian rose.

And it is precisely this image of cultural betrayal that Francesca and Paolo feel called upon to imitate.[8] As their life begins, out of desire, to imitate art, they are discovered and summarily dispatched. Francesca rather ungenerously places the blame on the book, on art and the artist, "Galeotto fu 'l libro e chi lo scrisse" [That book's a pimp, and so's the man who wrote it] (*Inferno* 5.137). This catastrophic encounter between reader and text requires the closest attention, as does Francesca's position that when things go wrong between reader and text it is not the reader but the writer and the text who are culpable.

Like Augustine, Dante places himself at the narrative center of his epic not out of pride but because he, like any man, can be read as Everyman; and because his art, like any *ars,* can be read as any work, or *labor.* It is in the light of Dante's multiple roles, within the poem as Pilgrim and Everyman but also outside the poem as exiled Florentine poet, that such a fatal encounter between reader and text as that between Francesca and the *Lancelot* must be understood. The encounter as depicted in *Inferno* 5 both embodies and figures forth all the imperatives and the dangers inherent in the delicate yet crucial relations that obtain, and that must obtain, between any writer (say, Dante), any text (say, the *Commedia*), and any reader (say, us).

Both the fictive world of the *Commedia* and the nonfictive world of Dante (which included, gradually, as each canticle "appeared," the *Commedia*) consisted of an array of texts: the books of men, the book of nature, and the books of God. Right reading was easily seen as a synechdoche of right living: both were considered chancy. If writers possessed, as Beatrice says Dante possessed, "falso imaginar," and if books, such as the *Lancelot,* were filled with "falli scritturi," then Everyman as Common Reader read and walked a landscape strewn with booby traps. Was there a criterion of corrigibility in the medieval theory of *recte legendi?* St. Augustine provides such a rule of interpretation, though it applied, in its original devising, only to the privileged texts of God. It is a hermeneutic of love; here is the key passage:

Therefore in figural locutions, the following rule will serve: that which is read should be subjected to diligent consideration until such time as an interpretation is reached that increases the reign of charity.[9]

There is an ancient tradition linking love and language that I shall touch upon further at the end of the chapter. Here it is enough to note that the linkage of word and love will eventually turn out to be as true and saving for Dante as it was false and killing for Francesca. Her love is not *caritas,* of course, but *amor,* in another of its driving forms: *cupiditas.* Cupidinous love impelled her action and thus at the center of her disaster is a nexus of love, text, and world gone wrong. What seems to have gone wrong is the faulty mediation between text and world by love.

All criticism I have read seems satisfied that Francesca's report of the encounter with the *Lancelot* completes her own map of misreading. I would suggest that she also, and equally as seriously, misreads the motives, if not the cadence, of the *dolce stil nuovo,* that new style that, Dante will later imply in *Purgatorio* 24, makes the *Commedia* possible. I also urge that Dante the Pilgrim, who enters Hell as the writer of the *Vita Nuova* (and *not* the *Commedia*), is far more deeply implicated in Francesca's catastrophe than critics have shown. Finally, I hope to render compelling an argument that says it is the recognition of himself as personally part of the pattern responsible for Francesca's disaster that, along with all the other pieces of the mosaic of canto 5, helps account for the psychological, dramatic, metaphysical, and theological rightness of the deathlike swoon at the end. These patterns of implication will in turn complete justification of the preliminary contention that Francesca is central, and not eccentric, to the program of the *Commedia* as a whole. Here is a first pass at *Inferno* 5.

In his descent to the Second Circle, the first abode of physical suffering, Dante confronts Minos, who warns him about entry and trust. He then becomes only gradually aware of the presence of the Circle's enormous host, not by visual images, but by sounds: notes, wailings, bellows, shrieking winds, hurricanes, moans, lamentations, and railings at Divine Power: all "in parte ove non è che luca" [in a part of Hell where no light shines at all] (*Inferno* 4.151). This cacophony is a kind of prototalk: the various noises are preverbal indicators of Hell's state of *nullus ordo* (no order or rule). He learns that here are the sinners who subjected *reason* (*ragion;* Dante's favorite word for discourse is the etymologically related *ragionare*) to *desire* (*talento*). Hearing this against the radical image of background noises makes us sense that in this phonic "prespace" of our soon-to-occur literary perception of these spirits, part of their punishment is to be always hovering just short of the brink of speech, on the frontier of *ordo.*

We must keep this sense of things sequestered in our minds when we later notice just how extraordinarily literate and articulate Francesca can be with the still living Dante. Francesca, through the grace of Hell, will *appear* to us in the mode of verbal articulation—an infernal accommodation to the "faculties" of the living. We have here, in the preliminary images of raucous noise, a hint of the *actual* state of those who gave all for love: the *nullus ordo* of an infernal love-talk that manifests itself in primal scream.

There follow three images of the host of damned lovers as birds. L. V. Ryan has gathered together all the necessary folklore we need in order for us to read the texts of these infernal birds.[10] The sum of the lore shows Dante clearly prefiguring what sort of beastliness we are finally supposed to "see" behind the elegant talk of Francesca and the accompanying pedal-point sobbing of Paolo.

There are three bird similes. The first two are stacked upon one another, in the fashion of many famous beast similes in the *Iliad;* they herald the approach of the errant host of love:

> And as, in the cold season, starlings' wings
> bear them along in broad and crowded ranks,
> so does that blast bear on the guilty spirits:
> now here, now there, now down, now up, it drives them.
> There is no hope that ever comforts them—
> no hope for rest and none for lesser pain.
> And just as cranes in flight will chant their lays,

arraying their long file across the air,
so did the shades I saw approaching, borne
by that assailing wind, lament and moan.

(*Inferno* 5.40–49)

Starlings were known for their capacity for imitating or parroting "real" speech, for their stupendous talents at defecation, and for the fact that they defecate and chatter most when coupling. This grim linkage of bestial fornication and love-talk is an inverted figure of paradisal love as revealed in the Logos made Flesh at the Annunciation. As for the cranes, they are gregarious and move to the south, a habit that—according to Benvenuto da Imola, an early commentator of Dante's—is in perfect harmony with the behavior of casual lovers. More important, Dante invests these cranes with their own verbal, narrative art: they fly by "cantando lor lai" [singing their lais]. Of course it is perfectly conventional in the medieval courtly tradition for birds to sing "lor latin" [their "latin," or language], and lais sung by cranes, however grating on the ear of the mind, might slip by as dead metaphor if it were not that a *lai* is not some defunct Latin genre, but precisely the popular sort of vernacular miniromance that Francesca will shortly recite to Dante.

Finally Paolo and Francesca descend to Dante as doves, not as the chaste turtle or "tortora," but as the ardent and promiscuous "colombe." Their descent as the wrong kind of dove bringing news of the wrong kind of love is an inverted figure of the descent of the Dove of the Spirit to Mary, correcting the figural *culpa* of *Eva* with the reverse *Ave* of Redemption. All this preliminary imagery from the infernal aviary provides the typological ground for reading "right" the confrontation between Dante and Francesca.

The second cluster of preliminary images consists of the catalog of lovers. There are seven identified: Semiramís, Dido, Cleopatra, Helen, Achilles, Paris, and Tristram. They all betray and die for love and thus they prefigure Paolo and Francesca in an appropriately anticipatory and retroactively reinforcing way. The first, most awful, and, in the light of the literary discussion that is to follow, most oddly consonant with Francesca is Semiramís. This is not because Francesca slept with her son as it is rumored Semiramís did but because Francesca, like Semiramís, "legitimized her lust by writing new laws":

182

Her vice of lust became so customary
that she made license licit *in her laws*
to free her from the scandal she had caused.
   She is Semiramís, *of whom we read*
that she was Ninus' wife and his successor.

[A vizio di lussuria fu sì rotta,
che libito fé licito *in sua legge,*
per tòrre il biasmo in che era condotta.
   Ell' è Semiramìs, *di cui si legge*
che succedette a Nino e fu sua sposa.]
(*Inferno* 5.55–59, my emphasis)

The perfect rhyme, or *rima equivica,* of "in sua *legge*" [in her *laws*]
and "di cui si *legge*" [about whom we *read*], generates both a phonic
and a textual mirror by which we hear the same sounds mean both
"the act of reading" and "the legitimizing of evil": this is anticipatory
reinforcement of precisely what it is that Francesca later does as a reader
of the *Lancelot*. According to the "rule" of verbal figuralism, our expectations will not be betrayed: the noise, birds, and lovers of the first
half of the canto do prefigure important aspects of the confrontation
between Dante and Francesca, which constitutes the second half, and
these expectations are richly fulfilled.

As noted, it is midway through the canto when Dante spies Paolo
and Francesca among the flying lovers and asks Virgil if an interview
is possible. He replies affirmatively, "e tu allor li priega / per quello
amore che i mena" [and you may appeal to them by that love which
impels them]. Here again, we have the proximity of speech and love
that we find counterpointed in the canto by Paolo's tears. What follows
is an extraordinary monologue of Francesca's. It is pervaded with a
mixed diction that is sweet, acrid, and brutal:

Love that can quickly seize the gentle heart,
took hold of him because of the fair body
taken from me—how that was done still wounds me.
   Love, that releases no beloved from loving,
took hold of me so strongly through his beauty
that, as you see, it has not left me yet.
   Love led the two of us unto one death.
(*Inferno* 5.100–106)

183

The fine rhetorical finish indicates she has said all there is to say. Dante pauses, head down. The pause becomes considerable enough for Virgil to ask, "Che pense?" Dante's answer indicates he is in trouble. Francesca's self-contained reply has only stimulated his erotic imagination: he wants more. He says to Virgil: "Oh lasso, / *quanti dolci pensier, quanto disio* / menò costoro *al doloroso passo!*" [Alas, *how many sweet thoughts, what deep desire* led them *to the dolorous pass*] (*Inferno* 5, 112–14, my emphasis). There is more than a trace here of *ex post facto* voyeurism in his concern about the number of sweet thoughts and the depth of the desire. This is not the first time he has heard the story. He knows who she is and he knows what happened to her. He wants to hear it all again, and again, and in certain terms. He calls her by name, and amplifies in his catechism his own mixed diction of erotic infatuation and the *via dolorosa:*

> . . . Francesca, i tuoi *martìri*
> a *lagrimar* mi fanno *tristo e pio.*
> Ma dimmi: al tempo d'i *dolci sospiri,*
> a che e come concedette *amore*
> che conosceste i *dubbiosi disiri?*

> [. . . Francesca, your *martyrdom*
> moves me to *tears of sorrow and pi(e)ty.*
> But tell me, in that time of *sweet sighs*
> by what and how did *love* grant you
> to recognize the *dubious desires?*]
>   (*Inferno* 5.116–20, my translation and emphasis)

While making verbal gestures toward the realm of religious martyrdom, the real fascination for the Pilgrim lies in sweet sighs and dubious desires in the context of sexual betrayal. He is not satisfied with *what;* he wants to know *how;* so Francesca accommodates his desire and speaks again, but in a different way, the "via narrativa," and we hear about the splendor in the grass triggered by an act of disastrous reading:

> One day, to pass the time away, we *read*
> of Lancelot—how love had overcome him.
> We were alone, and we suspected nothing.
>   And time and time again that *reading* led
> our eyes to meet, and made our faces pale,

and yet one point alone defeated us.
When we had *read* how the desired smile
was kissed by one who was so true a lover,
this one, who never shall be parted from me,
    while all his body trembled, kissed my mouth.
A Gallehault indeed, that book and he
who wrote it, too. That day we *read* no more.

(Inferno 5.127–38, my emphasis)

As one spirit spoke, the other wept, and for pity, Dante swooned, "as if I'd died and fell as a dead body falls." His heat for the story has backfired; Francesca has answered somehow with more than he bargained for. Her narration of the culmination of erotic desire in death suddenly becomes for the Pilgrim-Poet a narrative mirror, the perusal of which leads him to a pseudo death of his own. A mimesis of mirror *regressus* is generated: As Francesca reads the text of Lancelot, so Dante reads the text of Francesca. Each reading leads to a kind of death: this is implication of a first kind.

To establish implication of a second order, we must determine that Francesca's fascination with reading cuts deep and goes far beyond mere boudoir delight in trendy French fiction.

Some readers feel that although gracious enough to her visitors, Francesca neither knows who they are nor cares. I believe she is quite aware of their identity and reveals it by a sophisticated literary game of direct and oblique quotation. Let us look at the passage in which she replies to Dante's request for "the story":

. . . There is no greater sorrow
than thinking back upon a happy time
in misery—and this your teacher knows.
    Yet if you long so much to understand
the first root of our love, then I shall tell
my tale to you as one who weeps and speaks.

(Inferno 5.121–26)

The lines are rich in overtones. One echo comes from the *Consolation* of Boethius: "*Nam in omni adversitate fortunae infelicissimum est genus infortunii fuisse felicem*" [For in all adversity of fortune it is the most unhappy kind of misfortune to have been happy]. Another echo comes from even further back, the *Confessions* of St. Augustine: "*Aliquando et*

e contrario tristitiam meam transactam laetus reminiscor, et tristis laetitiam"
[Sometimes, on the contrary, in joy do I remember my forepassed
sorrow, and in sadness my joy].[11] Then, "this your teacher knows."
The teacher of course is Virgil, but does she know that? I think so.
The locus classicus for such glad/sad recollection is the same for
Boethius and Augustine as it is for Francesca: it opens book 2 of the
Aeneid. She reveals, by her oblique quotation, that she realizes she is
in a position similar to the one of Aeneas when asked by Dido to
recount the Fall of Troy. Not only are the sexual roles of questioner
and answerer reversed, as we would expect in such a literary mirror,
but so is the sentiment: for Aeneas must recall miserable times in the
context of a time relatively happy, whereas Francesca attempts to put
a good face on recollecting happy times in the context of eternal woe.

More than that, Francesca goes on to paraphrase and, to a great
extent, actually translate and transpose much of Aeneas's Virgilian
diction in his reply to Dido. First Virgil's line, and then Francesca's
echoing transpositions of Virgil:

Sed si tantu amor casus cognoscere nostros

(*Aeneid* 2.10)

"Ma s'a conoscer . . . nostro amor . . . cotanto affetto."

(*Inferno* 5.124–5)

Francesca transmutes Dido's express "desire so much to know our fall"
[*amor cognoscere nostros casus*] to what she suspects as Dante's "desire so
much to know our love" [affetto conoscer nostro amor], thereby hint-
ing at an equivalence between "our love" and "our fall." Then she
completes her gesture of literary tribute to the author of the *Aeneid* by
adapting the Virgilian formula that links speech and tears: "I shall tell
my tale to you as one who weeps and speaks" (5.125–26).

Although her diction is masterful here, she is not in full control.
Dante the Poet undercuts her pretensions quietly, but mercilessly. Her
phrase "prima radice del nostro amor" [the first root of our love] echoes
scholastic paranomasia. Dramatic irony surfaces as we realize there is a
deeper implication here than Francesca would perhaps wish to reveal.

Renato Poggioli, in his famous *PMLA* essay of 1957, actually quotes
and discusses this passage as if Francesca had said, "la prima radice del
nostro *male*" [the first root of our *evil*, i.e. misfortune or bad luck].[12]
In fact, only one of the major manuscripts, that of Toledo, has *male*

instead of *amor.*[13] Whether this was a Joycean slip on the part of Poggioli, or whether his edition simply departed from standard texts, the locution is informative. Through Francesca's diction, Dante is recalling the medieval tag: *radix malorum est cupiditas,* the tag that later becomes the leitmotif of Chaucer's Pardoner. Dante is playing, through Francesca's game of literary civility, his own scholastic game of *mots sous les mots:* under Francesca's *radice amore* lies *radix malorum,* under *malorum, cupiditas.*

Francesca continues her literary tennis. Having nodded graciously to Virgil, she now nods knowingly to Dante as she begins her lyric report of what lay behind her undoing: "Amor, ch'al cor gentil ratto s'apprende" [Love that can quickly seize the gentle heart] (5.100). To sense the range of literary tribute embedded in her diction here, we must first recall a quatrain from the famous manifesto of Guinizelli that declares the code of gentle hearts for the *dolce stil nuovo:*

> Al *cor gentil* rempaira sempre amore
> come l'ausello in selva a la verdura;
> né fe' *amor* anti che *gentil core,*
> né *gentil core* anti ch'*amor* natura.

[Love always repairs to the gentle heart like the bird in the woods to the meadow; nor is love in any way prior to the gentle heart, nor the gentle heart prior to natural love.]

Dante, in a critical moment of his *Vita Nuova,* refers back to Guinizelli as the wise one (*il saggio*) and paraphrases the sense of Guinizelli's quatrain in the swing canzone that signals the turning point of his own work:

> *Amore e'l cor gentil* sono una cosa,
> sì come il saggio in suo dittare pone.

[Love and the gentle heart are one and the same, as the wise one puts it in his verse.][14]

Just as Francesca indicates her awareness of the fact that it is Virgil she is talking to by means of quotation, she indicates the same recognition of Dante the Pilgrim in her first speech by sharing with him (as author of the *Vita Nuova*) the text of her own life as a conflation of the texts of Guinizelli and Dante the Poet: "amor ch'al cor gentil ratto s'apprende. . . ."

The trouble is, she has dreadfully misread her authors. Recall that Dante asks the two shades to descend in very gracious terms: "O anime affanate, venite a noi parlar." She responds with equal grace at first, echoing and amplifying his syntactic strategy—"O animal grazïoso e benigno!" [Oh living creature, gracious and benign!]—but then moves on to an image of violence: "che visitando vai per l'aere perso noi che tignemmo il mondo de sanguigno" [visiting us who stained the world with blood] (*Inferno* 5.80–90). Then comes the lyric tour de force of explanation quoted above in translation:

> Amor, ch'al cor gentil ratto s'apprende,
>   prese costui de la bella persona
>   che mi fu tolta e 'l modo ancor m'offende.
> Amor, ch'a nullo *amato amar* perdona,
>   mi prese del costui piacer sì forte,
>   che, come vedi, ancor non m'abbandona.
> Amor condusse noi ad una *morte*.
>
> [*Love* that can quickly seize the gentle heart,
> took hold of him because of the fair body
> taken from me—how that was done still wounds me.
>   *Love,* that releases no *beloved* from *loving,*
> took hold of me so strongly through his beauty
> that, as you see, it has not left me yet.
>   *Love* led the two of us unto one death.]
>
> (*Inferno* 5.100–106, my emphasis)

The shimmering patterns of repetition that rain down from the key words of Dante and Guinizelli have ultimately nothing to do with the "gentle heart," nor with the lucid, love-filled, light-drenched words (and worlds) of the *dolce stil nuovo*. What is being said by Francesca is quite the contrary: for her "gentle" love is gentle only in the sense of being "aristocratic," it is fire and ice; it is violent, entrapping, and self-absorbing; it leads to darkness and death. No matter how "gentil" the "cor", the verbs are violent and intrusive: *apprende* ("seizes"), *prese* ("snatched"), *tolta* ("taken away"), *offende, prese, abbandona, condussa noi ad una morte* ("led us unto death"). Yet all the violence is held suspended in a crossing pattern of anaphora: the thrice repeated noun incipits: *Amor—Amor—Amor* of lines 100, 103, and 106, and the additional triple repetition of *Amor* in different verb forms—*Amor— amato—amar*—in line 103.

In the final line of the passage we find a visual narro-linguistic mirror-metaphor of the kind of love-in-death Francesca is talking about (very similar to the Liebestod in Gottfried von Strassburg's *Tristan*): *Amor* leads us to un*A mor*te, a death in which the word for love is literally embedded. The principle of ordination figured in the double anaphora of love holds out, by its stable and intersecting axes, the promise of a new life (the sweet new style); what is actually said, however, counters with the death-dealing love of the violently self-absorbed. It is true that cupidinous love defeats the crossed trinity of heavenly love; but this defeat occurs only in Hell, in the damnably closed will of Francesca da Rimini. She brings the wrong words of a wrong love: bad news. It is Beatrice who will, in Paradise, bring the liberating trinity of good news: right reading, right speaking, right loving.

It is also important to note that Francesca is here speaking in the lyric mode, the self-absorbed and self-imprisoning mode of Heinrich von Morungen (see chapter 5), the appropriate genre for the troubadour tradition of courtly love. The Italian poet who most deeply explored the psychopathology of Francesca's kind of love is Dante's first friend, perhaps the greatest purely lyric poet of his age, Guido Cavalcante. We identify Francesca's mode in this passage as lyric partly because a desire to display the interior condition of the speaker drives the voice. But this does not satisfy Dante the Pilgrim, and he asks for the *how* in addition to the *what*. Francesca then shifts to the narrative mode and in an equally fashionable literary mode delivers herself of a *lai,* a short romance, in which a desire to narrate external history impels the voice. She "tells" it all twice, first as lyric, then as romance. Both modes are enclosed in and subsumed by the more inclusive genre of the *Commedia* itself, which is encyclopedic epic. Here is a tacit, yet strong, structural indication of generic criticism: for Dante, neither the romance nor the lyric is adequate in the service of salvation.

I have said that in the opening line of this passage Francesca obliquely alludes to the same line of Guinizelli as Dante does in the *Vita Nuova*. Dante the Poet would insist that his reading is the right one (*recte legendi*) because at that point in the *Vita Nuova* Dante as remembered Lover makes an interior move outward, from the prison of pure self-absorption to concern for his Lady. Francesca, on the other hand, although quoting the same code words of the manifesto of the *dolce stil nuovo,* remains adamantly and eternally self-willed and self-absorbed. She has misread the new style; for her the new is really the old: the old psychology of claustrophobia, entrapment, and death shared with the lyric and the romance.

In the implication that neither lyric nor romance are adequate to salvation lies another major point. For better or worse, these are the modes Francesca knows. One she clearly appropriated from twelfth-century France. This has only general implication for Dante the Pilgrim or Dante the Poet. The other, however, she got from recent Italian lyric writers she has identified as the *dolce stil nuovo.* That drives closer home. Dante clearly has more than a mere allegiance to that school. The fact that he swoons like a dead man upon witnessing the recitation of catastrophes between a reader and her texts, one of which he has in fact authored, reveals him as deeply aware of his own implication in that catastrophe, even if he bears no ultimate responsibility for it. And an equation emerges of how lost Francesca really is as we paraphrase a famous line of Wallace Stevens: "there never was a world for her except the one she read, and reading, made." Now for implication of a third and final order.

What is it that links our fascination with Francesca to the larger nexus of text, love, and world in the *Commedia* as a whole? There is a deep and ancient relationship between love and language that provides the ground for many central intimations throughout our cultural history. One path leads back at least as far as Plato of the *Phaedrus* and the *Symposium,* in which right discourse is analogous to right loving, and another leads back to Genesis, in which cosmogony is effected by the Word. Both traditions are linked and reconciled in St. John's seminal identities: *Deus erat verbum* and *Deus caritas est.* Francesca's *amor* is *cupiditas,* the mirror inversion of John's *caritas.* This fulfills the test of Paradise.

Dante's encounter with Francesca and the enabling *speculum* of Francesca's encounter with the text of *Lancelot* are parodic inversions of Dante's final encounter with Beatrice and the enabling *speculum* of the hypostatic union mirrored in her eyes. The entrapment of Francesca's *amor,* which leads to her real and eternal death and to Dante's sympathetic and mimetic swoon, is a parodic inversion of that true life in liberty that Beatrice's *caritas* brings. The deathlike silence of Dante's swoon after his encounter with Francesca figures forth and is corrected and fulfilled by his eloquent prayer of thanksgiving as he takes his final leave of Beatrice in Paradise: "Thou hast led me from slavery to freedom" [tu m'hae di servo tratto a libertate] (*Paradiso* 31.85).

* * * * *

Here we have examined the inverse mirroring power of the infernal figure. In the next chapter we shall test this power as we see it reflected in Chaucer's *Canterbury Tales,* pursuing the test through what Paul Ruggiers has termed "the range of the middle."[15] We will extend the examination of discourse and textual reference engaged in by three literary characters, namely the infernal Pardoner, the purgatorial Wife of Bath, and the paradisal Saint Cecilia; and we shall see how Chaucer reflects the spectrum of ethical possibility first instituted by Dante in the *Divina Commedia.*

CHAPTER 8

Knocking the Mary Out of the Bones: Chaucer's Ethical Mirrors of Dante

> But the difficultest rigor is forthwith,
> On the image of what we see, to catch from that
> Irrational moment its unreasoning,
> As when the sun comes rising, when the sea
> Clears deeply, when the moon hangs on the wall
> of heaven-haven. These are not things transformed.
> Yet we are shaken by them as if they were.
> We reason about them with a later reason.
> —Wallace Stevens, *Notes toward a Supreme Fiction*

Usually, when juxtaposing such formidable figures as Dante and Chaucer, one seeks first the shared ground, the contexts of comparability. In this case, we begin with a major alterity.

Perhaps the most celebrated feature of the *Commedia* is its astounding structural, ethical, thematic, theological, and literary clarity. Perhaps the most notorious feature about the *Canterbury Tales* is its comparatively messy sense of its own coordinates, its fragmentary, ambiguous nature—the more ambiguous for being so fragmentary. Surely some of the clarity of the *Commedia*, and the ambiguity of the *Canterbury Tales*, has to do with the existential venue each imitates and represents.

Part of the clarity of the *Commedia* is a result of depicting the world of the dead, the world of "*tunc facies ad faciem*," of "then face to face." Human will has revealed itself in its ultimate acts of self-exhaustion, the moment of "*in extremis mortuis*" has been passed, the story is told, and the shape of the life-now-lived reveals the curve of desire and knowing in action as complete, a figure in the past perfect.

Part of the ambiguity of *The Canterbury Tales* comes from depicting the world of the living, a world of *nunc* rather than *tunc,* reality seen in a glass darkly, this side of the eschaton, where choice is still real, where will is still discovering itself in the tensive, ongoing world of the present imperfect.

Along with this programmatic alterity, we also have the methodologically necessary counter of a programmatic commonality. Each work implies an inclusive, rather than an exclusive, horizon of expectation; each work depicts a world of affairs: political and social affairs, affairs of the heart and mind, of the body and soul. Each is a comedic, encyclopedic epic that both includes and transcends all other literary genres available to its epoch.

In addition to an inclusive epic program, the poems share political and social history, and it has been clear for many years that the *Commedia* exerted shaping pressure on the production of the *Canterbury Tales.* The problem is in assessing the nature of that pressure. Chaucer does not reveal his anxieties of influence in any systematic appropriation of theme or structure; he does seem to have engaged the *Commedia* on ethical grounds, in the ways in which the depiction of literary character both embodies and comments on human nature.

Dante in the *Canterbury Tales*

Dante's ghostly presence haunts the *Canterbury Tales* in three major modes; each seems important in inverse proportion to the ease of its identification. The most obvious, and least important, is the mode of open borrowings. There are three clear patches of such appropriation: the conversion of Dante's Ugolino (*Inferno* 33) to the Hugolino of the *Monk's Tale,* the use of St. Bernard's prayer to the Virgin (*Paradiso* 33) in the *invocacio* of the *Second Nun's Prologue,* and the discourse on *gentilezza* (*Convivio,* tractate 4) as it surfaces in the Loathly Lady's lecture to the young rapist in the *Wife of Bath's Tale.*

A second order of presence is to be found in the rich array of Dantean fragments of image and discourse distributed throughout the Chaucerian canon: these are far more pervasive and suggestive, and much harder to track. A reliable map of this territory is provided by Howard Schless's recent book, which is as provocative in its speculations as it is reliable in its inventory of references.[1]

194

The third mode of Dantean presence is even more difficult to track, and far more difficult to document; yet it is also far more interesting in terms of assessing the ways in which Chaucer appropriated his Italian master; that is, the way in which the living pilgrims of the *Canterbury Tales* reflect, in their ethical configurations, the dead souls of Dante's *Commedia*.

A number of provocative speculations regarding the issue of Chaucer's apppropriations of Dante were raised over twenty years ago by Paul Ruggiers. He suggested that we think of the Chaucerian modes of comedy and romance generically, and more specifically, in Dantean terms. According to Ruggiers, Chaucerian comedy reflects the ethos of the *Inferno,* Chaucerian romance the ethos of the *Purgatorio:*

> Wherever the tales deal with the unwillingness of the agents to surrender their instinctual incorrigibility, with the determined assertion of their appetites over social convention, they belong to the world of comedy.
> . . . Wherever the agents manifest powers of growth, submit themselves to a learning process, are in some way regenerated, they belong to the world of romance.[2]

This chapter will pursue some of the implications of Ruggiers's remarks in greater detail, by examining three "agents" in the *Canterbury Tales* as they reflect the ethos of discourse and quotation in all three canticles of the *Commedia*. We shall consider the Pardoner reflected in the infernal *figura* of Francesca da Rimini, the Wife of Bath reflected in purgatorial Statius, and Cecilia reflected in the paradisal Beatrice.

The Infernal Pardoner: A Dove Untunes the Skies

> O glotonye, ful of cursednesse!
> O cause first of oure confusion!
> O original of oure dampnacioun,
> Til Crist hadde boght us with his blood agayn! . . .
> Corrupt was al this world for glotonye.
> Adam our fader, and his wyf also,
> Fro Paradys to labour and to wo
> Were dryven for that vice, it is no drede. [doubt]
> For whil that Adam fasted, as I rede, [read]
> He was in Paradys; and whan that he

Eet of the fruyt defended on the tree [forbidden]
Anon he was out cast to wo and peyne.
O glotonye, on thee wel oughte us pleyne!

(6 [C].498–512)[3]

The Pardoner's *O Altitudo!* on the Fall as eating disorder is surely calculated to elicit the grin of his fellow pilgrims as well as of ourselves. Donald Howard recently sketched with a very deft hand the way the Pardoner uses the wiles of complicity in order to co-opt his audience on the Canterbury Road. In the Pardoner's ambivalent need to be liked and to vent his contempt, he must seduce his listeners congregating in the alehouse to join him in laughing at the imagined congregation of unknowing peasants to whom he would normally preach this sermon. Once that is done, they will be vulnerable to his contempt. But the Pardoner is ultimately too clever by half. He underestimates the perceptive powers of his fellows and he overestimates the success of his cosmetic virility, a fiction of attitude and gesture that he uses to screen his liminal and extremely vulnerable androgyny.

The irony resulting from epistemological discrepancy is multilayered. As he allows his fellow pilgrims to know more than his usual congregation, they in turn get to know more than he thinks they know. And we know more than they do—and ultimately more than he does. Their sense of him is epitomized in Chaucer the Pilgrim's summary in the *General Prologue:* "I trowe he were a geldyng or a mare."

We may well deduce, with the hindsight of Walter Clyde Curry and Beryl Rowland, that the Pardoner is a *eunuchus ex nativitate,* with all the inner senses of being cut off that the outward, visible sign signifies.[4] But if the pilgrims don't know everything, they know enough: he is ambiguous, as either this or that—either a gelding, a sexual construct lacking the physical equipment; or a mare, a sexual construct lacking male gender identity—he radiates a sense of both and neither. It is this sexual liminality that both fascinates and puts one off. Donald Howard dubbed him a "feminoid" and ticked him off smartly: "He is a mystery, an enigma—sexually anomalous, hermaphroditic, menacing, contradictory."[5]

His missing sexual identity is covered, and finally substituted for, by an enormous appetite for eating, drinking, and talking. Before he agrees to start his performance, he makes the company stop for cakes and ale. He eats and eats and eats, but waxes not full. In his prologue, he is all candor, letting the pilgrims in on his programmatic duplicity. He tells us that fundamentally, *"radix malorum est cupiditas,"* yet insisting that even in his rich personal duplicity resides a simple, saving, ultimate truth. And so it does, but the truth that resides there is not the truth he thinks is there. The ultimate layer of dramatic irony is that we, although we never get to know everything, realize at the end that we do know more than he does: we know that he has unwittingly exposed his own spiritual anatomy, and that his rhetorical ploy of pretended candor has, in spite of himself, become real.

The rhetorical games he plays in his discourse on gluttony, his cadenzas on the excesses of eating and drinking, and his piquant and willful misreading of authoritative texts all reveal a deep and terrible despair resulting from a perversely closed will. This is an energetically evil will, which in this orthodoxy is a will turned away from God, toward nonbeing, a will like Francesca's, whose self-representation is radically limited to anti-images of the truly Real; such souls can only image themselves forth as parody of the truly Other.

At first, his insistence that apple-eating in Eden be read as a cautionary exemplum of gluttony seems a harmless, hyperbolic joke. But he pushes the image further and further, far beyond the pseudopornographic giggles of schoolboys into a region of unlikeness where we begin to feel ourselves at the frontier of desolate hallucination:

> Allas the shorte throte, the tendre mouth,
> Maketh that est and west and north and south,
> In erthe, in eir, in water, men to swynke [work]
> To gete a glotoun deyntee mete and drynke!
> Of this matiere, O Paul, wel kanstow trete: [canst thou]
> "Mete unto wombe, and wombe eek unto mete, [meat, belly]
> Shal God destroyen bothe," as Paulus saith.
> Allas, a foul thyng is it, by my feith,
> To seye this word, and fouler is the dede,
> Whan man so drynketh of the white and rede
> That of his throte he maketh his pryvee
> Thurgh thilke cursed superfluitee. [through such]
>
> (6 [C].518–28)

We begin to sense a frisson of horror as the structure and logic of his amplification on the digestive tract enters into an image of existential middle as a radically reductive *confusio* of beginnings and endings: wine in, water out; bread in, excrement out. The gastrointestinal descant that follows develops into alimentary nightmare, again citing blasphemic legitimacy in Paul:

> The apostel wepyng, seith ful pitously
> "Ther walken manye of whiche yow toold have I—
> I seye it now wepyng, with pitous voys—
> They been enemys of Cristes croys
> Of which the ende is deeth: wombe is her god!" [their]
> O wombe! O bely! O stynking cod, [bag]
> Fulfilled of dong and of corrupcion!
> At either ende of thee foul is the soun. [sound]
> How greet labour and cost is thee to fynde!
> Thise cookes, how they stampe, and streyne, and grynde
> And turnen substaunce into accident
> To fulfille al thy likerous talent! [greedy, desire]
>
> (6 [C].529–40)

The scholastic joke on substance into accidence reveals the deeper, hidden agenda of the Pardoner: his word is the inverse of the saving Word; his news, like that of Francesca, is bad news. The eating of the bread and drinking of the wine are "fulfilled" in dung. The parable of the talents is willfully misread, deconstructed, and turned into an accidental stew resulting from the mashing, grinding, and straining of "thise cookes."

Both the Pardoner and Francesca are figured as doves; Francesca descending to Virgil and Dante from the endlessly circling lovers; the Pardoner stretches out his neck and nods to his congregation,

> As dooth a dowve sittynge on a berne [dove, barn]
> Myne handes and my tonge goon so yerne
> That it is joye to se my bisynesse.
> Of avarice and of swich cursednesse
> Is al my prechyng, for to make hem free [free/generous]
> To yeven hir pens, and namely unto me. [give, pence]
>
> (6 [C].397–402)

The doves of both Francesca and the Pardoner are the inverse, wrong kind of dove: theirs is not the voice of the turtle heard in the land, but the call of the notoriously promiscuous *columba*, who, in betrayal of the sanctity of marriage, copulates and defecates in mindless repetition, while parroting human speech; this dove deconstructs the world and untunes the sky, converting substance into squittering accidence.

The "bisynesse" of the Pardoner's "tonge" is an infernal *figura* soon to be corrected and fulfilled by the equally busy but paradisal tongue of St. Cecilia in the *Second Nun's Tale.* The Pardoner's "yerne tonge" is the living figure of his particular avarice, his misdirected love: his passion to devour and decreate reality with his words, to unwrite Genesis. To do that, he must deconstruct not only the apple-eating in Eden, but its figural fulfillment and correction in the Last Supper. These cooks, he goes on to say,

> Out of the hard bones knokke they
> The mary, for they caste noght awey [marrow/(mary)]
> That may go thrugh the golet softe and swoote. [sweet]
> Of spicerie of beef, and bark, and roote
> Shal been his sauce ymaked by delit, [be, made]
> To make him yet a newer appetit.
> But, certes, he that haunteth swich delices [delights]
> Is deed, whil that he lyveth in tho vices. [dead, those]
>
> (6 [C].541–48)

The tale the Pardoner tells is a dream-tally; all the images bump paratactically by, without an ordering narrative syntax to help us see them as part of an intelligible whole. This is a dream not of Prudentius, but of Bosch: an *insomnium,* a nightmare. Like all medieval dream poems, it strives toward allegorical signification, not outward, but inward: the imagery is an externalised imaginary landscape of the Pardoner's soul. As Donald Howard says, his tale of the three boys in search of death is "an extremely personal projection, so much so that everything in it can be related directly to the Pardoner's consciousness."[6]

One may well object that this is shameless psychologizing; perhaps it is. But I would argue that our modern distinction between theology and psychology can just as well be seen as protective of a parochial and naive desire to gain the illusion of control over a unified realm of reality by dividing it up and renaming the parts (a modern instance of verbal conversion of substance into accidence). For the medieval imagination, such a distinction between theology and psychology would be a false distinction, no distinction at all. In the world-model shared by Dante and Chaucer, practical theology was precisely that drama in which intellect, memory, and desire played out the love affair between the soul and its creating God. A psychology is a logic of the soul, and the soul's logic would lodge, almost by definition, in the center of the jurisdiction of theology, the logic of God. This central alterity between the medieval epoch and modernity, this unified understanding of the micro-as-macrocosm, illuminates the compelling power of Augustinian notions of sin and evil. As evil is a willing away from God to nonbeing, sin must be read as inversions of love: misdirected, too much, and too little.

In his personal psychomachia, the Pardoner plays all the parts. When he speaks of the cooks mashing, straining, and grinding, knocking the "mary" out of the bones, turning substance into accidence, he is speaking of himself. Past a certain point in the antipilgrimage to nonbeing, hope shrivels into the *attritio cordis* of despair; faith can no longer conceive or believe in a God generous enough to forgive, so high does pride heap up the stature of its own grotesque undoing. This *desperatio*, or paralysis of the will, does not lead to inactivity in the case of the Pardoner, but to a hyperactive spinning of the wheels in the direction of nullity.

The exemplary sinner for whom the cooks prepare the meal in the Pardoner's exordium is also a mirror of the Pardoner himself: he now has a "newer appetite" for haunting these delights in which his life is a living death. He is also the triune original of the three youths of his story, a parodistic *imago* of the trinity of his Maker, imploding as a result of a decreating will out of control. Finally, he is also the Old Man of his Tale. Having no male member, he knocks at his mother's gate with the staff of his tongue. His newer appetite for the fecal, teleological delights of bread and wine undoes the Eucharist; the brilliance of his rhetoric attempts to reverse the direction of meaning in an attempt to push the Word back out of the Flesh and thereby undo the Incarnation. The energy of his discourse is a devouring force; he is a sinkhole. Rather than blessing reality with his words, he sucks it into his vanishing self; his appropriation of others through the seductions of language is a kind of cannibalism. In his willful misreading of biblical authority he reverses, by his parody of *recte legendi*, the Pentecostal gift of tongues. In parodic inversions of Bread, Wine, and the mediating Word, he eats the world; he is the *imitatio Antichristi*, a zombie, "deed, whil that he lyveth in thos vices": he is degenerate in the purest and most desolate sense of the word.

The Purgatorial Wife of Bath: Alysoun the Looking Glass

The Wife of Bath, on the other hand, belongs to Ruggiers's taxonomy of romance; she is purgatorial, capable of regeneration. The Wife and the Clerk, Franklyn, Knight, Prioress, and Nun's Priest all "corroborate our inner convictions about human freedom. When they err and fall, in a sense we err and fall with them, but with them we also rise."[7]

> Experience, though noon auctoritee [even if no authority]
> Were in this world, is right ynogh for me [good enough]
> To speke of the wo that is in mariage;
> For, lordynges, sith I twelve yeer was of age [since]
> Thonked be God that is eterne on lyve, [eternally alive]
> Housbondes at chirche dore I have had fyve—
> If I so ofte myghte have ywedded bee—
> And alle were worthy men in hir degree, [their]
> But me was toold, certeyn, nat longe agoon is,
> That sith that Crist ne wente nevere but onis [once]
> To weddyng, in the Cane of Galilee, [Cana]
> That by the same ensample taughte he me [example]
> That I ne sholde wedded be but ones, [shouldn't, once]
> Herkne eek, lo, which a sharp word for the nones, [nonce]
> Biside a welle, Jhesus, God and man,
> Spak in repreeve of the Samaritan:
> "Thou has yhad fyve housbondes," quod he,
> "And that ilke man that now hath thee [same]
> Is noght thyn housbonde." thus sayde he certeyn.
> What that he mente therby, I can nat seyn.
>
> (3 [D].1–20)

The Wife's opening lines would seem to stress the primacy of experience over authority, until we realize that she develops instead a technique of furthering discourse that depends on a programmatic alternation between the tests of experience and the tests of authority. For her, each realm must prove true against the other; any final truth must prove out against both orders of reckoning.

In fact, even these celebrated words of her first sentence, which seem to privilege experience, themselves call on authority. They are a quotation, by loose translation, of some nearly equally famous words spoken by La Vieille, an earlier antifeminist construction of Jean de Meun: "Mais je sai tant par la practique / Esperiment m'en ont fait sage" [*Rose*, 12804–5]. Chaucer's balanced image of the Wife results in our sense of her, in equal parts, as literary construct and implied human being. In one of her most charming gestures of self-deprecation, in which we can nearly catch the glint in her eye, she says of her *modus vivendi* with her cheating fourth husband: "By God, in erthe I was his purgatorie, / For which I hope his soule be in glorie." Even here, this delicious moment of shared candor is, in another sense, not hers at all, but merely a bright re-articulation of a standard antifeminist commonplace. Christine Ryan Hilary quotes, as an example of such a commonplace, some lines of Golias: "*Quid dicam breviter esse conjugium? / Certe vel tartara, vel purgatorium*" [What shall I briefly say about the institution of marriage? Part hell and part purgatory!].[8]

One of the most intriguing debates of modern criticism has to do with the credibility of the Wife as a woman, whether or not she constitutes a viable "feminist" text. Almost every word she says is drawn by Chaucer from famous, even notorious, antifeminist texts. The miracle, as I have suggested, is that as she delivers this discourse, we sense the gradual generation of an autonomous center of energy that somehow renders credible the idea that a real woman is speaking this language. For us, as she is literary construct, everything she says reeks of antifeminist commonplace; as she is an implied human being, she weaves a compelling text of mind over the abyss of her unknowing. She functions as a mirror of our own pilgrimage of intellect, memory, and will as she suffers into truth. The question is not whether there is a real woman here. The question is how does Chaucer manipulate these antifeminist clichés so that the illusion of a real woman rises up so credibly before our eyes and hearts.

My sense is that Chaucer has tricked us wonderfully without particularly wishing to do so. Alysoun is, like all the other women in the *Canterbury Tales*, nothing more, yet nothing less, than a male image of woman. At key moments Dante and Chaucer, like most male poets, require a composite image of woman to fulfill certain central, specular functions.

A central thesis of this section, in fact of this entire chapter, is founded on a truism: Men have never known very much about women. That ignorance has been traditionally adumbrated, as well as veiled, by the development of a skein of innumerable male clichés about what men *think* or *wish* or *fear* women are and/or are up to. This stock of images, like any other stock of images, can be demeaning and/or useful for everyone regardless of personal gender.

The thesis founded on this truism is this: There are also certain moments in life that *nobody* seems to know very much about: moments such as the miracle of generation, the miracle of self-submission in the pursuit of love, the miracle of self-mastery in the face of love, the miracles of hope and faith, the miracle of wedding knowing and loving into just action. These moments of mystery in the drama of human capability require mediating figures; why not employ midwives? employ our collective, largely male-generated images of women? employ those always already hopelessly inadequate mirrors of the very mystery they are devised to reflect?

Like St. Augustine, the Wife of Bath, as she weaves her discourse in and around the events of her past and her desires for a future, saves her life as she narrates it. In so doing she demonstrates the way in which experience is converted, through the agency of triune *mens*—the medieval faculties of memory, will, and intelligence—*into* authority. She is especially impressive regarding the body's forces of generation and the will's powers of regeneration.

As Jane Cowgill demonstrated recently, the authority of the male arts of persuasion may rest in words alone, but women must demonstrate in action the validity of their arguments: they must "embody the virtues which they preach" in order to persuade the male side of the house of their intellectual and moral credibility.[9] Although Cowgill was speaking primarily of the narrative action of Prudence in the *Melibee,* her insight works as well for Cecilia and the Wife of Bath; the difference here is that for Cecilia and the Wife, narrative action is more a matter of how they speak than of what they do.

As Alysoun speaks of her fervid devotion to sex and engendering, she demonstrates, in her linguistic and narrative syntax, just how superlative a weaver of lace, or *textus* (Latin for fabric), she is, and that Chaucer the Pilgrim is correct in a more extended sense when, in the

General Prologue, he announces that "Of clooth-makyng she hadde swich an haunt [skill] / She passed [t]hem of Ypres and of Gaunt." Her way of talking is akin to the filament spun by Ovid's Arachne: it captures the flies of experience in an amber network of intelligibility, and the final figure of the discourse is a web of lace, with the warp and woof of *être* laid over and across the abyss of *néant.* Her discourse extends the reality of her personal history over time and is in imitation of Genesis in which the result of God's speech, or logos, was the cosmos caught in the warp and woof of space and time. Her kind of discourse is brilliantly figured much later in Virginia Woolf's *To the Lighthouse:* Lily Briscoe, while contemplating her painting, thinks of it and the discourse of Mrs. Ramsey, her model, in terms of an artist's desire to weave adequate texts:

Beautiful and bright it should be on the surface, feathery and evanescent, one colour melting into another like the colours on a butterfly's wing; but beneath the fabric must be clamped together with bolts of iron. It was to be a thing you could ruffle with your breath; and a thing you could not dislodge with a team of horses. [10]

A revealing test of Cowgill's thesis occurs in our present comparison between Dante and Chaucer as we observe the performances of Chaucer's Wife of Bath and Dante's Statius in the *Purgatorio.*

At first Dante's use of male Statius to mediate his complex notions of the generation of the body and the regeneration of the will might seem to run against my intimation regarding the naturalness of placing images of women in these roles. But closer examination will show that an important vector of Dante's literary instincts moved precisely in this direction.

Statius first appears as a mystery figure, unnamed, as the mountain shakes and voices call "Gloria in excelsis deo."

> I could feel the mountain tremble like
> a falling thing; at which a chill seized me
> as cold grips one who goes to meet his death.
> Delos had surely not been buffeted
> so hard before Latona planted there
> the nest in which to bear the sky's two eyes.
> Then such a shout rose up on every side

that, drawing near to me, my master said:
"Don't be afraid, as long as I'm your guide."
"Gloria in excelsis Deo," they all cried.

(Purgatorio 20.127–36)

The entire mountain shakes in love, framed in first and last images of
fear of death and joy in birth (Latona in the throes of giving birth to
Apollo and Diana); this, we learn, is the reaction of Purgatory when a
will surprises itself by its own death to self-imposed slavery and its
rebirth into freedom; has, by its own determination, suffered enough;
and has, as yet unbeknownst to memory and intellect, declared itself
free to ascend to Paradise. The soul who occasions this earthquake of
love is Statius. He appears to Virgil and Dante in a carefully drawn
figure:

And here—even as Luke records for us
that Christ, new risen from his burial grave
appeared to two along his way—a shade
    appeared; and he advanced behind our backs
while we were careful not to trample on
the outstretched crowd. We did not notice him
    until he had addressed us with: "God give
you, O my brothers, peace!"

(Purgatorio 21.7–14)

Statius appears as a figural mirror of the resurrected Christ on the
road to Emmaus, and yet, when he speaks, it is in recognizably human,
genial, and collegial terms. We sense afresh the power all have, in the
medieval imagination, of imperfectly figuring forth the hypostatic
union of Man and God in Christ.

Dante's thirst for knowledge regarding the shaking mountain is
couched in feminine biblical metaphor: "The natural thirst which is
never quenched, save with the water whereof the poor Samaritan
woman asked the grace, was tormenting me." Statius appears and asks
how Dante, still alive, has mounted the stairs. Virgil replies that
extraordinary help was required just because Dante had not passed
through the mystery of death. Again he clothes mystery in feminine
images:

> But since she who spins night and day had not
> yet spun the spool that Clotho sets upon
> the distaff and adjusts for everyone,
>   his soul, the sister of your soul and mine,
> in its ascent, could not—alone—have climbed
> here, for it does not see the way we see.
>
>   (*Purgatorio* 21.25–30]

The teller of the soul's saving dialectic with will and freedom may be male, but his demonstration is impossible without feminine gender grammatically structuring the discourse. This linguistic aspect is more clearly present, of course, in the Italian (*anima, alma,* etc.) than in any English translation. The shaking mountain, says Statius, cannot be a real earthquake in any sense of earthly weather, as Thauma's daughter, Iris, does not reach that far up the mountain in her mediations between storm and sunshine. But nonetheless the mountain trembles, and no one can provide an answer from the physics of this world. All we know is that the mountain trembles as a soul moves, in freedom, from the strictures of its own cleansing to its own release; I risk here some violation to Mandelbaum's translation in order to get a greater sense of the feminine presence in Statius's discourse:

> . . . it only trembles here
> when some soul feels [she's] cleansed, so that [she]
> rises or stirs to climb on high; and that shout follows.
> The will alone is proof of purity
> and, fully free, surprises soul into
> a change of dwelling place—effectively.
> Soul had the will to climb before, but that
> will was opposed [to her ascent] by longing to do penance
> (as once, to sin), instilled by divine justice.
>
>   (*Purgatorio* 21.58–66)

Similarly, Statius's involved description of the process of human generation and embryology is threaded with feminine images, just as his grammar is necessarily threaded with feminine genders. Linguistic gender in everyday language probably does not, in and of itself, strongly signal sociopolitical gender; but it surely has a powerful signifying potential. This potential signifying power in everyday language is activated, in Statius's lecture on fetal development, by the fact that it all takes place in the female body.

He begins with the "perfect blood" [sperm] dripping into "that natural receptacle" upon the "other's [menstrual] blood." The "mixture of active and passive" both "coagulates and quickens the fetus" into something "like a sea-sponge"—and in the third month, God wondering at nature's art, "breathes" a soul—a "spirito novo"—into the fetus: He *anima*tes it. This "masculine-into-feminine" discourse is a fulfilling, if slightly ironic, echo of the "masculine" empowering discourse in the previous canto, in which Dante explained to Bonagiunta da Lucca how God breathed into him (*poetà*) a new (masculine) style of poetry, a *dolce stil nuovo*.[11] After the lecture on generation and birth, Statius moves to ending. When death comes, again in the distaff imagery of weaving, the soul's faculties take on a fictive body in order to work through purgation intelligibly: out of biological death comes a new birth of the logos, imaged forth in the feminine *fiammella,* the flame, the "radiating power that gives form":

> And when Lachesis lacks more thread, then soul's
> divided from the flesh; potentially,
> it bears with it the human and divine;
> but with the human powers mute, the rest—
> intelligence and memory and will—
> are more acute in action than they were.
>
> (*Purgatorio* 25.79–84)

It may smack of the perverse to pick out male Statius as a Dantean mirror of the Wife of Bath, no matter how distant, but the pervasive presence of the feminine as a mediating power translating his otherwise rather scholastic arguments on the will's regenerative powers and the process of the body's generation provide an anticipatory echo for the hard (male?) edge of the Wife of Bath's weaving discourse as she "remembers her upon her youthe." As Statius, a male literary construct of a male, is surrounded by female images and language, so the Wife, a male literary construct of a female, speaks in the cracked, hand-me-down diction of the scholastic clerk. Here she is herself on the organs of generation:

Telle me also, to what conclusion
Were membres maad of generacion
And of so parfit wys a wright ywroght? [manner, maker, made]
Glose whoso wole, and seye bothe up and doun [gloss, will]
That they were maked for purgacioun
Of uryne, and oure both thynges smale [genitalia]
Were eek to know a femele from a male, [also]
And for noon oother cause—say ye no?
The experience woot wel it is noght so. [knows well]
So that the clerkes be nat with me wrothe, [angry]
I say this: that they maked ben for bothe: [be made]
That is to sye, for office and for ese [function (excretory)]
Of engendure. [engendering]

(3 [D]. 115–28)

As we hear her deliver this parody of male diction, we do well to remember that it is, after all, the only diction available to her; just as we do well to remember that we all are limited to the conventions of inherited diction and rhetoric as we seek to find and speak in our own voice. The Wife of Bath's transcendence over male language occurs in the denouement of her prologue, as her clerkly husband incessantly reads his fictive Book of Wicked Women at her. Her stunning triumph is figured forth in her nonverbal language of primal gesture: ripping the pages out of his book, her eloquent silence, and her even more eloquent left hook. These final, purgatorial gestures move in a redemptive parody of Augustine's final admission in *De Doctrina Christiana:* if you cannot make an eloquent speech, you can go one better by leading an eloquent life.[12]

As she fills her world with word in action, as she weaves structures of intelligibility by means of her discourse, she creates an analogue in language of human reality and its imaginable future. Her logos is the agency of her energy, which is another way of saying that for her, logos and love, the fire and the rose, are one. And though she is herself ironically barren in a biological sense, her "new progeny" springs from the refreshing seeds her discourse plants in the hearts of others. Alysoun of Bath, in her indomitable spirit, embodies the Holy Spirit of generation. In the guise of barley bread, she bestows "the flour of al myn age / In the acts and in fruyt of marriage" (3 [D]. 113–14).

Finally, and this is perhaps most purgatorial of all, the Wife, clothed as she is in the borrowed fictive weavings of male imagery, reveals a degree of self-knowledge that the will of the Pardoner denies to himself, in spite of his native intelligence. For the purgatorial Wife, as opposed to the infernal Pardoner, knowing is not antithetical to loving; rather it empowers loving. When she doesn't know, she says so: "What that he mente therby, I kan nat seyn." And what she knows, she shares. And as she borrows the words by which Jean de Meun invested La Vielle with literary life, she declares, in a miraculous act of self-appropriation, their shared independence from male generated diction:

> But—Lord Crist!—whan that it remembreth me
> Upon my yowthe, and on my jolitee,
> It tikleth me aboute myn herte roote. [heart's root]
> Unto this day it dooth myn herte boote [does, good]
> That I have had the world as in my tyme. [in my time]
> But age, allas, that al wole envenyme, [will envenom]
> Hath me biraft my beautee and my pith. [stolen from me]
> Lat go. Farewel! The devel go therwith!
> The flour is goon; ther is namore to telle;
> The bren, as I best kan, now moste I selle; [bran]
> But yet to be right myrie wol I fond. [merry will I try]
>
> (3 [D].469–88)

Cecilia as *Imago Dei:* "Memorie, Engyn, and Intellect Also"

Our sense of the Pardoner and Wife as "realistic" representatives of the human drama is always held in check by our simultaneous knowledge that they also exist as literary echoes of Jean de Meun's Faux Semblaunt and La Vielle. Their vitality is a function of their life in the mind as read, as living entities of the imagination spanning the texts of the *Canterbury Tales* and the *Roman de la Rose*.

The case of the *Second Nun's Tale* is more extreme in terms of a sense of artifice dominating the illusionistic mimetics of social reality. Cecilia is from the outset an inherited, "bookish" image. Chaucer not only openly informs us of the name of his alleged model ("Frater Jacobus Januensis in *Legenda*") but the Second Nun unaccountably identifies herself as a "sone of Eve" and as a writer rather than a tale-teller.[13] In fact, the Second Nun makes rather heavy weather about the fact that she has both the "wordes" and the "sentence" from the "authority" of Cecilia's *vita,* as found in the *Golden Legend.*

> Yet preye I you that reden that I write [that which]
> Foryeve me that I do no diligence
> This ilke storie subtilly to endite. [same, write]
> For bothe have I the wordes and sentence [meaning]
> Of hym that at the seintes reverence
> The storie wroot, and folwen hire legende,
> And pray yow that ye wole my werk amende. [improve]
>
> (8 [G].78–84)

The main argument here will be to attribute witty intention to Chaucer, to show how the uses Cecilia makes of her reading in the deployment of her arguments help counter the pressure we feel to view her as a static literary icon, and recuperate a sense of vivid humanity as she suffers toward the truth of her martyrdom. To make such an argument for Chaucerian intentionality is a special challenge, considering the explicit vow of the teller to stick "religiously" to the source(s).

The set of tales to which the Second Nun's belongs participates in a genre, or horizon of expectation, that has no traditional name. It includes the tales of Melibee, the Clerk, the Physician, the Prioress, and the Parson, which are often referred to as serious, ideal, and religious or, in a recent suggestion by Barbara Nolan, as tales of spirituality or tales of transcendence.[14] The lack of consensus in the matter of nomenclature indicates a lack of consensus regarding what the horizon of expectation is and what these stories are in aid of.

An additional set of concerns that I see as related to the question of genre is: Why, in so many of them, do women figure so prominently? And why are so many of them couched in the extravagant verse form known as rhyme royal? I would like to suggest some sketches of answers to these questions as I review the *Second Nun's Tale* in the framework of the current investigation: character in the *Tales* as reflective of the infernal, purgatorial, and paradisal capabilities of human discourse as fore-figured in the *Commedia.*

All of these tales of piety make the modern reader uncomfortable; it is just possible that something about them made the medieval reader uncomfortable as well. In the *Second Nun's Tale,* the discomfort for most readers lies in the quick, smart, and "uppity" way Cecilia converses with Almachius in the trial scene. Her fearless insistence on a literal logic reveals the scene as a clearly ludic, if highly serious, parody of the trial of Christ before the Sanhedrin. Where Christ employs silence as a central aspect of his eloquence, Cecilia is all "busynesse" with her tongue, which is never at a loss for words as she upbraids the Roman judge and cajoles, provokes, and lectures him to his distraction and to her martyrdom.

At the center of the trial is the insistence that Cecilia sacrifice to the stone gods of Rome. With more patience than modern magistrates tend to show to political protesters, Almachius promises to overlook any personal affront if she will just submit to the gods:

> Cecilia answerde, O nyce creature! [foolish]
> Thou seydest no word syn thou spak to me [since]
> That I ne knew therwith thy nycetee [stupidity]
> And that thou were in every maner wise [every way]
> A lewed officer and a veyn justise. [ignorant, foolish]
>
> "Ther lakketh no thyng to thyne outter yen
> That thou n'art blynd; for thyng that we seen alle
> That it is stoon—that may men well espyen—
> That ilke stoon a god thow wolt it calle. [same]
> I rede thee, lat thyne hande upon it falle [advise]
> And taste it well, and stoon thou shal it fynde [touch/test]
> Syn that thou seest nat with thyne eyen blynde.
>
> (8 [G].493–504)

She rebukes Almachius for being a dolt, for not knowing the difference between the signifier and the signified. As she argues bravely and shrewdly the difference between the letter (stone) and the spirit (god) and the nonconnection between the two in the Roman belief system, she puts to brilliant use her faculties of memory, will, and intelligence. She embodies the doctrine of right reading, of *recte legende,* even as she argues. Earlier on, as she was busy converting her brother-in-law Tiburce, she answered a question of his that she herself had inspired by talking of one God, but in terms of Father, Son, and Holy Ghost. How can God be both three and one? he asks. Her answer reveals a correct reading of St. Augustine's *De Trinitate:*

"That shal I telle," quod she, "er I go.
Right as a man hath sapiences three— [faculties]
Memorie, engyn, and intellect also [will]
So in o beynge of divinitee [one being]
Thre persones may ther right wel bee."

(8 [G].337–41]

Her answer is to urge Tiburce to see the mind as an image of its maker: as *mens* is an amalgam of memory, will, and intelligence, it mirrors back the triune nature of its Creator. This *ratio* is guaranteed in the creation formulae of Genesis 1.27: "*Ad imaginem Dei creavit illum, masculum et feminam creavit eos*" [In the image of God created He them, male and female created He them].

Cecilia is a living emblem of the fruit of her own Augustinian reading and preaching; as she lectures Almachius on the inanity of worshiping dead stone, she is quintessentially alive, figuring forth in her very discourse the correct *ratio* between image and original: she embodies the truth she preaches: she makes right use of "memorie, engyn and intellect also" in the unified discourse of her mind. She is a living emblem of the Trinitarian doctrine by which she converts the world to God. Cecilia ministers life, facing, with laughter, Almachius, who ministers death.

This question must now be raised: How can one argue such a rich skein of intentionality if Chaucer is, in fact, responsible for nothing, if he has "only" translated the *legenda aurea* of Jacobus de Voragine (as he says) or an earlier, longer *Passio* of Bosius (or Mombritius), as argued by Sherry Reames?[15] The answer is to be derived from an examination of the intra- and intertextual literary contexts of Chaucer's narrative.

First, let us deal with the intertextual tradition leading up to the *Canterbury Tales*. The axis from Augustine to Chaucer does not run through hagiographic tradition alone. Surely hagiography is crucial and central; but there is another axis of tradition that runs from Augustine to Chaucer by way of the *Roman de la Rose* and the final canticle of the *Divina Commedia*. To his tight translation of Jacobus's *Legenda Aurea*, Chaucer adds his own "new" prologue, which shapes additional context within which we may complete our "right reading" of his *vita* of Cecilia.

The voice of the faceless narrator-nun enters into our readerly consciousness by calling up entry images of the *Roman de la Rose*'s Garden of Delight, only to warn us away from them, reminding us of the genre of romance only in order to deny its validity. She recalls the Lady who opens the door of Deduit's Garden to Amant: the name of the Lady with the comb and the mirror is Oiseuse or, in Chaucer's own translation of the *Rose,* Ydelnesse.

> The ministre and the norice of vices, [nurse]
> Which that we clepe in English Ydelnesse, [call]
> That porter of the gate is of delices, [delights]
> To eschue, and by hire contrarie hire oppresse—
> That is to seyn, by leveful bisynesse— [lawful]
> Well oghten we to doon al oure entente, [ought, do]
> Lest that the feend thurgh ydelnesse us hente [snatch]
>
> (8 [G]. 1–7)

The word "ministre" in the first line establishes a primary context against which resonates the later colloquy between Cecilia and Almachius regarding who ministers life and who ministers death. The abstract idea of Ydelnesse is clothed in the iconography of a literary figure (Oiseuse as Guillaume de Lorris's porter of the gate of delights), and the *Rose* is thereby firmly established as a negative mirror for what is to come. A second negative literary mirror, one from the *Canterbury Tales* itself, is called to mind by the way in which the Second Nun develops, in the third stanza, an image of "slouth" as a variant of that *desperatio* that, in its emphasis on eating and drinking as acts of devouring, echoes the sin driving the Pardoner:

> . . . ydelnesse is roten slogardye,
> Of which ther nevere comth no good n'encrees;
> And syn that slouthe hire holdeth in a lees [on a leash]
> oonly to slepe, and for to ete and drynke
> And to devouren al that othere swynke. . . . [other's work]
>
> (8 [G]. 17–21)

The Second Nun then turns from negative exempla to ascend a ladder of positive models by means of some quick shifts of address. She moves into apostrophe by addressing St. Cecilia directly, and then, with an intervening subtitle in Latin, *Invocacio ad Mariam,* moves further upward to address the Blessed Virgin Mary. She invokes as her

213

ally in addressing the Virgin Dante's own paradisal mediator, St. Bernard, "who list so wel to write." And her praise-song begins by translating the opening lines from the famous poem to the Virgin delivered by St. Bernard in the opening lines of canto 33 of Dante's *Paradiso:* "Thou Mayde and Mooder, doghter of thy Sone" [Vergine Madre, figlia del tuo figlio]. As the Second Nun uses Dante's Bernard as a mediate bridge between Cecilia and her Ur-figura, Mary, so Dante, in the very moment translated from the *Paradiso,* is using Bernard as a mediate bridge between Beatrice and *her* Ur-figura, the same Mary. Chaucer's implied relation, then, is that the lateral model of Cecilia is Beatrice. Thus the Beatrice of Dante joins the Cecilia of Jacobus to form a double set of mirrors, an intertextual context in which to view Chaucer's Cecilia. In sum, the prologue to the *Second Nun's Tale* establishes a dual axis of prior tradition against which we are directed to "read" the narrative of St. Cecilia: that of the hagiographic tradition, and that of the literary tradition running through the *Roman de la Rose* and the *Divina Commedia.*

The second mode of contextuality is intratextual. Chaucer can effect his own rich intentionality, despite maintaining extreme verbal fidelity to his appropriated model, by means of the associated contexts of other Canterbury narratives of spiritual transcendence. Here we think of the *Clerke's Tale* of Griselda, Prudence in the *Tale of Melibee,* and the *Man of Law's Tale* of Custance. But more than all of these, we think of the Second Nun's employer, the Prioress, and her tale of the boy-child, tossed into the privy with his throat cut, singing his song to the Virgin: *Alma Redemptoris.*

The indispensable work on Chaucer's use of sources for the *Second Nun's Tale* is gathered in two recent articles of Sherry Reames. In the first, she argues compellingly that Chaucer's identification of Jacobus de Voragine is a major oversimplification. In the second, she argues that if one examines the narrative in a descending line of authority— from the longer *Passio* to Jacobus to Chaucer—one finds decreasing emphasis on fecundity, fruitfulness, and the exercise of intelligent and reasoned choice. One also finds an increasingly severe insistence on blind faith over reason, and a related emphasis on the intervention of miracle. Her arguments are persuasive, yet only partially so. In her second article, she attacks Donald Howard for ignoring the hagiographic axis in favor of a contextual reading anchored in the *Canterbury Tales* itself.[16]

A standard argument runs that since the Cecilia narrative was composed long before the *Canterbury Tales*, it has a "meaning" established prior to the composition of the *Canterbury Tales*. Yet Howard insists that we owe it to ourselves as well as Chaucer to reread the *Second Nun's Tale* in the new context that his prologue (which is late, not early) sets: as a deliberate part of the *Canterbury Tales*.[17] I side with Howard here, not only on the grounds argued above by which Chaucer brings Beatrice to the fore as a model for understanding Cecilia, but also on the grounds that the immediate context in the *Canterbury Tales* doubly reinforces a reading of Cecilia in which she is to be viewed not as a figure *beyond* reason, but precisely as a figure *embodying* reason. She may appear, in Reames's terms, more "theologically pessimistic" when compared to her earlier manifestation in the longer *Passio;* but when one compares her to the boy in the *Prioress's Tale*, she is a model of Augustinian will, intelligence, and memory. For the sake of brevity, perhaps a schematic might be tolerated at this point, suggesting the major similarities and contrasts obtaining between the *Prioress's Tale* and the *Second Nun's Tale:*

Prioress's Tale	*Second Nun's Tale*
1. Little boy, little book	1. Mature woman, Augustine
2. Doesn't understand the words he sings	2. Knows exactly what she is talking about
3. Song: sings for three days after throat cut	3. Discourse: talks for three days after throat cut
4. Mere repetition of words	4. Developed reasoning of words
5. Folk converted by miracle	5. Folk converted by words
6. No trial (no words)	6. Trial (with words)
7. Will alone	7. Will, intelligence, memory
8. Grace alone	8. Grace and works
9. Faith alone	9. Faith and reason

Perhaps the most important concession the critic must make as we struggle with Chaucer's poetics, particularly in the case of these difficult tales of spirituality, is that a lot of things are going on at the same time. One important relationship Chaucer is clearly intent on orchestrating with care is his ordinated distance between his readers and his characters. In these spiritual tales it is crucial that we feel close enough to the central characters to generate sympathy sufficient to admit their humanity, and distant enough from them to feel the mystery of autonomy at their centers. We must be able to imagine them fully, but not explain them fully; the mystery at the center of human nature must be protected even as it is revealed.

One of the functions of rhyme royal is to accomplish this sense of middle distance. The form itself is so lapidarian that we can never quite suppress our sense of it as a medium that stands between us and the narrative just as much as it mediates the narrative to us and us to it. It spatializes the narrative by converting it from an illusionistic flow of time into the tesserae of associated *picturae,* rather like the lead-outlined images in a "narrative" depicted in stained glass. It also makes the narrative "precious."

Another factor involved in the distancing game is the overwhelming use of women as the figures of mediation. As suggested in earlier sections of this chapter, Chaucer makes capital on the very fact that at the center of all the male clichés about women is a profound ignorance. He can use this hollow center of the male imagination to good ends: he can place male images of women at precisely those narrative points where problem evolves into mystery, where common wisdom regarding the human situation evaporates and we feel most keenly the need for access to those mysterious resources at the center of human being that only figures of radical liminality, whether infernal, purgatorial, or paradisal, seem able to call up to our imagination.

Thus all three figures studied in this chapter can help us better see the role of the male-engendered-feminine as mediator of the mystery at the center of engodded humanity: the feminoid Pardoner, the feminine Wife (with a male edge to her tongue), and the saintly Cecilia as she out-mans Almachius.

Each of these Chaucerian "agents" is a figure of literary androgyny whose liminality reaches into domains of knowing and loving that in the ordinary way of the world are conventionally only possessed by one sex or the other. The telling power of the hermaphroditic convergence of these three "characters" is legitimated in the foundational text of Genesis. In the first part of *Genesis* 1.27 God creates man in His image: "*Et creavit Deus hominem ad imaginem suam.*" The second part consists of two mirroring halves, implying identification of each part with the other: "In the image of God created He him; male and female created He them" [*Ad imaginem Dei creavit illum, masculum et feminam creavit eos*]. Because of antiphonal, parallel placement, the singularity of the first half, creating "him" in God's image, is equated to the pluralizing act of creating "them" as male and female. The implied subequation insists that the plurality of male and female equals the singularity of humanity as created in the image of God: the *imago dei* is androgynous.

All of these male images of the female engage in forms of love and marriage: the Pardoner with the Self, the Wife of Bath with the Other, and Cecilia with God. All engage in their manipulation of words as readers of the authoritative text of Life: willful misreading on the part of the Pardoner; the imperfect reading of the Wife (who, with the blessing of St. Augustine, strays from the path but, guided by love, arrives at the right place in the end); and *recte legendi,* right reading, on the part of Cecilia. Each figure stands in a richly resonant relation to corresponding figures in the three canticles of Dante's *Divina Commedia.* By appropriating the *Commedia* as an ethical mirror for his pilgrims in this indirect, yet illuminating way, Chaucer aknowledges his heritage, even as he establishes himself as the sole, true "makere" of his book, a book from which, at the end, he "taketh his leve."

* * * * *

So far in this study we have discussed the mirroring functions of text and image (Virgil, Ovid, and Augustine), genre (Heinrich von Morungen and Chrétien de Troyes), and literary character (Dante and Chaucer). This has moved us always and irrevocably into the mirror problematics of literary discourse, of the reflexivity of literature altogether. These problems of literary catoptrics will continue to direct our attention: in the next chapter, we examine the figural powers of language itself, and finally, in the conclusion, the mirroring powers of literary closure.

CHAPTER 9

Speculum of the Logos:
Latin in Dante and Langland

> . . . this hot, dependent orator,
> The spokesman at our bluntest barriers. . . .
> He tries by a peculiar speech to speak
> The peculiar potency of the general,
> To compound the imagination's Latin with
> The lingua franca et jocundissima
> —Wallace Stevens, *Notes toward a Supreme Fiction*

Although as English as anything in the *Canterbury Tales*, *Piers Plowman* embodies more Latin quotation than any other vernacular work of comparable dimension.[1] There are 619 Latin quotations in the three redactions of the poem, 514 of which are taken from the Bible. They are spread throughout the work, in greater and lesser density, and they range from a snatched word, tag, or phrase to sentences and clusters of sentences. Many of them end in "etc.," indicating that more, but not telling how much more, text is thereby referenced.

Skeat, the first great editor of Langland, contented himself with remarking that the text is "crowded" with Latin.[2] In 1932, Sister Carmeline Sullivan published a dissertation that is essentially a catalog of all the Latin articulated in the A, B, and C texts of Skeats.[3] She makes some diffident yet perceptive observations on the more immediately apparent functions (marginal gloss, ethical reinforcement, etc.) and points out that there are places in the text where understanding of Latin is crucial for the lewd reader, but where the Latin nevertheless remains neither translated nor glossed. Nowhere does she point firmly to the occasional yet crucial *function* of Latin as riddle or as gloss; nor does she ever suggest that in a poem in which language is the vehicle for meaning, and in which meaning is the prime and explicit object of the pilgrim's search, the consistently intrusive presence of an alternative language may possess a programmatic function.

More recent work focuses on the contexts of quotation, thereby richly enhancing our sense of the worlds of texts from which these tags come. But, with the exception of the recent work of John Alford, there still seems to be a lack of systematic attention to how these texts function in the larger text of *Piers Plowman* as a whole.[4] Alford reconstructs Langland's use of biblical and patristic concordance as a means of determining significant aspects of structure in the poem. This chapter will address the iconic and metaphorical functions of the presence of latinity in Langland's vernacular text.

A great deal of the criticism of the poem has been generically oriented. The assumption is reasonable enough: If we can find out what kind of poem it is, we will be in a better position to assess what it means. All these studies prove valuable; none exclusively convincing. Charles Muscatine seems very near the mark when he reiterates the various medieval gestalts that reverberate within the poem (modulation, dialectic, procession) and their related generic conventions (dream-vision, romance, allegory, sermon, etc.) and concludes that "the first thing to be observed about Langland is that although his work bears traces of almost all the large formal resources I have mentioned, it is finally controlled and explained by none of them."[5] No matter how cunningly critics reach for a metaphor of sustained coherence, most admit the presence of a fundamental and disturbing tendency toward instability, whether linguistic, rhetorical, generic, or even moral. This instability must be reckoned with, and I agree with Muscatine again when he insists that to refuse the threat of "an artistic breakdown" would be to refuse something fundamental about the artist and his epoch that the work is telling us.[6]

Muscatine then abandons the generic approach in favor of an all-too-brief examination of the ways in which Langland organizes space. Quite independently, Frank Goodridge, in the introduction to his translation of the B text, suggests, in a few tantalizing sentences, that one might also look at the ways in which Langland organizes (and disorganizes and reorganizes) time.[7] Continued pursuit of Langland's strategies for shaping the coordinates of space and time might well provide a clearer sense of the implied ontology of Langland's narrative mode; this would certainly bring us greater confidence as readers of this difficult, searching, and always shifting poem.

Some of the more recent work on *Piers Plowman* is most powerful as it reaches for Langland's epistemology as a way of dealing with the poem's deep instability. Of particular interest is the work of Julia Bolton Holloway and Laurie A. Finke. Holloway integrates *Piers* into the context of a broad-ranging discussion of paradigm shifts evident in pilgrimage narratives, concentrating on Dante and Chaucer as well as Langland. Finke reassesses the poststructuralist critique of allegory by Paul de Man and J. Hillis Miller and approaches *Piers* with a fresh sense of the presence of Augustinian incarnational thinking.[8] In line with these new directions, I hope to examine the ways in which the alternation of Latin and the vernacular in *Piers* figures forth the medieval sense of the human dialectic between epistemology and ontology in the face of the divine.

What we need is a model that displays iconically or schematically the values of each language (Latin and vernacular) as present in the medieval set of expectations. We should not be surprised if language, like any overarching social structure or process, generates ambivalence in the society it serves: we should not be surprised if both Latin and the vernacular, as they interact with other sociopolitical structures and processes, accrue both positive and negative values. And we should not be surprised if we find much of what we need for the construction of such a model in Dante.

First we have Dante's explicit, yet by no means consonant, remarks on Latin and the vernacular in the *Convivio* and *De Vulgari Eloquentia*. He insists, albeit in two different places, that each language is *nobilior* than the other.

In *De Vulgari* he says, in Latin, that the vernacular is nobler because it is natural and useful (and not artificial like Latin):

Harum quoque duarum nobilior est vulgaris: tum quia prima fuit humano generi usitata . . . tum quia naturalis est nobis, cum illa potius artificialis existat.[9]

Ten years later, in the *Convivio,* Dante says, in Italian, that Latin is sovereign over the vernacular in its nobility:

. . . non era subietto ma sovrano, e per nobiltà e per vertù e per bellezza. Per nobiltà, perche lo latino e perpetuo e non corrutibile. . . . [10]

In this newer context, then, Latin is nobler because it is immutable and perpetual and not corruptible like the vernacular.

Cecil Grayson opens his essay on the intricacies of this apparent contradiction by suggesting that this has become all but a *punctum dolens* in Dante studies.[11] And yet the contradiction is largely verbal, although a real tension exists. Here is a draft of a working schematic of resolution:

Latin:
  Positive: perpetual, incorruptible
  Negative: artificial

Vernacular:
  Positive: natural, useful
  Negative: unstable, mutable, corruptible

Dante provides much additional indirect assistance in both the *Vita Nuova* and the *Commedia.* One recalls the impressive dream of Amor in chapter 12 of the *Vita Nuova,* in which the god appears as a young man in white, reminiscent of the figure in white at Christ's tomb on Easter morning. Amor sighs and speaks in a Latin resonant with St. Paul's meditations on childhood and childish things. *"Fili mi, tempus est ut pretermictantur simulacra nostra"* [My son, it is time to put away our fictions]. This sentence makes no appreciable dent on the dreaming boy, and Amor falls to weeping. The boy asks, in Italian, "Segnore de la nobiltade, e perché piangi tu?" [But why, noble Sir, do you weep?] And then Amor answers in Latin, *"Ego tanquam centrum circuli, cui simili modo se habent circumferentie partes; tu autem non sic"* [I am like the center of the circle, equidistant from all points, but you are not]. The boy again fails to understand this reply at any level of engagement as an answer to his question and asks, in Italian, why his partner speaks "con tanta oscuritade" [with so much obscurity]. At this point Amor shifts from Latin to the vernacular and says, "Non dimandare più che utile ti sia" [Don't ask for more than is useful to you].[12] The failure of Amor's Latin rests not with Dante the Poet (as Curtius seems to imply) nor with the Latin itself, nor with Amor, but with the boy who is not at the center.[13]

The reason he is not at the center has to do with a failure of heart, nerve, intelligence, imagination, and love. As Amor, weeping, shifts from Latin to the vernacular, we see that move from one language to another as a figure of the *descensus ad humanitatem,* a stooping of Grace to the limitations of humanity. Latin is the higher mode of mediation between God and man; in the Bible and in the liturgy it is the vehicle of revelation, the mediator of first and last things. The narrator-boy, an invention of memory, trapped in the vernacular, is simply all unready, too fraught with middle; thus Amor stoops to conquer. In the *Vita Nuova,* then, the two languages are in significant tension; their value systems are in essential opposition and this reflects the primal disjunction between the eternal and the merely living.

In the *Purgatorio* and *Paradiso,* Latin generally comes in single lines that rhyme (more than phonetically) with the Italian in which they are embedded. Usually the Latin functions apodictically. It is as if in the great but momentary soarings of mind toward the *apex mentis* of truth, sudden proximity to deity reveals itself quasi-mimetically in the hieratic Latin of biblical and liturgical quotation. The corporate wisdom of the ages flashes through the narrative of a unique, personal history, and in this verbal flash, Latin functions momentarily as a radical apex of discourse, a mirror of the Divine Logos itself. The embedding of Latin within the vernacular is an iconic representation of the timeless in the schemes of time and thus suggests itself as a "backgrounding" figure of the world as redeemed by the Incarnation: the Word, or Logos, made Flesh.

To get a vivid sense of biblical quotation in Latin as a trope of the presence of God, it is only necessary to recuperate a vivid sense of the text itself as privileged, as itself a divinely instituted *imago* of the Incarnation: for the Bible is a continuous exemplar of the hypostatic union of God and Man insofar as it is the Divine Word made into the flesh of human language.

Evidence for negative aspects of Latin within the medieval set of expectations is legion. The richest tapestry for this is the *Canterbury Tales* and the extraordinary range of anticlericism Chaucer presents there. In addition, medieval drama and Langland's great poem itself are both pervaded by the attitudes of lay piety and fraught with instances of complaint against the use of Latin as a confidence trick to milk the unlettered multitudes.

We can now expand sufficiently our working schematic of values assignable to Latin and the vernacular:

Latin:
  Positive: perpetual, incorruptible; vehicle for revelation
  Negative: artificial; vehicle for fraud

Vernacular:
  Positive: natural, useful; language of the pilgrimage
  Negative: unstable, mutable, corruptible; mode of misunderstanding, un
  knowing, and error

Turning now to Langland, we see that, like the *Commedia, Piers Plowman* begins in disorder and early sorrow; radically unlike the *Commedia, Piers Plowman* ends in disorder and final sorrow. Langland's poem has the curves of Phaeton's flight; joy and insight, reconciliation and consolation are always fleeting, always penultimate. Dialectic does not counter entropy; it furthers it, and, as with Dante's infernal figure of the Old Man of Crete, tears of recognition serve only to feed the rivers of Hell.

To begin with, the poem as a whole as well as each of its parts or sections is framed in latinity. Skeat does not print a title as such for the A version, but B begins "INCIPIT LIBER DE PETRO PLOWMAN," which C amplifies to "HIC INCIPIT VISIO WILLELMI DE PETRO PLOUHMAN." Then each section of the poem is titled as a *passus,* a kind of step, and A concludes with *"Explicit Dowel,"* B with *"Explicit hic dialogus Petri Plowman,"* and C with *"Explicit Peeres Plouheman."* One can make too little and too much of this. It should suffice to point out that the framing of the vernacular with latinity lends a certain dignity, a sense of limit, reach, reference, and division that indirectly implies the elevation of vernacular English to a certain degree of poetic and doctrinal adequacy. This use of rubric also reflects the organizing principle informing the deployment of text in the Vulgate Bible. Thus the framing power of the Latin rubrics in organizing a vast and varied vernacular middle in *Piers* functions iconically as an image of the divine plan, the context within which our human, quotidian dramas play themselves out.

The prologue in all versions displays the famous "fair field full of folk," which is bounded above by the high tower and below by the dark dungeon. The allegorical force of this deployment of images may seem obvious to the reader, but the folk appear unaware of any organization of their field along the tower/dungeon axis and simply mill about. The king enters the field and with him the expectation of at least a secular order. Suddenly the people (in English) and a descending angel (in Latin) urge the king to act with mercy as well as justice. As matters seem to be moving toward some sort of social contract, a "glutton of words" speaks out in warning:

> Thanne greued hym a goliardeys y a glotoun of wordes,
> And to the angel an hei3 y answered after,
> *"Dum rex a regere y dicatur nomen habere,*
> *Nomen habet sine re y nisi studet iura tenere."*
> And thanne gan alle the commune y crye in vers of Latin,
> To the kynges conseille y construe ho-so-wolde—
> *"Precepta Regis y sunt nobis vincula legis."*
> With that ran there a route y of ratones at ones,
> And smale mys myd hem y mo then a thousande.
>
> (B Prologue, 139–47)[14]

Skeat assumed that *Sum rex, sum princeps* was probably Langland's invention.[15] J. A. W. Bennett has found the lines "on f. 147v of Ms. Lambeth 61, where they follow a sermon preached by Henry Harclay in 1315 whilst he was Chancellor of Oxford."[16] G. R. Owst argues that the angel is really Thomas Brunton, bishop of Rochester; that the goliard is Sir Peter de la Mare, spokesman of the Commons; and that the people suddenly shouting in Latin are backing him to the hilt.[17] First, I fail to see how the line of Latin the people shout backs up the goliard's legal distinction. The goliard is insisting that the king is king only as long as he maintains the law, whereas the people say his decrees have power equal to the law. More important, the ruminations of Bennett and Owst, as important as they are in any effort to link this text into a correct historical context, do nothing to help us understand what is going on in the text itself. Like the field, tower, and dungeon, the entire Latin colloquy is all pietistic portent without clue.

It is important to notice that although I have provided translations of the Latin, Langland does not: it goes unglossed and untranslated in the Middle English text. Thus all the dual-language colloquy really does is tell us two not unrelated things: (*a*) that there is tension between law and power, and (*b*) that to speak in Latin makes certain claims regarding rank, class, and authority. In fact, the scene is little more than a shouting match silenced by a radical shift in image to rats and mice and a debate among suddenly imagined rodents (a debate that proceeds with far more clarity than the one just ended among humans) about whether, and if so, how, to bell the cat. Although this little beast fable seems clear enough as an image of political instability in the face of time and fate, the narrator says, vatically, that the reader must interpret the dream image on his own. The rats disappear, the folk reappear, and, with cries of "God save ye, Dame Emma," and "Hot pies! Hot pies!" the prologue comes to a close. For all their energy and brilliant color, the images in the prologue lack an informing scale and are oddly anticipatory of the pell-mell scenes of Breughel; the Latin is hardly more than noise.

Passus 1 is a lecture delivered by Holychurch, interlaced with queries by the dreaming narrator, the implied author, Long Will. His two crucial questions concern meaning and salvation, and he will be some time discovering that they are the same thing. Looking at the disordered landscape of his dream, Will's eyes are drawn to the field of folk, and he asks Holychurch what it all means. Holychurch begins, not with the field, but with the tower, saying that its inhabitant is Truth (God), and that He is the proper goal of any quest for meaning. Will persists in seeking further instruction about the world, and Holychurch recapitulates the "render unto Caesar" episode from the gospel. She reiterates enough of the story so that the most inattentive reader knows where he is. When she comes to Christ's answer, she says: " '*Reddite Cesari*,' said God, 'what belongs to *Cesari, et que sunt dei, deo,* or else you do wrongly'" (B 1.52–53). The ease with which Christ engages in bilingualism indicates that in his mouth, as opposed to the mouths of the folk in the field, both languages are in some sort of accord. I shall expand on the nature and implication of this linguistic accord shortly, after further exploration of the thematic implications of this scene.

Deciding on what is Caesar's and what is God's demands knowledge of this world and the next and an awareness of Augustine's distinctions between use and enjoyment. And yet what is the ultimate criterion of corrigibility for making the right distinction in an ambiguous world, or in an ambiguous text? For in *Piers Plowman* world and word are one. Right reason, operating rationally, operates at Will's direction, but Will's actions are driven by the irrational impulse to love. Thus his second question of Holychurch, "How may I save my soul?" is intimately linked with his first, "What does this all mean?" She replies,

"When all treasures are tested, Truth is best. And to prove it and test what is true, I appeal to the text, *deus caritas*" (B 1.85–86). So we, if not Long Will, begin to see just how inextricably loving and knowing (and English and Latin, for that matter) are bound together in the search for Truth. This is sound Augustinian doctrine. In his *De Doctrina Christiana,* Augustine sets the rule for dealing with apparent Scriptural ambiguity:

Therefore in consideration of figurative expressions, a rule such as this will serve: that what is read should be subjected to diligent scrutiny until an interpretation contributing to the reign of charity is produced. If this result appears literally in the text, the expression being considered is not figurative.[18]

In his world as text, Will proves an extremely poor reader. He consistently makes two kinds of mistakes: he confuses the sign with the signified—i.e., he is unable to distinguish when the text, a given image in his dream, is literal and when figural—and he is unable, despite constant instruction, to apply the rule of love to interpretation. I amplify my remarks on these opening sections simply because they embody the fundamental problem of the poem: in a world of text, salvation is a matter of *recte legendi,* right reading. And when the stakes are that high, it behooves one to attend with extra care if and when that "wordworld" is driven in two languages.

The central panel of the *Visio,* the first great dream section of the poem, is devoted to the adventures of Lady Meed. This is a dramatic personification allegory of the highest order, a magnificent romp. Curiously enough, the dramatic "problem" is one of lexicology: when all is said and done, what does the word *Meed* really mean? In personification allegory, our primary image is of Words (such as Meed) getting married, getting sued, going to court, losing the suit, and being cast out for a whore. This is the literally literal level: these Words doing these Things. As Augustine says, all signs are things. But because not all things are signs, we are, in personification allegory, forced into a tighter mode of interpretation than usual. The issue with Meed is what she means: "reward" or "bribe." Reason and Conscience prosecute her for meaning bribery. They win the case by getting the votes, primarily by means of an admixture of rhetorical suasion and threat. Thus the problem of what Meed means is solved dramatically rather than argued epistemologically. And it is fitting that the role of Latin in the scene also be dramatic rather than epistemic. It is used as a rhetorical weapon in the courtroom battle, both by Conscience in his prosecution and by Lady Meed in her defense (again, to gain a sense of the power of the Latin in the original text, one must remember that the phrases translated here for convenience are *not* translated in Langland's text):

> But to Mohamet and Meed, will mishap come in time,
> for *melius est bonum nomen quam diuicie multe*
> {A good name is rather to be chosen than great riches].
> Mad as wind, grew Meed in a moment.
> "I don't know any Latin," she said, "Clerks know that's the truth.
> See what Solomon says in the book of Wisdom,
> that he that gives gifts, wins the victory,
> and much worship has withal, as holywrit tells,
> *Honorem adquiret qui dat munera, etc."* [gift givers get honor]
> "I agree mylady," said Conscience, "that your Latin hits true;
> But you are like a lady that once read a lesson,
> T'was: *omnia probate* {Try everything]; it pleased her heart.
> The line seemed no longer, it was at the end of a page.
> Had she seen the line's ending, if she'd turned the page,
> She would have found more words following these,
> *quod bonum est, tenete* [Hold fast to that which is good],
> which made the text true. And thusly you fared, madame!
> You could find no more, though you looked on Wisdom, sitting in
> your study. . . . but if you seek Wisdom often, you'll find what
> follows, a full bitter text, for him who takes Meed,
> and that is *animam autem aufert accipientium"* [But he taketh away
> the soul of him that receiveth bribes].

(B 3.328–46)

In passus 7, the last in the *Visio,* the problem of right reading is itself the core of the dramatic action. Truth sends Piers a pardon. A priest says, "Let me read your pardon, Piers. I will construe each article for you and explain it in English." He opens the pardon and begins to read, with Will reading over his shoulder. The pardon contains two lines of Latin: "*Et qui bona egerunt, ibunt in vitam eternam; Qui vero mala, in ignem eternum.*" "Peter," says the Priest, "I can find no pardon here. All I find is, 'Do-well and you will have well and God shall have thy

228

soul; Do-evil, and you will have evil, and the Devil shall have thy soul.'" Piers, in pure rage, tears the pardon to pieces, saying, "*Si ambulavero in medio umbre mortis, no timebo mala; quoniam tu mecum est*" [Yea, though I walk through the valley of the shadow of death, I will fear no evil, for Thou art with me]. Piers continues, "I shall cease my sowing, and not work so hard, nor worry so much about my belly-joy. From now on my plow will be penance and prayers." The priest and Piers begin to argue, and Will awakens (summary and quotations drawn from B 7.106–19).

The role Latin plays in this scene is definitive. Both the text of the pardon and the prayer of Piers are in Latin. In fourteenth-century England, ruined by the plague and threatened with civil war, lay piety and anticlericism rode high. There is an attendant ambivalence toward Latin. As suggested above, Latin, as the language of Scripture and the institution of the Church, is the vehicle of true revelation. As the language of the Church's officers, it can also be a vehicle of deception. In right use, moving from sign to signification in love, Latin leads to salvation. Used wrongly, Latin becomes a powerful tool of the enemy within. The fact that both the text of the pardon and the prayer of Piers are in Latin indicates that the problem here is not in the language of the text but in right reading.

Readers typically find it difficult to accept the tearing of the pardon as a good thing, sent, as it was, directly from God. They make the same mistake in reading that the priest makes. He mistakes the sign for the thing signified; he assumes that right words in right distribution on the right piece of paper constitute an act of divine pardon. This scene approaches a dramatization of a celebrated passage in Augustine:

He is a slave to a sign who uses or worships a significant thing without knowing what it signifies. But he who uses or worships a useful sign divinely instituted whose signifying force he understands does not worship what he sees and passes away, but rather that to which all such things are to be referred. Such a man is spiritual and free.[19]

Pier's anger is directed at the priest and his error, not at any specious duplicity in the pardon. An analogue from the Old Testament proves helpful:

And it came to pass, as soon as he came nigh unto the camp, that he saw the calf, and the dancing: and Moses' anger waxed hot, and he cast the tables out of his hands, and brake them beneath the mount. (Exodus 32.19)

Like Moses, Piers moves from the sign that he destroys to its (and his own) true signification: he prays the prayer of the pilgrim and abandons the plow for the prayers and the penance that it signifies. He has, indeed, followed the implicit commandment of the pardon; he is doing well. Will, the dreamer of all this, appears to get a glimmer of understanding, for he starts to use Piers as a *speculum,* as a glass in which he begins to see, however darkly, his own possibility of redemption.[20]

The last and longest part of the poem consists of the "lives" of Do-Well, Do-Better, and Do-Best. Do-Well (passus 8–14) portrays Will's search, in several dimensions, for Do-Well. Do-Better (15–18) presents Will's observance of the pattern of redemption as figured in the life of Christ. Do-Best (19–20) shows Will dreaming of the signifying pattern of apocalypse, figured antiphonally in images of universal and personal history.

Will makes it clear to us, particularly in the C version, that he has had a great deal of education and training. As he searches for Do-Well, then, it is more than slightly ironic that he consistently errs in method. He moves from one intriguing source of information to another; in dream after dream he catechizes Thought, Intelligence, Study, Learning, Scripture, and, in a deep dream-within-a-dream, Fortune and Trajan, Imagination and Anima. Yet no one can answer his question satisfactorily because he asks it incorrectly. He assumes Do-Well is a person, a quality, or a word: an interesting case of personification allegory backfiring in the act of reading. Infatuated with sign, he nevertheless fails to realize that this sign is an imperative verb, commanding the action of doing well.

With all the familiar orneriness of the prideful intellectual, he assumes that the inadequacy in the situation resides not in himself, but in these dreamed images of human faculties, and he reacts with rabid anti-intellectualism. With great wit, Langland has him lay out his theory of know-nothingism to Learning in a parody of scholastic dispute, replete with a passage out of Augustine, read wickedly out of context:

Ecce ipsi idioti repiunt celum, ubi nos sapientes in inferno mergimur [Lo, the ignorant arise and take heaven by force, while we, with all our wisdom, are plunged into hell]; which means, to Englishmen, neither more nor less than, "None are sooner ravished from right belief than those cunning clerks that know many books; and none are sooner saved or are firmer in faith than plowmen and shepherds and poor common laborers."

(B 10.455–59)

Faith and Reason, central counters in the dialectics of medieval thought, are here embodied in a psychomachia between Will and Understanding. Scripture has the last word and, as others do on occasion in the poem, lays on Long Will a Latin scourge:

Then Scripture . . . blamed me in Latin . . . and said, *"multi multa sciunt, et seipsos nesciunt"* [many know much, but do not know themselves]. Whereat I wept for woe and the anger of her speech, and in ill humor fell asleep.

(B 11.1–4)

Sunk into a dream-within-a-dream (he dreams he falls asleep), two mirrors of middle earth are displayed to him, but the "ill humor" in which he dreams lasts forty-five years and prevents him from reading those mirrors with the rule of love. He awakes back to the level of his primary dream to encounter Ymaginatyf, a figure who seems to combine a neo-Aristotelian faculty of imagination (which converts sensual data into images) with the faculty of memory. Ymaginatyf helps Will begin correcting his vision. Ymaginatyf's definitions of Do-Well provide a semantic frame that suggests right action: "Paul in his epistle . . . proves what Do-Well is: *Fides, spes, caritas*" (B 12.30). In addition he provides Will with a hint of the complex relationship that obtains between knowing and loving in a fallen world. Note how Latin and English function in contrapuntal fashion in the following passage:

Clergy and Natural Wit come of sight and teaching as the Book bears witness to those who can read: *Quod scimus loquimur; quod vidimus, testamur* [What we know we speak, what we see, we testify]. Clergy comes of *quod scimus,* as does knowledge of heaven; Natural Wit comes of *quod vidimus,* of what diverse people see. But grace is a gift of God and springs from great love. Never a clerk knew how it comes forth, nor natural wit the ways, *Nescit aliquis unde venit, aut quo vadit* [Thou knowst not, whence it cometh or whither it goeth].

Yet clergy is to be commended, and natural wit as well, and especially clergy, for the love of Christ is the root of clergy.

(B 12.66–73)

This is not the most lucid excursus on the relationship between divine love and human intellect that has come down to us. Yet the very confusion reveals how powerfully the poem is driven by the central idea of its age: Incarnation. It is Incarnation that informs and renders intelligible the created world—but there is a limit to our capacity to know it. The *what* (or *quia*) is intelligible; the *why*, emanating from the Trinity, is not. As one would expect, Dante's Virgil says far more than Ymaginatyf, and says it with far greater clarity:

> Bodies like mine, to bear pain, cold and heat,
>   That power ordains, whose will forever spreads
>   A veil between its working and our wit.
> Madness! that reason lodged in human heads
>   Should hope to traverse backward and unweave
>   The infinite path three-personed Substance treads.
> Content you with the *quia*, sons of Eve,
>   For had you power to see the whole truth plain
>   No need had been for Mary to conceive.[21]

One of the high points in the poem is the Banquet of Clergye (Learning) in passus 13. The densest point in the passus is a discussion in which Latin, once again, proves pivotal. Conscience asks Clergy to speak about Do-Well, and he answers:

A certain Piers Plowman has impugned us all, and set all sciences at a sop save love alone . . . and saith that Do-Well and Do-Better are two infinites, which infinites, by faith, discover Do-Best, which shall save man's soul.

(B 13.123–29)

Anne Middleton has suggested that here, at last, someone in the poem has begun to sort out the grammar of the problem. She points out that the Middle English "infinite" not only means "incomplete in itself" but is also the grammatical term for the infinitive aspect of a verb.[22] Patience then casts his gloss directly into the imperative form:

232

Disce [Learn!] . . . *doce* [Teach!], *dilige inimicos* [Love your enemies!]; *Disce* and Do-Well; *doce* and Do-Better; *Dilige* and Do-Best. Thus a beloved I loved taught me: Love was her name.

(B 13.136–39)

Here a possible matrix for solving the knowing/loving problem is displayed by laying out the elements in an order of ascent and by the repeated alternation of Latin "text" and English "gloss." It is first and foremost a linguistic, or grammatical, matrix. We begin the analytic breakdown of the problem by laying the elements out in the paradigms of adverbial possibility (positive, comparative, superlative: well, better, best). Then the realm of knowing is located in the language of time and space (English). And for limited us, the glossing direction moves from loving to knowing; the English glosses the Latin. Later on, Langland will show us moments in which the glossing goes the other way.

Patience's last gift to the discussion at the Banquet of Learning is a verbal riddle that has still to be solved to everyone's satisfaction. He weaves the words of the riddle as if they formed a thing to be opened and then insists it makes him invincible:

I carry Do-Well about with me . . . bound fast within these words—in a sign of that Saturday which first set the calendar, and the wit of the Wednesday the next week after; from the middle of the moon springs the power of them both. As long as I have it with me, I am welcome everywhere. . . . If you take this charm with you, neither pain nor poverty shall ever trouble you. *Caritas nichel timet* [Love fears nothing]. And by the might of this riddle you shall have at your asking absolute power over Earls and Emperors, Kings and Barons, Popes, and Patriarchs.

(B 13.152–66)

Whatever calendrical calculations are here implied, the force of the riddle has less to do with numbers and dates than with our sure invulnerability in the face of historical pressures brought by love.[23] The Latin phrase points to John. In the C version, Langland moves even more explicitly in that direction, where his "*Caritas expellit omnem timorem*" [Love expells all fear] paraphrases "*Perfecta caritas foras mittet timorem*" [Perfect love casts out all fear] (1 John 4.8). In a reversal of normal pattern, it is Latin that valorizes, if it does not finally illuminate, the riddle of English.

Passus 15 is transitional, leading into the second major narrative panel, the Life of Do-Better, in which the life of Christ is brilliantly and surreally woven into Will's dream of middle earth. Before this can begin, Will must be instructed into a more adequate theory of knowledge than lexical definition can provide. Thus he meets Anima. Anima has neither tongue nor teeth, but that doesn't stop Will. As he dreams the image he asks its name, assuming, as usual, that a name is an explanation. Anima then provides in the answer a model of a higher order of complexity than Will has previously been subjected to. Anima moves from name to function, and drawing authority from both Augustine and Isidore of Seville, says:

When I quicken the body I am called *Anima* (Life); but when I will and wish, my name is *Animus,* and since I know and understand, I am also called *Mens* (Mind) and when I make moan to God, my name is *Memoria;* when I make judgements and do as truth teaches, they call me *Racio,* Reason in English; when I hear what others say, my first name is *Sensus* . . . when I do or do not claim anything, then I am called Conscience; when I truly love our Lord, then I am called True Love, or *Amor* in Latin; and when I fly from the flesh and forsake the body, I am speechless spirit and am called *Spiritus.*

(B 15.23–36)

In Anima's mode of self-exegesis, name signifies action or function. And because of the way in which Latin and English act interchangeably with one another as glosses, name and function achieve a degree of equal, interdependent weight and validity. Will, of course, misses the point. He replies, "You're like a Bishop . . . they also have many names, *presul,* and *pontifex* and *metropolitanus* . . . *episcopus* and *pastor*" (B 15.40–43). Anima is not amused. Although Will always improves, he never does so to the point of adequacy; that is the most endearing and tiresome thing about him. It is also crucial to an understanding of his signification. He is Long Will, the Dreamer, but he also figures forth, of course, the psychological faculty of Will as well.

Fittingly enough, the discussion then turns to the nature of charity. In the course of the talk, Will reveals a certain improvement in his epistemology, although he still tends toward acceptance of name as explanation:

Clergy teaches me that Christ is in all places but I have never seen him really, except as myself in a mirror, *Ita in enigmate, tunc facie ad faciem* [Now darkly, then face to face].

(B 15.156–57)

Clergy says he never has seen Christ directly, only as he mirrors Christ forth: this he sees when he sees his own image in a looking glass. As Clergy links the *imago dei* of Genesis with the *per speculum in aenigmate* of 1 Corinthians, Will begins to win the values to be won in the speculative mode of knowing. He is delighted with Anima's discourse on Charity and exuberantly declares his desire to see "him" face to face. Anima says that is impossible without Piers Plowman, who sees more deeply into the nature of the human will than any cleric. Anima continues:

therefore not by colors nor by clergy shall you ever know him, nor through words nor works, but through will alone. And no clerk knows it, no creature on earth, but Piers the Plowman, *Petrus, id est, Christus.*

(B 15.203–6)

Here Anima provides the first explicit speculum in the poem of the figural relation that signifies the ladder of redemption. Piers is imagined as a local, historic, unique character, but in a redeemed world, he also figures forth and is a type, not only of Christ's first vicar, but, in the anagogical leap of Christian thinking, of Christ himself. At a point later in the dream vision, Christ jousts on the cross, hidden in Pier's "armour," glossed by Langland as *humana natura:* again the Latin serves as a gloss of the English; it is in the Latin, the mirror of divine nature, that we see the perfected image of our own. At another time Piers appears, bloody, carrying a cross. These images are dramatic displays of the specular power of the figural relation in poetic action— in fact they are only intelligible in the light of the figural relation.

The Life of Do-Better closes with the magnificent Harrowing of Hell. This declares the triumph of Christ and the triumph of the world. Here Latin speaks in such perfect accord with English that one moves toward musical analogy. Christ comes to Hell as light:

And the light bade them unlock and Lucifer answered,
"What lord art thou?" Lucifer said, *"quis est iste?"*

235

"*Rex glorie*," the Light soon said.
"And the Lord of might and main, and of all manner
of virtues *dominus virtutem;*
Dukes of this dim place, straightway unbar the gates that
Christ may come in, the Son of Heaven's King."
(B 18.312–18)

In the following celebration of the Four Daughters of God, which is accompanied by angels singing and harping, the musical analogy is no longer farfetched:

Many hundreds of angels harped and sang:
Culpat caro, purgat caro; regnat deus dei caro [the flesh
sins, the flesh atones for sin, the flesh of God reigns as God]
Then Peace piped a note of poetry:
clarior est solito post maxima nebula phebus,
post inimicitias clarior est et amor.
"After sharp showers," said Peace, "the sun is most brilliant;
there's no warmer weather than after watery clouds
nor no love lovelier, nor no friend dearer
than after war and woe, when Love and Peace are masters.
There was never a war in the world, nor evil so keen,
that Love, if he wished, could not bring to laughter
and Peace, through Patience, put an end to all perils."
(B 18.405–15)

These perfect accords of Latin and English function as linguistic metaphors of the reconciliation of opposites in Peace's song. The accord is a kind of linguistic figure of the hypostatic union in the triumph of redemption.

Passus 19 and 20, the Life of Do-Best, bring the poem to closure. After the establishment of *Unitas,* the Church, the poem moves mercilessly from triumph to dissolution to apocalyptic nightmare. Conscience tries to withstand the siege of all the sins of the world, and a crucial aspect of that battle is his attempt to maintain the integrity of language. There is willful misreading of the cardinal virtues, always called by their Latin names. The meanings slip; things fly apart. When the friars offer to assist, Conscience is perturbed that their number appears to be infinite. He urges them to:

236

Leave logic and learn to love. . . . And if you desire a cure, Nature will teach you that God made all manner of things in measure and set them at a certain and at a limited number . . . and named them new names and numbered the stars; *Quia numerat multitudinem stellarum* [He telleth the number of the stars]. . . . It is wicked to pay you [friars] any wages, you grow beyond number! Why, even Heaven itself has a fixed number of souls; only Hell is without number.

(B 20.249–68)

One cannot hear Conscience quoting the Psalms (the last significant Latin quotation in the poem) and bravely joke about Hell without sensing that he has put his finger on what is so utterly wrong: there is at the end of *Piers Plowman* (as at the beginning) no order of rule. The structural repetition is balanced by verbal repetition. Witnessing the universal breakdown, Will himself is mortally wounded by Death. He pleads to Nature for assistance, and Nature suggests he seek shelter in the crumbling House of Unity and wait until he is sent for. She also advises him to learn a craft. "What would you advise?" he asks. "Learn to love," says Nature, "leave off all the rest." The end recalls the beginning; the question and the answer are the same. One may be sympathetic to Elizabeth Salter's idea that Langland is anticipating Eliot, but there is not much evidence that Will actually "knows the place for the first time" when he finally arrives there.[24]

As sad and unsatisfying as Langland's final images may be, the ground rules of the poem call for them. The poem is millenarian, true to Langland's own time and to Scriptural revelation: fourteenth-century England, if not "the promised end," was certainly an apt "image of that horror." Dante must deal with this too, and does. But he embodies it in a showpiece allegory, the transformation of the Cart of the Church near the end of the *Purgatorio*. Dante the Poet stages the vision for Dante the Pilgrim much like Prospero stages the wedding masque for Ferdinand and Miranda. It is safe, performed in postlapsarian Eden, an island where nobody real really resides, not even a Caliban. The sense of hopelessness and helplessness we have in *Piers* is partly due to the fact that we witness the disintegration of *Unitas* through Will's dying eyes—we are dramatically trapped in his vision and cannot escape his point of view. We are freed from the poem, and from his vision, only by the last three words, when, hearing Conscience calling loudly on Grace, he releases us at last with the words: "I gan awake."

237

Dante's formal strategies reveal a profound and consistent intuition with regard to *telos*. The middle always makes sense because it is structured and hermetically enclosed in beginning and end. Langland is merely fraught with middle. Like Chaucer, he begins in the middle and he leaves in the middle. He does, after all, deal with the world of the living, the world of choice and error. Clarity for Dante is only possible in the world of the dead, where all decisions have been made and freedom exhausted. In a living, lapsed world, meaning is difficult because language slips and slides; people are still making up their minds as to what it is they want to say. But Langland's figures, as they speak their nonce English, speak against the Latin echos of a revealed, divine design. English is the mode of *Piers;* the Latin within it provides a speculum for the reader in which he can see language *qua* language: see its functions, its fate, and its promise—a promise that can only be totally fulfilled by the *Verbum,* the Logos that is Christ; and Christ triumphs fully only on the other side of death.

I would like to bring this discussion to a close with a brief consideration of a poem that, although something of a showpiece, has not been discussed in the recent major works on medieval lyric.[25] It is a Marian poem, probably of the early thirteenth century, and it pulls out a great number of stops. It is in two languages and develops, by brilliant intersection of the principles of verisimilitude and ordination, a linguistic figure of the Incarnation that is anticipatory of the figural power of dual-language structures we have discovered in the poetics of Dante and Langland:

> Of oon that is so faire and bright
>> *Velud maris stella* [as the star of the sea]
> Brighter thanne the dayes light
>> *Parens et puella* [mother and maiden]
> I crie to thee, thou see to me
> Lady preye thy Sone for me
>> *Tam pia* [so gracious]
> That I moot come to thee,
>> *Maria*
>
> Of care counseil thou are best
>> *Felix fecundata* [happy the wombfruit]
> Of alle wery thou art reste,
>> *Mater onorata* [honored Mother]

Beseech thou Him wyth mylde mood,
That for us alle shedde His blood
 In cruce [on the cross]
That we mote come to Him
 In luce [in the light]

Al this world was forlorn
 Eva peccatrice [through sinning Eve]
Til oure Lord was i-born
 De te genetrice [of thee genetrix]
Wyth *Ave* it went away
Thester nyght and cam the day [thester = dark]
 Salutis [of safety, salvation]
The welle spryngeth out of thee
 Virtutis [of virtue]

Lady flour of alle thyng
 Rosa sine spina [rose without thorn]
Thou bare Jhesu hevenes kyng
 Gratia divina [by divine grace]
Of alle thou berest the pris [pris = high honors]
Lady quene of paradys
 Electa [elected]
Moder mylde and mayden eke
 Effecta [created]

Wel He wot He is thy sone
 Ventre quem portasti [whom you carried in womb]
He wyl not werne thee thy boon [werne = refuse]
 Parvum quem lactasti [the boy you suckled]
So hende and so good He is
He hath broghte us all to blisse
 Superni [from on high]
That hath i-dut the foule put [i-dut = shut; put = pit]
 Inferni [of hell][26]

In terms of the mimetics of verisimilitude, this poem can be adequately read as a meditation, imitative of prayer, on the virtues and powers of the Virgin and a supplication for her assistance. The English carries the burden of argument and the Latin adds a delicate decorative touch in the form of rhyming snatches and tags from Marian liturgy. The real key to this poem, however, is to be found in the representational principle of ordination, which is that of a very precise pattern

of *alternation* between Latin and the vernacular. The "rule" of the poem
is that although the languages alternate predictably, they do not
merge. That rule is broken only once: but it is precisely at that point
of "breaking the rule" that we find the key to the mimetic function of
the presence of two languages in the poem. It is the programmatic
alternation of Latin and vernacular, with one sole intersection, that
generates a linguistic figure of Incarnation.

Keeping our model of medieval intuitions regarding Latin and the
vernacular with which we began this chapter, we return to the poem
under discussion. The English, with one stunning exception, makes
coherent grammatical sense if one removes the Latin. It is a "finished"
autonomous utterance. The Latin, although inflected so as to integrate
with the English, cannot stand grammatically alone. It nevertheless
has its own principle of coherence: the unified frame of reference constituted of Marian liturgy. The bits and pieces call up in the mind of the
reader (like the snatches of Psalms in the *Purgatorio*) the whole utterance
of which they are a part. But these Marian prayers are not private or
local, they are public and never end: somewhere on the planet they are
always being said.

The Latin also has greater reach than the English: by linking into
the text of the particular poem under discussion and into the liturgy
of Mary, it provides a kind of bridge between the particular poem and
the plenary meditations of humanity. The English is, then, private,
autonomous, and complete, while the Latin is public, liturgical, and
unending. The ordinating principle of linguistic alternation is thus
mimetic of the alternation of the private quotidian voice of the individual here and now in England and the public, eternal voice of revelation
in the texts of the Universal Church. English figures forth the human,
Latin the divine aspect of reality.

As indicated, at the one point, and at one point only, the rule is
broken. At that point both languages intersect (and become one) and
we are literally as well as figuratively at the center. In the middle of
the middle stanza we read, "Wyth *Ave* it went away." The Latin *Ave*
is the only Latin word required to complete the grammatical functioning of English in the poem. This is, of course, the same *Ave* that
announces redemption by means of the Incarnation. The embedding
of the Latin *verbum* in the "flesh" of quotidian English confirms our
sense that the ordinated disposition of the two languages mirrors forth
the Incarnation—that hypostatic union of human and divine nature

that was the primal fact of the historical Christ in the imagination of medieval Europe.

* * * * *

This study of modes and images of Roman and medieval mirroring is nearly complete. In the following conclusion, we shall examine how the work as a whole functions as a Pauline speculum and how closure, that frontier between the work and the world, sends the mind's eye, Janus-like, at once back into the work and out into the world.

Conclusion: Promised Ends

Lear:	I know when one is dead, and when one lives. She's dead as earth. Lend me a looking glass. If that her breath will mist or stain the stone, Why then she lives.
Kent:	Is this the promised end?
Edgar:	Or image of that horror?
Albany:	Fall and cease.

—Shakespeare, *King Lear* 5.3.261–65

In this quick colloquy, Kent and Edgar raise a central issue in general poetics even as they voice a more local question that must have been on the tongues of contemporary spectators. Surely in any preliminary sense the answer is no: a dead Cordelia is *not* the promised end. All Shakespeare's sources promise continued life and restoration of power. Yet Shakespeare brazenly breaks that promise. And he insists we weigh the implications by having Kent explicitly call this "new" version of the story into question in these terms. And by having Kent put the question when he does, at the end, as Cordelia lies dead in her dying father's arms, midst a call for a looking glass, Shakespeare calls into even more urgent question the traditional solutions of continuance and restoration.

So it is at the end, where we most want light, that we are left darkling. Oddly enough, ending is one of the most important, yet until recently one of the least-written-about, aspects of the narrative arts. The first full-scale studies to appear in English on this issue were published in the late 1960s: Frank Kermode's *Sense of an Ending* and Barbara Herrnstein Smith's *Poetic Closure*.[1] Each discusses provocatively various motives and features of closure and provides an intriguing set of conceptual frameworks for handling the issue. Neither deals quite

243

satisfactorily with the special needs of a narrative poetic both privileged by and burdened with the theological imperatives that helped form the worldview of the Middle Ages.

As a work relinquishes its claim *as* world, it concludes its final directives *to* the world that impelled it appropriately on the contiguous frontiers it shares *with* that world. This chapter tracks closing negotiations in a series of major texts and inquires, albeit obliquely, into the fundamental relationships obtaining between any work and the world to which it must submit, or at least succumb. As we move along toward the high Middle Ages, which appropriated the massive and reciprocal trope of the *liber mundi,* the World as Book and the Book as World, we shall see how the ending of the book can mirror the ending of life itself and, in the case of Chaucer, even more specifically, and rather technically, the *ars moriendi,* or the art of holy dying. We begin with the end of the *Iliad:*

And no one saw them, not a man or woman,
before Kassandra. Tall as the pale-gold
goddess Aphrodite, she had climbed
the citadel of Pergamos at dawn.
Now looking down she saw her father come
in his war-car, and saw the crier there,
and saw Lord Hektor on his bed of death
upon the mulecart. The girl wailed and cried
to all the city: "Oh, look down, look down,
go to your windows, men of Troy, and women,
see Lord Hektor now! Remember joy
at seeing him return alive from battle,
exalting all our city and our land!"
. . . .
In a golden urn they put the bones,
shrouding the urn with veiling of soft purple.
Then in a grave dug deep they placed it
and heaped it with great stones. The men were quick
to raise the death-mound, while in every quarter
lookouts were posted to ensure against
an Akhaian surprise attack. When they had finished
raising the barrow, they returned to Ilion,
where all sat down to banquet in his honor

244

> in the hall of Priam king. So they performed
> the funeral rites of Hector, tamer of horses.[2]

As we hear the final summons of Cassandra to come witness the return of Hector's body and listen to the valedictories of the keening Hecuba, Andromache, and Helen, our sense of things as moving forward is countered by Cassandra's specific command to reach back into memory for the living Hector. And as we think back, we hear the lamentations of Mother, Wife, and Friend in precisely the reverse order in which we heard the same three women engage in the ordered discourse of valediction with the living Hector upon his departure into battle in *Iliad* 6. In addition, the women's stately, lyric grieving for Hector flashes back, in an inverse manner, not only to the ritual sport of men in tribute to Patroklos in *Iliad* 23, but all the way back to the very beginning of the poem, to those fatal escalations of the shouting match between Agamemnon and Achilleus over the body of Briseis.

As we seek to assess Homer's moves at the close of the *Iliad*, it proves helpful to consider the functions of some of the rich and often daring ways in which he rhymes. This is not the rhyme of words, of course, but of images, moments, events, even poetic strategies across the entire canvasses of his poems. Such rhyming at the formal and thematic levels involves, like its phonetic namesake, repetition with a difference.

When Chaucer rhymes "cloister" with "oyster," the metaphoric potential of sounds bearing different meanings opens like a rose. The phonic similarity no longer seems quite so arbitrary and it invites, if only for a moment, a bit of lyric meditation on both difference and like. When this sort of partial pairing occurs on trans- or superlinguistic levels of a narrative, quite similar effects can be achieved. Again we are not speaking of verbal, formulaic repetition. We are speaking of a narrative technique that insists by more gentle strategies of repetition upon some essential identity between otherwise quite obviously different entities. Before pursuing the mirroring technique of thematic rhyming that Homer orchestrates in the final threnody of the *Iliad*, perhaps a brief excursus into Homeric simile will be tolerated: two similes, both from *Iliad* 4.

> And then the dark blood ran out of the wound,
> as when a Maionian or Kyrian woman

dyes ivory with purple, as a cheekpiece for horses—
and lays it up in the chamber; many an owner of chariots
would like to have had it, but it's stored up for the king,
as a treasure—for two reasons:
the beauty of the horse and the rider's glory;
just so, Menelaos, were your powerful legs dyed
bloody, the shins and the ankles, beautiful underneath.

(Iliad 4.140–47, my translation)

Similarity resides in the coloring over of white with red and an initial sense of movement. Then difference presides. We move from men in disorder in Troy to the ordering procedures of a single woman (abstracted slightly by means of placing her in two possible else-wheres). We move from martial to aesthetic precision, from blood, grit, and the danger of sudden death to a radiant and infinitely extend-able world. Yet as difference supersedes, the grammatical insistence on identity never quite loses force, is in fact verbally repeated when the narrative voice returns us to the battleground and the wounded flesh of Menelaos. The wound has now been elevated by the fabled identity it bears to the extended image of the purpled ivory treasure; and the initial incongruity of the two images subsides as we begin to sense the way in which a *tertium comparationis* looms. The poet has functioned here as the silent double of the ivoryworker, and as she transforms in our imagined memory the natural ivory into a king's treasure, so Homer has marmorealized Menelaos's bleeding wound into a poetic image of clarity and beauty, at rest in a sense of endlessly available time.

Then the spear pierced the right nipple and
ran him through the shoulder
and he fell to earth in the dust like a poplar
which, having grown in the wet earth of a great swamp,
is smooth and only has bright greening branches on top;
but the wheelwright has felled it with his bright axe
in order to bend it into a wheel for a royal chariot
and it lies now softening on the bank of the stream:
so Anthemion's son Simoisios was stretched
out under Ajax, offshoot of Zeus.

(Iliad 4.480–89, my translation)

246

Again, difference is most striking. Again, the governing image in the simile is a nameless artisan. And again, that governing image has no obvious parallel in the narrative that occasions and frames the simile. For the poplar we have the boy, for the axe the spear; but here congruity ceases. In the simile, our attention is focused on the care with which the wheelwright fells the tree. There is purpose. The nameless artisan transforms the tree into a wheel, a mediator between a burden and its ground, an object that enables movement, overcomes inertia. Then, from the world as meditation figured forth by the simile, which is drenched with water (the moistness of the earth in the swamp, the softening poplar in the river), we return to the dust of Troy, to the narrative of war, and find no artisan, but killer Ajax. As the tree was transformed by the hand of the artisan, we find the boy has simply died. But of course he does not simply die; he too is transformed, rescued from that imagined moment on the edge of oblivion and appropriated into an image of arcadian sublimity. It is again the narrator, the poet Homer, who has doubled as the wheelwright outside the poem and transformed an otherwise meaningless death into a vehicle of signification.

Such similes are frequent in the *Iliad* and are as insistent in their function as they are quiet in that insistence. At their onset, the narrative rush freezes into a cinematic "still," into an image that both triggers the simile and completes its frames of reference. As a result of the move into simile, the forwarding mode of the narrative radically shifts, enters a more lyrical mode of disposition. Our readerly attitude is now contemplative, comparative, more critical. A distance is thereby created (and carefully manipulated) that enhances our sense of control over the narrative as well as our isolation from it. Finally, we see that these similes are only a special case of a more general formal and thematic technique of rhyming that always involves the juxtaposition of partially congruent structures in greater or lesser proximity. Continuing the cinematic metaphor, I would like to suggest that the great threnody of burial that concludes the *Iliad* rhymes "positively" with the departure of Hector in *Iliad* 6, and "negatively" (or inversely) with the funeral games of *Iliad* 23 and the interview between Priam and Achilles at the beginning of *Iliad* 24.

As the women mourn at the end of the poem, they tell us directly, as well as in ways that are even more powerful for their indirection, that the ultimate devastation visited by the wrath of Achilles is the loss of the civilizing force of Hector, tamer of horses. He was the man who was not born with but learned his bravery. We have lost the man who, seeing his son's fear of a flashing helmet, can demystify, on the edge of doom, the masks of war and death by laughter. The magnanimity of his laughter is beautifully drawn as he puts his helmet down, picks up his boy, and tosses him into the air. Hector's gaiety, as in Yeats's wonderful line from "Lapis Lazuli," "transfigures all that dread." And the moral force of Hector's laughter holds firm, even in the face of our own terrible knowledge that Odysseus, in rhyming horror, long after the *Iliad* has surrounded itself in silence, will smash the child Astyanax into the rubble beneath the broken walls of Troy.

I have suggested that the image of the women engaging in formal obsequies around the body of Hector also acts as an inverse mirror, a kind of photographic negative. It calls to mind the Akhaian men engaged in formal funeral games in honor of the dead Patroklos in *Iliad* 23. We see, in the eye of recollection, Achilles mourning Patroklos. And as we look, we can see Hector reflected in dual aspect. In his victim Patroklos, we see a mirror of Hector as the quintessential military hero, the appropriate subject of funereal cynosure. But in Hector's killer Achilles, now playing the role of *magister ludi* in *Iliad* 23, we see another mirror of Hector performing as a civil governor. As we see Achilles in the civilizing virtues of Hector, as an ordering center, we see a redemptive possibility in Achilles, a redemptive possibility even more strongly foreshadowed later on in the tent with Priam. But this is a possibility that can never be fulfilled. Fate's grim irony has seen to it that at the very moment he destroyed Hector, Achilles started his own doomsday machine, a machine that will soon bring him his own death at the hands of the beautiful and vacuous Paris—a death to that aspect of the self that could have provided, in the alternative world of the listener's mind, an ethos sufficient in stability and stature to offer a true counter to Lord Agamemnon, whose madness and general stupidity triggered the devastating wrath of Achilles in the first place.

As desolate as things are, we find, at the very end, an image of implied continuance:

> They piled up the grave barrow and went away.
> And thereafter assembled in a fair gathering and held

a glorious feast within the house of Priam, king under god's hand.
Such was their burial of Hector, breaker of horses.

(*Iliad* 24.801–05)[3]

The positive image is that of ritual feast. Such feasting, then as now, constitutes a kind of contract among the living, a collective commitment to life and futurity. It is also the final tribute we pay to the dead. As we relinquish the dead as dead, we allow them their ultimate power over us, their radical difference. Before we pay such tribute, however, we often engage in negative rituals of avoidance of the truth. In our refusal to eat, to wash, to change clothes, we signify our temporary roles as still belonging to the dead, acting as psychopomps, as blind guides to the underworld. On our return from our private, imagined descents into Hell with those we grieve for, we change, we wash, we eat, and we sleep.

This closing image of ritual feasting not only affirms the final release of the dead Hector by the living women; it also rhymes with, and thus calls to mind, the scene just prior to the bringing of Hector's body back to Troy; the celebrated interview in the tent between Priam and Achilles. In that interview, each engages in a tribute to past and future, knowing that for each there is only past and no future. Each gazes on the other and remembers a double: Achilles sees Priam and remembers his father Peleus; Priam sees Achilles and remembers his son Hector. In this twilight silence of mutual recognition we reach our most intimate degree of proximity to the central ethos of the poem. As the moment passes, our distance to the narrative center increases as that between the heroes decreases, and we are deftly led outside the tent as Achilles and Priam eat together, clasp hands, and retire to sleep.

Such incidental end rhyming, in which the closing images complete a pattern of partial repetition, send us not out into the world but back into the poem. We become distanced observers whose roles are meditation, comparison, and judgment, but never identification. A field of silence surrounds the work as the funeral meats are eaten. It is probably true that the frequency of formal and thematic rhyming contributes to our sense of control and coherence even while we feel to the bone the ever-widening devastation of Achilles' wrath. Homer's maneuvers of repetition have a ritualizing effect that aids in memorializing the ethical values maintained by the heroes in the poem. At the same time the

rhyming in the *Iliad,* with its controlling principle of overriding difference in the face of apparent similarity, generates a profound sense of
severance. The work has been rendered inviolable to its witnesses. It
seals itself off from the world it joins even as it enters in.

As the *Iliad* comprises a catalogue of death, devastation, and breakdown, the *Odyssey* is a celebration of the possibilities of restitution and
reconciliation. From the beginning, the promised end is reunion of
Odysseus with Penelope and Telemachus, yet that reunion proves penultimate. It is only in the almost holy marriage bed of *Odyssey* 23 that
we learn of other closures. A set of wanderings must be undertaken to
propitiate Poseidon. A second homecoming must be fought for in
which death will come to Odysseus in bed, with a hand as mild as the
hand of Penelope. As we move toward the end of *Odyssey* 23, this
wonderful book of false closure, Penelope seems to sum things up
conclusively by saying, "If by the gods' grace age at least is kind, /we
have that promise—trials will end in peace." But she subsides; and
Odysseus begins to tally his odyssey all over again until sleep substi-
tutes for whatever other closure he may have had in mind.

In the morning, there is not only a new day; there is a new project
and a new book, *Odyssey* 24, the final and authentic closure to the epic.
After arising, Odysseus leaves the bed of Penelope to find his father
Laërtes. One must remember that this homecoming has been taking
place for the entire second half of the poem; the Phaiakians land him
asleep on Ithaca at the close of *Odyssey* 12. As we work our way through
Odyssey 24, we begin to catch on that this particular homecoming is
moving toward a kind of completion of the journey best articulated
over two and a half millenia later by T. S. Eliot in his *Four Quartets:*

> We shall not cease from exploration
> and the end of all our exploring
> will be to arrive where we started
> and know the place for the first time.[4]

The final section, *Odyssey* 24, consists of three narrative panels and
a coda: three resonant celebrations of different sorts of marriages and a
final tribute to the power of oblivion, which, though inimical to the
epic's own forwarding procedures, is ironically necessary for the poem's
successful emergence from the trap of its own plot.

The first panel celebrates an array of marriages (and near-marriages) among men and women and takes place in a second visit to Hell, the reversal of Odysseus's own descent in *Odyssey* 11. The obverse of the phantom, would-be marriage of Achilles and Polyxena is mirrored in the report of the death rituals of Achilles and the mixing of his ashes with those of Patroklos in the golden amphora of Haephaestos. The suitors are then questioned by Agamemnon. Amphimion regales the ghostly crowd with the tale of another phantom, almost-marriage, that of Penelope and Antinoös. Agamemnon, victim of a marriage destroyed, and brother of Menelaos (who leads, as we see in *Odyssey* 4, a mended but barren marriage with Helen), then counters with an encomium to the true Penelope, and praises the ideality of her own marriage of intelligence and faith, an ideality that has since formed, in Europe, the model of true mind.

The second panel celebrates the marriage of past and future by the coalescing presence of both aspects of time in mediating Odysseus. The reconciliation with his father moves from the position of Odysseus as testing strategist, through a compassion that breaks down the mechanisms of his control, to a reversal of the testing pattern in which the father, Laërtes, tests the son. The success of that test is embodied in the son's recollection of the gifts of his origin: the olive, the fig, and the vine. The dimension of futurity, in the figure of Telemachus, is then linked to the dimension of the past, in the figure of Laërtes by the figure of the present Odysseus, and the triple threat of Ithaca is thus affirmed in action, both in the ritual meal with Eumaeus and Dolios and in the final figure of the three in battle armor facing Antinoös's father, Eupeithes.

The final image of peace comes, but not until Athena has urged Laërtes to ultimate self-reassertion in the ritual killing of his opposite: Eupeithes, the father of Antinoös, Odysseus's would-be usurper. One line of filiation is thus brought down to final obliteration by another, and that act itself amplifies the validity of the surviving trinity of past, present, and future figured forth by the three who constitute the house of Laërtes. Such allegorizing may appear shameless, but it is precisely the Roman and medieval arts of reading we have been concerned with in this study, and such allegorization of Homer was one way by which Rome and the Middle Ages developed the coherence of western literary tradition.

The third narrative panel of *Odyssey* 24 celebrates the final dimension of marriage, that between king and subject. The claims of blood-revenge are real and not questioned in the *Odyssey:* they lead to a real and necessary sense of dilemma as they clash with the equally real and unquestioned claims of communal continuity. The answer is to arrange for the conversion of the kingship of Odysseus from election to dynastic succession, and this is done by one of the few really crucial acts of divine intervention in the poem: Zeus's gift of oblivion. Here is the final comic irony of the *Odyssey:* the poem that celebrates the continuance of the race by the self-generating power of memory closes with the plot-saving intervention of the act of forgetting. This ironic sense of paradoxy is appropriate and expected. As I suggested at the beginning of this study, the truly encyclopedic work includes at least once the inverse mirror image of its own forwarding principles. The *Iliad* does so in the funeral games of *Iliad* 23, and the *Odyssey* does so on several occasions: the song of the Sirens, the scenes in Hades (*Odyssey* 11), and the closing image of Zeus dispensing oblivion so that Ithaca can accept its survivor king—a king who has, as is pointed out in assembly in its final book, managed to lose all the men he took with him and kill a good portion of those who remained behind.

Thus, at closure, Homer goes to great lengths to bridge and link his comic work to the world it enters. One way he does this is to place sequels in that world: Odysseus will undergo another journey beyond the narrative boundaries of the *Odyssey* and will, in the imagination's eye, conclude his life at death's soft hand in the world beyond the work. In addition, the repeated emphasis on marriages and weddings, on reconstituting the links between man and woman, father and son, and king and citizen amplifies a concerted emphasis on linkage itself— as opposed to the *Iliad*'s insistence on severance. Finally, the many endings of the *Odyssey* constitute a figure of a refusal to end at all—every gesture in the poem made in the direction of ending has within it the seeds of a new problem, a new situation, a new concern—in short, a new beginning.

Virgil and Ovid approach closure with all the advantages and disadvantages of being clearly aware not only of Homer, but also of all the intervening Athenian, Hellenistic, and Alexandrine strategies of closure.

> Aeneas stood, ferocious in his armor;
> his eyes were restless and he stayed his hand;
> and as he hesitated, Turnus' words

began to move him more and more—until
high on the Latin's shoulder he made out
the luckless belt of Pallas, of the boy
whom Turnus had defeated, wounded stretched
upon the battlefield, from whom he took
this fatal sign to wear upon his back,
this girdle glittering with familiar studs.
And when his eyes drank in this plunder, this
memorial of brutal grief, Aeneas,
aflame with rage—his wrath was terrible—
cried: "How can you who wear the spoils of my
dear comrade now escape me? It is Pallas,
who strikes, who sacrifices you, who takes
this payment from your shameless blood." Relentless,
he sinks his sword into the chest of Turnus.
His limbs fell slack with chill; and with a moan
his life, resentful, fled to Shades below.

(*Aeneid* 12.938–52)[5]

The final image of the slaughter of Turnus, couched in Iliadic death formula, may seem to run counter to the ideological thrust of Virgil's narrative as apologia for Augustus's politics of *pax romana*. But, as I tried to elaborate in chapter 1, it is an end long promised.[6] All images of future restitution, reconciliation, peace, and tranquility are penultimate in Virgil, and all such images are followed by an image of violence, rupture, and breakdown. The advantage gained by the struggle for power and stability is always followed, if not preceded, by a detailed litany of the cost. In Roman economy, the value of anything is directly tallied by what one pays for it. This last image of the cost to Aeneas and of the universal Rome he is losing everything for turns the mind's attention, not forward to the next encounter or to an escape from Aeneas's world, but back into the world of the work in the hope of finding some sufficient justification for suffering that must otherwise be acknowledged as gratuitous and barbarous.

In a way, the violence at the end of *Aeneid* 12 sends us not only back to the reconciliation scene in heaven that immediately precedes it, but all the way back to the catabasis of *Aeneid* 6, that great canticle of Hell, and its alternative mode of closure: the exit of the hero, full of divine revelation, through the Ivory Gate of False Dream.

An important difference between Homer and Virgil, as suggested in chapter 1, is that Virgil always insists reflexively on the ficticity of his story, on the sense of his gleaming narrative as a polished artifact. Therefore, as the closural strategies of Virgil draw us back into the text, they also protect the ontological barrier between text as art and world as nature that Virgil has been at great pains to maintain all along. In both senses of end, cessation and telos, Virgil's final images are promised. The way Aeneas slaughters Turnus rhymes with the eyes full of sunflare with which Homer's Achilles picked up the Shield of Haephaestus and the wrath with which he slaughtered Hector. These resonances are appropriately reflexive of the design of the *Aeneid* as itself anti-Homeric. This is a design in which those who died in Troy, according to the Virgilian hero's first words, are *terque quaterque beati*—three, even four times blessed. This is a design in which the only release of the hero from personal suffering comes with the oblivion of death.

Ovid, on the other hand, shouts affirmation of immortality at the end of the *Metamorphoses:*

> The work is done. Neither Jove's wrath, nor fire,
> nor sword, nor the gnawing tooth of time can undo it.
> Let that day come, when it will, which only has power
> over my body, and cut off my uncertain span of years.
> In my better part, I shall be carried beyond the
> stars, and my name shall never die. Wherever in the
> world Rome extends her power, people will read and
> through eternal fame, if vatic intuition carries
> any truth, I shall live!
> (*Metamorphoses* 15.871–79, my translation)

As discussed in chapter 2, one of the constants of Ovid's marvelous book of changes is the way in which Poet and Nature keep wearing each other's clothes. Nature at her best in Ovid acts as artist, and as such she seems somehow better than the nameless god with whom she created the world in the first place (*deus et melior natura*). As we work through one transformation after another we begin to see that *natura* is a literary image that has been assigned by Ovid the task of representing both art and artist in the world. After we hear the lecture of Pythagoras, however, another final twist begins to assert itself.

In the scheme of real things, not of art, i.e., in the world to which Ovid at the close of the *Metamorphoses* submits his work, Ovid shows that he in turn has been assigned his role by Nature: his voice and his poetic powers are the momentary form through which the eternal force of *natura* speaks. Thus the *vivam* that closes the *Metamorphoses* is spoken only in the penultimate sense by the persona of Ovid the Poet. In a final submission that is in fact as humble as its appearance is arrogant, we discover that the voice we hear is *natura* herself, speaking through the death mask of her poet/*vates,* Publius Ovidius Naso. The closing *vivam* thus unites art with *melior natura* herself, the genetrix of the world; the link between the fabulous artifices of the *Metamorphoses* and the fabulous artifices of the world that the *Metamorphoses* now joins is complete.

St. Augustine's *Confessions* offers two closures. The first is the closure of the conversion story of the narrated Augustine, which we find executed by the narrating Augustine in book 10. After conversion, the two "nows" of the divided self, represented by the narrating Augustine-as-Subject and the narrated Augustine-as-Object, converge. The final closure is a trinity of expositions on the nature of beginning. The unified, converted Augustine presents three essays doing essentially the same thing: showing the redeemed mind at work, in which will, memory, and intellect perform in unified harmony. He demonstrates as well as argues the power of the Christian mind as it performs exegesis on Genesis, the foundational text of the world's beginning.

As we move into the high Middle Ages, it might prove useful to recapitulate briefly certain implications of chapter 4. What links the medieval poet to modern reader/writer expectations is his addiction to tough syntax, dense diction, paronomastic high jinks, and intricate sound/sense orchestrations as well as to visual tricks of juxtaposition. What sets the medieval horizon of reader/writer expectations apart from ours is a prior organizing cultural decision: the appropriation of a web of belief in which the Incarnation was taken as fact rather than as mere alternative.

The axiomatic, historic sense of the hypostatic union of divinity and man in the person of Christ meant that all previous accident had been redeemed: all had become significant. When an entire culture proceeds with an axiom of such total coherence embedded in its deepest mental and psychical network of resources, then all the particles of its individual and corporate utterances, verbal and nonverbal, claim resonance with a cosmic center. For medieval people, the Word had become Flesh, and texts therefore became privileged in ways it is difficult for us in the twentieth century to keep firmly in mind. Four lines of Alan of Lille help us to capture this crucial alterity:

> Sphaeram claudit curvatura
> Et sub ipsa clauditur.
> In hac Verbi copula
> Stupet omnis regula
>
> [The arc encloses the sphere
> and is enclosed within it.
> In this coupling of the Word
> every rule is broken.][7]

We are perhaps on even firmer ground as we reflect on ways the shape of the book mirrors the shape of the world. I have already referred to Curtius's chapter on the book as symbol in the Western tradition, and call to mind once again these equally famous lines of Alan of Lille from *De Incarnatione Christi:*

> Omnis mundi creatura
> Quasi liber et pictura
>   Nobis est et speculum
> Nostrae vitae, nostrae mortis,
> Nostri status, nostrae sortis
>   Fidele signaculum.
>
> [Every creature in this world
> resembles a book, a picture,
> and is to us a mirror,
> faithful image
> of our life, our death,
> our state, our fate.][8]

Perhaps the most important aspect of the medieval use of this trope is the often mannered delight with which these authors traded on its reversibility: not only is the World Book, but the Book is World. One of the final great images of the *Commedia* envisages the cosmos as a book read by the light of the Mind of God:

> In its profundity I saw—ingathered
> and bound by love into one single volume—
> what, in the universe, seems separate, scattered.
>
> (*Paradiso* 33.85–87)[9]

With this in mind, and with a schematic notion of two general modes of closure, Virgilian and Ovidian (the former principally Iliadic and the latter primarily Odyssean), we proceed to the medieval literary production with which this study has been primarily concerned.

In our examination of two central lyrics of Heinrich von Morungen, we discovered closure to be a cul-de-sac. As the reader turns back into the text in order to find liberation from Heinrich's parabolic syntax, he replicates the interior adventure of the speaker as the generator of the very utterance that sends him back. Heinrich will not let us have the illusion of explanation or consolation that literary closure often provides: his refusal to release the reader into clarity is an insistence that in art, as in life, there is no exit.

In chapter 6 I explored certain strategies of Chrétien de Troyes, including brief reference to closure, though not as a separate subject. Let me recapitulate briefly. In the *Erec,* Chrétien achieves an essentially Virgilian close: the final panel of the romance, the *joie de la court,* seals off the work. The closing image of the coronation of Erec and Enide is so amplified that it becomes an allegorical figure of the signification of the romance as a whole. It is not, I think, by chance that emblematic figures from the *Aeneid* play such an important role in the *Erec*— especially figures surrounding Enide, who embodies Chrétien's attempt to reconcile the values traditionally associated with Dido and Lavinia as figures of *amie,* or the mistress/lover, and of *fame,* or wife.

From then on, as Chrétien moves toward more pluralistic forms of social and literary criticism, he tends toward more Ovidian modes of closure. In the *Yvain,* the same trick is used to marry the same lady a second time. Closure as replication of an earlier event cancels, in an important way, all intervening action, which, in the case of the *Yvain,* acts as a very powerful reductive force on the entire enterprise of rehabilitation the hero struggles through. "Plus ça change, plus la même chose." As for the *Cligés,* its existence as a romance plays parodistic games with versions of the *Tristan,* and hence there is no great surprise about the fact that closure here is a great, reflexive joke. Only at the end do we learn that the entire production has been in aid of rendering a foundational explanation for the existence of harems in the East. Clearly such narrative buffoonery explodes any pretensions of any high-minded integrity we may have sought here. The *Lancelot* is another matter:

> Lords, if I were to say any more about this
> it would alter the material
> so I'll address myself to conclusion.
> Godfrey de Leigni, the clerk
> has brought The Cart to a close:
> but nobody should blame him
> for working on Chrétien
> for he did it with the good will
> of Chrétien who began it.
> He took the story from the point
> where Lancelot was walled up.
> This is how far the story goes.
> So far and no farther. He wouldn't put in any more
> or less, because that would disfigure the tale.
> So ends the romance of Lancelot of the Cart.
> *(Lancelot,* 7098–7113, my translation)[10]

Closure here is very tricky indeed. It would seem, at the very end, that our author Chrétien has long since abandoned the work, somewhere back at the point where Lancelot was shut in the tower longing for Guinever. Suddenly some clerk identifying himself as Godefroi de Leigni is addressing us; he hopes he hasn't disappointed us, and he goes on and on about how he won't go on and on for fear of spoiling the design. In his bid for final clarity of who did what, he closes the romance in irresolvable ambiguity: for lack of a firm pronoun reference (the "he" in the third line from the end could refer back either to Godefroi or to Chrétien), either Godefroi won't say any more now, or Chrétien wouldn't say any more then, after locking up Lancelot in the tower.

What are we to make of the fact that our author has abandoned both his story and us? In the opening lines of the romance he expresses his disaffection for this story and says he will tell it to us only because his patroness (Marie de Champagne) has ordered him to do so. During the depiction of the successful consummation of Lancelot's desire for Guinever, the narrator says that his story dares not speak of their joy. This is no Puritan scruple; Chrétien often delights in the candid depiction of sexual pleasures. The reluctance must stem from the fact that this particular consummation is so fatal to the court.

The slippery ending, with the early departure of the author, points to at least three possible closures. First is the one left unsaid: the disfiguring breakdown of Camelot. The second is the "authoritative" version, the ending desired by Chrétien, which is the point where he abandoned the romance: Lancelot is walled up, there is no escape, Guinever is never found, Arthur is never betrayed, and Camelot lives forever. The third, the overt ending brought us by Godefroi, is a lie within a lie. The final scene of the romance takes place in a garden that parodies Eden. Here, Meleagant, the alleged danger to the court, is beheaded in the presence of a distracted Arthur by the cuckolding Lancelot, hero of the West, gay betrayer of king and country. As the court cheers the decapitation of the wrong hero, and Godefroi suddenly identifies himself as an ersatz for the original author, only to refuse to tell us more, we have been served our happy ending. It is patently false. We do not have to wait centuries for Malory to know how it really turns out; the catastrophic ending of Camelot is available in Geoffrey of Monmouth. And the taste of this dessert of closure is more than a little compromised by the fact that we discover we are sitting at the table long after the host has gone home.

In the foregoing chapter, I discussed the closure of Langland's *Piers Plowman* at some length. For a Christian poem, there is a surprisingly deep sense of claustrophobia, entrapment, and labyrinthine plotting, with no apparent way out. But there is a way out, and it is essentially Ovidian in its strategies: we are ejected out of the poem into the world by a poem that, like the *Metamorphoses,* has been identified with the personal history of the hero/narrator. As the hero reaches the end, he says, "I gan awake." Whether this awakening is only to be taken literally as awakening from sleep, or also as a figure for death (he "awakens" from this life), there is no sure way to tell. Nonetheless we realize that our sense of imprisonment in this poem is derived from the fact that we are trapped in the relentless point of view of Will, the narrator, and we feel this most intensely even as we are released, spat out into the quotidian world only at the very end of the poem, as Jonah was spat out of the whale: feeling not so much a sense of relief as a refreshed imperative to seek meaning in our lives.

In the last canto of *Paradiso,* Dante the Pilgrim encounters his final image of God. He sees three circles, each of differing color, each occupying the same place. He literally cannot make them out. Like Augustine, he too engages in prayer, and the *Commedia* closes with his discovery of the Self, our collective *imago,* in this radical image of the ordinating Other:

> . . . in the deep and bright
>   essence of that exalted Light, three circles
> appeared to me; they had three different colors,
> but all of them were of the same dimension. . . .
>   That circle—which, begotten so, appeared
> in You as light reflected—why my eyes
> had watched it with attention for some time,
>   within itself and colored like itself,
> to me seemed painted with our effigy,
> so that my sight was set on it completely.
>   As the geometer intently seeks
> to square the circle, but he cannot reach,
> through thought on thought, the principle he needs,
>   so I searched that strange sight: I wished to see
> the way in which our human effigy
> suited the circle and found place in it—
>   and my own wings were far too weak for that.
> But then my mind was struck by light that flashed
> and, with this light, received what it had asked.
>   Here force failed my high fantasy; but my
> desire and will were moved already—like
> a wheel revolving uniformly—by
>   the Love that moves the sun and the other stars.
>
> (*Paradiso* 33.114–17, 133–45)

This final image is a figure of the Trinity limned with our own collective *imago.* But what sort of image is it? In what sense is this image a mirror image of the divine gesture in Genesis in which God creates us in *His* image? One feels that from the beginning of *Paradiso* 30, Dante has somehow shifted his basic poetic mode and that these final spectacular images: the river of intellectual light, the celestial rose, and the Circles of God shining forth our image belong to a world of radical, specular metaphor that differs from conventional poetry in kind as well as degree. Dante warns us of the necessity of such a shift from normal usage in the opening canto of the *Paradiso:*

> I was within the heaven that receives
> more of His light: and I saw things that he
> who from that height descends, forgets or can
> not speak; for nearing its desired end,
> our intellect sinks into an abyss
> so deep that memory fails to follow it.
>
> (*Paradiso* 1.4–9)

To his patron, Can Grande della Scala, he writes that true mystic vision brings with it precisely this problem: the compelling need to mediate a vision of which he has no detailed memory, and he cites Paul and Augustine as well as more recent theoreticians of elevation:

And where these examples (Paul, Matthew, Ezekiel) are not enough for the sceptics, let them read Richard of Saint Victor . . . let them read Bernard . . . let them read Augustine . . . and let them not be sceptical. . . . He does not have knowledge because he has forgotten, he has no power because, even if he remembers and retains the content, words nonetheless fail. For there are many things which we see by the intellect for which verbal signs are lacking, which Plato sufficiently suggests in his books by means of metaphors, for he saw many things by the light of his intellect that he could not express in suitable words.[11]

But if he has neither the knowledge nor the power to tell what happened, what is it that we are getting as we read of it? Let us return to the passage in the lecture Beatrice gives to Dante after his misprision of the situation of Piccarda in the sphere of the moon:

These are shown, not because they have been allotted to this sphere, but to make a sign of heavenly differentiation. It is necessary to talk this way to your faculty because only by apprehending data through the senses can it present them to your intellect. Thus Scripture condescends to your powers and attributes feet and hands to God, while meaning something quite altogether other.

(*Paradiso* 4.37–45, my translation)

Dante has followed Augustine, both at the end of the *Confessions* and at the end of *De Trinitate,* and provided us with a Jacob's ladder of ascending images, of "suppose we saw's," each image more adequate than the previous one, each image ultimately inadequate to the desired task, which is to incorporate the ineffable in language. Seeing this over and over again, we begin to feel as well as apprehend a figure of humanity's corporate desire for redemption: our desire to incorporate the ineffable, our desire that the Word be made Flesh. We see the impossibility of achieving the object unaided even as we sense the answering accommodations of Grace as it stoops to provide us with the requisite ladder of ascent. God has accepted, as Augustine says early on in *De Doctrina,* the tribute of the human voice.

The final image of Dante the Pilgrim gazing on our self-image as reflected back from the figure of the ultimate Other fulfills St. Augustine's image of our mind as figured in the schemes of time (chap. 3). Perhaps the most important question about these master images of the discovery of our self in the Other is not so much *what* they mean but *how* they mean. They reveal themselves as dramatizations of our own discovery of ourselves as heroes and heroines of memory, as revelatory masks of ourselves as authors of recollected youth, as our own invented figures of life-saving narrative. R. Allen Shoaf has argued eloquently that Dante's final image is an illuminating fulfillment and redemption of the lost Narcissus petrified before his own image in the pool; surely he is correct.[12] In fact, both of the opposed, conventional aspects of mirror-gazing, the negative image of a trapped and dying Narcissus and the positive image of a liberated and circumspect Prudentia, are reconciled and transcended in this final, specular *imago nostris in deo.*

As stupendous and as breathtaking as the closure of the *Commedia* is, part of its truth is to its own nature as language: to reveal its own limits as well as those of art altogether. As we stretch our imaginations to "remember" how three spheres could occupy the same space but be of differing color and as we begin to see, in a radical mirror image, of both the Incarnation and our own genesis as *imago dei,* Dante leaves us, just as Virgil left Dante at the edge of earthly Paradise. We are left not with real love really moving the real sun and the other stars but with words alone: the Italian line that allows everything to come to a unified close:

l'amor che move il sole e l'altre stelle.

The word *stelle* points outward, as all words point outward in some referential power, to incandescent heavenly bodies. But *stelle* also points back into the work itself. We have experienced the word *stelle* at the end of each preceding canticle of the *Commedia:* it is the last word of the *Inferno* and of the *Purgatorio* as well as of the *Paradiso.* This signals that each canticle is to be considered as a structural replication of its predecessor; the implication is that each goes a greater distance, but none takes us all the way. This triune ending both admits and celebrates the work's submission to the necessary limit of art. As the *Commedia* vanishes into silence, we have arrived at the liminal frontiers between being and knowing and we rediscover what we have known all along: earthly language is, after all, capable of only earthly pilgrimages.

If Dante is deeply affiliated with Virgil in his closural strategies, Chaucer affiliates with Ovid. Most readers have become accustomed to referring to Chaucer the Pilgrim when referring to the character in the *Canterbury Tales* and Chaucer the Poet when referring to the author. Chaucer the Pilgrim, however, is not the only representative or agent of Chaucer the Poet within the *Tales.* An absolutely minimal list would include the Clerk of Oxford, the Franklyn, and the Wife of Bath. And at the very end, there are two additional authorial voices as the "real" Chaucer surfaces to attach his recantation.

Of them all, perhaps the most interesting agent of Chaucer is the Wife of Bath, and an intriguing aspect of that agency is the way she handles closure of her own tale. By means of a formal trick of metrics, she incorporates her story of the rash young rapist and the protean witch who makes all better into her own "run-on" prologue, as the last in an ongoing series of exempla of the "wo that is in marriage." These marriages constitute her life, her frame of reference. Here is the end of her tale:

> And whan the knyght saugh verraily al this [saw truly]
> That she so fair was, and so yong thereto,
> For joye he hente hire in his armes two, [took]
> His herte bathed in a bath of Blisse.
> A thousand tyme a-rewe he gan hire kisse, [times in a row]
> And she obeyed hym in everything

That myghte doon him plesance or likyng. [might do]
And thus they lyve unto hir lyves end
In parfit joye; and Jhese crist us send
Housbondes meeke, younge, an fressh abedde,
And grace t'overbyde hem that we wedde. . . . [survive]

(3 [D]. 1150–60)[13]

The excessively drawn-out anaphora of the "and's," as well as the moon/june clanging of the rhymes, show the Wife of Bath gaily signalling a rush toward narrative closure. The penultimate line of the tale itself even ends with the word "end," and would seem to require, at least in the extremely conventional tricks of ending that the Wife is using, the completion of the following line in such a way as to bring both the rhymed couplet and the tale itself to a coterminous, appropriately happy ending. But no. The tale abruptly ends only two beats into the next line, "in parfit joye." The tale submits itself to its own ending in mid-sentence; it feeds itself into and is thus wrapped around and "consumed" by the endlessly elaborating web of the Wife's confession as she goes on with her task of saving her life by converting it into the significant forms of narrative, into the *enumeratio* of her marriages.

The Wife's technique of integrating her world by appropriating her narratives of desire into the lacework of her continuous, neverending "prologue," points to the ways in which Chaucer—who, if not her master, is at least, with Jean de Meun, her creator—linked the *Canterbury Tales* into *his* world at ending, that best of all possible worlds—best if only because it is the only world to which everything and everybody must finally submit.

Our sense of approaching ending in the *Canterbury Tales* does not, of course, flash out at us only at the last moment, upon our arrival at the dislocating Retraction. We have already been jolted by Harry Baily upon completion of the Manciple's tale. Although the original plan envisioned two tales apiece per pilgrim down to Canterbury and two tales back, Harry tells us after less than one go-around that it is all over, that the sun is going down—not only on this particular day, but on this day as a latter day. He does an ultimately fitting violence to our horizon of expectation. The original plan breaks down; we need to plan again, but in shorter shrift. Things are, as we should have expected, different than they seem:

> By that the Maunciple hadde his tale al ended,
> The sonne fro the south lyne was descended
> So lowe that he nas nat, to my sighte,
> Degrees nyne and twenty as in highte.
> Foure of the clokke it was, tho, as I gesse
> For eleven foot, or litel more or lesse,
> My shadwe was at thilke tyme, as there [that time]
> of swiche feet as my lengthe parted were [such]
> In sixe feet equal of proporcioun.
> Therewith the moones exaltation,
> I meane Libra, alwey gan ascende [evermore began to]
> As we were entryng at a thropes ende. [village's edge]
>
> (10 [I].1–12)

These crepuscular precisions of approaching night echo those even more famous precisions of springtime promise in the *General Prologue;* and this sense of sudden, proximate ending calls up remembrance of things beginning. If nature is well and forceful, we remember, once again, that we are not: we "long to go on pilgrimages," to Canterbury, "for that we are sick." Only one tale is left to tell: the tale of the Parson, who does not narrate, but tells, or tallies, the penitential way stations of the pilgrimage. The next station is not the Canterbury of man's design but death, the portal to the larger design of the city of God, Canterbury corrected and fulfilled as Jerusalem Celestial.

Recent work on Fragment 10, particularly the contributions of Olive Sayce, Siegfried Wenzel, and Douglas Wurtele, makes it almost impossible to deal with the *Retraction* in isolation; on the contrary, although disagreeing with one another on key points, these scholars have all taught us the need to view the *Parson's Prologue,* the *Parson's Tale,* and the troublesome *Retraction* as constituting an integrated "ending" to the *Canterbury Tales* as a whole.[14]

Sayce's major contribution was to make us see clearly just how conventional, in several crucial ways, the *Retraction* really is, and how important Chaucer's plural form, *retraccouns,* turns out to be in the play between the French and Latin semantic fields of *retractio.* Her discussion is particularly important in the way she demonstrates that the plural form of the word calls up as witness Augustine's *Retractationes,* which is not a work of denial but a review of one's career in the interests of increased self-knowledge and self-reform. Working against the value of Sayce's shrewd insight, however, is her insistence upon an either/or

decision that most of us now will not be willing to make. She insists
that in order to view Chaucer's ending as fulfilling the inherent imperatives of literary convention, we must deny that it could also be fulfilling
individual, personal intentions. That strikes me as an unnecessary,
even a false distinction. Wurtele sees this weakness in Sayce's argument
very well:

. . . nor does it follow, because Chaucer felt a concern over questions of
literary decorum and made use of a well-established form, that the "tacit or
explicit" assumptions about the Retraction's status as "autobiographical confession" are therefore wrong.

He then goes on to make an equally unnecessary, and, I would argue,
equally false distinction of his own:

. . . but it is not the literary work—the *Canterbury Tales* or even any major
element of it—that is under consideration. At issue is an incongruous yet
significant, passage inserted at the end of that work.[15]

Surely it is precisely the entire literary work that is in question.
No ending can "revoke" or "unmake" the work that it concludes: man
is not God; he cannot undo his own genesis. But ending can and does
add on to, mediate, transform, and complete the meaning of what
went before, and Chaucer's *Retraction,* if it is to mean in any nontrivial
way, must mean itself as a final, even a determinant, closure to the
entire *Canterbury Tales.*

Exactly how that might or might not work has been the issue in
question over the years for many critics, ranging from D. W.
Robertson and Bernard Huppé through Talbot Donaldson and Donald
Howard to David Benson and Derek Pearsall. And part of that debate
involves the matter of determining who is doing the writing and who
the talking. What about the rubric, "Here taketh the maker of his
boke his leve"? Is it scribal or authorial? What is the force for the rest
of the *Retraction* if it is scribal? And if it is authorial, is it Chaucer
speaking, or is it the Parson? Several critics, for one reason or another,
argue that the voice of the *Retraction,* at least at its beginning and
ending, must be understood to be the voice of the Parson rather than
the voice of the narrating, historical Chaucer. I would argue that there
is something very compelling and useful about identifying the speak-

ing voice as that of the Parson. But only at the beginning, and only for a while.

I would suggest that when we come to the catalogue of works that "sownen" into sin, we do not, as Wurtele and others have it, run up against a last-minute interpolation by a dying, panicked Chaucer. Rather we are then to understand that we have engaged in normal, human misprision; we discover that the voice speaking the *Retraction* is not that of the Parson, but has in fact been the voice of the implied Chaucer all along. A tentative ambiguity regarding the speaker's identity at the beginning allows for a richer, more welcome, even more appropriate range of implication than identifying the speaker at once and definitively as either the Parson or Chaucer. For instance, a conventional opportunity for amplification at ending, by which the Parson can recall his introductory remarks on penance, would be within the horizon of expectation signalled by the genre of the penitential handbook; and we work no real distortions at the closure of the *Canterbury Tales* as a whole if we assume, at least for a moment, that the voice speaking is that of the Parson, rounding off his theme.

But the true identity of the speaker, here as so often in real life, clarifies and resolves itself as more information comes to the fore. When that voice has finished quoting St. Paul and moves on to discuss a desire to "revoke in my retraccions" all those "werkes that sownen unto sinne," we understand that the Parson—who we have suspected was another secret agent of Chaucer all along—has, somewhere along the line, submitted to his author; just as Chaucer, the now clearly understood writer, the one who has "always already" been speaking in any ultimate sense, is getting ready to submit to his. Such a reading is not all that strained, and it does resolve a number of otherwise untenable anomalies. To get a fresh sense of how this all might work, here is the text of the *Retraction,* taken from the *Riverside Chaucer:*

Heere taketh the makere of this book his leve. Now preye I to hem alle that herkne this litel tretys or rede, that if ther be any thyng in it that liketh hem, that therof they thanken oure Lord Jhesu Crist, of whom procedeth al wit and al goodnesse. And if ther be any thyng that displese hem, I preye hem also that they arrette it to the defaute of myn unkonnynge and nat to my wyl, that wolde ful fayn have seyd bettre if I hadde had konnynge. For our book seith, "Al that is writen is writen for oure doctrine," and that is myn entente.

267

Up to this point the speaker could well be the Parson. From now on, however, we discover that if we thought this was the case, we must adjust our understanding. And such a shift in perspective, along with the admission of an attendant need to adjust understanding, is precisely the central message that the entire work is making clear about life here at closure: We are *not* in Canterbury, but "at a thropes ende." It is *not* morning, but early evening. At the point of closure, we discover we are neither where nor when we thought we were: it is precisely at this point of new awareness of the real situation that we must adjust our understanding. The *Retraction* continues:

Wherefor I besek yow mekely, for the mercy of God, that ye praye for me that Christ have mercy on me and and foryeve me my giltes; and namely of my translacions and enditynges of worldly vanitees, the whiche I revoke in my retracciouns: as is the book of Troilus, the books also of Fame . . . the tales of Caunterbury, thilke that sownen into synne. . . . so that I may been oon of hem at the day of doom that shulle be saved. Qui cum Patre et Spiritu Sancto vivit et regnat Deus per omnia secula. Amen.

HERE IS ENDED THE BOOK OF THE TALES OF
CAUNTERBURY, COMPILED BY GEFFREY CHAUCER,
OF WHOS SOULE JHESU CRIST HAVE MERCY: AMEN

(10 [I]. 1091–92)

Chaucer's shifts in modes of address and languages mirror the final transformation of the most significant work of his life to an image of the final and radical act of his life as significant work: the art of holy dying (*ars moriendi*). We move from the English prose of the penitent in recollection, confession, and retraction outward to the collective and institutionalized Latin of divine revelation to the final Hebrew syllables of plenary acceptance: Amen: So Be It. Finally there is the epitaph, writ large in the impersonal voice of an implied third person reporting one more passage among many.

Surely the moment linking continuance and severance at the point of literary closure is always a potential trope of the existential moment linking life and death. Yet in this special case, at the very end of the *Canterbury Tales,* Chaucer, in the form of his retraction, makes sure that the loop of life and art completes itself. After assisting at the recuperation of the work of art back into the life of the artist, we are issued a final directive by the artist as he ends that life: we are to complete the loop by relinquishing him as person and return back into the looking glass of his words. At the margin between life and death, Chaucer reads the past as figured in his "published" writing and then appropriates it into the liminal moment of his imagined final passing. As he does so, he engages, like the blessed Augustine he has his Parson so frequently quote, in a confession/conversion that is in its severest procedure an *imitatio Christi*. After taking back his work and making it part of his life at existential ending, he manages, through the very conversion of that act of appropriation into the more stable forms of remembrance that constitute the *Retraction,* to complete his *ars moriendi*, his art of dying, by reconverting the personal moment of his passing back into the sharable forms of public discourse. He offers up the private possession of his final moment *in extremis mortuis* on the altar of public good, thereby converting an image of our final experience into an image of our final authority: our dying flesh made living word.

The map of this looping is the final key to the signification of his manipulations of the levels and languages of discourse as the voice of the implied author passes through the implied point of dying. He moves in the discourse of the *Retraction* from an individuated sense of deliberation and prayer, couched in first-person English, to the quiet, collective Latin of liturgical prayer, to the plenary Hebrew of universal Judeo-Christian resignation and final, full acceptance. At the end, we hear a voice notifying us, in very ordinary third-person English, of Chaucer's passing, here and now in England. Whether that particular rubric was written by Chaucer or by a scribe may well be of interest, but it is only of secondary interest. What remains paramount is the haunting way in which Chaucer has, at the end, demonstrated rather than argued the underlying identity of the author as writer/creator and as creature/person; how he has illuminated in his *Retraction* the inextricable link between this particular individual moment and the collective meaning that it signifies for all of us. As we track his moves at closure and assess his registers of discourse within our minds, we find ourselves inevitably inquiring, however obliquely, into the fundamental relationships obtaining between *any* work and *any* life and the world to which they must both submit at the point of ending—including, of course, our own.

To sum up: As we read closure of the *Canterbury Tales,* we can see, in the mirror of Alisoun of Bath's appropriation of her story of the Rapist and the Hag into the tally of her own marriages, Chaucer's own judicious reappropriation of himself as fictive author of the *Canterbury Tales* both back into a personal self lived as a "real" pilgrim and back out to us again as a literary looking glass, a *figura* of ourselves. As we do so, we witness the reappropriation of art back into life and out again into the rituals of the final acts and arts of holy dying.

In his fictive art, Chaucer provided both the type, in the purgatorial figure of the Wife of Bath ("Lat go, farwel!"), and the infernal anti-type, that parodic inversion of paradisal desire figured in the speech of the Pardoner's Old Man:

> Ne Deeth, allas, ne wol nat han my lyf. [will not have]
> Thus walke I, lyk a restelees kaityf, [captive]
> And on the ground, which is my moodres gate, [mother's]
> I knokke with my staf, bothe erly and late,
> And saye 'Leeve mooder, leet me in! [dear mother]
>
> (6 [C].727–31)

Chaucer agrees in his poetics with Dante; we must be able to imagine well our capacity for Hell in order to credential our desire for Paradise. But the most telling speculum for Chaucer here in the *Retraction* was not so much Dante as St. Augustine, the master model for reading one's life as text: first in the *Confessions* of one's prime, then in the *Retractationes* of older age.

Yeats was right: we are the last romantics; yet we must not do Chaucer the disservice of romancing his final, intractable, illegible stone. The *Retraction,* as far as we can determine these things, is Chaucer's valedictory gift. It is authentic; it stands. But it is not, as some have thought, that the work has subsumed the maker or that the maker has in any way "betrayed" the work. It is that Chaucer, in a fitting reappropriation of his life-work at the point of apprehended death, has used the conventions of holy dying to mediate the completion of his personal and—*in figura*—our collective "troth": our truth to ourselves, to our work, and to our world.

* * * *

To bring both this chapter and this study to their own closure, perhaps a few final words will be tolerated regarding what I see as the nature of this undertaking. In talking about various modes of closure, for example, whether they be Iliadic or Odyssean, Virgilian or Ovidian, it seems right not only to admit but to insist upon the fact that such terms are not scientific but heuristic. Such strategies of closure, insofar as they point to anything real and nontrivial, would seem to point to basic impulses that simultaneously and continuously drive all narrative: the impulse to go on as well as the impulse to stop. Perhaps these fundamental narrative impulses mirror even deeper bio-psychological desires in all of us: a desire to live as well as a desire to die. At any given moment, one of these impulses triumphs over the other and helps constitute, for a while, a style. Such terms represent then not so much ideas as images of a fundamentally human procedure, and their validity probably resides more in their use to the mind than in their verifiability in the world.

David Hult has articulated very clearly both the anxieties and the tentative satisfactions that accompany studies of this sort. He concludes his own examination of reflexivity in Guillaume de Lorris's use of the myth of Narcissus by suggesting that reflexivity itself mirrors the modern reader's own role, that the "utter figural intangibility of Narcissus explains the reader's paradox, the human need for mystery, for unknowingness—that factor of human fictions that feeds the ongoing quest for knowledge but can never by definition satisfy it." Even more important, he insists, is the fact that Guillaume takes the myth beyond an image of pure atrophy and desolation by turning it into a generative paradigm of recreative self-knowing: "The shadowy and deceptive truth of the fountain is also a projection of the subject, an outward application of the individual's own perceptions."[16]

As we have toured some of the major modes of literary mirroring, we have observed how medieval writers depicted worlds in which literary art itself became a central mirroring counter in that vast and crucial game of love played out between medieval men and women and their God. But even as we observe that game, as we reconstitute it in the interior theaters of our own minds, we also see, in a glass darkly, our own mirror games. We see an image of the informing, but also revealing, role played by our deep desire to fulfill ourselves and thereby obey the Delphic and Socratic imperative to fully know ourselves. Thus reading medieval literature, like reading any literature, becomes, in Hult's happy play on the phrase, a "self-fulfilling prophecy," and, like the Wife of Bath, we test, in the act of reading, the full authority of our own experience.

Perhaps as we do so we dance on the edge of the abyss; but by sharing the added knowledge won by collective meditation and historical mediation, we acquire at least the tenuous consolation that we dance there together. Wallace Stevens, upon whose spirit I have relentlessly imposed the role of Virgilian guide for this journey through Roman and medieval looking glasses, provides us in one of his last poems, "The Final Soliloquy to the Interior Paramour," with fitting valediction:

> Here, now, we forget each other and ourselves.
> We feel the obscurity of an order, a whole,
> A knowledge, that which arranged the rendezvous
>
> Within its vital boundary, in the mind.
> We say God and the imagination are one . . .
> How high that highest candle lights the dark.
>
> Out of this same light, out of the central mind,
> We make a dwelling in the evening air,
> In which being there together is enough.

Appendix: Mirrors in
Modern Theory and Cultural History

SPIEGEL: noch nie hat man wissend beschrieben,
was ihr in euerem Wesen seid.

[MIRRORS: never yet has anyone fully knowing described
what in your essence you are.]
                                    —Rilke, *Sonette an Orpheus*, 2.3

This appendix makes no claims for either breadth or depth: rather it reviews a cluster of extraordinarily valuable approaches and perspectives encountered in the course of pursuing this project.

As with any project, some of the most intriguing reading turned out to be centered on issues that were relatively peripheral to my immediate concerns. Thus the following observations, findings, and queries written in response to that reading seemed too tangential to warrant systematic inclusion in this study of Roman and medieval literary catoptrics; yet the material itself not only formed a valuable echo chamber for my own thinking, it also proved, on its own terms, to be far too informative and provocative to let go entirely. The compromise that suggested itself was an appendix in the form of a review essay.

The following authors' viewpoints fall primarily, but not all that comfortably, into the domain of either cultural theory or cultural history; as time goes by one suspects that the inherited and often comforting division between theory and history is actually a division more accountable to mood and fashion than to real distinctions in subject or method.

Any consideration of mirrors and mirroring requires that attention be paid to the multiple, often extremely disparate aspects of the subject. One must at some early point be concerned with the physical nature of mirrors, with what mirrors are and were, what they were made of and how they were made. In short, we need to know more about mirrors as material culture: as things and as instruments; as decorative as well as functional adjuncts to walls and tables, to columns, ceilings, fortresses, magic theaters, and street corners. And as we consider mirrors historically as instruments, we see ever more clearly that it was primarily what people thought mirrors did and did not do, and how they thought mirrors did or did not do it, that helped Western Europe generate its self-informing and ever-shifting set of understandings and misunderstandings about how this world gets known, how the mystery of things gets taken on.

It would have been extremely helpful for this study of Roman and medieval literary catoptrics if the encyclopedic book on mirrors and mirroring were already written. But Rilke's lines quoted as brief epigraph are still correct: it has not yet been written; and this book could never have been that book. Yet the requisite prolegomenon for such a book lurks nevertheless in the aggregate contribution of a little over a dozen books and essays that have appeared, more or less independently, over the past thirty years or so.

Jorge Luis Borges once suggested in an interview that rather than spend a lifetime writing novels, one could perhaps proceed more efficiently by imagining the books as already written and the author dead. One would be asked to write a literary obituary of appreciation. This might well take the form of a postmortem review of an entire career's worth of literary remains, and its publication could then serve to accompany the interment of the imagined author who never wrote them.

Something resembling that strategy will be attempted here in order to deploy and demonstrate the ranges of aspect that both phenomenal and intellectual mirroring developed in the history of Western intellect and imagination. The difference, of course, is that the works treated in my synoptic eulogy have actually been written, and some of the writers called upon here in cerebral witness are very much alive. We will deal with five authors at somewhat greater length: Jacques Lacan,

Umberto Eco, Richard Rorty, David Lindberg, and Jurgis Baltrusaitis. The others will receive shorter shrift; not because they have lesser value, but because I have less of value to say about them.

Lacan's Mirror-Stage: Identity and Isolation

Perhaps our most commonly held image of the birth of self-awareness resides in the narrative of Narcissus. Yet that comes rather late in terms of literary history. I have found no version of the Narcissus narrative before Ovid that includes self-recognition as part of the denouement of the narrative. And though Ovid makes much of the element of self-discovery, medieval writers, for whom Ovid was often even more important than Virgil, nevertheless frequently neglect this aspect; many medieval references to Narcissus emphasize as the main point of the story the boy's stupidity at loving a water image and remain completely silent regarding the discovery that the image was, after all, his own. An important exception in this regard was the twelfth-century German court poet Heinrich von Morungen. In chapter 5 I attempted to show not only how Ovidian Heinrich is, but also how acutely he anticipates modern psychological thinking about the process of self-discovery in the mirror of the Other.

The modern theoretician of Narcissus is not so much Freud, of course, as his French Melanchthon, Jacques Lacan, for whom this encounter of the child and the mirror becomes the first, and remains the central, image of man's development toward self-awareness. Early on in his monumental *Ecrits,* we find a short essay that is seminal and indispensable: "Le Stade du miroir comme formateur de la fonction du Je."[1]

Lacan is compelling both in his description of the moment and in his reading of its implications. And he is implacable in his insistence that the discovery of the self as the Other in the mirror leads to a separation that is forever unbridgeable between the self and the Other in the real world.

This act, far from exhausting itself, as in the case of the ape, who achieves control by sensing the vacuity of the image, leads immediately, in the case of the child, to a series of gestures by which he proves out, in play, the relationship between the movements assumed [to be] in the image to those of his reflected environment; between the virtual image-complex and the reality which it doubles: the child's own body and the people, and the objects which are by his side. (*Ecrits*, 91)[2]

The veiled key to the operation is the function of the Other in the course of the discovery of the self. The child looks at the image of the self in the mirror and sees an Other. He then looks at the real other people and objects with him and sees them also in the mirror. This is patently a relationship of identity: the Others by his side are replicated in the virtual image of those Others in the mirror—except for one of those Others in the mirror. The shock of recognition comes with the realization that the remaining Other in the mirror not accounted for by the people and objects at his side must be himself. Here the presence of the Other mediates the child's discovery that his image in the mirror is not an Other, but indeed the self. This is accomplished ludically, and Lacan describes the child's reaction as accompanied by "l'assomption jubilatoire," a jubilant assumption, playing more than a little on the elevation of the Virgin Mary and on the pleasures of orgasm as well as on the idea of taking on something excitingly new.

This joy is not only intense; it is short-lived: soon and forever over. Why? Because the child's act of self-recognition inevitably foreshadows two things: "la permanence mentale du *je* en même temps qu'elle préfigure sa destination aliénante" [the mental permanence of the *ego* at the same time as it prefigures its alienating destiny] (*Ecrits*, 95).

One of the necessary disadvantages of a sense of identity is that it involves the placement of a firm barrier between the self and the Other. This is fairly self-evident to most of us—what is not self-evident is that this barrier between the self and the Other should be considered insurmountable. For Lacan the barrier is absolute. Here is the paragraph that foretells that vision:

This development is experienced as a temporal dialectic which projects decisively the formation of the individual into history. The mirror-stage is a drama in which internal pressure moves quickly from a sense of insufficiency to a sense of anticipation—and which, for the subject, caught in the lure of spatial identification, fashions fantasies which move from an image of a dismembered body to a form which we will call an orthopedic index of its own

276

totality—and to an armor, finally put on, of an alienating identity, which will mark, with its rigid structure, the child's entire mental development. Thus the rupture of the circle joining interiority and exteriority itself occasions the inexhaustible conjunctions [between the self and its virtual image] from which we derive the verifications of the ego. (*Ecrits*, 97)

That hidden key to the operations of self-identification, the Other, is now distinguished by a predestined and eternal absence from the one it helped toward self-discovery. For Lacan, identity necessitates isolation, a purer kind that leads to sainthood, desolation, or madness. The discovery in the mirror leads to the assumption of an orthopedic cast, a structure into which we must somehow fit, as if into a prefabricated shoe, our hitherto undifferentiated sense of self as limitless energy. This body, this sense of spatial limitation, is rigid, and will shape, as defensively as a medieval suit of armor—and with no accompanying odor of sanctity—the entire mental development of the child. Once the Other has mediated for the self its own discovery, that process of discovery itself initiates a developmental pattern that makes impossible any restorative mediation back to the Other. Lacan closes this bleak but crucial essay (of barely eight pages) by linking this process of individual discovery to its societal context, and his valedictions make one wonder that he didn't close up shop in 1949 and go home. As for the ties that bind, they are a "knot of imaginary servitude"; as for love, its destiny is never to join, but always to sever: "Psychoanalysis alone recognizes this knot of imaginary servitude which love must always untie or cut" (*Ecrits*, 100). As for the powers and limitations of his discipline, which would seem coterminous with those of his vision, Lacan writes:

In the resources [of recourse] which we preserve from subject to subject, psychoanalysis can only accompany the patient up to the ecstatic limit of "*That's you!*," where the token of his mortal destiny reveals itself to him, but it is not in our personal power as practitioners to lead him to the point where the real voyage begins. (*Ecrits*, 100)

According to Lacan's account of the confrontation with the mirror, we get, *per speculum*, by means of a mirror, *in aenigmate*, at or into the enigma of the self. But we cannot get back out again to the Other. What Lacan fails to account for is the positive effect of the distorting aspects of the mirroring system. The mirror tells its particular truth mercilessly, and we must learn with care the nature and the reach of that truth. But we also learn as much, perhaps more, from the ways in which we see how the truth of the mirror's image is *not* true to our sense of things.

We see in the mirror, as St. Augustine would insist we see, an image that is unlike as well as like the interior image of reality we have in our mind. To the extent that the mirror image is what we expect to see, we feel the affirming power of similarity. To the extent that it is different (via distortion, sense of inversion, chips, bumps, frames, bubbles in the glass, pockmarks in the metal, etc.), we begin to think. By triangulating what we see from where we look with what we know (or think we know), we figure out what it is that is incongruent and hence potentially faulty with either the image in the mirror or the image in our minds. It is only from that invaluable discrepancy between the mirror's image and the mind's eye that we can extrapolate new understandings of the "real" and move along.

Lacan speaks for and out of an age that has lost or rejected the coherence of relationship guaranteed to the medieval imagination by its appropriation of the Incarnation not merely as imaginable option, but as fact. The hypostatic union available in the physical, historical person of Christ was, for the Middle Ages, a final, unquestionable reconciliation of the intellectually required sense of differentiation between the self and the Other as well as the desperately desired similarity between them. It is no wonder, then, that Lacan—who is powerfully revelatory concerning contemporary anxieties, neuroses, and psychoses—is, like Everyman, limited by the perspectives of his age and is, in his theory of the mirror and self-discovery, of little direct use in attempting to understand the relationships between mirrors and epistemology (in general) and self-discovery (in particular) that obtained in earlier ages. Nor would he offer himself in that capacity. But because he is himself a telling mirror of the alterities of contemporary culture, we must test him in that capacity nonetheless. Drawing on his keen observations regarding the mediating role of the Other we can move forward, even in secular terms, from his essentially nihilistic position.

There is at least one way of arguing that the self can recognize in the mirror the Other along with the self as primal entities. As indicated above, that argument is double. The mirror provides, for a moment, the imaginable possibility, in both positive and negative aspects, of either a reconciliation or a contamination between the self and the Other. Positively charged, we assume for ourselves the value of the Other by possession, or complete our adoration of the Other by submission. Negatively charged, we loathe the cannibalistic destruction and incorporation of the Other by possession, and fear "la petite morte," that little death of the self, as it dies *into* the Other in submission. Near the end of his brief mirror essay, Lacan provides us with a "little list" of the atmospherics triggered by the mirror image: "inversion, isolation, reduplication, cancellation and displacement." Like Wallace Stevens's Snow Man, Lacan has a mind of winter. He is a connoisseur of "nothing that is not there and the nothing that is."[3] Thus it is not so much the brilliant surface of his argument, after all, but the cracks in the Lacanian looking glass that allow us, ultimately, to see the epideictic relationship that his work bears to a medieval sense of things.

Both Augustine and Dante continually reflect in their images a deep-seated and never-ceasing dialectic between an allegiance to the highly differentiated way things are (a love of texture, a respect for diversity and multiplicity) and an unquenchable desire for informing unity and coherence. The Trinity provided for them the final image of the reconciliation of this conflict as they sought to image forth Divinity as both many and one.

Perhaps our ultimate desire, now as well as in the Middle Ages, is to find the self unquestionably authenticated in the Other. For that, the Other must be absolutely other and the self must be undeniably present in it. But for those of us living in a post-Christian world, the deepest fear may be of falling into the abyss of solipsism, and it is probably more important that the Other be truly other, than that the desired agendas of encounter with the Other prove to be actually possible.

Eco: Images in Mirrors are *Not* Signs

The delight in reading Umberto Eco may well stem from his controlled schizophrenia: his consistency as both semiotic novelist and novelistic semiotician. Surely *The Name of the Rose* and *Foucault's Pendulum* embody both explicit and implied theories of catoptrics capacious enough for anyone. But his short monograph on mirrors recently made available in *Semiotics and the Philosophy of Language* deploys an explicit and lucid set of observations and warnings regarding our encounters with physical reflection that proves of more immediate use.[4]

Eco calls our longing for a world in which mirrors would do what we wished they would do a case of "catoptric nostalgia." More important, he shows us, in his deceptively amusing way, what it is we must not expect to find. His essay is a brilliant exercise in sustaining, for just as long as appears reasonable, a litany of negation: creating in a surprisingly jovial mood yet another inventory of nothing that is not there and the nothing that is:

It might be somewhat meaningless to discover that the mirror image is a sign, but it would be more interesting to discover that the mirror image is *not* a sign and why. Even though we assume we know everything about the mirror, excluding mirrors from the class of signs might help us better to define a sign (or at least to define what a sign is not). (*Semiotics*, 202)

Eco suggests that it might at first appear that Lacan has already said what there is to say on the subject, but he quickly points out that Lacan was concerned with mirror confrontations solely as they constituted threshold experiences of infant children. He suggests it might be equally interesting, perhaps even liberating, to think about the experience of mirrors we have as adults, when we already *know* what a mirror is and, at least to some extent, what it is we see in it. Eco is eager to instruct us about how exquisitely true the mirror is to the world. An amusing, if minor, shock comes when he insists that the mirror does not give us an inverse image:

A mirror reflects the right side exactly where the right side is, and the same with the left side. It is the observer (so ingenuous even when he is a scientist) who by self-identification imagines he is the man inside the mirror and, looking at himself, realizes he is wearing his watch on his right wrist. But it would be so only if he, the observer I mean, were the one who is inside the mirror (*Je est un autre!*). On the contrary, those who avoid behaving as Alice, and getting into the mirror, do not so deceive themselves. And, in fact, every morning, in the bathroom, each of us does use a mirror without behaving as a spastic. (*Semiotics*, 205)

For adults, the proper use of mirrors involves knowing we are facing them, or using them prosthetically to extend our range of sight (around corners, into dark places, etc.)—even when, in the fun house, or in the earlier, much more complicated catoptric theaters of ancient, medieval, and renaissance worlds (see the discussion of Baltrusaitis that follows), we play games that depend on pretending we *don't* know we are playing with mirrors. Eco is clear on what it is about mirrors that makes them useful:

You should not forget that the mirror image is not a double of its object, but, rather a double of the stimulating field one could have access to if one looked at the object instead of looking at its mirror image. The fact that the mirror image is a most peculiar case of double and has the traits of a unique case explains why mirrors inspired so much literature; this virtual duplication of stimuli (which sometimes works as if there were a duplication of both my body as an object and my body as a subject, splitting and facing itself), this theft of an image, this unceasing temptation to believe I am someone else, makes man's experience with mirrors an absolutely unique one, on the threshold between perception and signification. (*Semiotics,* 210)

For Eco there is nothing inherently wrong with wishing the situation to be otherwise as long as we don't forget that it isn't. One of these recurring yet usually fleeting desires is that the mirror, as we gaze into it, somehow absolutely capture us, the *real* us. But it is not a sign of ourselves we see, as enraptured as we may become. The haunting, fugitive nature of the outcome of such usually harmless habits of wishing is elegantly captured thus:

I may . . . happen to find a message in a bottle reading "I was shipwrecked in the Juan Fernandez islands": it would be clear to me that someone (someone who is not myself) was ship-wrecked. But, if I find a mirror in a bottle, after taking it out with considerable effort, I would always see myself in it, whoever may have sent it as a message. (*Semiotics,* 211)

Eco concludes his essay with a brief magical mystery tour of increasingly baroque uses of the mirror, showing that one can never break out of the antihermeneutic circle drawn above. There are two universes—the catoptric and the semiosic:

These two universes, of which the former is threshold to the latter, have no connecting points, the extreme cases represented by distorting mirrors being in fact "catastrophic points." There comes a time when one has to make up one's mind and choose which side one is on. The catoptric universe is a reality which can give the impressions of virtuality, whereas the semiosic universe is a virtuality which can give the impression of reality. (*Semiotics*, 226)

Looking at the present historically as well as contemporaneously, one can argue that Eco can find no connecting points between these two universes because he too has appropriated the givens of his time, one of which is the programmatic refusal to conceive of the Incarnation as a possibly relevant proposition outside the purview of medieval history or the realm of fiction. For example, the points of intersection that Eco describes as catastrophic were considered in the medieval mind of Alan of Lille as radically redemptive; as in fact they also are in the alternative worlds of Eco's own studies in medieval aesthetics and in his novels. This is yet another example of what Jauss means by the illuminating power of true medieval alterity. And again, it is not my intention to be so fatuous as to fault either Lacan or Eco with some fatal failure to get born again as Christians. I am merely examining the arsenal of our eclectic age in search of ideas concerning mirrors that will (*a*) help us get greater critical purchase on the a priori axioms we bring to *any* problem regarding mimetics and reflection, and (*b*) help us sort out more accurately the particular problems in understanding literary mirroring that obtained between the death of Caesar and the death of Chaucer.

What Eco teaches by both example and argument is that the most important thing we can learn from mirrors is what it is we cannot learn from them.

Rorty: Denaturing Mirrors to Untune the Skies

Richard Rorty's powerful and notorious book *Philosophy and the Mirror of Nature* combines witty history and devastating critique as he follows Philosophy's two-thousand-year love affair with its own image as a mental power both enabling and verifying the foundations of human knowledge.[5] Philosophy, he says,

sees itself as the attempt to underwrite or debunk claims to knowledge made by science, morality, art or religion. It purports to do this on the basis of its special understanding of the nature of knowledge and of mind. (*Mirror of Nature*, 3)

The problem is that this sense of privileged access to reality owes more to an array of successive metaphors than to verifiable propositions:

It is pictures rather than propositions, metaphors rather than statements which determine most of our philosophical convictions. The picture which holds traditional philosophy captive is that of the mind as a great mirror, containing various representations—some accurate, some not—and capable of being studied by pure, nonempirical methods. Without the notion of the mind as mirror, the notion of knowledge as accuracy of representation would not have suggested itself. Without this latter notion, the strategy common to Descartes and Kant—getting more accurate representations by inspecting, repairing and polishing the mirror, so to speak—would not have made sense. Without this strategy in mind, recent claims that philosophy could consist of "conceptual analysis," or "phenomenological analysis" or "explication of meaning" or examination of the "logic of our language" or of "the structure of the constituting activity of consciousness" would not have made sense. (*Mirror of Nature,* 12)

The attack, then, is not only on varieties of positivistic philosophy, but on their key offshoots: analytic philosophy, phenomenology, hermeneutics, language games, and psychology: a fairly significant hit list. His aim is not to be constructive, but openly deconstructive:

The aim of the book is to undermine the reader's confidence in "the mind" as something about which one should have a "philosophical" view, in "knowledge" as something about which there ought to be a "theory" and which has "foundations," and in "philosophy" as it has been conceived since Kant. (*Mirror of Nature,* 7)

Rorty's mode of deconstruction is designed not to express some deep-seated orneriness but, on the contrary, to open up our minds to a new and refreshing call to play: to reengage in adult, ludic conversation in which the point of the game is not to conclude the conversation but find new ways of continuing it. It is a therapeutic, not a systematic, book; it engages, in the tradition of the later Dewey, Heidegger, and Wittgenstein, in "edifying" philosophy—and recuperates for philosophy a liberating irony not systematically deployed since the dialogues of Plato. For both Plato and Rorty, the illusion triumphs—if not in the alleged mise-en-scène, at least in the mental "cabinet" of the attending reader—that such apparently spontaneous discourse mirrors the imaginable possibility of true dialectic, and that right talking can, after all, mediate right loving among civilized and civilizing citizens of a free republic.

Some of the weaknesses accompanying the strengths of Plato are also present in Rorty. There is, for some, an off-putting aristocratic tone combined with a sense that for the speaker (Rorty or Plato) evil, or at least ill will, is itself more a mistake than a crime and less, rather than more, troublesome for that. In fact evil seems for both Plato and Rorty a matter of too little information, not quite enough brain power, or bad manners. Yet the high spirits are catching. Rorty exhorts us to take advantage of an opportunity to free ourselves from present constraints by seeing them, as Alice does, as "nothing but a pack of cards." One of the minor ironies of the present age is that Rorty can undertake the project of undermining the foundation of received ideas with gay abandon, while someone like René Girard, for example, seems more often impelled by bitter anger.[6]

In addition, there is in Rorty a therapeutic modesty seldom found in Plato, and though it may not come through in this final assessment of his masters, the modesty of tone wields a cleansing power throughout this provocative and "edifying" book:

Great systematic philosophers are constructive and offer arguments. Great edifying philosophers are reactive and offer satires, parodies, aphorisms. . . . Great systematic philosophers, like great scientists, build for eternity. Great edifying philosophers destroy for the sake of their own generation. (*Mirror of Nature*, 369)

In his plea to free us from the dependence upon systematic analogical thinking, he is uneager to grant that this habit of perceiving metaphorically may be an unbreakable one, even that it may perhaps be the only available habit we can "wear" as we look. It may only be, in fact, for the purpose of engaging in rare, Rorty-like conversations that we can dispense with speculative metaphors, and even in such discourse one has the hunch that they would be chilly conversations if we did so. It seems then especially unlikely that we can dispense with the mirrors of metaphor as we attempt modest authenticity of being and knowing in that more quotidian world of building our temples, teaching our children, and cutting our corners. Our system of seeing things as mirrors paradoxically allows us to manage these balancing acts pretty well. As our organ of perception, the eye has this ironic, humdrum limitation: it has no unmediated access to its own center; it can only perceive itself in mirrors. We ask a lot of it—perhaps too much—to cut itself off from what may well be its sole instrument of self-discovery.

The net result of this minisurvey of three recent theorists of reflection, mirroring, and doubling is to see how close to bankruptcy our intellects and imaginations have come regarding these matters as we try to deal with medieval alterity. And so we push on backwards (an exercise Eco systematically engages in, Rorty encourages, and Lacan would call futile) in a search for more invigorating energies from the past.

Lindberg and the History of Vision Theory

David Lindberg, in his masterful narrative *The Theories of Vision from al-Kindi to Kepler,* lays out an extremely clear array of approaches to light, sight, and reflection that accounts for the main intellectual vectors driving the Greek imagination, and which held on, through myriad transformations, until the tenth-century Islamic synthesis of al-Hazen and its thirteenth-century Western appropriations by Roger Bacon. It was

A medical tradition, concerned primarily with the anatomy and physiology of the eye and the treatment of eye disease; a physical or philosophical tradition, devoted to questions of epistemology, psychology and physical causation; and a mathematical tradition, directed principally toward a geometrical explanation of the perception of space. Later, as Greek civilization went into decline, these same three traditions were transmitted to Islam and Latin Christendom, where they provided the framework and the materials for the medieval science of optics.[7]

Lindberg's careful history affirms Kuhn's intuitions regarding the history of scientific revolutions, that science proceeds according to partial and local agendas and only rarely receives the benefit (and disruption) of genuinely creative and synthetic minds.[8] The physicians, who want to cure the eye, and therefore require a physiology of the eye, don't give a tinker's damn about how light works. The mathematicians want to know how light works, but have no interest in the human eye. Only the philosophers of mind, in the service of understanding the new Christian dispensation, were able to take advantage of Chalcidius's early fourth-century Latin translation of the *Timaeus* and see useful analogies of ontology and epistemology in Plato's fables concerning the etiology of physics, light, reflection, and perception. One of the great ironies of history is that light, sight, perception, and reflection were thus available in a unified, coherent linguistic analogy long before they were integrated into a unified, coherent physical theory. In more than a merely casual sense metaphysics preceded physics.

We must free ourselves from the idea that a unified theory of light is in any way self-evident. After all, we are still more than a little embarrassed ourselves by our current need for two mutually exclusive theories of waves and particles in order to account for the behavior of light. The consolations of Niels Bohr's principle of complementarity are only partial; we impatiently await the final revelations of a unified force theory. We should, then, have some sympathy with the citizens of the period from Plato to the thirteenth century as they were both blessed and cursed with a plethora of mutually exclusive theories of light, sight, and reflection.

Lindberg shows that light was proposed variously as rays, corpuscles, spirits, pneuma—almost anything imaginable (except particles or waves). And the physiology of sight ranged from extramission (light went out from the eye to the object) to intromission (something went from the object to the eye) to theories that mixed both ideas. Lindberg shows how Lucretius, for example, suggests that objects are constantly flinging off extremely thin films that enter our eye through the pupil, while neglecting to explain how the film of a mountain, say, shrinks in the process sufficiently to enter the eyeball. Much earlier, Plato's combination theory of extramission and intromission has the inner fire move out from the eye, and then be joined and activated by the light of the sun, and, after having joined up at the object, return with the image as from a mirror and reenter the eye, and thence the soul. In addition, Aristotle postulated an entirely different theory in which the cone triangulated by the eye and the object defined a continuous medium that instantaneously mediated perception.

Lindberg goes on to show that it was by linking the agenda of the physician with that of the mathematician that al-Hazen was able to play the extraordinary role of mediating not only light and sight but East and West as he, a prince of Islamic learning, provided the base for Kepler's synthesis of a viable theory of light, vision, and catoptrics. It is important that we sense how deeply unstable the physics of light and reflection actually was through the thirteenth century, even as we read of a much more unified symbolic use of light in metaphysical and theological discourse.

But until al-Hazen, the wrangling continued for over fifteen centuries, back and forth, with the gallery of the theater peopled variously by Platonists, Aristotelians, Euclidites, Galenists, al-Kindians, and continued by various disciples of al-Hazen, culminating, as far as the Middle Ages are concerned, with the final fling of Aristotelianism in the writings of the Franciscan chancellor of Oxford (and later bishop of Lincoln), Robert Grosseteste, and that more stormy follower of St. Francis who lit alternate academic fires in Oxford and Paris even as he synthesized for the West a relatively coherent articulation of the theories of al-Hazen: Roger Bacon. In fact, the general muddle regarding sight, light, and the phenomena of reflection lingered in the minds of Europe long past Kepler. Gustav Hartlaub quotes an eighteenth-century encyclopedia that offers the following options to its reader regarding the mirror image:

Many think our image is actually in the mirror, that is, that the mirror replicates in itself an exact figure of our body. Others insist, on the contrary, that our image isn't in the mirror at all, but that the rays bounce back.

[Etliche meynen, es sey in dem Spiegel unser Ebenbild, das ist, dass der Spiegel eine gleiche Gestalt unseres Leibes bilde. Andere schliessen hingegen, dass unser Ebenbild nicht in dem Spiegel sey, sondern es prallen die Strahlen wider zurück.][9]

There seems little progress either backwards or forwards between this particular hedge on the matter and the ruminations of Seneca fifteen hundred years earlier in his *Quaestiones naturales* about whether the image really is in the mirror or not. We need to get firmly in our minds—and we can get it only from history, not from theory—a sense of irresolvable open-endedness regarding the physics of light and sight as we approach key reflective images and techniques in Roman and medieval literature.

Poets, particularly, work the vineyard relating the particular to the general, the physical to its extensions. They must have found it exquisitely frustrating even as it must have proved extremely liberating to inherit such profound ambiguity regarding the nature of something so central to human experience. The unwillingness of a culture to reach definitive closure on something this basic for so long a time betrays a set of fears and desires regarding the place of the self in its context that not only deserves, but cries out for, the cauterizing wit and restorative humor of Chaucer, Rabelais, Cervantes, Shakespeare, Voltaire, Heine, and Lewis Carroll.

Cultural History from Colie to Kristeva

In addition to the four authors so far discussed, the following contributions are extremely valuable for filling out a sense of the complexities involved. Hartlaub's *Zauber des Spiegels* (see n. 9 to this Appendix) is a history of the image of the mirror in the history of art and forms a model of how to conduct such an iconographic inquiry. He ranges from Greek vase painting to the quietly disturbing drawings of Aubrey Beardsley, but concentrates primarily on the medieval and Renaissance production of Europe. Herbert Grabes's work (in two redactions) is a detailed study of medieval and Renaissance titles in manuscripts and incunabula that contain, in Latin or in the vernacular languages, the word *mirror*. One of the most important phenomena that Grabes demonstrates is the extraordinary denotative as well as connotative range the term had for medieval thought and discourse. Both the noun and the verb often meant ways of thinking, reading, and talking sooner than they meant physical instruments that reflected images in the presence of light. Both the earlier German and later English redactions of Grabe's book are of great use. In addition to a copious synoptic catalogue listing 398 books produced throughout the Middle Ages and Renaissance England, he has analyzed and presented the material in such a way as to provide a relatively clean overview of the shifting ways people thought about light, sight, the eye, mirrors, and reflection for over one thousand years.[10]

Another important contribution to intellectual history is Marcia Colish's *The Mirror of Language;* this book is also available in two equally valuable, but significantly different, redactions.[11] Although

288

written more from the point of view of the interdisciplinary cultural historian of ideas than of the specialist in language, philosophy, or literary criticism, this book, with its tenacious and brightly illuminating focus on the issue of the speculative powers of language (how language mirrors epistemology), manages, by devoting extended attention to Augustine, Anselm, Aquinas, and Dante, to cover an enormous range of intellectual territory in a manner that is consistently revealing and judicious.

The work of Robert Javelet is at once ground-breaking and magisterial.[12] *Image et ressemblance au douxième siècle* is not only a major contribution to Latin patristics, it is also of enormous importance to the current polemic surrounding the general modes of signification known as imitation and representation.

Rosemary L. Colie's brilliant and underread *Paradoxia epidemica* provides, with splendid wit, vision, and minute learning, the *terminus ad quem* of paradoxical thinking as a time-honored mode of deconstructive thought and persuasion.[13] She demonstrates how paradox has provoked and plagued the Western intellect and imagination since Xeno first used it to confound the enemies of Parmenides. Of particular use to this project in literary mirroring are parts 3 and 4, which are concerned with ontological and epistemological paradox.

St. Paul's key articulation on mirrors in 1 Corinthians is the subject of Norbert Hugedé, in *La Métaphore du miroir dans les Epîtres de Saint Paul aux Corinthiens*.[14] This is a masterly study of all the textural vectors that could conceivably, either indirectly or directly, have converged on and branched out from Paul's key articulations regarding mirrors and knowing. Hugedé's coverage of patristics is as scrupulous as his coverage of pre-Christian, Hellenistic writings on mirrors; thus he has been useful for our concerns with later medieval as well as earlier Roman literature.

Hans Leisegang's article in Paully-Wissowa on "Physik" is of more than passing interest to this project. Even more important is his short but splendid article on the intellectual history of the Western idea that nature and the soul have the capacity to mirror God ("Die Erkenntnis Gottes im Spiegel der Seele und der Natur"). This extraordinary piece of wartime writing was first bootlegged into the academic world by the free French, and only became available to us in its original form after the war.[15]

One must remember that the phonic parallel to Narcissus is Echo; John Hollander, a master synesthesiast himself, provides a deft tour of echoes in literature in his *Figure of Echo*.[16] Although the book deals primarily with "Milton and After," Hollander has some dazzling observations to make on Ovid's uses (and abuses) of sound/sense patterns. His penetrating observations are always useful as models, no matter what particular time or place his literary attention is visiting at any given moment.

In her recent and extremely provocative *Tales of Love*, Julia Kristeva has situated two large sections that, taken together, comprise a brilliant survey of both the theoretical and cultural historical aspects of the mirror as psycho-social-literary reflector of the self-as-subject as it deals with the physical, psychological, and metaphysical reflections of the self-as-object in the world through which it travels. The relevant chapter titles give very efficiently a sense of the world Kristeva "covers" as well as a hint of the style with which she does it: "A Holy Madness: She and He"; "Narcissus: The New Insanity"; "God Is Love"; "Ego Affectus Est"; "Bernard of Clairvaux: Affect, Desire, Love"; "Ratio Diligendi, or the Triumph of One's Own"; "Thomas Aquinas: Natural Love and Love of Self."[17]

Baltrusaitis: Games in the Great Hall of Mirrors

We have already stipulated that the encyclopedic book on mirrors and mirroring is as yet unwritten, but there are several very useful works that cover basic ground. The classic general article is that of von Netoliczka, "Katoptron" in Paully-Wissowa's *Real-Encyklopaedie*.[18] This provides the basic information on mirrors in the pre-Christian world: what can be established concerning what they looked like, how they were made, and what constituted their everyday functions. In addition, it is worth glancing at the rich illustrations in Karl Schefold's "Griechische Spiegel," which analyzes the more important holdings in German museums and private collections of the earlier twentieth century.[19] Finally, the tedious but invaluable quotidian information regarding mirrors in the Middle Ages is available in the fine nineteenth-century study by Karl H. Wackernagel, "Über die Spiegel im Mittelalter."[20]

But it is Jurgis Baltrusaitis who provides much of what we now need in his dazzling concoction fittingly and baroquely titled *Essai sur une légende scientifique: le miroir: révélations, science-fiction et fallacies*. With a mix of self-deprecation and brashness, Baltrusaitis calls to mind, in his first sentence, his massive medieval model, the *Speculum Majus* of Vincent de Beauvais (d. 1264), which divided the universe of knowledge into four mirrors: the Mirror of Nature, the Mirror of Wisdom, the Mirror of Morality, and the Mirror of History. Baltrusaitis does not succumb to his clear temptation to appropriate the entire universe for his base of inquiry, but satisfies himself instead with displaying a spectacular pastiche of how that universe is mirrored, a marvelous bricolage of hard information, somewhat softer folklore, photographs, and many useful tidbits and odds and ends about mirrors drawn from a collection of sources ranging from Aristotle through Bosch to the latest solar research.[21]

Although he frequently reflects on the metaphorical and allegorical values mirrors have possessed over centuries, his primary focus is on the physical, on what mirrors did and how they did it. This is helpful, for it counters a consistent tendency on the part of many writers to leap too quickly to metaphoric extension, thereby engaging in premature foreclosure on the rich, varied spectrum of actual mirrors performing actual functions. It is, after all, necessary to gain some control over what it was that mirrors did before we can move on to explore the crucial but much more elusive and ethereal territories surrounding what it was that mirrors meant.

Baltrusaitis makes frequent use of one of the most important Renaissance thinkers about mirroring, Raphael Mirami. In fact, the headnote to the entire book is drawn from this extraordinary sixteenth-century Jewish thinker from Ferrara, and I translate it here from Baltrusaitis's translation simply because I have yet to gain access to a copy of the original text. The passage reveals the deep ambivalence mirrors have evoked in Western culture:

I say that for some, mirrors constitute a hieroglyph of truth in that they uncover everything which is presented to them, like the habit of the truth which cannot remain hidden. Others, on the contrary, hold mirrors for a symbol of falsity because they so often show things other than as they are. (*Miroir*, 6)

Of the many kinds of mirror functions Baltrusaitis discusses, I wish to draw attention to two that emphasize the depth of the dual sense of attraction and repulsion that governs our cultural attitude toward reflection. The first can be seen in the unquenchable delight the West has taken in the physical extensions of the *theatrum mundi* trope, in the construction of catoptric theaters of magic and transformation. The second is reflected in the identification of the natural world as constituting a set of "real" mirrors in which man can see God and live.

Human nature has been consistently fascinated with the ways mirrors are capable of distorting the world, which is the same, actually, as delivering up an alternative world: they can magnify and diminish, they can eliminate and multiply, they can open up vistas of infinite regression and they can close in on an object and, by focusing the power of the sun upon it, consume it by fire. But no epochal mentality took the techniques of reflection to the lengths and heights as did the baroque. The symptomology of catoptric mania is epitomized in one of the major monuments of the seventeenth century: Athanasius Kircher's *Ars magna lucis et umbrae* (Rome, 1646).

Kircher sketches out a series of metamorphic rooms in which the spectator can see himself change from the self into a variety of others—other sexes, other people—into a number of chimera limited only by the imagination itself. The gimmick that makes the room work is a box that hides an octagonal drum that rotates on its side. On each face of the drum is depicted the image of a desired transformation, and this image has a direct and open sightline, through a concealed slit in the box, to a mirror hanging above it, but angled in such a way (like the mirror in a periscope) that the spectator standing in front of the drum-hiding box can look up and see, not the humdrum, expected image of the self, but the hotly desired appropriation to the self of an alien other. With careful lighting, drapes, a hidden amanuensis to rotate the drum, and other adjuncts of baroque showmanship, the illusion of actual transformation can be effected. There is a precision and fastidiousness in Kircher that is almost alarming. It is clear that the baroque age took great pleasure in attending with exquisite care to the aesthetics of fraud.

Baltrusaitis has carefully delineated this particular symptomology and gone far, I would argue, in reaching a convincing diagnosis. He lists the names of the various museums and catoptric "cabinets" found in Rome, Milan, and as far north as Copenhagen:

Theatrum catoptricum
Theatrum polydicticum
Theatrum protei
Sista, sistula catoptrica
Mensa catoptrica
Speculum heterodicticum
Speculum polyphaton
Speculum multiplex
Tabula scalata

He continues, pointing out that:

The nomenclature of these "machineries" is itself revelatory of the presiding elaborating method, with its apparel of erudition. Multiplications, substitutions, reversals, magnifications, reductions, dilations, formal compressions, the entire operation is presented like a technical demonstration of the laws of reflection in the lecture hall of a professor. (*Miroir*, 37)

Baltrusaitis goes on to indicate his sense of the underlying patterns of desire that seem to be answered by this passion for hybridization of the world. These theater names, he suggests,

correspond to a single iconography, that of the multiplicity of creatures and things, of hybrids, and fabulous monsters. It also reveals the suppression of all spatial limit and a riddance of the laws of equilibrium which in turn opens the way to all manner of evasions. . . . It is an unprecedented spectacle made of reality and fiction in which the images double and redouble, appear and reappear in a region that has no existence but is nonetheless irrefutably available to the eyes. . . . A second world is revealed in these academic games and scenic diversions which illuminates afresh certain questions regarding appearance and reality. (*Miroir*, 38)

To show how easily one could then move from the physical world to the world of revelation and prophecy, Baltrusaitis again draws on the descriptive power of Mirami:

The science of mirrors is useful to astrology where it clarifies diverse questions regarding heavenly bodies, spots on the moon, eclipses and the projection of rays. The science of mirrors is useful to natural philosophy in that it explains the effects in the air of rainbows and haloes as well as the heat produced by the solar rays. The science of mirrors is useful to divine philosophy. Do we not read the following in Dante's great Commedia?

"Up there are mirrors, you call them Thrones,
from which shines to us the judging God"

—Several visions appearing to the elect of God were framed in the Hebrew language and not without great mystery, by a name equivalent to MIRROR.[22]

Here, I take it, and unfortunately I have to take it without any help from Baltrusaitis, that Mirami is referring to some earlier Jewish interpretive tradition of Exodus. I would think that out of his rabbinical background he might be thinking of the "JawehJaweh" self-declaration of God as a doubling paraphrase for "BEING squared," or "aming: 'AMING,'" thereby implying that the created world is in an exponential mirror relationship to its Creator. That is the only sense I can retrieve out of the "great mystery of the Hebrew language" in which the vision is designated "par un nom correspondant a celui de Miroir."

Baltrusaitis concludes his study by reminding us that our Western tenacity in seeking mirrors of God in the world was fed by both Greek and Hebrew traditions. As we look into those traditions, we are struck by the admixture of fear and desire we find there. Behind the generous portion of gaiety figured forth in Greek amatory narratives of childlike gods and goddesses lurks a darker intuition of an *imago dei* relationship that figures forth violence and death. This darker vision is incorporated in the myth of Perseus and the Gorgon as well as in the myth of Zeus, Semele, and the engendering of Dionysus in which Semele is literally consumed by her desire to be loved by an untrammeled Zeus, the Zeus who comes purely as the god-as-god, rather than the accommodating, mediating Zeus "disguised" as the god-in-man.

In the Hebrew tradition a comparable ambivalence deriving from desire and fear is reflected in the positive guarantee underlying Genesis 1.27 ("So God created man in his own image, in the image of God created he him; male and female created he them") and in the negative interdiction of Exodus 33.20 ("Thou canst not see my face: for there shall no man see me, and live").

Both Greek and Hebrew traditions of fear and desire coalesce in the Pauline text with which we began this study. Saul-become-Paul, that apostle of liminality, reinvents the frontier shared by old and new dispensations by writing us letters filled with what it is like to live there. For those of us still traveling our own roads to Damascus, he sets down afresh, in 1 Corinthians 13.12, how mirrors legitimately meet our postlapsarian needs as we, too, seek a way to the miraculously radical Other: videmus nunc per speculum in aenigmate: tunc autem facie ad faciem; "For now we see through a glass, darkly; but then face to face."

Notes

Introduction

1. The recent standard commentaries are Margaret E. Thrall, *The First and Second Letters of Paul to the Corinthians* (Cambridge: Cambridge University Press, 1965); C. K. Barrett, *A Commentary on the First Epistle to the Corinthians,* 2d ed. (London: Adam and Charles Black, 1971), and Hans Conzelmann, *A Commentary on the First Epistle to the Corinthians,* translated by James W. Leitch (Philadelphia: Fortress Press, 1975). In addition, cf. Herbert M. Gale, *The Use of Analogy in the Letters of Paul* (Philadelphia: Westminster Press, 1964), 127–29, and Elaine Pagels, *The Gnostic Paul: Gnostic Exegesis of the Pauline Letters* (Philadelphia: Fortress Press, 1975). Paul W. Gooch concludes his important philosophical examination of Paul with a penetrating essay that doubles as a gloss to 1 ORINTHIANS 13 in *Partial Knowledge: Philosophical Studies in Paul* (Notre Dame, Ind.: University of Notre Dame Press, 1987), 142–61.
2. The Judeo-Christian doctrine forbidding unmediated access to divinity is dramatized in the colloquy between God and Moses in Exodus 34.20–23, in which God, while denying access to His full being, nevertheless does allow Moses to stand behind a tree and, while God passes by, view His "hinder parts." In the Greco-Roman tradition, interdiction lies at the center of the story of Dionysus's birth, in which Semele is vaporized when Zeus, at her own request, comes to her as he comes to Hera, as the purely unmediated god. The same interdiction, in a more feminist version, is surely echoed in the narrative of Actaeon, who, upon discovering Artemis bathing nude in the pool, is transformed into a stag and killed by his own hunting dogs. Both narratives occur in, and help lend thematic coherence to, book 3 of Ovid's *Metamorphoses.*
3. See sections on Lacan and Kristeva in the Appendix.
4. See my discussion of Pygmalion in the *Roman de la Rose,* end of chapter 6.

NOTES TO PAGES 4-12

5. For a full sense of all the vectors that led into the Pauline articulation and all the major variants of reception in the patristic literature that followed, see the monumental study by Norbert Hugedé, *La Métaphore du Miroir dans les Epîtres de Saint Paul aux Corinthiens* (Neuchatel: Librairie Grôz, 1957).

6. Saintsbury, *History of Criticism and Literary Taste in Europe from the Earliest Texts to the Present Day* (New York: Humanities Press, 1961), 1:11.

7. Perhaps the clearest and most dispassionate guide to the recent ferment in critical theory is Jonathan Culler. See his *Structuralist Poetics* (1975), *The Pursuit of Signs* (1981), and *On Deconstruction* (1983), all published by Cornell University Press. For the work on medieval alterity see Peter Haidu, "Making It (New) in the Middle Ages—Towards a Problematics of Alterity," *Diacritics* (Summer 1974); Eugene Vance, "The Modernity of the Middle Ages in the Future," *Romanic Review* 64 (1973):140–51; Hans Robert Jauss, *Alterität und Modernität der mittelalterlichen Literatur* (Munich: Wilhelm Fink Verlag, 1977), and the entire issue of *New Literary History* 10, no.2 (Winter 1979). An important collection of Jauss's essays has recently appeared in English, translated by Timothy Bahti and introduced by Paul de Man: *Toward an Aesthetic of Reception*, volume 2 in the University of Minnesota Press series on Theory and History of Literature (Minneapolis, 1982). The fruit of Judson Boyce Allen's work on medieval commentaries is available in *The Ethical Poetic of the Later Middle Ages* (Toronto: University of Toronto Press, 1982). The mirroring capabilities of medieval literature were powerfully demonstrated by Paul Zumthor in his *Essai de poétique médiévale* (Paris: Seuil, 1972); it illuminates a central "paradigm shift" as compellingly demonstrated by Julia Bolton Holloway's recent *The Pilgrim and the Book: A Study of Dante, Langland, and Chaucer* (New York, Berne, and Frankfurt-am-Main: Peter Lang, 1987).

8. "Problemfeld Widerspiegelung," in Schlenstedt, ed., *Literarische Widerspiegelung: geschichtliche und theoretische Dimensionen eines Problems* (Berlin and Weimar: Aufbau-Verlag, 1986).

9. All the remarks quoted from Jauss are drawn from his extended discussion of horizons of expectation in "The Alterity and Modernity of Medieval Literature," *New Literary History* 10, no.2 (Winter 1979): 181–229.

10. Sister Ritamary Bradley, "Backgrounds of the Title *Speculum* in Medieval Literature," *Speculum* 29 (1954): 1–19. The first iteration of the Grabes study appeared as *Speculum, Mirror und Looking-Glass: Kontinuität und Originalität der Spiegelmetapher in den Buchtiteln des Mittelalters und der englischen Literatur des 13. bis 17. Jahrhunderts* (Tübingen: Max Niemeyer, 1973). It appeared nearly a decade later in English, with significant revision, as *The Mutable Glass: Mirror-Imagery in Titles and Texts of the*

Middle Ages and the English Renaissance (Cambridge: Cambridge University Press, 1982).

11. The classic article is the *Katoptron* entry by v. Netoliczka in Paully-Wissowa's *Real-Encyklopaedie* 11, cols. 29–45. The best monographic study is still that of Gustav Friedrich Hartlaub, *Zauber des Spiegels* (Munich: R. Piper, 1951). Of almost no use at all is the recently published monograph by Benjamin Goldberg, *The Mirror and Man* (Charlottesville: University of Virginia Press, 1985). Tobin Siebers has provocative things to say from an anthropological point of view, particularly concerning the mirroring in Benvenuto Cellini's *Perseo;* see his *The Mirror of Medusa* (Los Angeles: University of California Press, 1983).

12. The most useful and trustworthy study to date is David Lindberg's *The Theories of Vision from al-Kindi to Kepler* (Chicago: University of Chicago Press, 1976). This has been richly amplified by his recent anthologies of articles by himself and others: *Studies in the History of Medieval Optics* (London: Variorum Reprints, 1983); with Ronald L. Numbers, *God and Nature: Historical Essays on the Encounter between Christianity and Science* (Berkeley: University of California Press, 1986), esp. chaps. 1–5; and *The Discourse of Light: From the Middle Ages to the Renaissance* (Los Angeles: William Andrews Clark Memorial Library, 1986).

13. The conceptual basis of this study was greatly clarified by four rather recent books. The first, already mentioned supra, note 10, appeared in two redactions and comprises the mirror-title studies of Herbert Grabes. The second is the brilliant, witty, and disturbing analysis and critique of Western mind and thought by Richard Rorty, *Philosophy and the Mirror of Nature* (Princeton: Princeton University Press, 1979); see appendix. The other two are admonitory mirrors by mentors I despair of emulating, John Hollander's *The Figure of Echo: A Mode of Allusion in Milton and After* (Berkeley: University of California Press, 1981), and Richard J. Schoeck's *Renaissance Intertextuality* (Bamberg: H. Kaiser Verlag, 1985).

Chapter 1

1. For one of the most useful guides to the entire complex of literary reflexivity, see Bruce F. Kawin's *The Mind of the Novel: Reflexive Fiction and the Ineffable* (Princeton: Princeton University Press, 1982). In the first chapter, "Notes on a Haunted Form," Kawin wisely warns of terminological risk, "Along with 'reflexivity' and the ugly, redundant 'self-reflexivity,' 'self-conciousness' has often served as an amorphous critical

term that refers to arty art without saying much about it. Used with rigor, however, [they] can illuminate the problem of exactly how art presents itself as haunted . . ." (*Mind of Novel*, 14). The reflexive, specular images I have focused on in this study also bear an analogous relationship to the French heraldic term, *mise-en-abîme*, so judiciously described by Lucien Dällenbach:

The word *abyme* is a technical term. It is a reference to a treatise on heraldy: "Abyss" (Abîme) - the heart of the shield. A figure is said to be "en abyme" when it is combined with other figures in the centre of the shield, but does not touch any of these figures. *The Mirror in the Text*, translation of *Le récit spéculaire: essay sur la mise en abyme* by Jeremy Whiteley with Emma Hughes (Chicago: The University of Chicago Press, 1989), 8.

2. See David Thompson, "Allegory and Typology in the *Aeneid*," *Arethusa* 3 (1970): 151. Also cf. G. N. Knauer, who is as tentative as he is provocative in his suggestions along this line, in his "Virgil and Homer," in *Aufstieg und Niedergang der roemischen Welt* (henceforward *ANRW*), edited by Wolfgang Haase (Berlin and New York: Walter de Gruyter, 1981), II, 31.2: 889. The central thrust of both allegorical and typological readings has been to link Aeneas with Caesar Augustus. The question, since World War I, has been whether to do so positively, negatively, or in some more overarchingly complex fashion. Francesco Sforza, "The Problem of Virgil," *CR* 49 (1935): 97–128, argued that the *Aeneid* is a kind of *roman-à-clef* in which Virgil is writing a systematically anti-Augustan tract. Sforza wrote from Cyprus as the world headed for fascism, and that adds spice to his ingenious reading. R. Symes, on the brink of World War II, spoke in clearly anti-Augustan terms simply because it made sense to him, given the atrocities of the foundation of empire, but he denied such feelings to Virgil, making him look more than a little like Augustus's hack (*The Roman Revolution* [Oxford: Oxford University Press, 1971; first published at the Clarendon Press, 1939]). A more balanced view on the matter was sketched by W. F. Jackson Knight in *Roman Virgil*, rev. ed. (Harmondsworth, Eng.: Faber and Faber, 1966), 363ff.; first published under T. S. Eliot's imprimatur, 1944. More recently a strongly pro-Augustan reading was argued by Gerhard Binder in his *Aeneas und Augustus: Interpretationen zum 8. Buch der Aeneis* (Meisenheim am Glan: A. Hain, 1971). Adam Parry wrote the landmark essay in which the particularly postwar sense of Virgilian ambiguity is sounded, "The Two Voices of Vergil's *Aeneid*," *Arion* 2, no.4 (1963): 66–80. The most haunting and brilliantly sable view of how this Roman book relates to a Roman world is etched by W. R.

Johnson in *Darkness Visible* (Berkeley: University of California Press, 1976), esp. p. 4. The most recent ecumenical reading is Viktor Poeschl's "Virgil und Augustus," *ANRW* II, 31.2: 709–27. Rudolf Rieks offers the most recent survey of Virgil and Roman history in his monograph (with indices) "Vergil und die roemische Geschichte," *ANRW* II, 31.2: 728–868.

3. Domenico P. A. Comparetti, *Virgil in the Middle Ages* (New York: G.E. Stechert, 1929).

4. The indispensable study is G. N. Knauer's *Die* Aeneis *und Homer. Studien zur poetischen Technik Vergils mit Listen der Homerzitate in der* Aeneis, *Hypomnemata* 7 (Göttingen: Vandenhoeck and Ruprecht, 1964), reprinted 1979. His major conclusions are most readily available in his article in *ANRW*, cited in note 1 supra, 870–90. Virgil's debt to the cyclic epic has been displayed and analyzed by E. Christian Kopff, "Virgil and the Cyclic Epics," *ANRW* II, 31.2: 920–47. Robin Schlunk has provided preliminary work on Virgil's debt (if any) to the Homeric scholarship of Alexandria in *The Homeric Scholia and the* Aeneid (Ann Arbor: University of Michigan Press, 1974).

5. Many valuable studies have drawn on Knauer's work; one of the most important is G. K. Galinsky's "Vergil's *Romanitas* and his Adaptation of Greek Heroes," *ANRW* II, 31.2: 985–1010. The element of inversion or difference in Virgil's replications of Homer's images often constitutes the mirror relation we are concerned with here. The habit of constantly engaging in repetition with telling difference belongs to the deeper structures of Virgil's apparatus of apperception and also belies the rhetorical training of his age. W. F. Jackson Knight writes convincingly about the conventions of Roman translation (turning the old into the new) and about *retractatio*. Virgil is most Virgilian when he is about the business of repetition. See Knight's *Roman Vergil*, 350ff., and his "Repetitive Style in Vergil," *TAPA* 72 (1941): 212–25. The programmatic strategies of "same but different" generate ambiguity; see W. R. Nethercutt for one of the most intriguing discussions of systematic ambiguity in Virgil, "The Imagery of the Aeneid," *CJ* 67 (1971–72): 123–43. The capital Virgil invests in Homer-with-a-difference pays high interest. See, for example, Charles Segal's cadenza on Virgil's reworkings of Odysseus's unforgettable gesture of reaching out three times to clasp the ghostly image of Anticlea in "Vanishing Shades: Virgil and Homeric Repetitions," *Eranos* 72 (1974): 34–52.

More directly associated with the mirroring aspect of such imagery is the article by my colleague E. Christian Kopff in which he examines the inverted ways in which Dido mirrors Penelope (or, more accurately, in which Penelope mirrors Dido). Kopff sees Odysseus's romantic journey turned into high tragedy as Virgil makes Penelope/Dido not the fulfilling goal, but the final obstacle: "Dido and Penelope," *Philologus* 121 (1977): 244–48. Closest to the present inquiry is the article by Michael von Albrecht, "Die Kunst der Spiegelung in Vergils *Aeneis,*" *Hermes* 93 (1965): 54–64. Von Albrecht shows that the Dido encounter in Hell, in which Dido turns in silence from Aeneas to Sycheus, mirrors doubly. Many have seen the reversals involved in the way Dido's silence mimics the silence of Ajax in the Nekyia. Von Albrecht demonstrates conclusively the power of the double bind created by simultaneous internal and external mirroring as he reveals how Dido's silence in the face of Aeneas's plea for forgiveness also mirrors Aeneas's silence in the face of Dido's plea that he remain with her in Carthage. He also shows that the narrative sequence is deployed in mirror fashion: Dido silently leaves her lover to turn to the consolations of the past, whereas Aeneas left Dido to turn to the claims of the future. Von Albrecht's article argues the need for a more extended consideration of mirroring in Virgil, a need this chapter attempts to accommodate. Mirroring and typology are inseparable. Virgil's typology is generated by the creation in his poem of a hall of mirror images. He offers countless images that look like countless other images in terms of structure but differ sharply in particular matters of content. The impressive similarity demands that we seek in the poem the promises and consolations that the coherences of similarity seem to offer. But the telling, often disquieting differences insist that we look again. This generates a critical attitude on the part of the reader that makes for uneasiness in the face of any apparently direct state of affairs. Most of the *Aeneid*'s major images possess this mirroring/typological relationship, not only to other images within the poem but also to many collective literary images and historical events outside the poem as well.

The kind of typological thinking represented only slightly later by such thinkers as Philo Judeaus was already in the air. There was the related, if more general, Alexandrian willingness to consider Greek and Hebrew traditions together. There is also the agenda of Aeneas himself. Greco-Roman literature provides no ethical model for it, but the book of Exodus does: the sinning prophet is destined to follow unquestioningly a divine imperative to bring his people to a promised land he himself has no hope of entering. Finally, as discussed above, Virgil's own programmatic use of Homer is the additional, and probably more immediately compelling, reason for presuming the presence, in the *Aeneid,* of a typological principle of composition.

6. Robert Fitzgerald, *Homer, the Odyssey* (New York: Anchor Press/ Doubleday, 1963, 142). With the permission of Vintage Books, I have

used, throughout this study, Robert Fitzgerald's translation of Homer's *Odyssey* (copyright 1961, 1963 by Robert Fitzgerald). Where I argue directly from the Greek I use my own translations, noting that.

7. Richmond Lattimore, *The Iliad of Homer* (Chicago: University of Chicago Press, 1970), 162. With the permission of the University of Chicago Press, I have used, throughout this study, *The Iliad of Homer,* translated with an introduction by Richmond Lattimore (copyright 1951 by the University of Chicago). Where I argue directly from the Greek I use my own translations, noting that.

8. P. Vergilii Maronis, *Opera,* ed. R. A. B. Mynors (Oxford: Oxford University Press, 1976). Throughout this study I have used, with the permission of Bantam Editions, the translation of Allen Mandelbaum, *The Aeneid of Virgil* (New York: Bantam, 1978, copyright 1972 by Allen Mandelbaum). Where I argue directly from the Latin, I use Virgil's text and my own translations, noting that.

9. For a review of filiation, see E. Black, "Failure to Thrive: The Theme of Parents and Children in the *Aeneid* and Its Iliadic Models," *Ramus* 11 (1980): 128–49; and M. Owen Lee, *Fathers and Sons in Virgil's* Aeneid (Albany: SUNY Press, 1979). Neither deals satisfactorily with the typological force of the imagery on Apollo's temple doors at Cumae.

10. "Leda and the Swan," *The Collected Poems of W. B. Yeats* (New York: MacMillan, 1956), 212.

11. My argument for a move from time to space, from movement to stasis, from freedom to control, must remain partial, even tentative. R. D. Williams argues that there is, in addition to the rigidities of pictorial rendering, an implied interior narrative of Aeneas's observations and interpretation of the frozen *pictura inani;* hence the episode is "story as well as an art gallery" ("The Pictures on Dido's Temple," *CQ* 54 [n.s. 10, 1960]: 145–51). Thomas Greene senses this shift as well, but suggests it may have as much to do with the exigencies of the Latin language as with Virgil's poetic strategy:

> Because its syntax is intricate and hypotactic and its meter so heavily punctuated, Latin poetry tends to render physical movement less well than it renders static situations. . . . This failure to represent movement is typical of Virgil and is compensated for by an ability to render great areas within a single perspective. . . . Virgil indeed is a great poet of geography. (*The Descent from Heaven* [New Haven and London: Yale University Press, 1963]: 95–96).

I hope my understanding of the mutually mirroring panels of art (on the temple of Juno at Carthage in *Aeneid* 1 and on the temple of Apollo at Cumae in *Aeneid* 6) enriches rather than counters W. R. Johnson's splendid pages in *Darkness Visible* (99—114) entitled "Aeneas and the Monuments." And though Charles Segal would presumably support my contentions regarding the importance of Virgilian mirroring, particularly in the effect of repeated uses of *labor,* he too, like Williams, sees more of interest in the implied movement than in the stasis:

> The mirror-within-mirror effect [of Aeneas as both participant in and observer of depicted action in the temple art-work] is doubled as the scene shifts from Aeneas's perception of the Trojan past as aesthetic object to his increasing response to it as lived reality. . . . Within the description, however, the intricate movement from narrated event to lived actuality is also expressed in the change of tenses from pluperfect to imperfect to present. There is a shift from indirect statement (466—73) to direct description (474—84, 490—93) or participial constructions (485—89). (Segal, "Art and the Hero: Participation, Detachment, and Narrative Point of View in *Aeneid* 1," *Arethusa* 14, no. 1 [1981]: 67—82).

Two of the most provocative essays on the Daedalian panels are H. C. Rutledge, "The Opening of *Aeneid* 6," *CJ* 67 (1971—72): 110—15, in which Daedalus does a double mirroring of both Augustus and Aeneas; and A. G. McKay, "Apollo Cumanus," *Virgilius* 19 (1973): 51—63. I have not yet been able to see Victor Poeschl's "Die Tempeltüren des Daedalus in der *Aeneis,*" *WJA* (NF1, 1975): 119—23.

12. Fitzgerald, *Odyssey,* 136.
13. Stevens, "The Pure Good of Theory," *The Collected Poems of Wallace Stevens* (New York: Alfred A. Knopf, 1964 [first Collected Edition published 1954], copyright 1954 by Wallace Stevens). Here is a larger context:

> Yet to speak of the whole world as metaphor
> Is still to stick to the contents of the mind
> And the desire to believe in a metaphor.
> It is to stick to the nicer knowledge of
> Belief, that what it believes in is not true.

Special acknowledgment is made to Holly Stevens, Alfred A. Knopf, Inc., and Random House for permission to use excerpts from the poetry of Wallace Stevens as epigraphs of all numbered chapters of this book, as well as throughout the argument of this study.

14. Knox, "The Serpent and the Flame: the Imagery of the Second Book of the *Aeneid,*" *AJP* 71 (1950): 379—400.

15. Brooks, *"Discolor aura:* Reflections of a Golden Bough," *AJP* 74 (1953): 260–80. Segal has written the equivalent of a monograph on the Golden Bough that is extraordinarily rich and provocative: C. P. Segal, *"Aeternum per saecula nomen:* The Golden Bough and the Tragedy of History," *Arion* 4 (1965): 617–57; *Arion* 5 (1966): 34–72; followed by a brief codicil: "The Hesitation of the Golden Bough," *Hermes* 96 (1968): 74–79.

16. Brooks, *"Discolor aura,"* 280.

17. Two related articles, impressive in their own right, also offer brief bibliographies of the controversy surrounding the crux: Brooks Otis, "Three Problems of *Aeneid* 6," *TAPA* 90 (1959): 165–79; and E. Christian Kopff and Nanno Marinatos Kopff, "Aeneas: False Dream or Messenger of the Manes?" *Philologus* 120 (1976): 246–50. Useful in providing archeological and anthropological background are E. L. Highbarger's *The Gate of Dreams: An Archeological Examination of Virgil, Aeneid VI, 893–899* (Baltimore: Johns Hopkins University Press, 1940); and Raymond J. Clark, *Catabasis: Vergil and the Wisdom Tradition* (Amsterdam: Gruner, 1979).

18. Fitzgerald's *Odyssey,* 371. See my discussion on infernal ordination in *Inferno* 33 near the beginning of chapter 5 and the digression on infernal figuration at the beginning of chapter 7.

19. Fitzgerald, *Odyssey,* 206.

20. Donald Howard quotes Augustine from the *Soliloquia* (PL 32:393, and in Howard's translation):

On the stage [the actor] Roscius was a false Hecuba by choice, a true man by nature; but by that choice also a true tragic actor because he fulfilled his purpose, yet a false Priam because he imitated Priam but was not he. And now from this comes something amazing, which however no one doubts . . . that all these things are true in some respects for the very reason that they are false in some respects, and that only the fact that they are false in one sense helps them towards their truth. (Howard, *The Idea of the Canterbury Tales* [Berkeley: University of California Press, 1976], 344–45).

21. Socrates gives a similar answer to Glaukon's question about the possibility of instituting the ideals reflected in the discussion, suggesting, at the end of *The Republic* 9, that the true republic is more likely to turn out to be the pattern of a just man's mind than a real city.

22. Stevens, "Angel Surrounded by Paysans," *Collected Poems,* 496.

Chapter 2

1. The indispensable bibliography on the *Metamorphoses,* aside from the annual reviews in *Année Philologique,* is H. Hofmann, "Ovids 'Metamorphosen' in der Forschung der letzten 30 Jahre (1950-1979)," *ANRW* II, 31.4: 2161–273. I find Brooks Otis's radically revised *Ovid as Epic Poet,* 2d ed. (Cambridge: Cambridge University Press, 1970) still to be one of the most provocative full-scale studies, even though its date is inevitably beginning to show. See also G. Karl Galinsky, *Ovid's Metamorphoses* (Los Angeles: University of California Press, 1975), especially the final chapter, "Ovid, Vergil and Augustus," 210–61. For the best of modern European work, see the anthology published as *Ovid,* edited by Michael von Albrecht and Ernst Zinn (Darmstadt: Wissenschaftliche Buchgesellschaft, 1968). It includes Franz Boemer's incisive essay on Ovid's verbal resonances with Virgil, "Ovid und die Sprache Vergils," (1959), 173–202. More recent essays relevant to my approach are A. Crabbe, "Structure and Content in Ovid's 'Metamorphoses'," *ANRW* II, 31.4: 2274–327; and M. von Albrecht, "Mythos und römische Realität in Ovids 'Metamorphosen'," *ANRW* II, 31.4: 2328–42. Also see E. J. Kenny, "The Style of the Metamorphoses," in *Ovid,* edited by J. W. Binns (London and Boston: Routledge and Kegan Paul, 1973), 116–53. Also useful are Kenny's introduction and notes to the recently published A. D. Melville translation of the *Metamorphoses* (Oxford: Oxford University Press, 1986). Two excellent books on medieval Ovid are John Block Friedman, *Orpheus in the Middle Ages* (Cambridge: Harvard University Press, 1970); and John Fyler, *Chaucer and Ovid* (New Haven and London: Yale University Press, 1979). In addition, two articles by Charles Segal prove particularly useful in terms of problems surrounding Ovid's poetics: "Circean Temptations: Homer, Vergil, Ovid," *TAPA* 99 (1968): 419–42; and "Ovid's Orpheus and Augustan Ideology," *TAPA* 103 (1972): 473–94.

2. "Two Aspects of Language and Two Types of Aphasic Disturbance," in R. Jakobson and M. Halle, *Fundamentals of Language* (The Hague: Mouton, 1956). Jakobson argues that there are two driving forces that simultaneously impel all sane discourse. The first is the force for metaphor, which is essentially lexical; it is the organizing principle that chooses this item rather than that item as the sentence moves along. The second is the force for metonymy, which is essentially syntactical; it is the organizing principle that places this item next to that item as the sentence moves along. His argument seems to me analogous to the musings of Stephen Dedalus as he walks Sandymount strand with his eyes closed in the third chapter of Joyce's *Ulysses.* When Jakobson speaks of meta-

phor, I hear Stephen thinking of the "ineluctable modality" of the audible, the *nacheinander:* one thing after or instead of another. When Jakobson speaks of metonymy, I hear Stephen's words about the "ineluctable modality" of the visible, the *nebeneinander:* one thing next to, near to, or far apart from another. The idea of such forces at work is no doubt of greater heuristic than scientific value, but nevertheless helpful in a limited way. It is useful to think of several forces driving language simultaneously at any particular moment in an utterance, and the idea has some value that the domination of one such force over another might conceivably constitute a style.

3. Only in the poetic setting of the *Metamorphoses,* of course. Ovid was personally fascinated by history, particularly in exile. See Ronald Syme, *History in Ovid* (Oxford: Clarendon Press, 1978).

4. The text used is *P. Ovidius Naso Metamorphosen,* vol. 1, books 1–7 with commentary by von Moriz Haupt; vol. 2, books 8–15 with commentary by Otto Korn, edited by Rudolf Ehwald, corrected and with additional bibliography by Michael von Albrecht (Zurich and Dublin: Weidmann, 1966). Indispensable is the monumental, multi-volume commentary still in progress: *P. Ovidius Naso Metamorphosen: Kommentar von Franz Boemer* (Heidelberg: Carl Winter, Universitätsverlag, 1969–). For translations, I use the project initiated in the eighteenth century by Sir Samuel Garth, who gathered the work of many hands in addition to his own into an extraordinary collective project that included translations by Pope, Dryden, Addison, Gay, Congreve, and others: *Ovid's Metamorphoses in Fifteen Books* (New York: The Heritage Press, 1961). At times I argue from my own translations, and note that.

5. "The Idea of Order at Key West," *Collected Poems of Wallace Stevens,* 130.

6. See Kenneth J. Knoespel, *Narcissus and the Invention of Personal History* (New York and London: Garland, 1985), for a useful study of both Ovid's own narrative and its literary fortune in the Middle Ages. Cf. relevant sections of Julia Kristeva, *Tales of Love,* translated by Leon S. Roudiez (New York: Columbia University Press, 1987); see the Appendix.

7. My translation. John Hollander suggests this solution to the double entendre of *coeamus* in his *Figure of Echo,* 25.

8. Three excellent books trace the myth of Orpheus over time: Friedman, *Orpheus in the Middle Ages;* John Warden, ed., *Orpheus: The Metamorphoses of a Myth* (Toronto: University of Toronto Press, 1982); and Charles Segal, *Orpheus: The Myth of the Poet* (Baltimore and London: Johns Hopkins University Press, 1989). The following articles have proven particularly useful regarding mythic aspects of the narrative: C. M. Bowra, "Orpheus and Eurydice," *CQ,* n.s. 1 (1951): 113–26; Peter

Dronke, "The Return of Eurydice," *C&M* 21 (1960): 198–215; W. S. Anderson, "The Orpheus of Virgil and Ovid: *flebile nescio quid*," in Warden, *Orpheus*, 25–50; and David Sansone, "Orpheus and Eurydice in the Fifth Century," *C&M* 36 (1985): 53–64. Two helpful articles on Orpheus and the problematics of art and the artist are Eleanore Winsor Leach, "Ekphrasis and the Theme of Artistic Failure in Ovid's *Metamorphoses*," *Ramus* 3 (1974): 102–42; and Donald Lateiner, "Mythic and Non-Mythic Artists in Ovid's *Metamorphoses*," *Ramus* 13 (1984): 1–30.

9. Galinsky, *Ovid's Metamorphoses*, 86.

10. See Douglas F. Bauer, "The Function of Pygmalion in the *Metamorphoses* of Ovid," *TAPA* 93 (1962): 1–21; and Simone Viarre, "Pygmalion et Orphée chez Ovide (*Met.* X, 243–97)," *REL* 46 (1968): 235–47.

11. Iamque opus exegi, quod nec Iovis ira nec ignis
nec poterit ferrum nec edax abolere vetustas.
cum volet, illa dies, quae nil nisi corporis huius
ius habet, incerti spatium mihi finiat aevi:
parte tamen meliore mei super alta perennis
astra ferar, nomenque erit indelebile nostrum,
quaque patet domitis Romana potentia terris,
ore legar populi, perque omnia saecula fama,
si quid habent veri vatum praesagia, vivam.

(*Meta.* XV.871–879)

Chapter 3

1. A. W. Haddam, trans., *On the Trinity*, revised and annotated by W. T. Shedd, in *A Select Library of the Nicene and Post-Nicene Fathers of the Christian Church*, edited by Philip Schaff (1887; reprint, Grand Rapids: W. B. Eerdmans, 1956), 127. Cf. *De Trinitate*, in Sancti Aurelii Augustini, *Opera Omnia*, J. P. Migne, ed., *Patrologiae Cursus Completus, Series Latina*, vol. 42 (Paris: Garnier, 1886) (henceforth *PL* 42); and Sancti Aurelii Augustini, *De Trinitate Libri XV*, edited by W. J. Mountain, with Fr. Glorie, *Corpus Christianorum, Series Latina*, vols. 50 and 50A (Turnholt: Brepols, 1963), (henceforth, *CCSL*). For biography, the indispensable book remains Peter Brown, *Augustine of Hippo* (Berkeley: University of California Press, 1967). Still very useful is Roy W. Battenhouse's edition of *A Companion to the Study of St. Augustine* (New York: Oxford University Press, 1955). An important philologically based study of Augustine's theories of mind is Gerard O'Daly, *Augustine's Philosophy of Mind* (Berkeley: University of California Press, 1987). The

most valuable work published recently on evil and the problem of the will is Gillian R. Evans, *Augustine on Evil* (Cambridge: Cambridge University Press, 1982). Several monographs proved particularly helpful: Pierre Courcelle, *Recherches sur les Confessions de Saint Augustin* (Paris: Boccard, 1950); Ronald H. Nash, *The Light of the Mind: St. Augustine's Theory of Knowledge* (Lexington: University Press of Kentucky, 1969); Eugene TeSelle, *Augustine the Theologian* (New York: Herder and Herder, 1970); Oliver O'Donovan, *The Problem of Self-Love in St. Augustine* (New Haven: Yale University Press, 1980); Jaroslav Pelikan, *The Mystery of Continuity: Time and History, Memory and Eternity in the Thought of St. Augustine* (New Haven: Yale University Press, 1985). For a radically different reading of the nature and role of freedom and will in Augustine's thinking, see Elaine Pagels's *Adam, Eve and the Serpent* (New York: Vintage Books, 1988). Pagels emphasizes Augustine's pessimism regarding human depravity as it fatally limits our collective capacity for free political government. She seems to carry over that pessimism, unjustifiably, I would argue, into the more private domain of the self-government of the individual soul. Augustine was surely of many minds at various times on the will and its range of freedom; but I would argue that even his darkest views centered not on the *impossibility*, but rather on the extraordinary *difficulty* involved in exercising the awful gift of free will in the give and take of human affairs. More important for this study is Pagels's insistence that Augustine's dark denial of freedom shaped European thought in the later Middle Ages: such an assertion flies directly in the face of religious orthodoxy and the implications of narrative as well as explicit pronouncements on free will to be found in the secular, but ultimately theocentric, epics of Dante, Chaucer, and Langland that are at the core of our concern.

Also very helpful were a number of articles and chapters: Eugene Vance, "Augustine's *Confessions* and the Grammar of Selfhood," *Genre* 4 (1973): 1–28, and the first two chapters from his recent book *Mervelous Signals* (Lincoln: University of Nebraska Press, 1986): "Augustine's *Confessions* and the Poetics of the Law," and "Saint Augustine: Language as Temporality." Also Kenneth Burke, "Verbal Action in St. Augustine's *Confessions*," in his *The Rhetoric of Religion* (Boston: Beacon Press, 1961), 43– 171; Margaret Ferguson, "St. Augustine's Region of Unlikeness: The Crossing of Exile and Language," *Georgia Review* 29 (1975): 842–64; the first and third chapters in Charles Dahlberg's *The Literature of Unlikeness* (Hannover and London: University Press of New England, 1988): "The Literature of Unlikeness: Augustine, Boethius and Chaucer," and "The Rhetoric of Unlikeness: Augustine, Dionysus, and Alanus"; Marcia Colish, "St. Augustine's Rhetoric of Silence Revisited," *Augustinian Studies* 9 (1978): 15-24, and "Augustine: The Expression of the Word," in her *The Mirror of Language: A Study in the Medieval Theory of Knowledge*, rev. ed. (Lincoln: University of Nebraska Press, 1983), 9-54; Patrick Grant, "Redeeming the Time: The *Confessions* of St. Augustine," in *By Things Seen: Reference and Recognition in Medieval Thought*, edited by David Jeffrey (Ottowa: University of Ottowa Press, 1979), 21-32; Ralph Flores, "Double-Making St. Augustine's *Confessions*," in his *The Rhetoric of Doubtful Authority* (Ithaca: Cornell University Press, 1984); and Dennis A. Foster, "Three Exemplary Readings," in his *Confession and Complicity in Narrative* (Cambridge: Cambridge University Press, 1987).

2. See Nash, *Light of the Mind*, chap. 4, on Augustinian notions of physical sensation. Nash shows that Augustine's theories of sensation were, from a modern perspective, in a fundamental muddle due to a hopelessly inadequate physics. In his alterity essay, Jauss speaks of:

> an understanding of the world which C. S. Lewis so impressively knew how to present in all of its pre-Copernican features . . . a model which allowed for "saving the appearances" and harmonizing the contradictions of heterogeneous authorities in such a manner that one can place this medieval world-model alongside with Thomas Aquinas's *Summa* and Dante's *Divina Commedia* as its greatest work of art. ("Alterity," 183)

The map he refers to is delineated in more detail in C. S. Lewis's *The Discarded Image* (Cambridge: Cambridge University Press, 1964), 51ff. Augustine, in his refusal to wait for a harmonic and unified physics, helps create this "work of art" even as he moves forward impatiently into metaphysical speculation. In addition, Augustine's "paradoxes" (the intellect is active and passive; the forms are distinct from and not distinct from the human mind; the mind is and is not the light that makes knowledge possible) are capable of resolution if and as one sees Augustine as absolutely fearless in his intellectual honesty and tenacity, given the state of knowledge that he inherited concerning the physical universe. On these paradoxes, see Nash, *The Light of the Mind*, 104-11.

3. Cf. TeSelle, *Augustine the Theologian*, 308: " . . . it is necessary not only to know the mind but to know that it is an image and 'refer' what is known to the God whose image it is; otherwise we will see only the mirror."

4. For useful insights into the ways in which Augustine anticipates modern situationalist "realism," see TeSelle, *Augustine the Theologian*, 63; and R. A. Markus, *Christianity in the Roman World* (London: Thames and Hudson, 1974), 122.

5. 10.3, *PL* 42:975.

6. *CCSL* 50A, 15:9; Haddam, *Trinity.* 207.

7. Ibid., 208.

8. Concerned with a different but related duality of aspect and point of view, Ernst Kantorowicz quotes Seneca thus: "[*duas personas habet gubernator...*] Two persons are combined in the pilot: one he shares with all his fellow-passengers, for he also is a passenger; the other is peculiar to him, for he is the pilot. A storm harms him as a passenger, but it harms him not as a pilot." *The King's Two Bodies: A Study in Medieval Political Theology* (Princeton: Princeton University Press, 1957), 498.

9. *Corpus Scriptorum Ecclesiasticorum Latinorum,* vol. 33, Sancti Aurelii Augustini *Confessionum,* Libri Tredecim, ed. Pius Knoell (Prague, Vienna, and Leipzig, 1896; reprint, New York and London: Johnson Reprint, 1962), (henceforth *CSEL* 33), 2.3. My translation.

10. For Augustine's reception of Plato by the Neoplatonists and others, see Joseph A. Mazzeo, "St. Augustine and the Rhetoric of Silence," *Journal of the History of Ideas* 23 (1962): 175–96. See also his chapter "Dante and the Phaedrus Tradition" in his *Structure and Thought in the* Paradiso (Ithaca: Cornell University Press, 1958). See also Marcia Colish, works cited in note 1 supra, and note 10 in the Appendix for her useful deliberations on the *translatio studii* of Plato and Aristotle to Augustine, esp. 63–69 of the first edition of *The Mirror of Language.*

11. *PL* 42:1071; *CCSL* 50A:15.10; Haddam, *Trinity,* 209.

12. *CSEL* 33:1.1. My translation.

13. Pine-Coffin, trans., *Confessions* of Saint Augustine (New York: Penguin, 1961), 25; *CSEL* 33:1.6.

14. Pine-Coffin, *Confessions,* 26; *CSEL* 33:1.6.

15. Pine-Coffin, *Confessions,* 26–27; *CSEL* 33:1.6.

16. See *Physics,* Book I, in "The Student's Oxford Aristotle," translated by R. P. Hardie and R. K. Gaye, in Justin D. Kaplan, ed., *The Pocket Aristotle* (New York: Pocket Books, 1958), 12–14.

17. *Phaedrus,* 242D; Plato, *Phaedrus,* translated with an Introduction by W. C. Hembold and W. G. Rabinowitz (New York: Liberal Arts Press, 1956), 23.

18. Lattimore, *Iliad,* 97.

19. *Phaedrus,* 246A; Hembold and Rabinowitz, *Phaedrus,* 28.

20. St. Augustine, *On Christian Doctrine,* translated with an introduction by D. W. Robertson, Jr. (Indianapolis: Library of Liberal Arts, 1958), 10.

21. Ibid., 10–11.

22. Ibid.

23. *CSEL* 33:1.13. My translation.

24. Ibid.

25. Ibid., 7.21

26. Ibid., 7.9. Cf. John 1.1–14.
27. Ibid.
28. Ibid., 8.2.
29. As discussed in the introduction, there is much ambiguity in Paul's dictum. C. K. Barrett refers to other interesting aspects of that ambiguity in his *Commentary on the First Epistle to the Corinthians:*

> Looking glasses were made in Corinth. . . . Always the glass is an instrument of revelation, sometimes the stress lies simply on the revelation, sometimes on its indirectness . . . but the ambiguity of the metaphor accounts for the addition (for which some odd explanations have been supplied) of a further qualification, obscurely (literally, in a riddle, [*en ainigmati*]) . . . probably dependent . . . on *Num* XII.8, where God says that he will speak to Moses face to face, not obscurely (through riddles [*di' ainigmaton*]), but the expression would be fully comprehensible to Corinthians unfamiliar with the Greek Old Testament. The Chorus complains of Cassandra that she speaks in riddles [*ex ainigmaton*] (*Agamemnon* 1112); this is because she is inspired by Apollo, whose custom it is to deliver obscure oracles.

30. *CSEL* 33:6.3, my translation and emphasis.
31. Ibid., 6.4, my translation.
32. Ibid., 8.1, my translation.
33. Ibid., 8.12, my translation.
34. Pine-Coffin, *Confessions*, 198; *CSEL* 33: 9.10.
35. *CSEL* 33:11.9, my translation.
36. Ibid., 11.13, my translation.
37. Pine-Coffin, *Confessions*, 264; *CSEL* 33:11.15
38. Pine-Coffin, *Confessions*, 269; *CSEL* 33:11.20.
39. Pine-Coffin, *Confessions*, 274; *CSEL* 33:11.26.
40. Pine-Coffin, *Confessions*, 276; *CSEL* 33:11.27.
41. Pine-Coffin, *Confessions*, 277; *CSEL* 33:11.28.
42. Pine-Coffin, *Confessions*, 279; *CSEL* 33:11.29.

Chapter 4

1. For Alan of Lille, a central Neoplatonic image parallel to that of the mirror is that of painting ("*O nova picturae miracula!*"). In an amplified reference to the ways in which *Aeneid*-like images in a painting dance between the lie and the truth ["*Virgilii musa mendacia multa colorat, Et facie veri contexit pallia falso*" (Alanus de Insulis, *Anticlaudianus,* PL 210:491)] he places Nature, whose desire to reform her own imperfection

triggers the narrative of the entire poem, leading her to ask God's help in forming the New Man, as a "mirror in which we can see the possibility of our own perfection" [*Sit speculum nobis, ut nos speculemur in illo; /Quae sit nostra fides, quae nostra potentia, virtus / Quae sit, et in quantum melius procedere possit*] (Ibid., 493).

2. My translation and parenthetic commentary. See discussion of irresolvable linguistic ambiguity in Paul's mirror dictum in the first pages of my introduction.

3. Jauss, "Alterity and Modernity," esp. 181–91. This is Timothy Bahti's translation of the first chapter of Jauss's *Alterität und Modernität*.

4. Friedman, *Orpheus in the Middle Ages*, 1–2.

5. Ibid.

6. Knoespel, *Narcissus*, 55, my emphasis.

7. Ibid.

8. See Kristeva, *Tales of Love* and Segal, *Orpheus: The Myth of the Poet*.

9. Knoespel, *Narcissus*, 39.

10. Jauss, in "Alterity and Modernity," 192, follows up on a penetrating suggestion that C. S. Lewis laid out in *The Discarded Image* (Cambridge: Cambridge University Press, 1964).

If one follows C. S. Lewis's direction, namely, to imagine the pre-Copernican view of the cosmos, then the alterity lies in the fact that the medieval observer looked into and upon the starry sky at night, as if looking over the outermost wall of a city, while we look *out;* that to him the whole universe appeared as a bound ordering of spaces, already layered and populated with angelic essences, and filled with light and the music of the spheres, while we feel Pascal's horror of the "silence éternel de ces espaces infinis" when faced with the endless, empty, dark and mute universe. ("Alterity and Modernity," 192).

11. My translation of a passage quoted by Knoespel in *Narcissus*, 42–43.

12. Ibid., 33.

13. Ibid., 34. See also "A Critical Colloquy: Conrad of Hirsau," in A. J. Minnis and A. B. Scott, *Medieval Literary Theory and Criticism, ca. 1100–ca. 1375: The Commentary-Tradition* (Oxford: Clarendon Press, 1988), esp. 56–57.

14. The attribution of the *Commentum super sex Libros Eneidos Virgilli* is now a vexed question; see an adumbration of the issues by Julian W. Jones and Elizabeth R. Jones in the introduction to their edition of the text *The Commentary on the First Six Books of the Aeneid of Vergil Commonly Attributed to Bernadus Silvestris* (Lincoln and London: University of Nebraska Press, 1977), ix–xi. Where one stands on this issue depends on many things, not the least of which is one's assessment of the real status of the so-called

school of Chartres during the twelfth century. For the classic statements on the side of deflating the Chartrian reputation, see R. W. Southern, "Humanism and the School of Chartres," in his *Medieval Humanism* (New York and Evanston: Harper and Row, 1970), 61–85, and his more recent "The Schools of Paris and the School of Chartres," in Robert L. Benson and Giles Constable, eds., *Renaissance and Renewal in the Twelfth Century* (Cambridge: Harvard University Press, 1982), 113–37. See also Gillian Evans, *Old Arts and New Theology* (Oxford: Clarendon Press, 1980). For useful texts and commentaries on Bernardus Silvestris as well as William of Conches and Arnulf of Orleans, see Minnis and Scott, *Medieval Literary Theory,* 113–64. See also Allen, *Ethical Poetic,* for additional texts and commentaries on Aegidius Romanus, as well as Bernardus Silvestris and Arnulf of Orleans. For Bernardus Silvestris's important role in European intellectual history, see Brian Stock's indispensable *Myth and Science in the Twelfth Century: a Study of Bernard Silvester* (Princeton: Princeton University Press, 1972).

15. *Commentary on the First Six Books of Virgil's Aeneid by Bernardus Silvestris,* translated by Earl G. Schreiber and Thomas E. Maresca (Lincoln and London: University of Nebraska Press, 1979), 38–39, after Jones's critical edition, 37 n. 10]).

16. Beryl Smalley, *The Study of the Bible in the Middle Ages* (Oxford: Clarendon Press, 1941). See also the recent appreciation by R. W. Southern, "Beryl Smalley and the Place of the Bible in Medieval Studies, 1927–84," in Katherine Walsh and Diana Wood, eds., *The Bible and the Medieval World* (Oxford: Basil Blackwell, 1985), 1–16. Three recent works on medieval commentary are of inestimable value: Allen, *Ethical Poetic;* Minnis, *Medieval Theory of Authorship: Scholastic Literary Attitudes in the Later Middle Ages* (London: Scolar Press, 1984); and Minnis and Scott, *Medieval Literary Theory.*

17. Smalley suggests that Hugh's greatest flaw was to continue, at least in his theorizing, a traditionally Alexandrian *contaminatio* that confused the subject matter of Scripture and its mode of exposition, though she says he is consistently clear in practice (*Bible,* 63). Robert Hollander feels rather that the issue is a lack of expressed distinction between Hugh's *two* sets of threes: *historia, allegoria,* and *tropologia* and *littera, sensus,* and *sententia.* Implicitly, Hollander suggests, the former are to be reserved exclusively for Scripture's historical images and the latter for either Scripture or secular literature, but reserved exclusively for *non*-historical images ("Dante: *Theologus-Poeta," Dante Studies* 94 [1976]: 91–136, esp. 94).

18. Dante, *Epistola* 10, Paget Toynbee, ed., *Dantis Alighierii Epistolae* (Oxford: Clarendon Press, 1920): 160–211. Cf. Philip H. Wicksteed, *A*

Translation of the Latin Works of Dante (London: Dent and Sons, 1934): 343–68.

19. Hugh of St. Victor, *Didascalicon* 5, ii; translated by Jerome Taylor (New York and London: Columbia University Press, 1961): 120–21.

20. Smalley, *Bible,* 68.

21. Ibid., 68–69.

22. Ibid., 77.

23. Ibid., 83.

24. Minnis and Scott quote this passage from Richard's commentary on *Benjamin minor* in their provocative discussion on the Dionysian imagination in chapter 5 of *Medieval Literary Theory,* 168.

25. Smalley, *Bible,* 97.

26. cf. Baudelaire's "Le Cygne." Of course I run my own risks here in attributing this sense of outward/inward duality to the Middle Ages as a Jaussian alterity in which we can see, however darkly, our own modernity. This sense of relating the directions of signification both outward and inward at the same time has become increasingly important to readers of the modern theoretics of Northrop Frye:

> Whenever we read anything, we find our attention moving in two directions at once. One direction is outward or centrifugal, in which we keep going outside our reading, from the individual words to the things they mean, or, in practice, to our memory of the conventional association between them. The other direction is inward or centripetal, in which we try to develop from the words a sense of the larger verbal pattern they make. . . . These two modes of understanding take place simultaneously in all reading. (*Anatomy of Criticism* [Princeton: Princeton University Press, 1957], 73–74). For a recent discussion that assesses the current importance of this idea in aesthetic theory, see Deanne Bogdan, "From Stubborn Structure to Double Mirror: The Evolution of Northrop Frye's Theory of Poetic Creation and Response," *The Journal of Aesthetic Education* (1989): 33–43.

27. See Toynbee, *Dantis Epistolae,* Epistola 10. Cf. Wicksteed, *A Translation of the Latin Works,* 348.

28. Allen, *Ethical Poetic,* 41–42.

29. Ibid., 14.

30. James J. Sheridan, trans., *Anticlaudianus; or, the Good and Perfect Man* (Toronto: Pontifical Institute of Mediaeval Studies, 1973), 63. Latin text: Alanus de Insulis, *Anticlaudianus, PL* 210:497.

31. Evans writes "Alan's proposed alternative is therefore a topic of some philosophical and theological daring, and one which he himself would appear to reject in the *Contra Haereticos.* . . . If Alan's scheme in the

Anticlaudianus provides an acceptable alternative, then the Incarnation was not the absolute necessity which Anselm argues that it was. Nature herself could have saved mankind." *Alan of Lille: The Frontiers of Theology in the Later Twelfth Century* (Cambridge: Cambridge University Press, 1983), 149.

32. Sheridan, *Anticlaudianus,* 160; *PL* 210:542.

33. Sheridan, *Anticlaudianus.* 161; *PL* 210:543.

34. Sheridan, *Anticlaudianus,* 165; *PL* 210:545.

35. St. Bonaventure, *Itinerarium mentis in Deum,* with an introduction, translation, and commentary by Philotheus Boehner (St. Bonaventure, N.Y.: Franciscan Institute of St. Bonaventure University, 1956), 100–101.

36. This potentially specular relationship between "form" and "content" seems to be at the heart of the way Dante divides up the ten aspects of *forma tractandi* into two sets of five in his Letter to Can Crande. He also calls it *modus tractandi:* he says:

Forma sive modus tractandi est poeticus, fictivus,
descriptivus, digressivus, transumptivus, et cum hoc
diffinitivus, divisivus, probativus, improbativus, et
exemplorum positivus.

If we lay out the sets of five in parallel, we can see an implied equivalence linking each member of each set:

Form or mode of treatment consists of these things:

They are:	at the same time they are:
poetry	definition
fiction	division
description	proof
digression	refutation
metaphor	citing of examples

No one would be foolish enough to argue for systematic identity across the members of these two sets of lists (i.e., poetry = definition; description = proof, etc.), yet one senses an informing resonance when one meditates upon them in such paired lists. The main thing is to see how the list on the left more or less fits in with our modern vocabulary of poetry and literary criticism and how the list on the right fits our vocabulary for the logic of analysis and the rhetoric of persuasion. This reflects an emergent "premodernist" dialectic in Dante's thinking that is beginning to exert counter-pressure upon his dominant "centrist" sense of harmonious integration as he faces the project of casting the world into the structures of language. For Dante, we need to have a sharp sense of both the dominant sense of unity and the emerging sense of split. For St. Bonaventure, who flourishes half a century before Dante, it is the clear dominance of his sense of unity that characterizes his unfettered confidence as he engages the *forma duplex*. Curtius does everything short of coming out and saying this in his brilliant analysis of Dante's treatment of the *forma duplex* in the Letter to Can Grande. See E. R. Curtius, *European Literature in the Latin Middle Ages* (New York: Harper and Row, 1963): 221–25.

37. Boehner, *Itinerarium*, 32–33.

38. Boehner, *Itinerarium*, 40–41.

39. See R. A. Shoaf, *Dante, Chaucer, and the Currency of the Word: Money, Images, and Reference in Late Medieval Poetry* (Norman, Okla.: Pilgrim Books, Inc., 1983), 21–100.

40. See Julia Kristeva's *Tales of Love* (New York: Columbia University Press, 1987), 127–30.

41. *Dante's Convivio*, translated into English by William Walrond Jackson (Oxford: Clarendon Press, 1909), Tractate 2.1, 73.

42. Robert Hollander also seems to feel this way about the minimalist presence of Orpheus—that is, if I read correctly the end of his last note in his "Dante: *Theologus-Poeta*," 136.

43. Allen, *Ethical Poetic*, 13.

44. *Purgatorio* 31.112–17; 121–26. With the permission of Bantam Books, I have used, throughout this study, *The Divine Comedy of Dante Alighieri: A Verse Translation* with introductions by Allen Mandelbaum (Berkeley: University of California Press, 1980–82, copyright 1980, 1982, and 1984 by Allen Mandelbaum; henceforward *California Dante*). When I need to argue closely from the Italian, I occasionally quote Dante's text and use my own translations, noting that.

45. See the two chapters on light metaphysics in Joseph Mazzeo's *Medieval Cultural Tradition in Dante* (Ithaca: Cornell University Press, 1960).

Chapter 5

1. Rosalie Colie, *Resources of Kind: Genre-Theory in the Renaissance*, edited by Barbara K. Lewalsky (Berkeley and London: University of California Press, 1973). Jauss's major articulations are conveniently collected as chapters 9–11 in *Alterität und Modernität*: "Epos und Roman—eine vergleichende Betrachtung an Texten des XII. Jahrhunderts," "Theorie der Gattungen und Literatur des Mittelalters," and "Paradigmawechsel in der Rezeption mittelalterlicher Epik." The second essay is available in English translation by Timothy Bahti as "Theory of Genres and Medieval Literature," in Jauss, *Toward an Aesthetic of Reception*, 76–109. See also

David F. Hult, *Self-Fulfilling Prophecies: Readership and Authority in the First* Roman de la Rose (Cambridge: Cambridge University Press, 1986), especially chapter 3: "Lyric and Romance."

2. "I would like to present genre-theory as a means of accounting for connections between topic and treatment within the literary system, but also to see the connection of the literary kinds with kinds of knowledge and experience. . . . The kinds honor aspects and elements of culture and in their conjunctions help make up culture as a whole. . . . Experience can be seen as searching for its own form, after all: the kinds may act as myth or metaphor for a man's new vision of literary truth." Colie, *Resources of Kind*, 29–30.

3. For the Christian, of course, the problem of *philautia* or *amour-propre* has always been a nagging one. Some sort of self-love seems justified in the great summary commandments: " 'Thou shalt love the Lord thy God with all thy heart, and with all thy soul, and with all thy mind, and with all thy strength': this is the first commandment. And the second is like it, namely this, 'Thou shalt love thy neighbour as thyself.' There is none other commandment greater than these." (Mark 12.31). See the discussion of this problematic, particularly as it relates to St. Augustine, in O'Donovan, *The Problem of Self-Love*.

4. Prudentia, with her capacity to extrapolate from the mirror the kind of self-knowledge requisite for reform, resides more on the pictorial rather than the literary side of the developing iconographic tradition. There is, of course, the stunning "textual" exception of Prudentia-Phronesis-Sophia in Alan of Lille's *Anticlaudianus* (see chap. 4). A charming rendition of the "Seven Virtues" by Francesco Pesinello, currently owned by the Birmingham (Alabama) Museum of Art, has a particularly interesting iconography surrounding the image of Prudenza (reproduced on the dust-jacket of this book). It includes a second face looking *away* from the mirror, a richly ambiguous snake, and an implied relationship of superiority over pre-Christian Greek culture as figured in the arrangment by which Pesinello's Prudenza gazes toward our right into a mirror; while at her feet, the male figure of Solon, starkly reduced in scale, gazes in reverse symmetry toward our left into a text. Perhaps Prudentia's most famous depiction is by Giotto, in which she gazes down on the observer with extreme severity from the surface of her fresco in the Arena Chapel in Padua. It is, of course, a commonplace that human nature delights more in Hell than Heaven and tends to expend greater imaginative resources in depicting vices than in practicing virtues. Thus the richer tradition is that which develops around the figure of Narcissus. Hard evidence supporting Heinrich von Morungen's debts or legacies in the development of this tradition is hard to come by. It seems clear he

died in Leipzig in 1220. It is also clear he was long a member of the court of Dietrich von Meissen, who himself was the son-in-law of Hermann von Thüringen, one of the great patrons of the Hohenstaufen establishment. It is very likely that Heinrich both originated from Thuringia and afterward visited there on the progresses of Dietrich von Meissen. It is also at Hermann's court that Hendrik van Veldeke was finally able to finish his translation of the *Aeneid* (through the mediation of French texts) and where, in 1210, Albrecht von Halberstadt completed his translation of Ovid's *Metamorphoses,* directly from the Latin. Cf. Joachim Bumke, *Maezene im Mittelalter* (Munich: C. H. Beck, 1979), 113, 159–60, and 172–73. Hermann Menhardt speculates provocatively that Heinrich von Morungen (as well as Friedrich von Hausen) joined the court of Friedrich Barbarossa on one of the great state occasions when he engaged on imperial progress with his wife, Beatrix of Burgundy. The possibility is not only intriguing but reasonably strong that Heinrich was present at a two-day fête in Arles in 1178, when Barbarossa had himself crowned king of Burgundy. This is an especially tantalizing possibility because Bernard de Ventadorn, the Provençal poet who incorporated Narcissus as a central image in his famous "can vei la lauzeta mover," and who was a member of the household of Raimon V of Toulouse, was also there. Cf. Menhardt, "Heinrich von Morungen am Stauferhofe? Zu MF 122,1ff and 134,14ff," *Zeitschrift fuer deutsches Altertum* 73 (1936): 253–60.

The narcissan imagery of Bernard probably precedes Heinrich's own Narcissus poem. The implied or latent psychologizing in Heinrich's poem is in any case far richer than that of Bernard, much more probing, more in the direction taken by Guillaume de Lorris (ca. 1235) in the first part of the *Roman de la Rose.* Although a romance, the *Rose* is deeply affiliated with the central agenda of the lyric insofar as it is a psychological allegory, an externalization of the interior drama of erotic infatuation (see Hult, chapter 3 in n.1 supra, and my discussion of the *Rose* in the final section of chapter 6). Guillaume's narrative of the Lover gazing into the Fountain of Narcissus and the way the crystals reflect and refract the garden with great accuracy, but deceive the Lover catastrophically, is a culminating as well as a seminal moment in the history of literary reflection. The following four books are indispensable in gathering together the explicit and implicit ramifications of that moment in literary history, even though none of them takes into account the German and Italian aspects of that development: D. W. Robertson, *Preface to Chaucer* (Princeton: Princeton University Press, 1962); John Fleming, *The Roman de la Rose* (Princeton: Princeton University Press, 1969); Hult, *Self-Fulfilling Prophecies,* chapter 4; and Knoespel, *Narcissus,* 67–104. Jauss seems to point to the way I understand Heinrich's lady as continually disappearing behind our images of her when he speaks of the Rose in the *Roman de la Rose* as pointing to "the lady whose essence remains hidden behind a series of personifications" ("Alterity and Modernity," 186).

5. Although generally restricted to Carolingian literature, one of the best books on the subject of significant form is Wolfgang Haubrich, *Ordo als Form* (Tuebingen: Max Niemeyer, 1969). Two recent anthologies of essays by several hands are particularly useful: Caroline Eckhardt's *Essays in the Numerical Criticism of Medieval Literature* (Lewisburg, Pa.: Bucknell University Press, 1979); and David Jeffrey's edition of *By Things Seen*. L. V. Ryan has some spectacular notes in his essay "Conrad Celtis and the Mystique of Number," in *From Wolfram and Petrarch to Goethe and Grass: Studies in Literature in Honour of Leonard Forster*, edited by D. H. Green et al. (Baden Baden: V. Koerner, 1982). The discussion of medieval order in this chapter as well as the close reading of Heinrich's meadow poem originally appeared, in shorter versions, in an essay of mine entitled "Order's Image: Heinrich von Morungen, Dante, Chaucer and Two Middle English Lyrics," in *Hypatia:* Essays in Philosophy, Classics, and Comparative Literature presented to Hazel E. Barnes on her Seventieth Birthday, edited by William M. Calder III., Ulrich K. Goldsmith and Phyllis B. Kenevan (Boulder, Colorado: Colorado Associated University Press of Colorado. Copyright 1985 by Colorado Associated University Press): 139–50. Special acknowledgment is made to Luther Williams and the Colorado Associated University Press for permission to quote and revise passages from my essay.

6. *Itinerarium mentis in Deum, Bonaventurae Opera Omnia* (Florence: Studio et Cura P. P. Collegii a S. Bonaventura, 1891), 5.209ff.

7. Mandelbaum, *Inferno,* xx.

8. Text from Hugo Moser and Helmut Tervooren's edition of *Des Minnesangs Frühling* (Stuttgart: S. Hirzel Verlag, 1982), 268–69, with several minor emendations of my own drawn from the facsimile edition of the *Grosse Heidelberger Liederhandschrift,* and Ulrich Mueller's *Heinrich von Morungen: Abbildungen zur gesamten handschriftlichen Ueberlieferung* (Göppingen, 1971). This poem is notorious for the difficulties it presents. My translation indicates to those for whom it matters where I stand on the cruxes. For example, I read *an truren kranc* as Carl von Kraus did the first time around (*Des Minnesangs Fruehling* [Leipzig: S. Hirzel, 1939]) as "full of sorrow" in opposition to "rich in joy," consonant with the ambivalent erotic-literary syndrome of the lover who has mastered the *ars amatoria.* Since then, most critics, including von Kraus (who changed his mind, see his *Heinrich von Morungen* [Munich: Carl Hanser Verlag, 1950]), agree that the locution is an intensive, to be read as a

reinforcement of *froidenrich,* rather than in opposition to it, and is thus a negative periphrasis: *kranc* as "poor," or "wanting" in sorrow, hence as "carefree." One exception, Franz Rolf Schroeder, allows my now eccentric reading: "Heinrich von Morungen 139,19," *GRM* 46 (1965): 117. Another example: I read, on no authority but my own, a phrase in strophe 3, line 2, as *zuo zaln* in the manuscript, and then, on the authority of *Lexers Mittelhochdeutsches Taschenwörterbuch* (Stuttgart: S. Hirzel Verlag, 1969), 410, col. 1, as an adverbial of time past, "zur gegebenen Zeit," hence "then." I also read "dâ si an dem morgen mînes todes sich vermas" in a less than orthodox fashion: not as "on the day she signed my death warrant" (presumably by refusing sexual favors), nor as "ordered my execution," nor as "had received the (apparently false) news of my death," but, against the critics, yet with the authority of the words, as "she had taken the measure of my death" or "had foreseen my death" (by the imaginative sympathy common to intelligent lovers). As the burden of proof for these readings rests with me, I hope a more extended essay of mine regarding systematic ambiguity in the lyric of Heinrich von Morungen will appear soon as an introduction to a diplomatic edition of the text, and present my arguments in convincing detail. Professor Gerhard Hahn of the University of Regensburg devoted several sessions of his Oberseminar in Mediävistik to my querulous contentions regarding this poem in the spring of 1984; he and the members of the Oberseminar have my gratitude, affection, and continued, if now only partial, disagreement. The major critical stances on the cruxes in the poem are cited and well summarized in H. Tervooren, *Heinrich von Morungen: Lieder* (Stuttgart: Philipp Reclam Jun., 1975).

9. It is difficult to imagine the subject of this chapter ever having come to mind without the leavening presence of Fredrick Goldin's *The Mirror of Narcissus in the Courtly Love Lyric* (Ithaca: Cornell University Press, 1967). Upon rereading the book recently, I found no specific instance of direct influence, but a constant resonance to the sense of the alienating impact of artistic convention upon the poet is pervasive in Goldin and thus foundational to the thinking that has produced this study.

10. Text from Tervooren, *Heinrich von Morungen,* 130–32, with several emendations from "e," the "Würzburger Liederhandschrift" (University Library, Munich, 20 Cod. ms731 [=Cim4]). My translation. Cf. Ulrich Mueller, *Heinrich von Morungen.* The classification of the poem as MF 145.1 accords with the conventions used in the Moser and Tervooren edition of *Minnesangs Frühling.*

11. See Roswitha Wisniewski, "Narzissmus bei Heinrich von Morungen," in *Festschrift fuer Helmut de Boor* (Tübingen: Max Niemeyer, 1966), 20–42; Antonin Hruby, "Historische Semantik in Morungens 'Narzissus-

lied' und die Interpretation des Textes," *Deutsche Vierteljahresschrift* 42 (1968): 1–22; and Otto Ludwig, "Komposition und Bildstruktur: Zur poetischen Form der Lieder Heinrichs von Morungen," *Zeitschrift für deutsche Philologie,* 1968 (Special issue 87): 48–71. The best summary of the various interpretations discussed in an overarching concern for the Morungen canon as a whole can be found in Helmut Tervooren's *Heinrich von Morungen.* The standard bibliography was also compiled by Tervooren: *Bibliographie zum Minnesang und zu den Dichtern aus "Des Minnesangs Fruehling"* (Berlin: E. Schmidt, 1969). In 1985 a number of important articles appeared in a special issue of *Deutsche Vierteljahresschrift:* Elisabeth Schmid, "Augenlust und Spiegelliebe des mittelalterlichen Narziss"; Ernst von Reussner, "Hebt die Vollendung der Minnesangskunst die Moeglichkeit von Minnesang auf?" and Christoph Huber, "Narziss und die Geliebte: zur Funktion des Narziss-Mythos im Kontext der Minne bei Heinrich von Morungen (MF 145,1) und anderen." See also K. Speckenbach, "Gattungsreflexion in Morungens Lied 'Mir ist geschehen als einem kindeline (MF 145.1)," *Jahrbuch des Instituts fuer Fruehmittelalterforschung der Universität Münster* 20 (1986): 36–53.

12. Text from Tervooren's *Heinrich von Morungen,* 185. My translation.

13. The Provençal poem was first identified as Heinrich von Morungen's model by Karl Bartsch and published in *Germania* 3 (1858): 304ff. For the major argument against this identification, or at least against this simple kind of identification, see Peter Hoezle, "'Aissi m'ave cum al enfan petit': eine provenzalische Vorlage des Morungen-Liedes 'Mirst geschen als eime kindeline' (MF 145.1)?," in *Mélanges d'histoire littéraire, de linquistique et de philologie romanes offerts à Charles Rostaing par ses élèves et ses amis* (Liège: Association des Romanistes de l'Université de Liège, 1974), 447–67. Hoezle argues strongly for the case that the Provençal poem we have cannot be Heinrich's literary model. His position is that it is demonstrably later, and he even implies it might be either a hoax or some figment of Karl Bartsch's imagination. Hoezle fields an interesting set of arguments that are partly linguistic and partly a result of not finding the original or copy of the manuscript to which Bartsch referred. They are not ultimately compelling. Even if his point turns out to be true, and it is hard to imagine the hard evidence that would clinch the argument one way or another, the fact of the matter is that the use of the Narcissus theme throughout the Middle Ages (the "can vei la lauzeta mover" of Bernard de Ventadorn, the late twelfth-century Norman *Lai de Narcisus,* and both parts of the *Roman de la Rose*) is consistent with its use in the so-called Provençal model; thus my argument that Heinrich's poem implies a critique of that use as characteristic of contemporary

usage stands. See Knoespel's careful study of the Narcissus myth throughout the Middle Ages in his *Narcissus.* See also Peter Dronke, *The Medieval Lyric* (Cambridge: Cambridge University Press, 1968), 131–35. For further background on Ovidiana in the Middle Ages, see Simone Viarre, *La survie d'Ovide dans la littérature scientifique des XIIe et XIIIe siècles* (Poitiers: Université de Poitiers, 1966).

14. Knoespel, *Narcissus,* 23–58, 62–64; and Hult, *Self-Fulfilling Prophecies,* 264–65.

15. *Ovid's* Metamorphoses: *The Arthur Golding Translation,* 1567, edited by J. F. Nims (New York: Macmillan, 1965), 75–76.

Chapter 6

1. The narrative summaries in this essay and the section on reductive images contain some substantially revised passages from an article of mine originally published as "Toads in the Garden: Mythopoetic Evolution in Chrétien de Troyes," *Symposium* 25 (1971): 139–61. Special acknowledgment is made to the editors of *Symposium,* Syracuse University Press, and the Helen Dwight Ried Educational Foundation for permission to quote and revise passages from my article. The texts of Chrétien are drawn from the edition of Mario Roques, *Les Romans de Chrétien de Troyes* (Paris: H. Champion, 1981–84), 6 vols. (*Cligés* was edited by Alexandre Micha, 1982). All translations from the work of Chrétien de Troyes in this book are mine. Chrétien study has been made easier for Americans by Douglas Kelly's *Chrétien de Troyes: An Analytic Bibliography* (London: Grant and Cutler, 1976). See also a special issue on Chrétien de Troyes: *Europe: revue littéraire mensuelle,* no. 642 (October, 1982). Rupert T. Pickens published much important work eventuating from the Kentucky Foreign Language Conference of 1981, including essays by Peter Haidu, Douglas Kelly, Karl Uitti, and others in *The Sower and his Seeds: Essays on Chrétien de Troyes* (Lexington: French Forum Publishers, 1983). Equally important was the publication of *The Romances of Chrétien de Troyes: A Symposium,* edited by Douglas Kelly (Lexington: French Forum Publishers, 1985), with an essay dedicated to each romance, written by a series of scholars, including Haidu, Kelly, Pickens, Uitti, Edward J. Buckbee, and Michelle A. Freeman, scholar-critics whose work over the past two decades warrants their identification as the Chrétien establishment of North America. For a model of computer-aided organization of romance diction, see the impressive collation of Helmut Peter Schwake, *Der Wortschatz des "Cligés" von Chrétien de Troyes* (Tübingen: Max Niemeyer, 1979).

2. Chrétien's last and unfinished romance, *Li Contes du Graal,* is not included in the discussion as it moves rather beyond the scope of the inquiry. Unlike the fiction of the artistically "unfinished" *Lancelot,* the *Perceval* really *is* unfinished, biologically unfinished; it is a true fragment, hence affords no verifiable means of comparison with his finished works in terms of our discussion. My hunch is that Wolfram von Eschenbach, of all the continuators, tagged Chrétien's direction best. What Chrétien was apparently developing, at least what he seemed to be moving toward, was a new set of narrative paramaters within which the Arthurian court discovered itself as only one of a more inclusive secular group of societies. He seems to have envisioned a vast Grail society that included the court of Arthur, a society not in ontological opposition to the Arthurian court (like the Forest of Broceliande or the domain of Morgan), but as an imaginable fulfillment of it. My sense is that he would have approved of Wolfram's closure, which allows a kind of stable, moral sufficiency for Gawain and Feirefiz, as well as for Parzival, while still managing to project a future beyond closure for Lohengrin. Chrétien seems, in *Li contes du Graal,* to be reaching for a narrative form capacious enough to accept the explicit need for a radicalizing second chance, and to provide a welcome for the comedic penetration of divine grace, forgiveness, and redemption into the secular structures of human society.

3. I am grateful for a recent conversation with Elisabeth Kirk on the subject of the strategies of dislocation in Chaucer's *Clerk's Tale.* The paper she gave at a University of Colorado conference on "Piety and Passion: Chaucer's Religious Tales," held in Boulder in February 1989, is scheduled for publication as "Nominalism and the Dynamics of the *Clerk's Tale:* Homo Viator as Woman," in C. David Benson and Elisabeth A. Robertson, eds., *Chaucer's Religious Tales* (Cambridge, Eng.: Bodell and Brewer).

4. These lines from "Poetry" are reprinted with permission of Macmillan Publishing Company from *Collected Poems* of Marianne Moore. Copyright 1935 by Marianne Moore, renewed 1963 by Marianne Moore and T. S. Eliot.

5. Cf. Jean Frappier, "Chrétien de Troyes," in *Arthurian Literature in the Middle Ages,* edited by R. S. Loomis (Oxford: Clarendon Press, 1959), 167. For a more recent reading, see Glyn S. Burgess, *Chrétien de Troyes' Erec et Enide* (London: Grant and Cutler, 1984).

6. Frye, *Anatomy,* esp. 203–6. Especially important for this dimension of Chrétien's meaning is Donald Maddox, *Structure and Sacring: The Systematic Kingdom in Chrétien's Erec et Enide* (Lexington: French Forum Publishers, 1978).

7. This solution to the public demands of *fame* and the private demands of

amie anticipates Chaucer's Franklyn. See Jauss on this anticipatory power of Chrétien's image of marriage in "Alterity and Modernity," 193. He in turn draws attention to Arno Borst, *Lebensformen im Mittelalter* (Frankfurt and Berlin: Propyläen Verlag, 1973), 65, 70; and R. R. Grimm, "Die Paradiesehe: Eine erotische Utopie des Mittelalters," in *Festschrift W. Mohr* (Göppingen, 1972), 1–25.

8. Primary evidence of the *matière/sens* distinction and its relation to *conjointure* can be argued from Chrétien's own diction in the opening lines of the *Charette* (ll. 24–27). But there are real difficulties regarding denotation, not to mention connotation. See Karl D. Uitti, "Chrétien de Troyes' *Yvain*: Fiction and Sense," *RPh* 22 (1969): 473n, for a précis of the relevant argumentation. See also Douglas Kelly's *Sens and Conjointure in the Chevalier de la Charette* (The Hague and Paris: Mouton, 1966).

9. For a recent and provocative close reading of the *Cligés*, see Michelle A. Freeman, *The Poetics of Translatio Studii and Conjointure: Chrétien de Troyes' Cligés* (Lexington: French Forum Publishers, 1979). See also Lucie Polak, *Chrétien de Troyes: Cligés* (London: Grant and Cutler, 1982).

10. See D. W. Robertson, Jr., "The Doctrine of Charity in Medieval Gardens," *Essays in Medieval Culture* (Princeton: Princeton University Press, 1980), 21–50.

11. Cf. Peter Haidu, *Aesthetic Distance in Chrétien de Troyes: Irony and Comedy in Cligés and Perceval* (Geneva: Librarie Drôz, 1968). Robert Hanning argues for quite another kind of distancing: that effected by the deployment of narrative strategy in such a way as to make us aware of a sense of autonomy of character in the romance. Hanning sees this occurring in fully developed ways as early as the *Erec;* see his *The Individual in Twelfth-Century Romance* (New Haven and London: Yale University Press, 1977), esp. 61–79.

12. Erich Auerbach, *Mimesis* (Princeton: Princeton University Press, 1953), 123–42.

13. The text I have translated here is that of Wendelin Foerster's 1912 edition, reprinted in T. B. W. Reid, *Chrétien de Troyes' Yvain* (Manchester, Eng.: 1942), ll. 295–307, 323–32. The first-person address by the Vilain makes the point a trifle clearer (e.g. in Roques, the reply of the Vilain is in indirect discourse: "Et il me dist qu'il ert uns hom").

14. Frappier, "Chrétien de Troyes," 183–84. See also Stefan Hofer, *Chrétien de Troyes: Leben und Werke des altfranzoesischen Epikers* (Graz-Cologne: Herman Boehlau Nachfolger, 1954), esp. 45-86.

15. Kratins, "A Comparative Study of the Structure and Meaning of Chrétien de Troyes's *Yvain,* Hartmann von Aue's *Iwein,* and the Middle English *Ywain and Gawain*" (Ph.D. diss., Harvard University, 1964), 150–51.

16. F. Whitehead, "Yvain's Wooing," in *Medieval Miscellany Presented to Eugene Vinaver*, edited by Frederick Whitehead et al. (New York: Barnes and Noble, 1965), 333.

17. See Tom Artin, *The Allegory of Adventure* (Lewisburg, Pa.: Bucknell University Press, 1974). A more adequate sense of symbolism in Chrétien was greatly furthered by Peter Haidu's *Lion-queue-coupée: l'ecart symbolique chez Chrétien de Troyes* (Geneva: Librarie Drôz, 1972); and Wolfgang Brand, *Chrétien de Troyes: Zur Dichtungstechnik seiner Romane* (Munich: Wilhelm Fink, 1972). See also Lucienne Carasso-Bülow, *The Merveilleux in Chrétien de Troyes' Romances* (Geneva: Librarie Drôz, 1976). More recent is Norris J. Lacy, *The Craft of Chrétien de Troyes: An Essay on Narrative Art* (Leiden: E. J. Brill, Davis Medieval Texts and Studies, 1980).

18. See D. D. R. Owen, "Profanity and Its Purpose in Chrétien's *Cligés* and *Lancelot*," *Forum for Modern Language Studies* 6 (1970): 37–48.

19. Robertson, *Preface to Chaucer*, 96.

20. Ibid., 93–94.

21. Knoespel, *Narcissus*, 101–3.

22. Robertson, *Preface to Chaucer*, 90.

23. *Romance of the Rose*, translated by Charles Dahlberg (Princeton: Princeton University Press, 1971), 345.

24. See the introduction to Colie, *Resources of Kind*.

Chapter 7

1. *Purgatorio* 15. 73–75. Except where noted, texts and translations of the *Divina Commedia* used in this chapter are taken from Allen Mandelbaum's *California Dante* (see supra, chapter 4, n. 44).

2. Canto 5 is inexhaustible. A landmark essay in postwar criticism, to which this and every essay on canto 5 written since owes much, was Renato Poggioli's essay, "Tragedy or Romance? A Reading of the Paolo and Francesca Episode in Dante's *Inferno*," *PMLA* 72 (1957): 313–58. Another important essay that takes into account many of the insights won by the structuralist and semiotic flares of the 1960s and 1970s is the monograph by D'Arco Silvio Avalle, *Analyse du récit de Paolo et Francesca: Dante Alighieri, Enfer, V* (Krefeld: Scherpe Verlag, 1975). Indispensable to any considerations of the act of reading are two books by Harold Bloom: *The Anxiety of Influence* (New York: Oxford University Press, 1973), and *A Map of Misreading* (New York: Oxford University Press, 1975).

3. For a rich and seminal discussion of the tensions obtaining between theological and dramatic imperatives in the *Commedia,* see Erich Auerbach's *Dante als Dichter der irdischen Welt* (Berlin: de Gruyter, 1969 [Berlin and Leipzig, 1929]). For an equally rich discussion of the development of figuralism in Western literature, see his landmark essay, "Figura," in his *Neue Dantestudien* (Istanbul, 1944), 12–71.

4. Most recently, Stephen Popolizio moved in some of the directions I pursue, but goes elsewhere, in his article "Literary Reminiscences and the Act of Reading in *Inferno* V," *Dante Studies* 102 (1984): 19–33. See also John Demaray, *The Invention of Dante's* Commedia (New Haven: Yale University Press, 1974), esp. 93–129. The most wide-ranging and most penetrating recent study of Dante's immediate literary contexts is Teodolinda Barolini, *Dante's Poets: Textuality and Truth in the* Comedy (Princeton: Princeton University Press, 1984). She deals specifically with self-quotation; her term is "auto-citation," in her first chapter, 2–84, and has a valuable bibliographic note on previous work on the topic, 3–4.

5. Cf. Robert Hollander, "Dante: *Theologus-Poeta,*" 91–136.

6. Singleton's *The Divine Comedy* (Cambridge: Harvard University Press, 1972), *Inferno,* 2 (Commentary), 626.

7. Chrétien's *Lancelot,* edited by W. W. Kibler (New York and London: Garland, 1981), ll. 4677–81.

8. See René Girard's *To Double Business Bound* (Baltimore: Johns Hopkins University Press, 1978), 1–8. Girard uses *Inferno* 5 to launch the opening salvo of his most polemic book to date on mimetic desire.

9. *De Doctrina Christiana, CSEL* 36:3.54; *On Christian Doctrine,* translated by D. W. Robertson (Indianapolis and New York: Liberal Arts Press, 1958), 93.

10. L. V. Ryan, "Stornei, grue, colombe: The Bird Images in *Inferno* V," *Dante Studies* 94 (1976): 25–41. For useful work on other aspects of the dove in Dante and medieval thought, see Charles Singleton, "The Irreducible Dove," *Comparative Literature* 9 (1957): 129–35; John Freccero, "Casella's Song," *Dante Studies* 91 (1973): 73–80; and R. A. Shoaf, "Dante's *colombi* and the Figuralism of Hope in the *Divine Comedy,*" *Dante Studies* 93 (1975): 27–59. For slightly more recent bird-lore, see Meredith J. West and Andrew P. King, "Mozart's Starlings," *American Scientist* 78 (March–April, 1990), 106–14.

11. *Commentary,* 93, in Singleton's *The Divine Comedy: Inferno.*

12. Cf. *La Commedia,* secondo l'antica vulgata, a cura di Giorgio Petrocchi (Florence: Società Dantesca Italiana, 1966), 95. Cf. Poggioli, "Tragedy or Romance?" 335. Poggioli says he followed the 1921 Società Dantesca Italiana edition, which I have not been able to locate.

13. *Commentary*, 89, in Singleton's *The Divine Commedy: Inferno.*
14. See Singleton's note to *Inferno* 5, 100, on the resonance of Francesca's diction to both Guinizzelli and Dante's *Vita Nuova* in his revision of Grandgent's edition of *La Divina Commedia* (Cambridge: Harvard University Press, 1972), 53.
15. Title of the third section of Part 1 of Paul Ruggiers, *Art of the Canterbury Tales* (Madison: University of Wisconsin Press, 1967).

Chapter 8

1. Schless, *Chaucer and Dante: A Revaluation* (Norman, Okla.: Pilgrim Books, 1984).
2. Paul G. Ruggiers, *The Art of the Canterbury Tales* (Madison: University of Wisconsin Press, 1965), 48. The idea of viewing Chaucer's pilgrims as *dramatis personae* was first christened by George Lyman Kittredge, "Chaucer's Discussion of Marriage," *Modern Philology* 9(1911):435–67, and revised in *Chaucer and His Poetry* (Cambridge: Harvard University Press, 1915), 185–210. The major development of the idea for current generations of scholars is to be found in R. M. Lumiansky, *Of Sondry Folk: The Dramatic Principle in the Canterbury Tales* (Austin: University of Texas Press, 1955). A systematic critique of this idea forms the main argument of a recent book by C. David Benson, *Chaucer's Drama of Style: Poetic Variety and Contrast in the Canterbury Tales* (Chapel Hill: University of North Carolina Press, 1986). The most powerful recent study of Chaucer in terms of generic modes is Derek Pearsall, *The Canterbury Tales* (Winchester, Mass.: Allen and Unwin, 1985).
3. By special permission from Houghton Mifflin, all Chaucerian texts quoted in this study are drawn from Larry D. Benson, ed., *The Riverside Chaucer*, 3rd ed. (Boston: Houghton Mifflin, 1987).
4. Curry, *Chaucer and the Medieval Sciences*, rev. ed. (New York: Barnes and Noble, 1960). Beryl Rolwand, "Animal Imagery and the Pardoner's Abnormality," *Neophilologus* 48 (1964): 56–60, and "Chaucer's Idea of the Pardoner," *Chaucer Review* 14 (1979): 140–54.
5. Donald Howard, *The Idea of the Canterbury Tales* (Berkeley: University of California Press, 1976), 344–45.
6. Ibid., 358. Alfred David also insists that "the tale *is* about the Pardoner." David is especially compelling in his analysis of ending, in which the society "reappropriates" the Pardoner, after his mocking offer of the opportunity to kiss his "piggesbones." The Pardoner's silence in the face of the final kiss of peace arranged by the Knight renders moot

the question of his own redemption. See David, *The Strumpet Muse* (Bloomington: Indiana University Press, 1976), 193–204.

7. Ruggiers, *The Art of the Canterbury Tales,* 48.

8. Benson, *Riverside Chaucer,* 869, col. 2.

9. Jane Cowgill, in a paper discussing feminine arts of persuasion in the prose tales, delivered at the University of Colorado conference on "Piety and Passion: Chaucer's Religious Tales," February 1989; scheduled for publication in Benson and Robertson, eds., *Chaucer's Religious Tales.*

10. Woolf, *To the Lighthouse* (New York: Harcourt, Brace and World, 1976), 255.

11. John Freccero shows brilliantly how Dante plays biological and poetic generation against one another in *Purgatorio* 24 and 25; see "Manfred's Wounds and the Poetics of the *Purgatorio*," in his *Dante: The Poetics of Conversion* (Cambridge: Harvard University Press, 1986), 195–208, esp. 204.

12. "... ita conversetur, ut non solum sibi praemium comparet sed etiam praebeat aliis exemplum, et sit eius quasi copia dicendi forma vivendi" [let him conduct himself so as not only to deserve a reward for himself, but also to offer an example to others; and in his case, let the form of his life be a flowing speech]. S. Aurelii Augustini, *De Doctrina Christiana: Liber Quartus,* edited by Sister Therese Sullivan (Washington, D.C.: Catholic University of America, 1930), 189.

13. Elizabeth Robertson insists that the prologue reveals a kind of learning unavailable to medieval women and that the resulting discourse, in addition to the self-identification of the narrator as a "son of Eve," proves that the narrator was originally conceived of as a male ("Aspects of Female Piety in the Prioress' Tale," scheduled for publication in *Chaucer's Religious Tales,* see n.9 supra). A long tradition in Chaucer scholarship holds that the St. Cecilia narrative is much earlier and was bootlegged into the *Canterbury Tales* as a last-minute maneuver. Howard makes an important point regarding such a move: he insists that it indicates a deliberate choice on the part of Chaucer, that he really meant us to read it as if narrated by a nun—no matter what novelistic slips of Chaucer might lead us to a contrary notion. Howard also suggests that the very facelessness of the Second Nun frees us from any need to read the story in terms of a teller, allowing us to read it in a neutral fashion (*Idea,* 290). This also keeps the Second Nun from acting as a filter to her own story and her own heroine, with the result that Cecilia, although a character within a tale, is nearly as unmediated as the pilgrims who tell tales, and hence can be compared with them more confidently (more confidently, say, than one could compare wife Alison of the Miller's Tale with Alison, the Wife of Bath).

14. Remarks given on a panel at the University of Colorado conference on "Piety and Passion: Chaucer's Religious Tales," February 1989.

15. Sherry Reames's ground-breaking work is to be found in "The Sources of Chaucer's 'Second Nun's Tale,'" *Modern Philology* 76 (1978–79): 111–35. Her interpretation of Chaucer's maneuvers is in "The Cecilia Legend as Chaucer Inherited It and Retold It: The Disappearance of an Augustinian Ideal," *Speculum* 55 (1980): 38–59. Other important articles include: R. A. Peck, "The Ideas of 'Entente' and Translation in Chaucer's *Second Nun's Tale*," *Annuale Medievale*, 1967: 17–37; Paul M. Clogan, "The Figural Style and Meaning of *The Second Nun's Prologue* and *Tale*," *Medievalia et Humanistica* n.s., 3 (1972): 213–40; Paul Beichner, "Confrontation, Contempt of Court, and Chaucer's Cecilia," *Chaucer Review* 8 (1974): 198–204; Carolyn P. Collete, "A Closer Look at Seinte Cecile's Special Vision," *Chaucer Review* 10 (1976): 337–49; Marc D. Glasser, "Marriage and the *Second Nun's Tale*," *Tennessee Studies in Literature* 23 (1978): 1–14; V. A. Kolve, "Chaucer's *Second Nun's Tale* and the Iconography of Saint Cecilia," in Donald M. Rose, ed., *New Perspectives in Chaucer Criticism* (Norman, Okla.: Pilgrim Books, 1981), 137–74 (see also his *Chaucer and the Imagery of Narrative* [Stanford: Stanford University Press, 1984], for similar essays on central "narrative" images in the *Canterbury Tales*); Hanemarie Luecke, O.S.B., "Three Faces of Cecilia: Chaucer's *Second Nun's Tale*," *American Benedictine Review* 22 (1982): 335–48; Anne Eggebroten, "Laughter in the *Second Nun's Tale*: A redefinition of the Genre," *Chaucer Review* 19 (1984): 54–61; and Saul Nathaniel Brody, "Chaucer's Rhyme Royal Tales and the Secularization of the Saint," *Chaucer Review* 20 (1985): 113–31.

16. Reames, "Cecilia Legend," 40.

17. Howard, *Idea,* 292.

Chapter 9

1. This is a much expanded version of a short paper delivered at the Fourth International Congress of Neo-Latin Studies in Bologna, Italy, in 1979. That paper, "Beyond Macaronic: Embedded Latin in Dante and Langland," has been published in the proceedings of that congress, *Acta Conventus Neo-Latini Bononiensis,* edited by R. J. Schoeck (Binghamton: SUNY Press, Medieval and Renaissance Texts and Studies [MRTS], 1985), 539–48; copyright 1985 by Center for Medieval & Early Renaissance Studies, University Center at Binghamton, State University of New York. My thanks to CMERS for permission to use my article here.

2. W. W. Skeat, ed., *The Vision of William Concerning Piers the Plowman*, 2 vols. (London: Oxford University Press, 1969 [1886]). In spite of the recent recensions by Kane, Donaldson, and Pearsall, the Skeat edition is still valuable because one can see the relationships of A, B, and C texts at a glance. This poem comes to us in growing and shifting redactions, its true nature as a text.

3. Sullivan, *The Latin Insertions and the Macaronic Verse in Piers Plowman* (Washington, D.C.: The Catholic University of America, 1932).

4. John A. Alford, "The Role of the Quotations in *Piers Plowman*," *Speculum* 52 (1977): 80–99.

5. Charles Muscatine, *Poetry and Crisis in the Age of Chaucer* (Notre Dame: University of Notre Dame Press, 1972), 74.

6. Ibid., 72.

7. F. Goodridge, trans., *Piers Plowman* (Baltimore: Penguin, 1959), 45.

8. See Mary Carruthers, *Search for St. Truth* (Evanston: Northwestern University Press, 1973); Priscilla Martin, *The Field and Tower* (New York: Barnes and Noble Books, 1979); Julia Bolton Holloway, *The Pilgrim and the Book* (New York: Peter Lang, 1987); and Laurie A. Finke, "Truth's Treasure: Allegory and Meaning in *Piers Plowman*," in *Medieval Texts and Contemporary Readers*, edited by Laurie A. Finke and Martin B. Shichtman (Ithaca: Cornell University Press, 1987), 51–68.

9. *De Vulgari Eloquentia*, edited by Aristide Marigo (Florence, 1957), 8.

10. *Il Convivio*, edited by Busnelli and Vandelli (Florence, 1954), 1:33.

11. Grayson, "*Nobilior est vulgaris:* Latin and Vernacular in Dante's Thought," in *Centenary Essays on Dante* by members of the Oxford Dante Society (Oxford: Clarendon Press, 1965), 54–76.

12. *Vita Nuova*, ed. Fredi Chiapelli (Milan: Mursia, 1971), 30–31.

13. Curtius, *European Literature*, 352–53.

14. Skeat, *Piers Plowman*. See n.2 supra. For the sake of convenience, I will henceforward translate the Langland text into "lean unlovely" English and include glosses for the Latin in parentheses when they are not glossed by Langland himself.

15. Skeat, *Piers Plowman* B 2:15–16.

16. "Date of the B-text of *Piers Plowman*," *Medium Aevum* 12 (1943): 57–59.

17. G. R. Owst, *Literature and Pulpit in Medieval England* (Oxford: Blackwell, 1961), 584–85.

18. *De Doctrina Christiana*, CSEL 80:3.14.

19. Ibid., 2.9.

20. Mary C. Schroeder was, if not the first, one of the first to see the analogical relationship obtaining between the tearing of the pardon and Pier's "pure tene" and the anger of Moses and his dashing the tablets against the mountain. See her "*Piers Plowman:* The Tearing of the Par-

don," *Philological Quarterly* 49 (1970): 8–18. She sees the *Visio* as representing an England in which grace is not meaningful, and thus Piers, in tearing the pardon, acts not as Do-Well, but merely as an imperfect everyman who is angry to see that grace involves work. Elizabeth D. Kirk suggests yet another useful analogue from the Old Testament: Job and his anger at God for treating him "unjustly," followed by the devastating demonstration of divine power and Job's acquiescence, see *The Dream Thought of Piers Plowman* (New Haven and London: Yale University Press, 1972), 71–100. Rosemary Woolf rests her solution on an excessive bit of casuistry: "The document was not a pardon when it was received, but it was a pardon after Piers had torn it . . . [as] a sentence of death, when torn up, might appropriately be called a reprieve" in her "The Tearing of the Pardon," *Art and Doctrine,* Heather O'Donoghue, ed. (London and Ronceverte: The Hambledon Press, 1986), 130–56.

21. *Purgatory,* translated by Dorothy L. Sayers (Baltimore: Penguin Books, 1967).

22. Anne Middleton, "Two Infinities: Grammatical Metaphor in *Piers Plowman*," *ELH* 39 (1973): 169–88.

23. Cf. R. E. Kaske, "'Ex vi transicionis' and Its Passage in *Piers Plowman*," *JEGP* 62 (1963): 21–60; and Edward C. Schweitzer, "'Half a Laumpe Lyne in Latyne' and Patience's Riddle in *Piers Plowman*," *JEGP* 73 (1974): 313–27.

24. *Piers Plowman,* edited by Elizabeth Salter and Derek Pearsall (Evanston, Ill.: Northwestern University Press, 1967).

25. See Peter Dronke, *The Medieval Lyric,* 2d ed. (New York: Cambridge University Press, 1977); Douglas Grey, *Themes and Images in the Medieval English Religious Lyric* (London and Boston: Routledge and Kegan Paul, 1972); Edmund Reiss, *The Art of the Middle English Lyric* (Athens, Ga.: University of Georgia Press, 1972); and Rosemary Woolf, *The English Religious Lyric in the Middle Ages* (Oxford: Clarendon Press, 1968).

26. My transcription of British Museum ms. Egerton 613, f.2. The discussion of the poem here is a revision of an earlier discussion published in my essay, "Order's Image: Heinrich von Morungen, Dante, Chaucer and Two Middle English Lyrics," in *Hypatia:* Essays in Philosophy, Classics, and Comparative Literature presented to Hazel E. Barnes on her Seventieth Birthday, edited by William M. Calder III., Ulrich K. Goldsmith, and Phyllis B. Kenevan. (Boulder, Colorado: Colorado Associated University Press of Colorado. Copyright 1985 by Colorado Associated University Press, 139–50). Special acknowledgment is made to Luther Williams and the Colorado Associated University Press for permission to print a revision and expansion of that discussion here.

Conclusion

1. Frank Kermode, *Sense of an Ending* (New York: Oxford University Press, 1967); Barbara Herrnstein Smith, *Poetic Closure* (Chicago: University of Chicago Press, 1968).

2. *Homer: The Iliad,* translated by Robert Fitzgerald (Garden City, N.Y.: Anchor Press, 1975), 590–94.

3. Lattimore's *Iliad,* 496.

4. T. S. Eliot, *Complete Poems and Plays, 1905–1950* (New York: Harcourt, Brace and World, 1952), 145.

5. Mandelbaum, *The Aeneid,* 347–48.

6. For a brilliant discussion of the ending of the *Aeneid,* see the last chapter of W. R. Johnson's *Darkness Visible.*

7. From Alan of Lille's *De Incarnatione Christi, PL* 210:578, my translation.

8. Ibid., 579, my translation. See Curtius, *European Literature,* who provides the course of study needed to grasp fully the historical development of this trope in chapter 16, "The Book as Symbol," 302–43. For Dante's senses of the Book of World and Book of God, see John Demaray's wide-ranging study, *The Invention of Dante's Commedia* (New Haven: Yale University Press, 1974). Donald Howard develops valuable insights into the significance of this trope for reading medieval literature generally, and Chaucer in particular, in his *Idea,* 1–76 and 380–87. For the best current study of the medieval understanding of the book, see Jesse M. Gellrich, *The Idea of the Book in the Middle Ages* (Ithaca: Cornell University Press, 1985).

9. All translations from the *Commedia,* with the exception of a few of my own, which are so noted in the text, are from Mandelbaum's *California Dante.* See n. 44, chapter 4.

10. My translation derives from W. W. Kibler's edition.

11. Toynbee, *Epistolae Dantis Aligherii,* Epistola 10.

12. Shoaf, *Dante, Chaucer, and the Currency of the Word* (Norman, Okla.: Pilgrim Books, 1983), 67–100.

13. Benson, *Riverside Chaucer.*

14. Sayce, "Chaucer's Retractions: The Conclusion of the *Canterbury Tales* and its Place in Literary Tradition," *Medium Aevum* 40 (1971): 230–248; Wenzel, see esp. his commentary and notes on Fragment 10 in the *Riverside Chaucer,* 954–65; Wurtele, "The Penitence of Geoffrey Chaucer," *Viator* 11 (1980): 335–59. See also Larry Sklute, *Virtue of Necessity: Inconclusiveness and Narrative Form in Chaucer's Poetry* (Columbus: Ohio State University Press, 1984). Donald Howard compares the *General Prologue* and the *Parson's Tale* as analogues of the mirrors of St. Vincent of Beauvais: "The General Prologue is like a *speculum humanae*

vitae reflecting the individuals and the society which produce the tales; the Parson's Tale is like a *speculum moralitatis* reflecting values which apply to the society and the individual. From either end we see the whole reflected from the viewpoint of the individual or the society and then see it reflected again in reverse, and we see the author and ourselves in the picture trying to see it clearly." *Idea*, 217.

15. Wurtele, "Penitence," 340.
16. Hult, *Self-Fulfilling Prophecies*, 314.

Appendix

The epigraph is from Rainer Marie Rilke, *Die Sonette an Orpheus*, Part 2, no. 3, in *Werke: Auswahl in zwei Bänden* (Frankfurt/Main: Insel Verlag, 1957), 1.286.

1. Lacan, *Ecrits* (Paris: Editions du Seuil, 1966), 91–100. I have used my own translation of Lacan. Alan Sheridan has published a translation of Lacan's own selections from *Ecrits* as *Ecrits, A Selection* (New York: Norton, 1977); the mirror essay opens the volume. Book 11 of the *Seminaire* has been made available by the same translator, and appears as *The Four Fundamental Concepts of Psycho-Analysis* (New York: Norton, 1978). Anthony Wilden translated the *Discours de Rome* and published the work with notes and commentary as *Speech and Language in Psychoanalysis* (Baltimore: Johns Hopkins University Press, 1971). See also Jane Gallop, *Reading Lacan* (Ithaca: Cornell University Press, 1985), esp. 74–92.
2. For recent evidence that the ape does in fact recognize himself in the mirror, see Gordon G. Gallup, Jr., "Self-Recognition in Primates: A Comparative Approach to the Bi-directional Properties of Consciousness," *American Psychology* 32, no. 5 (May 1977): 329–38. My thanks to colleague Gordon Hewes for this reference.
3. Stevens, *The Collected Poems*, 9.
4. Eco, *Semiotics and the Philosophy of Language* (Bloomington: Indiana University Press, 1984).
5. Rorty, *Philosophy and the Mirror of Nature* (Princeton: Princeton University Press, 1979).
6. Girard's theories regarding mimetic desire provide important contemporary counters to medieval epistemological concerns with mirroring. See his *To Double Business Bound*, especially the introduction and opening chapter on Paolo and Francesca. This book is an extension of the implied theory deployed in *The Violent and the Sacred* (Baltimore: Johns Hopkins University Press, 1977) and *Choses cachées depuis la fondation du monde*,

written in collaboration with Jean-Michel Oughourlian and Guy Lefort (Paris: Grasset, 1978).

7. Lindberg, *The Theories of Vision from al-Kindi to Kepler* (Chicago: University of Chicao Press, 1976), see n. 12 to my introduction.

8. Thomas S. Kuhn, *The Structure of Scientific Revolutions* (Chicago: University of Chicago Press, 1967).

9. Hartlaub, *Zauber des Spiegels* (Munich: R. Piper, 1951), 13.

10. Grabes's study first appeared in German as *Speculum, Mirror und Looking-Glass: Kontinuität und Originalität der Spiegel Metapher in den Buchtiteln des Mittelalters und der englischen Literatur des* 13. bis 17. Jahrhunderts (Tübingen: Max Niemeyer, 1973). A decade later, he published the English redaction, with significant revision, as *The Mutable Glass: Mirror-Imagery in Titles and Texts of the Middle Ages and the English Renaissance* (Cambridge: Cambridge University Press, 1982).

11. Colish, *The Mirror of Language: A Study in the Medieval Theory of Knowledge* (New Haven: Yale University Press, 1968; rev. ed. Lincoln, Neb.: University of Nebraska Press, 1988).

12. Javelet, *Image et ressemblance au douxième siècle: de saint Anselme à Alain de Lille* (Strasburg: Editions Letouzey and Ane, 1967).

13. Colie, *Paradoxia Epidemica* (Princeton: Princeton University Press, 1966).

14. Hugedé, *La Métaphore du miroir dans les Epîtres de Saint Paul aux Corinthiens* (Neuchatel: Delachaux et Niestlé, 1957).

15. Leisegang, "Physik" in Paully-Wissowa, *Real-Encyklopaedie*, (1941), 19:1034–63. See also "Die Erkenntnis Gottes im Spiegel der Seele und der Natur," *Zeitschrift für Philosophische Forschung*, 4 (1949–1950): 161–83.

16. Hollander, *The Figure of Echo: A Mode of Allusion in Milton and After* (Berkeley: University of California Press, 1981).

17. Kristeva, *Tales of Love*, translated by Louis Roudiez from her *Histoires d'amour* (New York: Columbia University Press, 1987).

18. Paully-Wissowa, *Real-Encyklopaedie*, 11:29–45.

19. Schefold, "Griechische Spiegel," *Die Antike* 16 (1940): 11–37.

20. Wackernagel, *Kleinere Schriften*, vol. 1 (Leipzig, 1872).

21. Baltrusaitis, *Essai sur une légende scientifique: le miroir: révélations, science-fiction et fallacies.* (Paris: Elmayan/le seuil, 1978). All translations are mine, including, unfortunately, my translations of Baltrusaitis's translations of Raphael Mirami. The only copy of Mirami's *Compendiosa* I could track down in the United States was at the Folger, and that was unavailable to me, for understandable technical reasons, when I was able to get there to look at it.

22. From chapter 1 of the *Compendiosa introduttione alla prima parte della*

specularia (Ferrara, 1582) entitled "Utilità che si cavano della scienza degli specchi," my translation by way of Baltrusaitis's translation (see supra, n.21).

Index